Black Earth, Red Star

Black Earth, Red Star

*A History of Soviet
Security Policy, 1917–1991*

R. Craig Nation

Cornell University Press

Ithaca and London

First published 1992 by Cornell University Press.

Library of Congress Cataloging-in-Publication Data

Nation, R. Craig.
  Black earth, red star : a history of Soviet security policy, 1917–1991 / R. Craig Nation.
     p.   cm.
  Includes bibliographical references and index.
  ISBN 0-8014-2725-8 (cloth : alk. paper).
  1. Soviet Union—National security.   2. Soviet Union—Foreign relations—1917– I. Title.
DK266.3.N28   1992
327.47—dc20   92-3717

Printed in the United States of America

For Marc Julien

Contents

Preface

The reform process that began in the USSR in 1985 challenged almost every particular of what once passed as conventional wisdom concerning the Soviet experience. Nowhere was this more the case than in the domain of national security affairs. Until very recently the entire western security agenda was built around the primacy of what was presumed to be an expanding Soviet threat. The Soviet Union was portrayed as a study in paranoia, a state whose obsession with external threats and grim determination to pursue, in Jonathan Alford's phrase, "the mirage of total security in a hostile world" created a situation whereby the prerequisites for Soviet security could be achieved only at the expense of increasing insecurity for all others.[1] The weight of a history replete with catastrophic invasions, the sense of isolation that was the legacy of the state's revolutionary origins, and the privileged role of the armed forces in the political system ensured that the preferred mechanism for maintaining security was military power, and Soviet militarism was repeatedly described as a real and present danger to the entire international community. Not least, the Soviet Union continued to be regarded as the heir of the messianic ideology of Marxism-Leninism, a non—status quo power with little or no stake in a stable world order.

The sweeping transformations affected under the aegis of Mikhail Gorbachev's *perestroika* ("restructuring") called most such assumptions seriously into question. Under the impetus of Gorbachev's "new thinking" the climate of fear and hostility that once characterized East-West relations melted away and began to be replaced by new patterns of security cooperation. Perestroika was a high-risk undertaking, however,

---

1. Jonathan Alford, "Introduction," in Jonathan Alford, ed., *The Soviet Union: Security Policies and Constraints* (New York, 1985), p. xii.

ix

and it has culminated in the collapse of Soviet communism and a major crisis of political order. Though the eventual consequences of this crisis for the peoples of the former USSR and for the entire international community are impossible to predict, it is clear they will be profound. Whatever the future may hold, the changes provoked by the reform experience have been sufficiently dramatic to make mandatory a reassessment of our own inherited assumptions about the Soviet quest for security, the motives that shaped it historically, and the forces that will account for its transformation in a new context during the years to come. This book provides a foundation for addressing such issues by offering a systematic reevaluation of Soviet security policy from 1917 to the autumn of 1991.

What is security? Although much of what is written about the theme concentrates upon military-related issues, in order to grasp the security dilemma in its full contours we must go much further. Security is not coterminous with military capacity, and one of the basic sources of Soviet perestroika was the conviction that in the past an attempt to achieve security by maintaining unassailable military strength actually undermined the USSR's more enduring interests. A study of national security policy must first of all address active measures undertaken to ward off external threats, but security policy is not only concerned with denial. It also seeks to preserve and confirm positive allegiances, which for want of a better term we might call "core values." Such values are usually defined by a deeply rooted political culture as well as by the priorities of governments currently in power. They are flexible but not entirely so, and their cogency makes a clear distinction between the internal and external dimensions of security very difficult to draw. Were Soviet core values more threatened by a potentially hostile military presence in adjacent territories, or by the dynamics of ethnic rivalry and separatism within the boundaries of the USSR? By the economic dynamism of international competitors, or by the Soviet Union's own technological lag? Such questions, impossible to answer if addressed in isolation, serve to point out the complexity of the security problem.

Over the years Soviet analysts attempted to elaborate a formal framework for the development and implementation of security policy. The first element in that framework was policy itself (*politika*), defined in classic Marxist terms with an emphasis on the economic determinants of political behavior, but with the caveat that only a consideration of the complex interactions among many variables allows for a full understanding of the policy environment. Policy was subdivided into more specific areas, including military policy (*voennaia politika*), the closest approximation to the dominant western concept of security policy in traditional Soviet usage. Military policy integrates the various factors relevant to establishing an adequate national defense and, according to a recent Soviet commentator, "determines the entire complex of ideological, moral-political, military-patriotic, economic, scientific-technical, foreign policy, and also purely military measures which . . . are implemented in the interest of maintaining the security of the state."[2] Military policy in turn determines the parameters of military doctrine (*voennaia doktrina*), encompassing both sociopolitical and military-technical dimensions (with the latter covering the more familiar categories of military strategy, operational art, and tactics). Military doctrine is concerned with the effort either to deter war or to wage it successfully, and is thus the domain where the actual planning of military operations goes on, but it is carefully subordinated to the larger political context within which preparations for the contingency of war are being made.[3] These distinctions are often highly abstract, but they are not entirely scholastic. The categories themselves reveal inherited perceptions and patterns of thought, and until recently they were used consistently to analyze the past and recommend changes for the future.

Here I use a broad definition of security compatible with traditional Soviet categories which encompasses military, political, and socioeconomic dimensions. The interaction between these various dynamics is examined in comparative historical perspective. My goal, to borrow the words of Robert Legvold, is to put aside "simple assumptions and begin to deal directly with the notions that actually shape the Soviet approach to the primary issues of power, security, and order" by using the past as "a hill from which to judge the evolution of Soviet perspective."[4] It might be charged that such an approach voids the notion of security policy of its relevance by merging it with that of foreign policy in the more traditional sense. So be it; security has always been the essential goal of foreign policy, and to opt for a narrow focus is inevitably to neglect what are often highly relevant variables. To the extent that a working definition of security might be useful, I prefer a larger one, such as that provided by Bruce Parrott: " 'National security' is here taken to mean military, economic, and political protection against external threats. By this definition, Soviet national-security policy encompasses

---

2. V. P. Khalipov, *Voennaia politika KPSS* (Moscow, 1988), p. 16, and the entire discussion on pp. 15–24.

3. Raymond L. Garthoff, *Deterrence and the Revolution in Soviet Military Doctrine* (Washington, D.C., 1990), pp. 37–40, elaborates on these distinctions. See also the discussion in Makhmut Akhmetovich Gareev, *M. V. Frunze, Military Theorist* (Washington, D.C., 1988), pp. 79–143.

4. Robert Legvold, "The Concept of Power and Security in Soviet History," in Christoph Bertram, ed., *Prospects of Soviet Power in the 1980s* (London, 1980), p. 6.

military programs, diplomatic interactions, economic choices affecting the state's geopolitical position, and policy toward foreign economic and cultural contacts."[5]

The Soviet approach to security has often been described as a function of fixed determinants such as geostrategic constraints (vague and open frontiers, limited access to the high seas), Russian national traits (a tradition of autocratic government, a strain of xenophobic nationalism), political ideology (the messianic strain in Russian political culture, the concept of the world revolution), or the "anarchic" character of the international political system. *Black Earth, Red Star* postulates that although such underlying themes lent some continuity to Soviet policy, the importance of fixed determinants has been exaggerated. Explanations concentrating on "immutable" motivation often fail to come to terms with the texture of policy making itself, and they are least of all satisfying at a moment that is witnessing a fundamental change of orientation. I second the observation of Helmut Sonnenfeldt and William G. Hyland that "it seems obvious that the question of what constitutes security has been answered differently at various times in the history of the Soviet Union."[6] My intention is not to suggest that Soviet policy was consistently pragmatic, but rather to note the importance of recent situations and events in pushing the evolution of that policy.

All states are compelled to come to terms with the security dilemma: the absence of effective supranational authority in world affairs, the need to accumulate power resources in order to defend against external threats, and the tendency for incremental increases in power capacity to heighten levels of insecurity and fear within the system as a whole. For the USSR, in common with other self-proclaimed revolutionary polities, the dilemma included a special twist. The October revolution was originally justified as an act of revolutionary internationalism. The Bolshevik regime based its claims to legitimacy on a set of assumptions that portrayed Soviet power as an agent of progressive social change, called down judgment on the dominant international order, and sought to negate the very idea of "national" security as traditionally understood. These aspirations were profound and could not easily be surrendered, but from the first day of its existence the search for security, and the compromises with principle that it imposed, became an essential formative experience for the Soviet state.

5. Bruce Parrott, "Soviet National Security under Gorbachev," *Problems of Communism* 6 (Nov.–Dec. 1988): 2. Barry Buzan, *People, States, and Fear: An Agenda for Security in the Post–Cold War Era* (New York, 1991), provides a good introduction to the problem.

6. Helmut Sonnenfeldt and William G. Hyland, "Soviet Perspectives on Security," in Alford, ed., *The Soviet Union*, p. 3.

The attempt to pursue an effective national security policy in a hostile world without sacrificing at least a pro forma commitment to its founding ideals is the essence of what might specifically be described as the *Soviet* security dilemma. Once Lenin's original hope that the revolution begun in Petrograd would expand to include Russia's more developed European neighbors had proved vain, a state that had been founded as an agent for the subversion of the established order confronted the need to "coexist" with its declared enemies more or less indefinitely. The resulting dilemma was never entirely resolved, and in consequence Soviet approaches to security were chronically ambiguous. A constant alternation between internationalism (in a variety of incarnations) and national self-interest, and the persistent need to justify actions in terms of an overarching ideology, lent Soviet policy its own distinctive patterns and rhythms. The attempt to monitor these rhythms and to identify the dominant motives shaping policy at any given point in time constitutes one of the main tasks of this book.

The *content* of Soviet policy as it was drawn up within a constantly changing national security environment can be described and evaluated more precisely. I suggest that, far from being immutable, Soviet security policy moved through a series of more or less distinct phases in response to changing perceptions of external threat, altered diplomatic circumstances, the emergence of new domestic elites, and the maturation of Soviet society itself. These phases are defined by what I call *security paradigms;* that is, sets of theoretically grounded assumptions about the nature of world politics, the Soviet Union's vocation within the community of states, the content of security threats, and the nature of appropriate responses. Seven distinct security paradigms (with related variants) are identified: *revolutionary internationalism* (1917–1921); *accommodation and retreat* (1921–1929); *collective security* (1933–1939); *survival* (1939–1944); *retrenchment* (1947–1953); *competitive coexistence* (1953–1985); and *mutual security* (1985–1991). These categories structure the text's eight chapters, which describe and interpret Soviet policy as it unfolds chronologically.

The concept of the security paradigm is intended to be suggestive and approximate. It is obviously impossible in the majority of cases to specify precise dates at which one set of dominant assumptions gives way to another, and in at least two cases (the periods 1929–1933 and 1944–1947), with policy in flux and equilibrium being sought, no single characterization seems appropriate. I have no desire to force interpretations into a Procrustean bed of inflexible ideal types, or to insist that the categorization I have chosen is necessarily the only or best one available. The point is to give form to the argument that the Soviet approach to security was characterized by adaptability and dynamic evolution as well as by continuity. Within the poles defined by the Soviet security dilemma, leaders in Moscow developed a succession of contrasting approaches to the security problem, approaches sufficiently distinct to allow them to be ordered around loosely defined models. The seven security paradigms I identify are used to characterize clearly discernible phases in the evolution of policy, to structure the attempt to understand its motive forces, and to represent the evolution in Soviet thinking about the security problem somewhat more formally.

Two additional points should be made concerning my underlying assumptions. First, I believe that the process of perestroika was in many ways a logical consequence of the Soviet past. It was also an attempt to redeem that past by thoroughly eliminating the legacy of Stalinism and finding a way back to the original progressive inspiration of the October revolution. Gorbachev's aspiration was to effect a revolutionary transformation of Soviet society and of the Soviet Union's relations with the external world without surrendering the basic premises of Soviet power. By decisively posing the issue of fundamental reform, the architects of perestroika accomplished a task of historic proportions. But their program ran headlong into the essential contradictions of Soviet society, with its profoundly undemocratic political culture, its history of repression and fear, its ethnic and linguistic complexity, and its conservative elites strongly resistant to change. As the tenacity of opposition to reform became clear, Aleksandr Iakovlev lamented that "the processes of healing are complicated and may go forward unevenly" and warned of the possibility for destabilizing tendencies to gain the upper hand, leading to "the triumph of an aggressive, vengeful conservatism."[7] The processes of healing have been more than complicated: it has proved to be impossible to eradicate the legacy of Stalin without shattering the very foundations of the USSR itself, and the Soviet peoples have been swept into an unprecedented crisis that is likely to last for years. My study rests upon the assumption that it is only in the light of the Soviet past that both the strengths and the limitations of the Soviet reform project, and the ambiguous character of its outcome, can be grasped.

It is also perhaps worth noting that the theme of this book still matters. The instability that has been provoked by perestroika, the likelihood that such instability will continue for some time, and the disengagement from a leading role in world affairs that has resulted have led many to conclude that Moscow has no choice but to default from its accumulated international responsibilities, and no option other than precipitous

7. A. Iakovlev, "Otvet—v nas samikh," *Voprosy ekonomiki* 2(1989): 12. Aleksandr Iakovlev is generally considered to have been one of the intellectual fathers of Soviet perestroika.

decline. Soviet power, so long feared and execrated for its alleged desire to inherit the earth, has become, overnight, a chimera deserving little more than contempt. Such perceptions, in some ways merely a mirror image of the exaggerated preoccupation with Soviet ambition that went before, are potentially misleading. The "victory of the West" in the Cold War will no doubt prove to be Pyrrhic; a just and viable international security order is tragically far from having been achieved. Whatever the outcome of the storms through which the old Soviet Union is passing, a reformed confederation of former Soviet republics or its Great Russian core will remain a significant member of the community of states. And the Soviet experience will not just go away. It contains both darkness and light, and will continue to represent one of the essential poles of twentieth-century politics.

Black Earth, Red Star is a work of historical synthesis. Its conclusions rest upon the pioneering efforts of generations of scholars whose attempts to come to terms with the Soviet experience have created a rich and diverse foundation for inquiry. The issues that I range over are controversial, and it would be surprising if my judgments did not on occasion generate some heat. I have attempted to state these judgments clearly and to defend them open-mindedly. As new archival materials become accessible to independent scholars in the years to come, some points of controversy will, I hope, be addressed more definitively.

My more ambitious goal is to attach the theme of security policy to a larger reevaluation of the entire Soviet experience and to bring to the study of the national security problem, too often examined in a very narrow frame of reference, an element Stephen Cohen has defined as "an intellectual passion for Russian-Soviet civilization."[8] My title juxtaposes the two elements from which the distinctive character of the Soviet security dilemma derived: the black earth of the Slavic east as a symbol of inherited national values, and the red star of Soviet power as the emblem of the political experiment born of the October revolution. I believe that only by making the effort to empathize with Soviet decision makers whose options were defined by these elements, and to see the world as it appeared when viewed from Moscow, can the dynamics of Soviet policy be grasped in all their complexity. The book's larger purpose is to offer an adequately researched, conceptually ordered, and intellectually consistent foundation for understanding these dynamics more completely.

I began this book as a resident fellow with the Peace Studies Program at Cornell University and completed it as a visiting scholar at Duke

---

8. Stephen F. Cohen, *Rethinking the Soviet Experience: Politics and History since 1917* (Oxford, 1985), p. 10.

University. I particularly thank Richard Ned Lebow of Cornell for his enthusiasm for the project and for making it possible for me to work in the stimulating environment of the Peace Studies Program. Thanks also to Warren Lerner for inviting me to Duke, where I was able to complete the manuscript with the benefit of reduced teaching and administrative responsibilities. The bulk of my work was accomplished in Switzerland and Italy, where the library staffs of the Eastern European Institute in Bern and the Johns Hopkins University Bologna Center were consistently helpful in making materials available to me. *Chaleureux remerciements* to Marie-Madeleine and Albert Geneux for the use of the Chalet Bon Accueil, "si loin du monde," where Chapters 7 and 8 were written. Matt Evangelista, David Glantz, John Harper, Otto Pick, and Anthony Radev offered their time to read the manuscript, and their comments have improved it immeasurably (within the limits of my own ability to take advantage of them). Many thanks also to my research assistant, Farzin Mirmotahari, and to my student assistants in Bologna, Léa Drouet, Nina Novikova, and Klaus Wiegrefe. I owe a particular debt to my wife, Kate Cucugliello-Nation, and our son, Marc Julien, whose patience and love have been beyond measure. I hope the result represents a useful contribution to a fuller understanding of the Soviet experience.

R. CRAIG NATION

Durham, North Carolina
Bologna, Italy

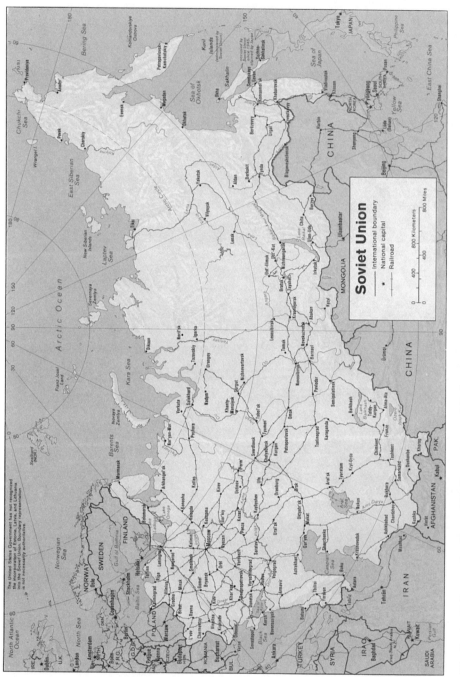

The Soviet Union, 1989. From U.S. Department of Defense.

CHAPTER ONE

The Age of World Revolution, 1917–1921

> The capitalists call that piece of earth which they surround with bayonets their fatherland, but we say that our fatherland, given to us by nature, is the entire earth, that in this fatherland, that is, in the earth as a whole, we want to organize one common fraternal economy, where there will be no frontiers, no bayonets, no enmity . . . so that people may live, not like wild beasts fighting over a piece of bread, but as brothers in harmony, who cultivate the earth together and transform it into one flowering garden for all humankind.
>
> —Lev Trotsky, 9 June 1918

Upon his appointment as the first Soviet people's commissar of foreign affairs in November 1917, Lev Trotsky claims to have remarked, "What diplomatic work are we apt to have now? I will issue a few revolutionary proclamations to the peoples of the world, and then shut up shop." The quip is often cited as an example of the naïveté with which the Bolsheviks set out to confront the unfamiliar world of international relations, but in fact it was made ironically. Trotsky's intention was to signal the desire to bring a whole new set of priorities to bear upon the conduct of foreign affairs.[1] Although lacking experience in the craft of diplomacy, the Bolsheviks came to power with a coherent image of the international system derived from their experience as revolutionaries during World War I and from the categories of classical Marxism. True to their roots, they rejected what were considered to be the discredited canons of bourgeois diplomacy and sought to put in their place an internationalist alternative.

Soviet security policy during the years of revolution and civil war from 1917 to 1921 can be understood only if one looks beyond the conceptual

---

1. Trotsky recounts the remark proudly, a dozen years after the fact, in his autobiography. Leon Trotsky, *My Life: An Attempt at an Autobiography* (New York, 1930), p. 341.

framework of traditional European statecraft. The dominant paradigm of the Bolsheviks was *revolutionary internationalism,* a commitment to the radical transformation of an imperialist world order judged to be historically bankrupt. The Russian revolution of 1917, Vladimir Il'ich Lenin was convinced, was not an isolated and fortuitous event, but rather a part of a general crisis of capitalist imperialism. The October revolution represented the first flash point in what Lenin called an "era of international socialist revolution," and it was assumed that unless the revolution that had begun in Russia spread to include at least one of the leading industrial states, it would be doomed to defeat.[2] "We place all our hopes upon our revolution igniting the European revolution," Trotsky stated in the wake of the Bolshevik seizure of power. "If the rising of the peoples of Europe does not crush imperialism, we will be crushed . . . that is unquestionable."[3] The key to the success of the revolution lay in its ability to function as a catalyst for what Lenin called the "world revolution."

Elements of utopianism and adventurism were attached to these expectations, but Lenin and his comrades were neither fanatical extremists nor cynical opportunists. The world war in progress was generating explosive social tensions, and real grounds existed for supposing that a new round of revolutionary confrontations was inevitable. What is more, the Bolsheviks' attachment to internationalism was deeply rooted in their party's entire theoretical development. "The workers have no fatherland," claimed *The Communist Manifesto* in a passage Lenin described during 1914 as "a fundamental truth of socialism."[4] It was to the legacy of Karl Marx and Friedrich Engels, rather than that of Otto von Bismarck or Camillo Cavour, that the Bolsheviks turned in defining their attitude toward the problem of international security after 1917.

Imperialism and World Revolution

Marx and Engels did not write systematically about the problems of international relations, but the implications of their work in this domain were considerable. In broad outline, the fathers of "scientific socialism" attempted to combine a radical image of the future of international society with a realistic appraisal of its limitations in the present. Both Marx and Engels adopted a pragmatic approach to the

2. Vladimir Il'ich Lenin, *Polnoe sobranie sochinenii* [hereinafter cited as *PSS*], 5th ed., 55 vols. (Moscow, 1958–64), 36:58–59.

3. *Vtoroi vserossiiskii s"ezd sovetov* (Petrograd, 1917), pp. 24–25.

4. Karl Marx and Friedrich Engels, *Werke,* 39 vols. (Berlin, 1961–68), 4:479; Lenin, *PSS,* 26:2.

international conflicts of their era, taking sides on the basis of highly subjective criteria. Oppressed classes were admonished "to master themselves the mysteries of international politics" and to make use of the institutions of bourgeois statecraft for their own ends.[5] On the other hand, Marxist political theory identified the "centralized state mechanism" as a guarantor of class privilege that would have to be superseded in the course of a social revolution. Victorious socialism, it was implied, would gradually eliminate the need for the coercive authority of the nation-state, which would eventually begin to "wither away" and give place to a universal socialist federation.

The agent of the bourgeois state's transformation was to be capitalism's dispossessed class, the industrial proletariat. The cumulating structural crisis inherent in the capitalist mode of production, it was argued, would eventually provoke proletarian revolution and initiate a restructuring of the contemporary world order. In the context of capitalist class society and during the transition to socialism the state was presumed to possess a measure of autonomy that made it a relevant actor in world politics. But Marx and Engels also offered the vision of a truly international society in which the national form and its related imperatives of sovereignty and security would be altered beyond recognition.[6]

Marx's internationalist vision achieved institutional expression in 1864, with the creation of the International Workingman's Association (First International), a confederation of socialist and labor parties pledged to embody the international solidarity of the proletariat. Though the First International collapsed in 1876 as a result of strife within its ranks between followers of Marx and the Russian anarchist Mikhail Bakunin, it established a significant precedent. In 1889 a Second International was created in Paris as the centerpiece of a social democratic labor movement inspired by Marxist theory and outspokenly pledged to the cause of internationalism.

Until the outbreak of World War I in August 1914, the primacy of internationalism in the social democratic program was unquestioned. All the greater the shock, then, when in the war's first days the International's leading parties abruptly abandoned their oft-expressed commitments to oppose war and rallied instead to a posture of "socialist defensism," urging support for their respective national military efforts. The contrast between words and deeds could hardly have been greater. The national principle, it seemed, had triumphed, and socialist internationalism proved a chimera when put to the test.

5. Marx and Engels, *Werke*, 16:13.
6. For a general discussion see Alan Gilbert, *Marx's Politics: Communists and Citizens* (New Brunswick, N.J., 1981), pp. 139–58.

It was as a reaction to the debacle of internationalism in August 1914 that the foundations of what would become the Soviet approach to international affairs were established. During the war's first months a movement of opposition to defensism gradually took form on the left-wing of the international socialist community. In September 1915 in the Swiss village of Zimmerwald (near Bern) a conference of oppositionists gave rise to the "Zimmerwald movement," a loose association of socialist parties and factions committed to work for peace. The Zimmerwald movement, however, was not united over strategy. A minority "Zimmerwald Left" faction organized and led by Lenin posed a challenge to the peace orientation of the movement's majority on several grounds. Lenin insisted that hopes for a democratic peace under bourgeois hegemony were vain. Socialists should abandon "bourgeois pacifism" and make use of the crisis provoked by the war to force revolutionary transformations. Where the Zimmerwald majority hoped to win back the errant defensists by reasserting traditional commitments to peace and internationalism, the Zimmerwald Left scorned the traitorous "social patriots" and demanded their expulsion from the movement. The Second International, the Left insisted, was dead. The task of the Zimmerwaldists was to break with its discredited remnant and to built a new, third international upon the principles of revolutionary Marxism.[7]

Lenin justified the line adopted by the Zimmerwald Left with a series of postulates marked by a radical rejection of any and all compromise with nationalism. To suggest that the world war was a "national" contest, he asserted, was the purest cant and hypocrisy. It was a predatory war of imperialism, waged by the great powers for domination of world markets, that had nothing to do with real popular aspirations. The proper attitude for Marxists to assume toward their national governments was revolutionary defeatism, the premise that defeat represented a "lesser evil" from the perspective of the working class, which was admonished to turn its weapons against the "enemy at home" and "transform the imperialist war into a civil war for socialism."

The theoretical foundation for these slogans was provided by Lenin's *Imperialism the Highest Stage of Capitalism,* written in Zurich during 1916.[8] The tract offered nothing new in the way of underlying assumptions; the concept of imperialism had become a commonplace on the

7. The history of the Zimmerwald Left is recounted by R. Craig Nation, *War on War: Lenin, the Zimmerwald Left, and the Origins of Communist Internationalism* (Durham, N.C., 1989), and from a traditional Soviet perspective by Ia. G. Temkin, *Lenin i mezhdunarodnaia sotsial-demokratiia, 1914–1917* (Moscow, 1968).

8. Lenin, *PSS,* 27:299–426, and for a useful commentary, Anthony Brewer, *Marxist Theories of Imperialism: A Critical Survey* (London, 1989), pp. 109–35.

socialist left prior to the war, and Lenin drew on what was already a considerable literature in developing his arguments. It was in applying the concept to the conjuncture created by the war and using it as the foundation for a series of politically barbed conclusions that *Imperialism the Highest Stage of Capitalism* broke new ground.

Imperialism was defined as a stage in the evolution of modern capitalism, which in the age of monopoly control and finance capital had burst the bounds of the nation-state and emerged as an interdependent world system. By stimulating the concentration and more rational organization of production, imperialism gave a boost to productive capacity, and as such it represented capitalism's "highest" phase. But it also contained destabilizing tendencies that, as Rosa Luxemburg put it in her own study of capitalist imperialism in 1913, take "forms which make the final phase of capitalism a period of catastrophe."[9] The most visible consequence of imperialism was the colonial system, accompanied by sharpened rivalry among the great powers for hegemony within the colonial domains. Super-exploitation of the colonies allowed the metropolitan centers of industrial capitalism temporarily to ward off crisis at home, but it also created an inevitable political reaction in the world at large. Lenin insisted that in the age of imperialism support for "national liberation movements" had become a necessary dimension of an emerging global struggle for socialism, even when the primary goal of such movements was national rather than social revolution. Even more important, with the bulk of the world already divided into colonial preserves, heightened imperial rivalry between the great powers was ineluctable. The present war, Lenin concluded, was only the first in a series of imperialist wars and catastrophic international dislocations. Its political implications were correspondingly immense.

As an antidote to the open-ended crisis that the imperialist war was presumed to have initiated, Lenin offered the concept of world revolution. Capitalist imperialism was riven by intractable contradictions, he asserted, and could not achieve an enduring peace. The present war revealed the bankruptcy of the international system of developed capitalism, the futility of reformist illusions, and the urgent need for a revolutionary alternative. The world revolution would develop as a response to a disintegrating imperialism, encompassing revolutionary national struggles in the colonial world as well as proletarian revolution in the imperial metropoles. It represented a process rather than an event, an era of revolutionary change with the ideal of social justice as its goal. There was a visionary strain in such analysis, but also a degree of

9. Rosa Luxemburg, *Gesammelte Werke*, 5 vols. (Berlin, 1983), 5:392.

hard-minded realism. The world war was an unprecedented catastrophe, and after several years of terrible battles revolutionary prospects were more than hopeful inventions.

When in March (February) 1917 what had begun as a spontaneous strike movement in the Russian empire's capital, Petrograd culminated in a popular insurrection that destroyed the tsarist autocracy and elevated a democratically oriented "Provisional Government" in its place, Lenin immediately interpreted the events as the first stage of "the proletarian revolution that is *beginning* in Europe."[10] Upon his return to Petrograd in April, Lenin shocked much of his own party by denouncing the Provisional Government and urging preparations for a new, socialist revolution. The industrial working class and its socialist representatives, came the obvious response, were too weak in underdeveloped Russia to take and maintain power. Lenin's rejoinder was that to view the Russian revolution in exclusively national terms was to misperceive its origins in a general crisis of capitalist imperialism. The era of world revolution had begun, and it had fallen to the Russian proletariat to fight its first battle. The Bolsheviks could strike for power confident that their example would fan the flames of revolution in the heartland of industrial Europe.

Lenin was well aware of the possibility that the socialist revolution might triumph first of all in a single state, where it would be required to maintain itself in semi-isolation until such time as new revolutionary conjunctures developed elsewhere. In "The Military Program of the Proletarian Revolution," written during 1916, he specifically justified armed defense of the revolution in terms of its international aspirations.

> The development of capitalism increases to the highest degree inequalities among various nations. . . . From this fact an unchallengeable conclusion emerges; socialism cannot triumph simultaneously *in all* countries. It will triumph first of all in one or several countries, while the remainder, for some time, will remain bourgeois or pre-bourgeois in character. This will create not only conflict, but direct attempts on the part of the bourgeoisie of other countries to destroy the victorious proletarian socialist state. In these circumstances, war will be necessary and just from our perspective. This will be a war for socialism, for the liberation of other peoples from bourgeois hegemony.[11]

In the autumn of 1917 Lenin and his comrades calculated the interval during which the revolution was likely to remain isolated in weeks or months, not in years. Their evaluation later proved badly flawed, but it

10. Lenin, *PSS*, 31:2.
11. Ibid., 30:133.

was essential to justify the decision to seize power. During the interval when the revolution would be left on its own, the Bolsheviks took it for granted that everything necessary must be done to ensure its survival. The struggle would be difficult, but by defending the revolution they could make a tangible contribution to the realization of their internationalist ideals. National survival was not at issue. The referent for security had become the struggle against the imperialist world order. Beyond the Bolsheviks' triumph in Russia stretched the world revolution and Marx's millenarian vision of communist society, in which the sources of war and national enmity would be purged away.

Revolutionary Internationalism and Realpolitik

Despite their high hopes for the progress of the world revolution, by assuming power within the confines of a sovereign state the Bolsheviks had placed themselves in an anomalous position. With power came obligation. Russia was still at war, and the survival of the revolution depended upon the ability of the new government to defend the state's territorial integrity. A certain duality in Bolshevik policy, torn between national responsibilities and internationalist priorities, was inherent in the situation that emerged after the October revolution. The Soviet security dilemma had been born.

The Soviet regime demonstrated its disdain for the conventions of bourgeois diplomacy by announcing the confiscation without compensation of foreign property, publishing and renouncing the tsar's secret treaties, and releasing a steady stream of inflammatory agitational statements intended to encourage fraternization at the fronts and stimulate popular unrest. The example provided by the revolution was powerful, but cut off from the remainder of Europe and of necessity preoccupied with their own lot, the Bolsheviks could do little to assist revolutionary forces elsewhere. Efforts to launch a third International proceeded slowly. At the 7th party congress in March 1918 the Bolsheviks renamed their organization the Russian Communist party (it had formerly been the Russian Social Democratic Labor party) and called on left-wing factions worldwide to follow them in breaking with the compromised social democratic heritage of the Second International. Gradually an international communist movement sprang to life, distinguished by its allegiance to the goal of revolution and support for the Bolsheviks in Russia. The founding conference of the Third, Communist International (Comintern) was held in Moscow during March 1919, but the movement was still in its infancy. Meanwhile, the Bolsheviks confronted problems that brooked no delay.

The most urgent of these problems was peace. It was an open secret that the Provisional Government's fate had been sealed by its inability to extract Russia from a war that its peoples were no longer willing to fight. The Bolsheviks won many converts by emphasizing their antiwar credentials, and they came to power pledged to secure an immediate end to hostilities. Moreover, during the winter of 1917–1918 the Imperial Army effectively ceased to exist.[12] The need for some kind of arrangement with Germany and its Austro-Hungarian, Bulgarian, and Turkish allies was obvious.

A willingness to make concessions in pursuit of peace was made evident by the very first act of the revolutionary government, the famous "Decree on Peace" promulgated by the 2nd Congress of Soviets on 8 November (25 October) 1917.[13] For those familiar with the fiery proclamations once issued by the Zimmerwald Left, the decree struck a surprisingly moderate tone. Calling for a "just and democratic peace" without annexations or contributions, urging a ceasefire as a prelude to negotiations, and expressly stating that Soviet conditions were not ultimatums but merely suggested points of departure, it was an earnest plea for a general armistice quite free of revolutionary rhetoric. The decree was a "diplomatic" text, though it was not necessarily perceived as such by those to whom it was addressed. Although the Bolsheviks themselves were probably dubious about the decree's prospects, by asserting the will to peace they had demonstrated good intentions and provided a veneer of legitimacy for the politically unpalatable but potentially necessary step of a separate peace with the Central Powers.

The Decree on Peace went unanswered, and on 20 November General Nikolai Dukhonin, commander in chief of what remained of the Imperial Army, was instructed to contact the German high command with the offer of an armistice. Unable to accept this affront to his conception of national honor, Dukhonin refused. He was cashiered several days later and eventually murdered by a revolutionary mob. On 26 November his successor, General Nikolai Krylenko, finally succeeded in conveying the

12. The fate of the Imperial Army is discussed in the complementary volumes by Allan K. Wildman, *The End of the Russian Imperial Army: The Old Army and the Soldiers' Revolt (March–April 1917)* (Princeton, N.J., 1980), and *The End of the Russian Imperial Army: The Road to Soviet Power and Peace* (Princeton, N.J., 1987). See also M. Frenkin, *Russkaia armiia i revoliutsiia, 1917–1918* (Munich, 1978).

13. The text is in *Dokumenty vneshnei politiki SSSR* [hereinafter cited as *DVP*], 21 vols. (Moscow, 1957–77), 1:11–14. Traditional Soviet evaluations laud the Decree on Peace as a summary of the basic premises of Soviet foreign policy. See, e.g., Iu. V. Vygodskii, *Leninskii dekret o mire* (Leningrad, 1958), pp. 3–6.

Soviet offer. "It is possible to negotiate with these people?" asked the perspicacious General Erich Ludendorff from his headquarters in Spa.[14] When he was assured that it was not only possible but much to hard-pressed Germany's advantage, peace talks were scheduled to open on 3 December at the border town of Brest-Litovsk.[15]

The Brest-Litovsk talks demanded a "deal with the devil" in the person of imperial Germany, and to some they seemed to betray prospects for a German revolution. With their proposal for a general peace in abeyance, however, it is difficult to see what choice the Bolsheviks had. Efforts were made at least to temper the effect of the offer. The Soviet delegation to Brest-Litovsk provided a quixotic representation of the ideal of a people's peace. Headed by Adolf Ioffe, a member of the Bolshevik Central Committee, it included living exemplars of the revolution in the persons of a peasant, worker, soldier, and sailor. On 21, 28, and 30 November, and again on 6 December and 12 January, the Soviet government wired appeals to the Entente powers urging their participation in the talks.[16] All remained unanswered. As negotiations began within the ancient Brest fortress, a fitting symbol for the hoary traditions of European statecraft, Ioffe sought to use them as a platform for broadcasting the Bolsheviks' revolutionary message. In a diplomatic innovation undertaken at Soviet insistence, a full stenographic account of the proceedings was kept and released to the world press at the end of each day. When pressed, however, Ioffe was required to admit that he had not even received a mandate from his government to approve a ceasefire on the eastern front. It was only after returning to Russia for consultation that he could sign the armistice, which went into effect on 15 December along the entire length of the front from the Baltic to the Black Sea.

Ioffe returned to Brest-Litovsk on 22 December armed with the "Outline Program for Peace Negotiations" written by Lenin, which contained little more than general guidelines.[17] His intention remained to delay the negotiations while seeking somehow to involve the Entente powers, but

14. Cited in Max Hoffmann, *Die Aufzeichnungen des Generalmajors Max Hoffmann*, 2 vols. (Berlin, 1930), 2:319.

15. Good general accounts of the negotiations are provided by John W. Wheeler-Bennett, *Brest-Litovsk: The Forgotten Peace, March 1918* (London, 1938); Richard K. Debo, *Revolution and Survival: The Foreign Policy of Soviet Russia, 1917–18* (Toronto, 1979), pp. 45–169. There is a large Soviet literature reflecting traditional interpretations, including A. O. Chubar'ian, *Brestskii mir* (Moscow, 1964); G. L. Nikol'nikov, *Vydaiushchaiasia pobeda leninskoi strategii i taktiki. Brestskii mir: Ot zakliucheniia do razryva* (Moscow, 1968). A more balanced contemporary evaluation is presented by A. V. Pantsov, "Brestskii mir," *Voprosy istorii* 2 (1990): 60–79.

16. *DVP*, 1:16–17, 28–30, 31–32, 41–42, and 76–79.

17. Lenin, *PSS*, 35:121–22.

within a week it became clear that such hopes were vain, and that Russia, alone, was confronting a vindictive and uncompromising German rival. On 28 November, Ioffe felt compelled to request a recess in order for the Soviet government to prepare a more precise negotiating strategy. Contemplating a very limited range of options, on 31 December, Lenin presented the Council of People's Commissars (Sovnarkom) with a project resolution recommending an intensification of revolutionary propaganda, an effort to reorganize Russia's armed forces, and an attempt to buy time by dragging out the Brest talks for as long as possible.[18] On 9 January the Soviet delegation reappeared at Brest-Litovsk with People's Commissar of Foreign Affairs Trotsky at its head. Trotsky proved adept as a revolutionary tribune, but it was painfully clear that the Soviet position rested on sand. On 18 January the German foreign minister Richard von Kühlmann presented an ultimatum, threatening a resumption of hostilities and demanding the outright cession of Lithuania, Courland, and Russia's Polish provinces, with the fate of the Ukraine to be left to separate negotiations with the separatist Ukrainian National Council (or Rada). The tactic of delay now seemed to be exhausted.

The Soviet regime confronted its first foreign policy crisis with the leadership badly divided. A significant portion of the Central Committee, led by the respected young theorist Nikolai Bukharin, adopted a "Left Communist" orientation premised upon the need to wage revolutionary war against Germany.[19] In his minority report to the 7th party congress Bukharin specified what this implied—nothing less than a readiness to court defeat if no principled alternative remained.

> We always said that sooner or later the Russian revolution . . . would clash with international capitalism. This moment is upon us. Already at the very outset of the revolution we said that either the Russian revolution would be saved by the international revolution, or it would perish under the blows of international capitalism. This was our most fundamental thesis, and it is completely correct, since we have spoken about the very possibility of the

18. Ibid., p. 181.
19. Left Communism as a political tendency defended a program with implications that extended well beyond the debate over a separate peace. See Robert Vincent Daniels, *The Conscience of the Revolution: Communist Opposition in Soviet Russia* (Cambridge, Mass., 1960), pp. 70–91; Leonard Schapiro, *The Origin of the Communist Autocracy: The First Phase, 1917–1922* (London, 1955), pp. 130–46; Stephen F. Cohen, *Bukharin and the Bolshevik Revolution: A Political Biography, 1888–1938* (New York, 1973), pp. 62–69.

Russian revolution's defeat, that no one should reproach us now with not having foreseen these difficulties, these weighty prospects which now stand before us.[20]

Rejecting attempts to rebuild a conventional army, calling instead for the creation of "flying partisan detachments" and a general mobilization of the armed people, Bukharin appealed to the fundament of his party's revolutionary doctrine.[21] Revolutionary war was not a desperate last resort necessitated by the German ultimatum. It was a means for the revolution positively to affirm its rejection of diplomatic hypocrisy and faith in popular alternatives. The world revolution, Bukharin implied, was an absolute priority, and it was only under its sign that the Bolsheviks would conquer.

Lenin had also mentioned the possibility of revolutionary war in his draft program of 31 December, but he soon became convinced that it was not a viable option. On 19 January he presented the Central Committee with a set of twenty-one unambiguously entitled "Theses on the Question of the Immediate Conclusion of a Separate and Annexationist Peace," in which he attempted to justify acceptance of the German ultimatum by redefining the pace of the world revolution.

> There is no doubt that the socialist revolution in Europe must occur and will occur. All our hope for the *final* victory of socialism is based upon this conviction, this scientific conclusion. . . . But it would be a mistake to construct a tactic for the socialist government of Russia on the attempt to determine whether the European, and especially the German revolution, will or will not break out in the next six months (or after a similarly brief interval). Because this can in no way be determined, all similar attempts, objectively, come to resemble a blind game of chance.[22]

Reliance upon revolutionary prospects in Europe, Lenin seemed to be saying, could only be part of a long-term strategy. Soviet power confronted immediate choices, and a "tactic for the socialist government of Russia" would have to include a degree of flexibility. Harshly refuting charges that a separate peace represented a betrayal of proletarian internationalism, he insisted that the first priority of any revolution was to ensure its own survival. If survival demanded a temporary deal with one

20. *Sed'moi ekstrennyi s''ezd RKP (b). Mart 1918 goda. Stenograficheskii otchet* (Moscow, 1962), p. 24.

21. See ibid., pp. 101–9, for Bukharin's attempt to demonstrate the feasibility of citizens' defense in the face of an attack by regular armed forces.

22. Lenin, *PSS*, 35:245.

or another bloc of imperialist states, there was no choice but to "crawl in the mud" and submit. "No matter which way we turn," he pointed out, "we cannot wholly escape this or that imperialist group. That is impossible without the complete destructon of world imperialism." Rather, "from the time a socialist government is victorious in any one country, questions must be decided . . . solely from the point of view of what is best for the development and consolidation of the socialist revolution which has already begun."[23] This was more than a justification for the Brest peace. It was a sophisticated argument against revolutionary intransigence and in support of a tactic of maneuver.

It remained for Trotsky to present a stop-gap alternative to the stark choice between revolutionary war and annexationist peace. He suggested further stalling, backed up, if the Soviets' bluff was called, by a unilateral declaration of peace. The proposal was bizarre, but it was not without its merits. Berlin was engaged in a life-or-death struggle on the western front, and there were powerful forces within Germany determined to avoid further military operations in the east at all cost; moreover, Germany's allies were outspoken advocates of peace. Trotsky's suggestion also allowed the postponement of a decisive confrontation within the Central Committee, where Lenin's position was by no means secure. With the party's reluctant approval, Trotsky carried what would become known as his "no war, no peace" solution back to Brest-Litovsk on 29 January.

After further delays and in response to a new German ultimatum, on 10 February, Trotsky announced that Russia was leaving the war without a negotiated settlement. German military authorities now secured approval for a resumption of the war in the east, and on 16 February, Berlin issued an ultimatum containing even more severe conditions, including cession of the entire Ukraine. On 18 February, German forces were set in motion, unopposed and moving in relative comfort along the main rail lines.

With disaster looming, Lenin was now able to override opposition and force acceptance of the German terms upon the Central Committee.[24] Communication with the German high command proved difficult, and as troops continued to advance the Bolsheviks scurried to mobilize their meager means of resistance. On 21 February the Sovnarkom issued an appeal entitled "The Socialist Fatherland in Danger," and on the

23. Ibid., p. 247.
24. Stenographic accounts of these debates appear in "Deiatel'nost' Tsentral'nogo Komiteta partii v dokumentakh," *Izvestiia TsK KPSS* 2 (1989): 176–96. V. V. Zhuravlev, "Rubicon Bresta," *Voprosy istorii KPSS* 7 (1990): 29–45, emphasizes the positive spirit of the debate as a Leninist model for inner-party democracy.

following day the Central Committee agreed to petition the Entente powers for military assistance, a decision that prompted Bukharin's temporary resignation.[25] Concern over German intentions was understandable but unnecessary. What was occurring was not an attempt to overturn the revolutionary government, whose willingness to make concessions suited German purposes, but merely a land grab. When the treaty of Brest-Litovsk was signed on 3 March, troop movements in the east came to an end.[26]

At Brest-Litovsk and in association with the Russo-German supplementary treaty of 27 August, the German-Finnish treaty of 7 March, and the German-Romanian treaty of 7 May, the Bolsheviks surrendered Russia's former Polish provinces, Lithuania, Courland, Livonia, Estonia, the Ukraine, a portion of the Grodno and Bessarabia regions, and ceded three districts in the Caucasus to Turkey (Kars, Ardahan, and Batum)— in toto over a million square kilometers of territory, including rich industrial and agricultural regions and more than 50 million inhabitants. No clearer object lesson in the consequences of weakness and exposure could be imagined. But the Bolsheviks had gained something as well. Their revolutionary institutions remained intact and they won access to what Lenin called a "breathing space." Chastened by events, the 7th party congress and the 4th All-Russian Soviet Congress during March approved and ratified the Brest treaty by comfortable margins.

The severity of the settlement was partially attributable to the ill-fated experiment with Trotsky's "no peace, no war" formula, and the people's commissar has been mockingly criticized for his "illusions" during the negotiations. The historians Mikhail Heller and Aleksandr Nekrich, for example, characterize the confrontation between Trotsky and Max von Hoffmann (the German military representative) at Brest-Litovsk as "an encounter and collision between utopianism and realism."[27] This is a peculiar conclusion in view of the treaty's outcome. Within months the policy defended by the "realist" Hoffmann would lead to defeat and debacle, while the Bolsheviks managed to recoup most of their losses on the battlefields of the civil war. What is more, Trotsky's policy served other than narrowly diplomatic ends. It allowed Lenin to avoid what might have become a damaging confrontation with the partisans of

25. The text of the appeal is given in *Sed'moi ekstrennyi s"ezd RKP (b)*, p. 218. For Bolshevik overtures to the Allies, see Jacques Sadoul, *Notes sur la révolution bolchevique* (Paris, 1920), pp. 241–43; D. V. Oznobishin, *Ot Bresta do Iur'eva: Iz istorii vneshnei politiki sovetskoi vlasti 1917–1920 gg.* (Moscow, 1966), pp. 91–92. The confrontation with the Central Committee is described in Trotsky, *My Life*, p. 389.

26. For the text of the treaty, see *DVP*, 1:119–205.

27. Mikhail Heller and Aleksandr Nekrich, *Utopia u vlasti: Istoriia Sovetskogo Soiuza s 1917 goda do nashikh dnei*, 2 vols. (London, 1982), 1:49.

revolutionary war, and it allowed the revolution to reassert its internationalist credentials by demonstrating that the decision to accept a
separate peace was made only under the most extreme compulsion. Karl
Radek defended the "no peace, no war" formula in precisely these terms
in an evaluation of Brest-Litovsk written in October 1918, reminding his
readers that in order to inspire world revolution, "the Russian revolution must appear before the world proletariat as a fighter, as an opponent of world imperialism." Because it "demonstrated to the European
working masses . . . that we concluded the rapacious peace with Germany only at gun point," Radek argued, Trotsky's policy had been more
than justified.[28]

In many ways the role of Brest-Litovsk as a "lesson" for the Bolsheviks
in the dog-eat-dog world of international politics has been exaggerated.[29] Soviet leaders entertained no illusions concerning the tender mer-
cies of their imperialist rivals, and they emerged from Brest-Litovsk with
their faith in world revolution unshaken. In an important sense their
willingness to accept the Draconian settlement, which dismantled the
physical base of the state's power and was opposed by every other organized Russian political faction, revealed an underlying scorn for the tradition of *raison d'état* and a confident identification with revolutionary
alternatives.

The Brest negotiations nonetheless affected Soviet perceptions of security in important ways. First, they served to discredit extremist formu-
las such as those represented by Bukharin. Revolutionary war simply
could not be defended as a feasible strategy under the conditions prevailing in 1918. Lenin's tactic of maneuver, urging compromise in order to
benefit from contradictions within the imperialist camp, would hence-
forth go unchallenged. Second, an awareness of the need for a capacity
for self-defense was reinforced. World revolution was still considered to
be the Soviet regime's most important ally in its long-term confrontation
with imperialism, but to secure its own survival, the revolution would

28. Karl Radek, *Vneshniaia politika sovetskoi Rossii* (Moscow-Petrograd, 1923), p. 17.
29. Richard Debo, for example, in an often highly insightful study, arrives at the exaggerated conclusion that "in March 1918, Soviet Russia had adopted a new foreign policy"
that "frankly repudiated" world revolution. Debo, *Revolution and Survival,* p. 300. For
Adam Ulam, Brest-Litovsk "marked the end of the age of innocence as far as the Bolsheviks
were concerned. They went into the negotiations as world revolutionaries; they emerged as
men solicitous mainly about their own state and power." Adam B. Ulam, *Expansion and
Coexistence: Soviet Foreign Policy, 1917–73,* 2d ed. (New York, 1974), p. 75. Evan Mawdsley, *The Russian Civil War* (Boston, 1987), p. 34, joins the chorus, calling Brest-Litovsk "a
sea change" where "revolutionary dreams had been abandoned for diplomatic reality."
Pantsov, "Brestskii mir," p. 79, is perhaps more correct in describing the treaty as a "maneuver" and "defeat" for the revolution, and noting that "despite this defeat the Bolsheviks' general strategic course . . . remained practically unchanged."

have to be strong. We signed the Brest peace, claimed Trotsky, "clench-ing our teeth, conscious of our weakness. . . . Yes, we are weak, and this is our greatest historical crime, because in history one must not be weak. Whoever is weak becomes a prey to the strong. Utopian preaching, lofty, beautiful words will not save us here."[30] What might save them was a competent army, and after Brest-Litovsk its construction became the highest priority of the revolution.

The Red Army of Workers and Peasants

The official date of birth for the new Soviet "Red Army of Workers and Peasants" (RKKA), long celebrated as a Soviet national holiday, is 23 February 1918. In fact, the date commemorates nothing more than an inconsequential or perhaps apocryphal encounter between a small group of Red Guards and an advancing German column in the area of Narva and Pskov. Intentionally chosen in 1922 from among many available alternatives, the date was intended to immortalize the de-fense of the revolution from an external threat.[31]

During the months following the October revolution the Soviet repub-lic's "armies" amounted to a chaotic mix of undisciplined Red Guards-men, stray units of the disintegrating Imperial Army, and so-called internationalist units organized among prisoners of war. Certain actions by the revolutionary government, such as the decree of general demobi-lization, the abolition of titles and ranks, and the introduction of direct election for officers up to the brigade level, helped feed the confusion. An order by Krylenko on 7 January confirmed that the Imperial Army had ceased to exist. The 3rd All-Russian Congress of Soviets on 25–26 January approved a plan to build a new army, and on 28 January a de-cree was published calling for voluntary enlistments. But the response was disappointing, and such units as were formed proved to be unruly and ineffective. The decision to press ahead more rapidly with the con-struction of a regular army came in the wake of Brest-Litovsk. Upon the appointment of Trotsky as commissar of war during March the effort

---

30. L. Trotskii, *Kak vooruzhalas' revoliutsiia* [hereinafter cited as *KVR*], 3 vols. (Mos-cow, 1923–25), 1:92–93.

31. Stalin made the point unambiguously in an address on 23 Feb. 1942. I. V. Stalin, *Sochineniia*, vol. 2 [XV], ed. Robert H. McNeal (Stanford, Calif., 1967), p. 37. In the Brezhnev era's official history of Soviet foreign policy one finds the dubious assertion that "as a result of the resistance which German forces encountered in the area of Narva and Pskov, they were denied the possibility of seizing Petrograd." A. A. Gromyko and B. N. Ponomarev, eds., *Istoriia vneshnei politiki SSSR*, 2 vols. (Moscow, 1980), 1:62.

received a dynamic leader with a clear perception of his goals and the power to achieve them.[32]

As products of the European social democratic tradition, the Bolsheviks inherited a corpus of doctrine concerning the role of organized military force in socialist society. Engels wrote at length on military affairs, including their more technical aspects. Marx evinced much less interest in such matters, but in his famous evaluation of the Paris Commune of 1870–1871 he praised the commune's abolition of the standing army and reliance upon the "armed people" to provide for its defense. During the era of the Second International the goal of replacing standing armies by a democratically controlled popular militia became the centerpiece of the social democratic military program.[33] In *State and Revolution,* written on the eve of the Bolshevik seizure of power, Lenin specified that the elimination of the standing army was a critical dimension of the democratic transformation that the revolution aspired to bring about.[34]

There was another edge to Bolshevik attitudes to the military question, however, which was particularly well represented in Lenin's wartime writings. Here the Bolshevik leader passionately condemned the influence of pacifist ideas upon the workers' movement and insisted upon the need for organized armed force (*voisko*) as the mailed fist of a victorious proletarian revolution. During 1915 Lenin carefully read the work of the Prussian military theorist Carl von Clausewitz, noting particularly his characterization of war as a continuation of politics "by other, namely violent means."[35] In *Socialism and War,* written during 1915, and in his contributions to the Swiss military debate in 1916, Lenin introduced a taxonomy of war which included four categories: (1) imperialist wars, (2) wars of national liberation, (3) revolutionary civil wars,

32. Detailed chronicles are provided by V. M. Cheremnykh, *Na zashchite zavoevanii revoliutsii: Voenno-organizatorskaia deiatel'nost' VTsIK v pervye gody sovetskoi vlasti* (Moscow, 1988), pp. 96–130; Iu. I. Korablev, *V. I. Lenin i zashchita zavoevanii Velikogo Oktiabria* (Moscow, 1979), pp. 100–288. See also John Erickson, "The Origins of the Red Army," in Richard Pipes, ed., *Revolutionary Russia* (Cambridge, Mass., 1968), pp. 224–58. The Red Guard phenomenon is described in Rex A. Wade, *Red Guards and Workers' Militia in the Russian Revolution* (Stanford, Calif., 1984).

33. The program is summarized in the classic study by Jean Jaurès, *L'armée nouvelle* (Paris, 1915).

34. Lenin, *PSS,* 33:79.

35. The intellectual encounter is described in Werner Hahlweg, "Lenin und Clausewitz: Ein Beitrag zur politischen Ideengeschichte des 20. Jahrhunderts," *Archiv für Kulturgeschichte,* vol. 36 (Munich-Cologne, 1954), pp. 20–59 and 357–87. See also Lenin's notebooks on Clausewitz in *Leninskii sbornik,* 36 vols. (Moscow, 1924–59), 12:387–452. A sympathetic description of Lenin's debt to Clausewitz is provided by N. N. Azovtsev, *V. I. Lenin i sovetskaia voennaia nauka* (Moscow, 1981), pp. 10–45.

and (4) wars in defense of a successful socialist revolution.[36] These categories rest upon a "just war" assumption that sanctions wars under specific political circumstances and by implication justifies concern for military expediency in the quest for victory. As the Russian civil war heated up during the summer of 1918, a shift in Bolshevik priorities, away from politically optimal and toward militarily efficacious forms of organization, was bound to occur. The revolution, as Lenin admonished Bukharin during the Brest-Litovsk debate, could not afford to "play with war."

The transformation of the RKKA into a centralized and disciplined armed force was embodied by the person of Trotsky. A revolutionary intellectual having no previous experience as a soldier or military administrator, Trotsky came to terms with the responsibilities of his new position with remarkable facility. His policies were shaped by a personal preference for tight organization, but also by the RKKA's first experiences in combat during the summer of 1918, where discipline proved to be woefully lacking. Gradually implemented in the course of the year, Trotsky's organizational design was to leave a lasting mark upon the Soviet military tradition.

To begin, the notion of a democratic militia was shelved as unachievable in a time of general war. A thoroughgoing militia system, Trotsky told the 5th All-Russian Congress of Soviets during July 1918, "is the necessary regime for a period of peaceful democratic construction. But we are living in conditions of open civil war, of class against class."[37] In April a general military training requirement was introduced for men between the ages of eighteen and forty, and on 29 May conscription replaced voluntary enlistments. By late July, though it was still chaotically organized, the RKKA claimed nearly 500,000 men at arms, and by January 1919 the figure had risen, at least on paper, to 1.7 million.[38] Equally significant was the decision to reverse the disorganizational legacy of the revolution, with its traditions of *komitetshchina* ("committee-mindedness") and what Trotsky called "military syndicalism." An effort to rebuild a central command authority culminated on 2 September in the creation of the Revolutionary Military Council (Revvoensovet) and the appointment shortly thereafter of the Lett Jukums Vacietis,

36. For the text of *Socialism and War* see Lenin, *PSS,* 26:209–65; for Lenin's writings on the problem during 1916, ibid., 30:131–43, 151–62, and 196–222.

37. Trotskii, *KVR,* 1:309.

38. Peter Gosztony, *Die Rote Armee: Geschichte und Aufbau der sowjetischen Streitkräfte seit 1917* (Vienna, 1980), p. 58. By way of comparison, at its height during World War I the Imperial Army numbered more than 9 million.

formerly a colonel in the Imperial Army and a graduate of its General Staff Academy, to replace Krylenko as commander in chief. Decrees of 21 March and 22 April brought an end to experiments with the elective principle, drastically reduced internal democracy in Red Army units, and reintroduced severe disciplinary measures, including the death penalty.[39]

Most controversially, Trotsky insisted that the mass army he was building could properly be led only if Russia's one available source of military expertise—the former officers of the Imperial Army—were tapped. Dubbed "military specialists," they would be recruited aggressively beginning in March with the invaluable help of the former Imperial Guard Officer M. A. Bonch-Bruevich. During the civil war 48,409 former tsarist officers enlisted with the RKKA, and although there were several spectacular betrayals, the vast majority served with distinction.[40] Traditional military ranks and insignia were eliminated (Red Army men on all levels addressed one another as "comrade"), but pay differentials and other perquisites did make the commander's status a modestly privileged one.

The institution of the political commissar was created to deal with the problem of political loyalty that the influx of former tsarist officers brought with it. This was not entirely an innovation. Political representatives, as Trotsky was well aware, had marched with the armies of the French revolution, and Aleksandr Kerenskii had made use of them during his tenure at the head of the Provisional Government. Within the RKKA political commissars were assigned to military units above the company level and tasked with ensuring the loyalty of the military specialist charged with the operational command function. In addition, they were given responsibility for maintaining revolutionary morale and discipline. Beginning in April the commissar was also required to countersign operational orders, a system of "dual command" that would become a constant bone of contention in the years ahead. The commissar system originally developed somewhat haphazardly, but by July political sections were established in armies and fronts, and in May 1919 the Main Political Administration was set up to coordinate the system.

Trotsky's new army was to be visionary in its ends but prosaic in its means. Ridiculing arguments in support of "guerrillaism" and "revolutionary" tactical innovations, he insisted that waging war required first

39. N. N. Azovtsev et al., eds., *Grazhdanskaia voina v SSSR*, 2 vols. (Moscow, 1980 and 1986), 1: 170–78.

40. A. M. Iavlev and D. A. Voropaev, *Bor'ba kommunisticheskoi partii za sozdanie voennykh kadrov* (Moscow, 1955), p. 18; A. G. Kavtaradze, *Voennye spetsialisty na sluzhbe respubliki sovetov 1917–1920 gg.* (Moscow, 1988), pp. 165–218.

of all a mastery of basics.⁴¹ Red Army commanders should be taught how to defend their flanks and strike at the enemy's weak point, and soldiers "to exterminate lice . . . to oil rifles and polish boots."⁴² It would nonetheless be incorrect to assume that Trotsky's regime as war commissar marked an abandonment of revolutionary priorities, or what one historian describes as a "return to normal conditions."⁴³ Trotsky's military writings, unique in their genre and filled with emotional exhortations to social ideas, make clear how nontraditional his outlook was. In combating "arbitrariness, slovenliness, and dishonesty," he sought to enforce a highly politicized conception of revolutionary virtue. The Red Army was "defined by the presence of a moral idea—therefore it triumphs."⁴⁴ Red Army commissars were "a new order of communist samurai" whose cause demanded total self-abnegation.⁴⁵ The RKKA adopted methods resembling those of its enemies because of the common environment imposed by the battlefield, but in its aspirations it remained distinct. These were twofold: not only to defend the revolution but also to make it strong, "in order that at the moment when the European proletariat rises up, we will be able to come to their aid fully armed and together with them, with our combined forces, bring down forever the power of capital."⁴⁶

Trotsky's program, in combination with his often abrasive personality, provoked a strong reaction. The Menshevik leader Iulii Martov criticized it at the 4th All-Russian Congress of Soviets from a traditional social democratic perspective and recommended the familiar alternative of a democratic militia. On the communist left Bukharin questioned the entire relevance of a national army in view of the revolution's internationalist priorities. Trotsky's army, he suggested in a set of theses coauthored with Valerian Osinskii, would prove incapable of fulfilling its self-proclaimed tasks.

"National" armed forces (as opposed to class forces) with former generals at their head cannot become permeated with a revolutionary class spirit; such a force will inevitably degenerate into a de-classed mercenary band

41. Trotskii, *KVR*, 2, book 1:59–64.
42. Ibid., 3, book 2:215 and 239–40.
43. Michael Morozow, *Die Falken des Kreml: Die sowjetische Militärmacht von 1917 bis Heute* (Munich, 1982), p. 26.
44. Trotskii, *KVR*, 2, book 1:126. For a confirmation of this emphasis, see John Erickson, *The Soviet High Command: A Military-Political History, 1918–1941* (London, 1962), pp. 40–41.
45. Trotskii, *KVR*, 2, book 2:7.
46. Ibid., 1:28.

and cannot serve as a point of support for the armed intervention of the Russian proletariat in the international revolution.[47]

The most significant dissent emerged from within the RKKA's high command. What would become known as the "military opposition" tended to express the views of a younger group of radical commanders who, though with a firmer grasp of military realities than Bukharin, were anxious to emphasize the army's revolutionary character. Trotsky, they suggested, underestimated the flexibility of the militia concept. His exaggerated "aping of bourgeois methods," overreliance upon constraint rather than persuasion, and cultivation of an officer "caste" gave rise to a form of Soviet militarism that could ultimately lead to Bonapartism. A deep and abiding distrust of the military specialists is evident in the critique, but also lingering class resentments. Many voices were raised on behalf of a strengthened role for party organs within the armed forces to balance the supposedly militaristic ethos of the command. Finally, there was considerable support for a greater degree of operational independence and encouragement for partisan style-methods emphasizing daring and initiative. Such criticisms were not always well founded. Francesco Benvenuti describes them as a typical example of the "idealist tendencies" attached to all great social transformations.[48] But cumulatively they represented a significant challenge to Trotsky's program.

The conflict between Trotsky and his antagonists came to a head at the 8th party congress in March 1919. Trotsky did not appear in person, but a set of theses on the military question was presented on his behalf by Grigorii Sokol'nikov.[49] After a vigorous debate in closed session the theses were approved unanimously as an expression of solidarity on the eve of the decisive battles of the civil war.[50] But Trotsky's position did not emerge unscathed. In the congress's resolution defining "active measures" for immediate implementation, the military opposition's views reappeared, particularly in recommendations for expanding the role of party organs within the army, and in June, Sergei Kamenev replaced Trotsky's favorite Vacietis as commander in chief. In effect, the congress had deferred to Trotsky in his role as commissar of war while

47. Cited in Francesco Benvenuti, *I bolscevichi e l'armata rossa, 1918–1922* (Naples, 1982), p. 54. This important book has been translated into English as Francesco Benvenuti, *The Bolsheviks and the Red Army, 1918–1922* (Cambridge, 1988).

48. Benvenuti, *I bolscevichi e l'armata rossa*, p. 117.

49. For the majority and minority reports on the military question presented to the 8th party congress by Sokol'nikov and V. M. Smirnov, respectively, see *Vos'moi s"ezd RKP (b). Protokoly. Mart 1919 goda* (Moscow, 1959), pp. 144–59.

50. A stenographic record of the debate appears in "VIII s"ezd RKP (b), Zasedaniia Voennoi sektsii," *Izvestiia TsK KPSS* 9 and 10 (1989): 135–86 and 171–89.

simultaneously asserting its own prerogatives. The RKKA as it emerged from the 8th party congress was structured on the basis of a compromise, basically corresponding to Trotsky's priorities but incorporating ideas drawn from the opposition as well.[51]

The controversy should not obscure what had been achieved. In the space of a single year a defeated nation presumed to be at the end of its tether had mobilized a mass army, assured it a qualified leadership, and successfully projected an inspirational vision of its goals. It was an army that, as events were to demonstrate, could fight and win.

A Pact with Death

The first battles of the Russian civil war were small in scale, with large destinies decided by almost insignificant forces. After the collapse of efforts to rally loyal elements within the Imperial Army against the Bolshevik regime, counterrevolutionary officers determined to continue the fight gravitated toward the periphery of the empire, where they found a sympathetic social base among Cossack communities.[52] A Cossack host under the command of Ataman Aleksei Dutov took control of Orenburg at the end of November 1917, but it was driven out during January 1918 by several detachments of Red sailors led by Vasilii Bliukher. More effective resistance was raised by the Ataman Aleksei Kaledin, who attempted to declare an independent republic in the Cossack country of the Don and Kuban. By February 1918 a small force of 6,000–7,000 Red Guardsmen led by Vladimir Antonov-Ovseenko had driven Kaledin's rickety government from Rostov-on-the-Don and Novocherkask, though a small anti-Bolshevik force including the tsarist generals Mikhail Alekseev, Lavr Kornilov, and Anton Denikin managed a difficult withdrawal into the Kuban, where they reorganized as the Volunteer Army. An army under the nominal command of Antonov-Ovseenko also attempted to clear the Ukraine. Soviet forces were forced out by the German occupation, however, with remnants of the Red Fifth Ukrainian Army led by Kliment Voroshilov limping eastward to arrive in Tsaritsyn (Volgograd) during June. Fortunately for the Bolsheviks, at

51. The final resolutions are given in *Vos'moi s"ezd RKP (b). Protokoly,* pp. 412–23. The best general account of the controversy and of army-party relations in the civil war period is Benvenuti, *I bolscevichi e l'armata rossa,* pp. 17–182.

52. A. P. Ermolin, *Revoliutsiia i kazachestvo (1917–1920 gg.)* (Moscow, 1982), pp. 54–84, describes the contradictory impact of the revolution upon Cossack communities. He explains Cossack sympathy for the counterrevolution on the basis of "caste traditions and prejudices, petty property holdings, deceit, bribery, and most of all coercion" (p. 200).

this time of maximum exposure the counterrevolutionary "White" armies were only beginning to draw together.[53]

A more serious threat arose in May, with the revolt of the so-called Czechoslovak legion.[54] This large body of more than 40,000 men, originally formed from among Czechoslovak prisoners of war and deserters as a division within the Imperial Army, found that by the spring of 1918 it was the most significant armed contingent in all of Soviet Russia. Plans to evacuate the Czechoslovaks via the Trans-Siberian railway went awry during May, when an order to disarm them following a lynching incident in Cheliabinsk provoked a full-scale rebellion.[55] Encouraged by local Socialist Revolutionary (SR) oppositionists organized as a Committee of Members of the Constituent Assembly (Komuch), the Czechoslovaks took control of key stations along the Trans-Siberian, thus cutting at a stroke Moscow's lifeline to the east. It was in response to the sudden and unexpected menace that on 16 July the royal family was put to death in Ekaterinburg (Sverdlovsk), the provincial city in the Urals where they had been held under house arrest. Assisted by the treason of the former Left SR Mikhail Murav'ev, the erstwhile Red commander of the Volga front, Czechoslovak and White forces seized important towns along the middle Volga, culminating with the capture of Kazan on 7 August. The abandonment of the city was accompanied by scenes of panic, as ill-trained Red Army units broke ranks and melted away. From Kazan the highway stretched some 700 kilometers over Nizhnii-Novgorod (Gorkii) to Moscow. The capture of the city, remarked one euphoric White commander, was "one of the greatest feats in military history."[56]

August 1918 marked a low point in Soviet fortunes. Germany was astride the Ukraine and in touch with White forces in the Kuban, and counterrevolution triumphed in the Baltic states and Finland. During July, after a desperate attempt to shatter the Brest-Litovsk peace by

53. On the first encounters with "counterrevolutionary mutinies" see Azovtsev et al., *Grazhdanskaia voina*, 1:74–90. The confused events in the south are described in Peter Kenez, *Civil War in South Russia, 1918* (Berkeley, Calif., 1971).

54. Gerburg Thunig-Nittner, *Die tschechoslowakische Legion in Russland* (Wiesbaden, 1970); Edward Palmer Huyt, *Army without a Country* (New York, 1967); and A. Kh. Klevanskii, *Chekhoslovatskie internatsionalisty i prodannyi korpus: Chekhoslovatskie politicheskie organizatsii i voenskie formirovanie v Rossii, 1914–1921 gg.* (Moscow, 1965), describe the episode of the Czechoslovak legion.

55. Victor M. Fic, *The Bolsheviks and the Czechoslovak Legion: The Origins of Their Armed Conflict, March–May 1918* (New Delhi, 1978), pp. 227–38.

56. Cited in David Footman, *Civil War in Russia* (London, 1961), p. 102. On the anti-Bolshevik movement on the Volga see Stephen M. Berk, "The Democratic Counterrevolution: Komuch and the Civil War on the Volga," *Canadian-American Slavic Studies* 37 (1973): 443–59.

assassinating the German ambassador Count Wilhelm Mirbach, the Left SRs, the only political party to join with the Bolsheviks in the revolutionary government after October, launched a coup in Moscow that had to be put down by armed force. Red armies had been driven from the middle Volga and were hard-pressed at Tsaritsyn in the south. Foreign intervention forces arrived in Murmansk during March, in Vladivostok during April, and in Arkhangel'sk by July. On 10 March the capital was moved from Petrograd to Moscow so that the government would be out of the range of a German thrust. The Soviet Republic's zone of effective control had shrunk to an area approximately equivalent to that of medieval Muscovy.[57] On 29 July, Trotsky called for the declaration of a state of emergency. The "socialist fatherland" would not be defeated, he intoned, for "we have made a pact with death."[58]

After 7 August, Trotsky sped to the small town of Sviiazhsk thirty kilometers west of Kazan and pulled out all stops in an effort to stabilize the front and prepare for a counterattack. The effort already devoted to constructing the RKKA now paid dividends, and on 10 September Kazan was retaken. Two days later the Red First Army under Mikhail Tukhachevskii reoccupied Simbirsk (Ul'ianovsk), and on 7 October, Samara (Kuibyshev) fell. Tsaritsyn was also successfully defended against the Don Cossacks of General Petr Krasnov. A corner of sorts had been turned. Though still far from being victorious, the regime had avoided being swept away during its first critical hours.

The decisive campaigns of the civil war came in 1919, and it was then that the full value of the breathing space won at Brest-Litovsk became clear. The Germans, compelled to evacuate the Ukraine under the terms of the ceasefire in the west, were no longer a factor, although Turkey's defeat opened the Black Sea to the navies of France and Great Britain. Most significantly, the RKKA was becoming a mass army, and though plagued by manifold weaknesses, it would prove to be more than a match for its White rivals.

An unpredictable element was added by the presence on Russian territory of foreign interventionist forces. By the spring of 1919 military contingents large and small representing no less than a dozen sovereign states had poured across Russia's undefended borders. In some cases the incursions were attempts to seize disputed border regions. In the case of the large Japanese intervention in the Far East, the goal was to establish a sphere of influence in a strategically significant region where a power

57. William Henry Chamberlin, *The Russian Revolution, 1917–1921*, 2 vols. (New York, 1935), 2:42.
58. Trotskii, *KVR*, 1:229.

vacuum had been allowed to develop.[59] Most worrisome was the U.S., British, and French presence in the White and Black Sea regions. Initially justified as an attempt to reestablish the eastern front and to guard weapons depots, the Entente powers' presence after Germany's defeat was less disguised, more clearly counterrevolutionary.[60] Much resented and constantly referred to in Soviet sources, foreign interventionist forces did make a real contribution to the White cause by providing secure rear areas and material assistance, but intervention never took the form of meaningful involvement in combat operations. Allied councils concerning engagement in Russia were divided. Some voices, such as that of the French marshal Ferdinand Foch, were raised on behalf of a "unified Allied push" to bring down Bolshevism, but they remained isolated.[61] After the trials of the world war a popular consensus for such adventuristic policies simply did not exist. As the key interventionist power, Great Britain found itself paralyzed by a political battle between the proponents of disengagement led by David Lloyd George and those supporting more determined action led by Winston Churchill. The presence of small and reluctant interventionist forces helped the Whites to organize and mount their campaigns, but it was not sufficient to turn the tide of battle.[62]

The first challenge of 1919 emerged from Siberia, where a counterrevolutionary government led by Admiral Aleksandr Kolchak, the self-designated "Supreme Ruler of Russia," had seized control in Omsk on 7 November 1918. With a large but poorly organized army that would grow to more than 450,000 men (including noncombatants), Kolchak advanced toward the Volga in March. By the end of May he had been thrown back and routed by a series of counteroffensives in which the young revolutionary commanders Tukhachevskii and Mikhail Frunze

59. See James William Morley, *The Japanese Thrust into Siberia, 1918* (New York, 1957).

60. Michael Jabara Carley, *Revolution and Intervention: The French Government and the Russian Civil War* (Kingston, Ont., 1983), p. xii, describes the French intervention as "a premeditated attempt to overthrow a menacing revolutionary government."

61. Described in John M. Thompson, *Russia, Bolshevism and the Versailles Peace* (Princeton, N.J., 1966), pp. 181–85; Arno J. Mayer, *Politics and Diplomacy of Peacemaking: Containment and Counterrevolution at Versailles, 1918–1919* (London, 1968), p. 461.

62. There is large literature addressed to the various interventions. John Bradlee, *Allied Intervention in Russia* (London, 1968); Carley, *Revolution and Intervention;* Richard Goldhurst, *The Midnight War: The American Intervention in Russia, 1918–1920* (New York, 1978); E. M. Halliday, *The Ignorant Armies* (New York, 1960); John Silverlight, *The Victors' Dilemma: Allied Intervention in the Russian Civil War* (New York, 1970); A. D. Skaba, *Parizhskaia mirnaia konferentsiia i inostrannaia interventsiia v strane sovetov (ianvar'-iiun' 1919 g.)* (Kiev, 1971).

distinguished themselves. The RKKA swept into Ufa on 9 June and continued to lunge forward, eventually entering Omsk on 14 November. Frustrated in an attempt to flee eastward along the Trans-Siberian by his now resentful Czechoslovak allies, Kolchak was turned over to the Reds and shot at dawn on 7 February.

With these dramatic events under way, a new threat appeared in the south. From their base in the Kuban the Armed Forces of South Russia assembled around Denikin's Volunteer Army prepared to launch a three-pronged advance on Moscow. White armies fought their way into Khar'kov on 24 May, Tsaritsyn on 1 July, and both Kiev and Kursk on 23 August. Making good use of the disruptive raids staged by the White cavalry under generals Konstantin Mamontov and Andrei Shkuro, by 14 October, Denikin had arrived in Orel, 120 kilometers from the Red arsenal at Tula and only 300 kilometers from Moscow.

Faulty command decisions and breakdowns in morale once again plagued the RKKA during Denikin's advance. A major reorganization was undertaken in the wake of the defeats, including a turnover in command and the creation in November 1919 of what would become the famous First Cavalry Army under the swashbuckling leadership of Semen Budennyi.[63] Drastic measures were in order, for during October, at the height of Denikin's offensive, another menace appeared on the Petrograd front. On 12 October a small force of about 14,000 men, based east of Lake Chud on Russian territory, was led by General Nikolai Iudenich toward Petrograd. By 21 October the Whites could look out from the palaces of Tsarskoe Selo and Pavlovsk onto the spires of the imperial capital, but this was their high-water mark. A determined defense of "Red Petrograd" soon drove the dispirited remnants of Iudenich's forces into Estonia. Offended by Iudenich's impolitic Great Russian nationalism ("There is no Estonia, it is a piece of Russian soil," he had remarked earlier in the year) and fearing reprisals, the Estonian government disarmed his army.[64]

Almost simultaneously the threat on the southern front also collapsed. In trying to reach Orel, Denikin had left himself badly overextended; his control over Cossack and Ukrainian base areas was never strong, and the pillages and anti-Semitic pogroms perpetrated by his troops alienated

63. Legendary in stature in its day, the First Cavalry Army spawned an influential group of commanders, including three future commissars of war and ministers of defense: Voroshilov (1925–40), Semen Timoshenko (1940–41), and Andrei Grechko (1967–76). For an attempt to debunk its heroic reputation see Vitaly Rapoport and Yuri Alexeev, *High Treason: Essays on the History of the Red Army, 1918–1939* (Durham, 1985), pp. 35–44.

64. Iudenich's remark is cited by Louis Fischer, *The Soviets in World Affairs: A History of the Relations between the Soviet Union and the Rest of the World, 1917–1929*, 2 vols. (Princeton, N.J., 1951), 1:207.

both local and international support. The Red Army had little difficulty in retaking Orel on 20 October, and on 24 October Budennyi's cavalry threatened an encirclement by seizing Voronezh. During November the Volunteer Army was in full retreat, and by January 1920 it had pulled back into the Kuban. In March 1920 a part of Denikin's broken army was transferred in Allied ships from Novorossiisk to the Crimea, where on 20 April Baron Petr Vrangel (known to the Red Army as the Black Baron) succeeded to Denikin's command. The threat from the south was not entirely eliminated, but with the repulse of Denikin the RKKA had withstood its major test.

Allied support was clearly important to the viability of the White armies, and the Soviet Republic seized at any opportunity to achieve negotiated arrangements with the Entente powers in order to bring intervention to an end. When in January 1919 the United States proposed that a reconciliation conference be convened on the Turkish island of Prinkipo, to include all major powers and Russian political factions, the Soviet response was favorable. On 8 March 1919 the American William Bullitt arrived in Petrograd on an unofficial mission seeking to explore the terms of a modus vivendi with the Soviet regime and was offered a friendly reception. Nothing came of such feelers, however, and in the end the Entente sided, albeit ineffectively, with the counterrevolution.

As a result 1919 became what E. H. Carr called "the year of isolation."[65] Not a single world power accorded diplomatic recognition to the Soviet Republic, which was also subjected to a full-scale economic boycott. Foreign armies pressed into Russia's exposed border areas and openly contributed to the White cause. Under such circumstances the Red commitment to the world revolution, of necessity, became reinforced. "These catastrophic developments," writes Carr, "left a lasting mark on Soviet thought. The action of the allies confirmed and intensified the ideological aspect of Soviet foreign policy and made international revolution once more its principle plank."[66]

Revolutionary prospects in Europe were real. Popular reaction to the defeat of the Central Powers in November 1918 swept the kaiser from his throne and shattered the Dual Monarchy. In March 1919 the Comintern was created, and during March and April, Soviet Republics were declared in Hungary and Bavaria. None of these promising developments, however, led to the stabilization of a revolutionary regime. Preoccupied with their own civil war, the Bolsheviks were forced to watch helplessly as a communist insurrection in Berlin during January 1919

65. E. H. Carr, *The Bolshevik Revolution, 1917–1923*, 3 vols. (New York, 1953), 3:109–47.
66. Ibid., p. 89.

was drowned in blood, a workers' uprising in Vienna was beaten down, and the Hungarian and Bavarian Soviet Republics were defeated by foreign and mercenary armies. Inspired by its own victories but frustrated by the failure of revolution elsewhere, the RKKA could but undertake one last effort to carry the world revolution to the reluctant West.

The Revolution from Without

In 1920 the Russian civil war spilled over into an undisguised interstate conflict. There is no consensus concerning the origin of the Russo-Polish war of that year. Traditional Soviet interpretations date the war from the Polish attack of April 1920, whereas "pro-Polish" accounts generally assert that a state of war had existed since February 1919.[67] Beyond dispute is the ambition of Polish ruler Józef Pilsudski to extend Poland's boundaries and to exploit the weakness of the Soviet Republic to that end. A series of incidents plagued Polish-Soviet relations through 1919, and between July and December, Julian Marchlewski, as Soviet emissary to Warsaw, searched in vain for a negotiated settlement. With the outcome of the Russian civil war still in doubt, Pilsudski held back; no greater enemies of Poland than the leading White commanders could be imagined. Once the Bolsheviks had turned the tide, this inhibition no longer applied, and on 25 April, Pilsudski set his troops on the march in Galicia. Still plagued by the chaotic circumstances prevailing in the Ukraine and partially tied down by the anarchist-inspired "Green" army of Nestor Makhno, the RKKA could not offer effective resistance. On 7 May, Pilsudski's armies entered Kiev. Seeking to benefit from the confusion created by the Polish advance, in June 1920 Vrangel's rechristened "Russian Army" broke out of the Crimea and advanced to the lower Dnieper.

After more than two years of existence and several trials by fire, the RKKA now represented a considerable force, and it was able to react quickly to these temporary setbacks. After regrouping to confront the offensive, the First Cavalry Army on 5 June led a breakthrough that made the Polish position at Kiev untenable. In the north Tukhachevskii's Western Front pushed forward to the Berezina. With the Polish thrust rolled back, the Soviet command suddenly confronted a major decision.

---

67. Compare Norman Davies, *White Eagle, Red Star: The Polish-Soviet War, 1919–20* (New York, 1972), pp. 19–61, and P. N. Ol'shauskii, *Rizhskii mir: Iz istorii bor'by sovetskogo pravitel'stva za ustanovlenie mirnykh otnoshenii s Pol'shei (konets 1918–mart 1921 g.)* (Moscow, 1969), pp. 8–51. See also James M. McCann, "Beyond the Bug: Soviet Historiography of the Soviet-Polish War of 1920," *Soviet Studies* (Oct. 1984): 475–93.

On one level Russian reactions to the Polish attack exposed an unrepentant strain of traditional nationalism. The famous tsarist general Aleksei Brusilov was the most prominent of many dignitaries who offered their support to the Soviet regime against a traditional rival during the spring of 1920. No doubt bemused by such reactions, the Soviet leadership was not visibly influenced by them. At one point Trotsky saw fit to suspend the military journal *Voennoe delo* (Military Affairs) for printing an ethnic slur against Poles.[68] More cautious councils opposed pursuing the retreating Polish armies, arguing that eliminating Vrangel should take priority. But within the Central Committee and among responsible officers there was considerable sentiment for a more aggressive approach. A permanent Polish-Soviet border had yet to be determined, and by continuing to advance, the Soviets could place themselves in a position to effect a settlement to their advantage. Moreover, a capitalist Poland linked to the West was regarded by some as a permanent threat to Soviet power. Pilsudski's attack, it was implied, provided an opportunity to eliminate a security risk by allowing the Red Army to assist the Polish proletariat in seizing power. Even more tantalizing was the prospect of creating a "bridge" across Red Poland to the revolutionary proletariat of Germany and seizing the elusive world revolution by force majeure. A group of "Moscow Poles" attached to the Soviet government, including Radek, Marchlewski, and Feliks Dzierzynski, sought to pour cold water on these heady prospects; the Polish proletariat, they argued, would perceive any campaign by the Red Army on Polish soil as old-fashioned Russian imperialism, and the political base of the young Polish communist movement was still too weak to allow it to maintain state power. Such reasoned arguments, in the flush of military success and after years of frustration with revolutionary prospects in the West, could not prevail. "Soldiers of the revolution," read Tukhachevskii's order of the day for 2 July, "in the West the fate of the world revolution is being decided. Across the corpse of White Poland shines the road to world conflagration. On our bayonets we will carry peace and happiness to laboring humanity."[69] In defiance of an ultimatum issued by the British foreign minister Lord Curzon, by 24 July, Tukhachevskii had forced the Bug, the Rubicon of the Polish campaign, and prepared to occupy the city of Bialystok.[70]

68. Trotskii, *KVR*, 2, part 2:153. The phrase in question referred to the "innate jesuitry of Polaks."

69. Cited in Iu. Stepanov, *S Krasnoi Armiei na panskuiu Pol'sku* (Moscow, 1920), p. 78.

70. Defying the Curzon ultimatum meant courting reprisals. That the Bolsheviks were ready to accept such a risk was a measure of their commitment. See the discussion in Mawdsley, *The Russian Civil War*, pp. 253–55, and the comment in Trotskii, *KVR*, 2, part 2:157–61.

Though it is never easy to rein in triumphantly advancing armies, the Bolsheviks also provided the Polish campaign with a theoretical gloss in the form of the doctrine of the "revolution from without."[71] The phrase was embarrassingly frank, but the concept that inspired it had ample precedent. No one questioned Marx's aphorism that "the liberation of the proletariat must be the work of the proletariat itself," but the presumption that the Red Army might be called upon to assist the revolutionary proletariat in neighboring states was commonplace. At its inception the RKKA actively recruited for an "International Department"; Trotsky made repeated references to the army's internationalist obligations; Lenin inquired on several occasions during 1919 whether the RKKA might be able to link up with Béla Kun's embattled Soviet Republic in Budapest; and the Left Communists built their entire critique around the absolute priority of the army's international mission.[72] At issue was merely a fine point of interpretation. The army must be assisting an indigenous popular revolution, not seeking to impose revolutionary institutions artificially.

It remained for the twenty-seven-year old front commander Tukhachevskii to give the doctrine of revolution from without its most extreme formulation. Between 7 July and 8 August the 2nd world congress of the Comintern met in Moscow. The conference hall was adorned by a large map upon which the progress of Soviet armies was indicated daily. On the eve of the congress Tukhachevskii addressed a letter to its chair, Grigorii Zinoviev, in which he pledged that the Red Army would bring Soviet power to Poland and begin "a world offensive of all the armed forces of the proletariat against the arms of world capitalism."[73] The Comintern

71. The genesis of the concept is described in Warren Lerner, "Attempting a Revolution from Without: Poland in 1920," in Thomas T. Hammond, ed., *The Anatomy of Communist Takeovers* (New Haven, Conn., 1975), pp. 94–106.

72. On the "International Department" see A. Rhys Williams, *Through the Russian Revolution* (New York, 1923), pp. 185–87. Lenin's call in 1918 for the creation of a new army specified that it should be tasked "to help the international workers' revolution." Lenin, *PSS*, 50:186. The *Sovnarkom* decree of 28 Jan. 1918 describing plans for a new army called it "a support for the coming socialist revolution in Europe." Martin McCauley, ed., *The Russian Revolution and the Soviet State, 1917–1921: Documents* (London, 1975), p. 140. For efforts to aid the Hungarian revolution by maneuvering troops closer to Budapest see Fischer, *The Soviets in World Affairs*, 1:194–96, and the relevant operational orders issued by commander in chief Vacietis in *Direktivy glavnogo komandirovaniia Krasnoi Armii (1917–1920)* (Moscow, 1969), nos. 184, 193, and 195. In a moment of enthusiasm during 1919 Trotsky went so far as to suggest that in the name of world revolution the Red Army might consider "a military thrust against India." Jan M. Meijer, ed., *The Trotsky Papers 1917–1922*, 2 vols. (The Hague, 1964 and 1971), 1:673–75. A letter published in *Ogonek*, 20–27 Feb. 1988, p. 4, points out that instruction in Esperanto was also a part of Red Army internationalist training during 1921–23.

73. M. N. Tukhachevskii, *Voina klassov: Stat'i 1919–1920 gg.* (Moscow, 1921), pp. 57–59. For the text in English see Erickson, *The Soviet High Command*, pp. 784–85.

was urged to create an "international general staff" to supervise the "global civil war" that was beginning, and the RKKA encouraged to abandon its "national" character altogether. Trotsky later described these effusions as "naive exaggeration" and commented laconically that the creation of an international command could only follow the progress of the world revolution, not precede it.[74] Nor is there any evidence that Tukhachevskii's suggestions were ever seriously considered. Still, several years later Tukhachevskii would continue to refer to the "lost opportunity" of 1920. "There is not the least doubt," he wrote in 1923, "that had we been victorious on the Vistula, the revolution would have swept up all Europe in its flames. . . . A revolution from without was possible. Capitalist Europe had been shaken to its very foundation, and except for our defeat on the battlefield, perhaps the Polish War would have been the link uniting the October revolution and the revolution in Western Europe."[75]

For better or worse, the Red Army was not victorious on the Vistula. Tukhachevskii's western front, brilliantly led, was able to advance rapidly toward Warsaw, but in the process a gap was allowed to open between itself and the southwest front, still engaged in the area of L'vov. Exploiting the opportunity to the full, Pilsudski directed a flanking attack on 16 August that cut off three Soviet divisions and forced Tukhachevskii's armies into a precipitous retreat. Fixing responsibility for the defeat would become one of the more contentious issues in the history of Soviet arms. The failure of the Polish proletariat to rally to the cause—the fact that there was no indigenous revolution to support—seems to have surprised some. Operational errors, inadequate planning, and poor communication between the commanders may also be cited. Trotsky would later blame the Southwest Army command for its preoccupation with taking L'vov, and at the height of the Stalin era the red herring of "treason" on the part of Trotsky and Tukhachevskii was trotted out. Perhaps the most fundamental source of the defeat, however, was simple overreaching. In 1920 the young Red Army still displayed major operational and logistical shortcomings. By the time of his appearance before Warsaw, Tukhachevskii's forces were dangerously strung out, with morale declining and supply services in chaos. The Polish armies, drawn back around their capital, well armed, effectively led, and aided by a large French military mission under General Maxime Weygand, performed better at the decisive moment. As a result the

74. Leon Trotsky, *The Revolution Betrayed: What Is the Soviet Union and Where Is it Going?* (New York, 1937), p. 211.

75. Cited in B. M. Shaposhnikov, *Na Visle: K istorii kampanii 1920 goda* (Moscow, 1924), p. 21.

RKKA was badly beaten in a campaign that probably should never have been undertaken.[76] On 12 October, after Soviet forces had pulled back beyond the Nieman, an armistice was concluded. The Treaty of Riga, which officially ended the war on 18 March 1921, defined a territorial settlement to Poland's advantage. But more than territory was at stake. The Bolsheviks' one great gamble on behalf of the world revolution had come to naught.

The Legacy of the Civil War

The RKKA now turned to deal with Vrangel's forces—the last significant White army on Soviet territory. By November the Black Baron had been forced back into the Crimea, and on 7 November, after several failed assaults, Soviet forces broke through the Perekop bottle-neck. Now irrevocably beaten, Vrangel disbanded his army, and in the days that followed some 140,000 of his men were evacuated from the Crimea in British ships. Fighting continued in distant corners of the vast country for some time, but to all intents and purposes the civil war was over. Gradually the remaining interventionist contingents were withdrawn, concluding with Japan's evacuation of Vladivostok in November 1922. Pockets of warlordism such as those presided over by Makhno in the Ukraine and Aleksandr Antonov in Tambov province were inexorably strangled and crushed. In the Caucasus the Red Army campaigned to enforce Soviet power through 1921; in Central Asia, despite ongoing resistance, Red Army units held Moscow's authority in place; and in the Far East, where a Far Eastern Republic has been established in April 1920 as a buffer state with Japan, an expeditionary corps under Bliukher successfully reasserted central control. On 15 December 1922 the Far Eastern Republic was abolished and its territory reattached to the Soviet Republic.[77] Two weeks later, on 30 December, the Union of

76. Erickson, *The Soviet High Command*, pp. 95–102, and Manfred von Boetticher, *Industrialisierungspolitik und Verteidigungskonzeption der UdSSR 1926–1930: Herausbildung des Stalinismus und "äussere Bedrohung"* (Düsseldorf, 1979), pp. 238–80. An official evaluation prepared during the 1980s vaguely concludes, "The basic reasons for the defeat of the armies of the Western Front were the serious mistakes of the Soviet command in its evaluation of the military-political circumstances and in planning operations" but also implies that southwest front commander Aleksandr Egorov and his political commissar Iosip Stalin defied orders by persisting in the effort to take L'vov. Azovtsev et al., *Grazhdanskaia voina*, 2:279 and 285–86.

77. On the Far Eastern Republic, see M. A. Dersits, *Dal'nevostochnaia respublika i Kitai: Rol' DVR v bor'be sovetskoi vlasti za druzhbu s Kitaem v 1920–1922 gg.* (Moscow, 1962).

Soviet Socialist Republics was officially created as a federation of technically autonomous regions within boundaries, with the exception of the western borderlands and Transcaucasia, that approximated those of Imperial Russia.

The Bolsheviks' victory provided a lasting foundation for Soviet power. A revolution whose original justification lay exclusively in its ability to serve as a catalyst for world revolution, merely by surviving had accomplished what its creators once dismissed as impossible. The Soviet Republic, confronting a "united front of the forces of world reaction," had rallied its forces and, in defiance of all odds, prevailed.

The experience of the civil war inevitably affected Soviet perceptions of security, in some cases reinforcing inherited notions and in others necessitating their revision or elimination. Revolutionary internationalism was the dominant paradigm through which Bolshevik leaders conceptualized the revolution's meaning in 1917, but in two critical ways its underlying assumptions had been challenged. First, the world revolution had proven to be much more elusive than expected. The embarrassing failure of a coup attempt in Germany during March 1921, coming on top of the disasters of 1919 and the abortive Polish campaign of 1920, represented a kind of full stop for revolutionary expectations. What *were* the implications of a protracted failure of the revolution to expand? Second, the Russian revolution itself had proven more resilient than expected. By 1921 the suicidal "revolutionary war" line pushed by the Left Communists in 1918 seemed naive. The stabilization of Soviet institutions and the demonstrated capacity of the revolution to fight its own battles opened up perspectives that were not part of original ideological assumptions. How had Soviet power managed to maintain itself in isolation? In addressing the question at least three factors could be adduced.

Revolutionary Internationalism. Commitment to the priority of revolutionary internationalism obviously had to be moderated because of the failure of revolution in Europe, but certain aspects of the doctrine were also strengthened by the outcome of the civil war. World revolution had not materialized, but the hostility of international capitalism toward the world's first socialist state certainly had. Over a quarter-million soldiers representing fourteen states (Austria-Hungary, Czechoslovakia, Finland, France, Great Britain, Greece, Italy, Japan, Poland, Romania, Serbia, Turkey, and the United States) violated Russia's territorial sovereignty in the course of the civil war and made measurable contributions to the White movement. Alone and unaided, the Soviet Republic confronted the reality of capitalist encirclement. Stalinist interpretations of the civil war, absorbed into official Soviet legend, would characterize it as primarily a confrontation with externally sponsored counterrevolution and describe its decisive campaigns as the "three campaigns of the Entente."[78] Belief in the inevitable hostility of the leading capitalist powers which these events reinforced would become one of the most entrenched of Soviet assumptions.

Internationalism also made a positive contribution to the Soviet struggle for survival. The international communist movement was launched successfully and came to represent a substantial new political reality. Domestic discord and the threat of a reaction at home placed meaningful constraints around the Bolsheviks' rivals' ability to contemplate large-scale intervention. The revolutionary workers of Europe, Lenin commented, had "supported us by halves, since they weakened the arm that was raised against us."[79] Even without a seizure of power, the international labor movement could play a role in helping to maintain the Soviet Republic.

Revolutionary priorities stood the Bolsheviks in good stead within Russia as well. Bolshevism represented social and political ideals that were intelligible and appealing to the broad masses of the Russian people. Accumulated class resentments, the peasants' land hunger, yearning for greater autonomy on the part of national minorities, and the breakdown of the ancien régime during the world war all contributed to the forcefulness of that appeal. By way of contrast the Whites could never shake the image of Great Russian nationalists and restorationists (nor did they always try). The Bolsheviks inherited the power of a great social revolution—the Whites sought to resist it. In consequence, the White armies remained dependent on foreign support and "top-heavy," with a superfluity of officers and lack of recruits. The RKKA placed great emphasis upon agitation and propaganda, and to good effect. The Bolsheviks' ability to draw upon the social energy that the revolution had unleashed was a real source of strength.

The Bolsheviks' revolutionary élan had its dark side. Statistics concerning the civil war are notoriously inaccurate, but there is no doubt that it was immensely costly. Over large parts of the country conditions of semi-anarchy prevailed. In addition to combat casualties, armies and

78. See *Istoriia grazhdanskoi voiny SSSR*, 5 vols. (Moscow, 1947–60), 4: chap. 2 and 6, and 5: chap. 2; N. N. Azovtsev and N. R. Naumov, "Izuchenie istorii voennoi interventsii v grazhdanskoi voine," *Istoriia SSSR* 6 (1970): 18–19.

79. Lenin, *PSS*, 42:25. I. I. Mints, "Stalin v grazhdanskoi voine: Mify i fakhty," *Voprosy istorii KPSS* 11 (1989): 35–49, while criticizing the Stalinist conception of the war as a contest "imposed" upon Russia by imperialism, nonetheless goes on to emphasize the importance of external support for the Bolshevik cause, especially on the part of the labor movements of the most important interventionist powers. See also Nikol'nikov, *Vydaiushchaiasia pobeda leninskoi strategii*, pp. 313–24.

the civilian population were stalked by hunger and epidemic disease.[80] To maintain their fragile hold on power, the Bolsheviks resorted to the most extreme measures. The humanistic standards of nineteenth-century social democracy crumbled as the revolutionary government systematically eliminated political opposition and launched a Red Terror including arbitrary arrest, the taking and execution of hostages, and numerous other barbarities. Mass reprisals against rebellious Cossack communities in the Don region took on a particularly odious form.[81] In the Cheka, created in 1918 and led with icy determination by Dzierzynski, the regime resurrected a secret police tradition that was once considered to be a hated emblem of tsarism. The militarization of Bolshevik attitudes and a certain brutalization of Soviet power were legacies of the civil war that would weigh heavily in the future.

The RKKA. The revolution inherited the rotten shell of the Imperial Army in the throes of disintegration. It emerged from the civil war with a new army, more than 5 million soldiers organized in fifty-five rifle and twenty-three cavalry divisions, tried and tempered in battle. Extremist notions such as the doctrines of revolutionary war or revolution from without had been discredited and Trotsky's essentially cautious approach to administration and command enforced, but the RKKA clung to its identity as a revolutionary armed force. With its commissar system, its varied organizational innovations, and the prominent role of the Communist party within its ranks, the Red Army was significantly distinct from its "bourgeois" counterparts. The civil war had bequeathed it a tradition of its own—an inheritance of songs, exploits, heroes, and the like—something of inestimable importance to any military organization. Henceforward the capacity to mobilize for self-defense would be an integral dimension of Soviet security.

The RKKA also drew on a number of coincidental advantages in crafting its victories. Though surrounded by enemies, the Bolsheviks commanded interior lines of communication, a more developed railway net than that available to their adversaries, and a significantly greater pool of exploitable manpower. The civil war was fought by what were, by the standards of the world war, quite small contingents, primitively

---

80. According to the calculations of V. M. Ustinov, "'Voiuiushchaia partiia' (gody grazhdanskoi voiny i voennoi interventsii)," *Voprosy istorii KPSS* 1 (1990): 82–97, a total of 8 million deaths resulted from the civil war, including approximately 1 million combat casualties. The majority of deaths resulted from disease and hunger, in part occasioned by an estimated 40% drop in agricultural production.

81. Described in Sergei Starikov and Roy Medvedev, *Philip Mironov and the Russian Civil War* (New York, 1978), pp. 101–32.

armed and operating on noncontinuous fronts. By rigidly enforcing its authority, the Soviet regime was able to field significantly larger armies than the Whites, and to direct them more effectively to threatened sectors. In comparison, the White armies were dispersed and uncoordinated, lacked a unifying strategic conception, and were often poorly led. Only the large-scale introduction of interventionist forces as a combat element could have overcome the Reds' advantages, and that was not forthcoming.

Not all advantages lay with the Reds. The classic allies of Russian armies under siege, the famous generals "winter" and "space," were denied to the Red Army in the civil war. The RKKA faced a Russian rival, and it had only a limited amount of room for strategic withdrawal. The civil war saw the temporary surrender of the entire middle Volga, fighting in the suburbs of Petrograd, and Denikin's penetration to within 300 kilometers of Moscow at Orel. In these dire moments it was only the fighting capacity of the RKKA that saved the day.[82]

Tactical Flexibility. Internationalism was integral to the Bolsheviks' revolutionary ideology and could not easily be abandoned. But by 1921 it was no longer possible to avoid examining the implications of the absence of world revolution. At Brest-Litovsk, Lenin fought for a policy of flexible diplomatic maneuver designed to take advantage of divisions within the imperialist camp. The treaty of Brest-Litovsk was only the most dramatic manifestation of the new approach. Various diplomatic overtures to both Germany and the Entente powers, peace negotiations with Pilsudski, and a determined effort to defend Russia's state interests all indicated that the Bolsheviks had no intention of enclosing themselves in enragé extremism. The justification for compromise was nothing less than revolutionary expediency. The Russian revolution would do all that was in its power to stimulate the world revolution, but its first responsibility remained to ensure its own survival.

Following the defeats of Kolchak and Denikin, with the attitude of the Entente powers toward the Soviet Republic beginning to soften, Soviet diplomacy began more actively to court international recognition and to encourage economic exchange. On 2 February, 12 July, and 11 August 1920, treaties with Estonia, Lithuania, and Latvia were signed, the regime's first permanent agreements with European states. The push for a more stable relationship with the capitalist world was temporarily interrupted by the revival of internationalist enthusiasm during the Polish

82. Mawdsley, *The Russian Civil War*, pp. 272–85, and Edgar O'Ballance, *The Red Army* (London, 1964), pp. 42–73, provide cogent evaluations of the Red Army's victory.

war, but only temporarily. By the autumn of 1920 it was clear that the Soviet Republic was condemned to exist for some time in a world of capitalist states, that encirclement could become a semi-permanent state of affairs. Intransigent revolutionary internationalism was incapable of resolving the dilemmas that the new situation posed. As a result of victory in the civil war, Lenin commented in November 1920, "we have not only a breathing-space, we have a new stage in which our fundamental right to an international existence in the framework of the capitalist states has been won."[83] The new stage that the revolution now prepared to enter demanded more emphasis upon formalizing relations with the capitalist world in order to secure the "fundamental right" that had been achieved at such cost.

In 1917 the Bolsheviks seized power in the expectation that their revolution represented the first wave of a world revolution, born of the world war and the crisis of capitalist imperialism that had given it birth. The assumption was flawed, and by 1921, though the Russian revolution had survived, it remained isolated and encircled by rivals.

Given the immense expectations bound up with the concept of world revolution, it is in some ways remarkable how brief its tenure as a dominant strategic assumption seems to have been. And yet the legacy of the "Age of World Revolution" was substantial. It opened up a chasm between the Soviet Republic and the rest of the world, strengthened the assumption of fundamental hostility on the part of the leading capitalist powers, underlined the need for a capacity for self-defense, and, insofar as the revolution was able to prevail despite the odds against it, reinforced a perception of the long-term vulnerability of capitalist imperialism. The role of interventionist forces in the civil war and the pariah status to which the Soviet Republic was consigned by the peace of Versailles encouraged a sense of separateness, just as the Bolsheviks' victories created a militant self-assurance and a conviction of the ultimate rightness of their cause.

By 1921, however, awareness had dawned that the world revolution was no deus ex machina, no panacea for the travail of the revolution in Russia. Weakened by war, racked by famine and social unrest, still exposed to the threat of external aggression, the Soviet Republic found itself compelled toward a temporary modus vivendi with the world around it.

83. Lenin, *PSS*, 42:22.

CHAPTER TWO

Accommodation and Retreat, 1921–1928

> An *internationalist* is one who, unreservedly, without wavering, without conditions is ready to defend the USSR, because the USSR is the base of the world revolutionary movement, and to defend, to move forward this revolutionary movement is impossible without defending the USSR.
>
> —Iosip V. Stalin, 1 August 1927

At its 10th party congress in March 1921 the Russian Communist party drew a balance sheet for three years of civil war. The revolution had triumphed, but at great cost. Although the political and economic regime imposed during the war, labeled War Communism, had enabled mobilization for the fight against counterrevolution, it was painfully obvious that it did not provide a context for peaceful reconstruction. Economic ruin and growing popular disaffection made a change of direction essential. The short-lived anti-Bolshevik rebellion of the Kronstadt naval garrison, which occurred with the 10th party congress in session, provided a vivid illustration of the risks involved in a failure to adjust.[1]

Urged on by Lenin, the 10th congress responded by replacing the eclectic mechanisms of War Communism with the famous New Economic Policy (NEP). The state grain monopoly and forced requisitioning were eliminated in favor of a tax in kind, and market relations were restored in the entire agricultural sector. Restrictions on internal trade were reduced and small private enterprises and industrial cooperatives

---

1. See Paul Avrich, *Kronstadt 1921* (Princeton, N.J., 1970); and Israel Getzler, *Kronstadt, 1917–1921: The Fate of a Soviet Democracy* (Cambridge, 1983). The rebellion was a desperate venture that did not really threaten the regime, but it symbolized potentially explosive social unrest. It has been interpreted in traditional Soviet historiography as a provocation inspired by White Guardists operating from Finland.

legalized, with only the "commanding heights" of the economy (heavy industry, transport, banking, and foreign trade) left to be administered centrally. The NEP was clearly a retreat from the radicalism of the civil war, an acknowledgment that socialism was not on the order of the day and that a long-term program was required merely to establish its prerequisites. The underlying social aim of the new policy was reconciliation with Soviet Russia's dominant social class, the peasantry, an imperative that existed in part because of the failure of the European revolution. But liberalization in economic policy was paralleled by retrenchment in the political realm. The 10th congress reacted to organized manifestations of inner-party dissent on the part of the Workers' Opposition and Democratic Centralists groups with an absolute ban on "factions" that went some distance toward stifling open debate and laid a foundation for Stalin's conquest and abuse of the party apparatus in the years ahead.

The NEP had its equivalent in international policy. Grigorii Chicherin, Trotsky's successor as people's commissar of foreign affairs, enunciated its key premise as early as June 1918, when he proposed that, so long as the Soviet Republic remained isolated, it must seek "accommodation" with the capitalist world in order to win time for the stabilization of Soviet power.[2] During the civil war it was still possible to hope that the pace of the world revolution could be accelerated, but by the spring of 1921 the prospect had been abandoned. In his opening address to the 10th congress Lenin stated bluntly that only "madmen" could count on a successful proletarian revolution emerging within a "brief interval" (*korotkii srok*).[3] Isolated, weak, and nursing its wounds, the Soviet Republic could no longer afford to entertain illusions. After 1921 *accommodation and retreat* became the leitmotifs of a new approach to security premised upon the need temporarily to shelve revolutionary expectations and to prepare for a period of what Lenin called "peaceful coexistence" with the capitalist world.

Lenin's career was cut short by a series of strokes that left him totally incapacitated after March 1923 and occasioned his premature death at age fifty-three in January 1924. So long as he remained active, Lenin never swerved from an ultimate faith in world revolution, and in his last

2. For the text of this important speech see G. V. Chicherin, *Stat'i i rechi po voprosam mezhdunarodnoi politiki* (Moscow, 1961), pp. 37–62. Chicherin is a key figure in the history of Soviet diplomacy. For sympathetic Soviet accounts of his career see E. M. Chossudovsky, *Chicherin and the Evolution of Soviet Foreign Policy and Diplomacy* (Geneva, 1972); I. Gorokhov, L. Zamiatin, and I. Zemskov, *G. V. Chicherin: Diplomat leninskoi shkoly* (Moscow, 1973). Timothy Edward O'Connor, *Diplomacy and Revolution: G. V. Chicherin and Soviet Foreign Affairs, 1918–1930* (Ames, Iowa, 1988), provides a good overview.

3. Lenin, *PSS*, 43:19.

writings he could still question whether the Soviet Republic would or would not "hold out until . . . the capitalist states of Western Europe have completed their development to socialism."[4] "Holding out" demanded concessions—concessions to the peasantry in order to stabilize Soviet power, concessions to capitalist concerns in order to encourage investment and trade, and concessions to the leading world powers in order to secure the Soviet Republic's place in a community of states. Though the threat of intervention would not disappear, it was presumed that the inherent contradictions of imperialism provided room for a tactic of maneuver designed to prevent the emergence of powerful anti-Soviet combinations. Lenin made no secret of the fact that the need to accommodate with the capitalist world order represented a retreat, forced upon the revolution by its inability to expand.[5] Accommodation was possible and justifiable, but it was also a second-best and inherently fragile solution. What the Bolsheviks sought was the relative degree of security necessary to ward the revolution over a difficult period of transition.

The Politics of Accommodation

Lenin considered commercial relations with the capitalist powers to be a necessary foundation for a policy of accommodation, and even during the darkest moments of the civil war the Soviet government made occasional efforts to establish trade contacts with the West.[6] All were rebuffed, but by 1920 motivation to restore contacts grew stronger on both sides. The Soviet regime was in desperate need of any and all economic assistance, and it hoped to use mutually beneficial exchange to attract the capital and technology needed for reconstruction. Lenin replied to the argument that such interaction would have the counterproductive effect of strengthening imperialism with the famous quip that "the capitalists themselves will be happy to sell us the rope which we will use to hang them."[7] The western powers also had positive incentives; in the strained postwar economic environment access to the

4. Ibid., 45:402.

5. See Cohen, *Bukharin*, pp. 138–39.

6. Described in M. E. Sonkin, *Okno vo vneshnii mir: Ekonomicheskie sviazi sovetskogo gosudarstva v 1917–1921 gg.* (Moscow, 1964), pp. 72–138.

7. This cogent phrase, while often cited, may be apocryphal. Perhaps closer to Lenin's real view is his remark that the "political interest" of the quest for economic integration lay in the fact that it would be more difficult "for capitalist powers that enter into deals with us to take part in military action against us." Lenin, *PSS,* 42:96 and 111. See also V. I. Kas'ianenko and O. V. Kas'ianenko, "Leninskie idei ob aktsionernom predprinimatel'stve," *Voprosy istorii KPSS* 9 (1990): 17–34.

Russian market, with its immense human and material potential, was a real attraction. After the defeat of the Whites it was clear that the route to Russia's bounty passed through the Bolsheviks.

Soviet economic overtures included efforts to revive trade relations and to attract foreign investment through concession agreements and joint ventures. Barriers to progress in all these areas existed as a legacy of the revolution. As prerequisites for cooperation the western powers demanded that the Bolsheviks agree to cease all hostile propaganda, return nationalized foreign property, repay all debts accumulated by the tsarist government, and grant extraterritorial privileges to foreign concerns. In many cases the Soviets came toward these demands, promising to refrain from revolutionary agitation, offering to "take into consideration" the interests of foreign property owners, agreeing to pay prewar debts with the help of foreign loans, and bidding to regulate debts accumulated during the war with the aid of compensation for the damages wrought by intervention. Underlying hostility proved difficult to overcome, however, and the policy of concessions never achieved significant results.

The quest for expanded trade relations was more successful. Great Britain was the principle target, and a Soviet trade delegation headed by Leonid Krasin opened talks in London as early as 31 May 1920. Negotiations stalled against the background of the Polish war, but on 16 March 1921, in conjunction with the unveiling of the NEP, a formal trade agreement was concluded. The Soviet Republic, Lenin remarked, had "forced open a window," and similar agreements with Germany, Norway, Austria, Italy, Denmark, and Czechoslovakia followed in the course of the year.[8]

A more significant breakthrough appeared to arrive on 6 January 1922, when the Supreme Allied Council meeting in Cannes scheduled an international economic conference and approved Soviet participation. The invitation, though conditioned by demands for the repayment of debts and compensation for nationalized property, seemed to represent an opportunity for the Soviet state to reenter the European community. Lenin urged careful preparation upon the Soviet delegates, insisting that they conduct themselves as "merchants." When the conference opened in Genoa on 10 April 1922 with twenty-nine states represented, the Soviet delegation appeared in top hats, silk gloves, and cutaways.[9] In a much-awaited opening address Chicherin professed his country's desire for

---

8. Lenin, *PSS*, 43:187–88.
9. Fischer, *The Soviets in World Affairs*, 1:320–21. Lenin's policy toward the Cannes project was opposed by some Bolsheviks as too conciliatory. The debate was eventually resolved in Lenin's favor. See Anna Di Biagio, *Le origini dell'isolazionismo sovietico:*

"general economic renewal" but also made an urgent appeal for disarmament which grated upon the conservative audience and sounded a sour note for the negotiations to follow.[10] The Genoa conference stretched from 10 April through 19 May and proved to be a frustrating experience. Chicherin hoped to take advantage of Europe's economic weakness in order to secure concessions and cement a strong bilateral relationship with Great Britain. These goals were not achieved; the conditions imposed by the Entente powers remained too severe and the Soviets' willingness to compromise was too limited. In its own perception the Soviet Republic continued to confront what one commentator called a "bourgeois united front."[11]

When the Genoa deliberations resumed at The Hague during July, a similar pattern of frustration reemerged. The second ranking member of the Soviet delegation and future commissar of foreign affairs Maksim Litvinov described the results as "a step backward from Genoa."[12] Rather than serving as a turning point, meetings at Genoa and The Hague made clear the limitations to economic and diplomatic interaction that the Soviet Republic's status as a revolutionary polity continued to impose.[13]

On the diplomatic front the policy of accommodation proceeded more smoothly. Already during and immediately after the civil war Moscow moved to regularize relations with its immediate neighbors. The independence of Poland, Finland, and the Baltic states was recognized, though grudgingly (Radek referred to the latter case as "in essence a question of their annexation by the Entente"),[14] and in 1920 and 1921 friendship treaties were signed with contiguous states in the Middle East and Central Asia, including Iran, Afghanistan, Turkey, and Mongolia. The attainment of recognition from the Entente powers proved to be more difficult, in part because of the Soviets Republic's oft-expressed

---

L'Unione Sovietica e l'Europa dal 1918 al 1928 (Milan, 1990), pp. 37–38; Stephen White, *The Origins of Detente: The Genoa Conference and Soviet-Western Relations, 1921–1922* (Cambridge, 1985), pp. 102–17.

10. Chicherin, *Stat'i i rechi*, pp. 208–212; White, *Origins of Detente*, pp. 133–35. Ironically, Chicherin had originally protested against presenting what he personally considered to be a "bourgeois pacifist" position.

11. Iu. Steklov, "Finita la comedia," *Izvestiia*, 22 July 1922, p. 1.

12. M. Litvinov, "Gaagskaia konferentsiia," *Izvestiia*, 18 July 1922, p. 1.

13. Traditional Soviet accounts portrayed the meetings at Genoa and The Hague as victories for Soviet policy to the degree that they thwarted attempts to exclude the Soviet Union from a role in European affairs. See V. F. Lopatin, *Proval antisovetskikh planov SShA: Genuia-Gaaga, 1922* (Moscow, 1963); V. A. Shishkin, *Sovetskoe gosudarstvo i strany Zapada v 1917–1923 godakh: Ocherki istorii stanovleniia ekonomicheskikh otnoshenii* (Leningrad, 1969), pp. 294–337.

14. Radek, *Vneshniaia politika sovetskoi Rossii*, p. 44.

scorn for the "Versailles system" and its central institution, the League of Nations. Chicherin's commitment to honor diplomatic protocol only partially masked his profound conviction that the stability of the bourgeois world order remained precarious—even with its representatives dressed in top hats, the Soviet Republic represented a symbolic challenge to the status quo. Moscow persevered nonetheless, though it was not until 1924 that the governments of Great Britain, France, and Italy bowed to the inevitable and established relations with the Soviet state.

Formal interstate relations were not a sufficient foundation for security. In addition, a larger diplomatic strategy was required aimed at preventing the emergence of anti-Soviet combinations. The exclusion of the Soviet Union from the League of Nations, the testiness of its relations with the Entente powers, and the *cordon sanitaire* of authoritarian states lined up against its western border made the danger of isolation seem particularly acute. Moscow's response was a policy that would become the foundation for its diplomacy throughout the 1920s, a "special relationship" with defeated Germany.

Soviet-German relations were proper but strained under the regime defined by the treaty of Brest-Litovsk. After the kaiser's fall, in part because of Soviet support for the revolutionary aspirations of the German Communist party, relations disintegrated considerably and had to be rebuilt in conjunction with the turn toward accommodation. A provisional Soviet-German trade pact of 6 May 1921 provided for the establishment of consulates and opened the door to extended contacts. Both parties, though for very different reasons, confronted a common dilemma—exclusion from the Versailles system and isolation from the mainstream of European affairs. In January 1922 Radek, the Bolshevik leader most attuned to the German domestic scene, arrived in Berlin for a series of consultations that established a basis for broader cooperation.[15] Radek was followed by Chicherin, who stopped in Berlin en route to the Genoa conference and, together with his German counterpart, Foreign Minister Walter Rathenau, developed the outline of a diplomatic agreement. On 16 April 1922, after initial disappointments at Genoa, the Soviet and German delegations convened separately in the nearby resort of Rapallo where, to the horror of the Entente, they concluded a formal treaty.[16]

15. Radek informed the Germans with whom he consulted, including General Hans von Seeckt and Walter Rathenau, that the Soviets had received an offer from France of de jure recognition and trade credits in exchange for endorsing Versailles. Kurt Rosenbaum, *Community of Fate: German-Soviet Diplomatic Relations, 1922–1928* (Syracuse, N.Y., 1965), pp. 26–27.

16. These events are described in Herbert Helbig, *Die Träger der Rapallo-Politik* (Göttingen, 1958), pp. 73–101; Th. Schieder, "Die Entstehungsgeschichte des Rapallo-Vertrags," *Historische Zeitschrift* 204 (1967): 547–609; White, *Origins of Detente*, pp. 147–63. For the text of the treaty see *DVP*, 5:223–24.

With the treaty of Rapallo, Germany and the Soviet Republic established full diplomatic relations, placed commercial exchange on a most-favored-nation basis, and mutually renounced claims to compensation for war damages. Word of the agreement created shock waves in Europe, even though it apparently amounted to nothing more than a restoration of conventional bilateral relations. It was the exclusion of Soviet power from the affairs of the continent which had come to seem the norm.[17] Lenin hailed the treaty as the "only proper avenue" to follow, and Soviet evaluations have consistently praised it as a "model for normal relations with capitalist states."[18] But as the basis for a multifaceted relationship with a leading European power, the treaty of Rapallo had a considerably greater immediate significance.

It was the treaty of Rapallo, rather than Brest-Litovsk, that represented the Soviet Republic's real coming to terms with the dilemma of coexistence. The treaty corresponded to the demands of the Soviets' new security environment in a number of ways. First, it broke the ring of isolation that had been cast around the Soviet Republic by allying it with a major European power. By accentuating postwar divisions within the imperialist camp, it blocked the emergence of a united anti-Soviet coalition. More concretely, it made foreign-sponsored aggression launched from Poland on the model of 1920 less likely by placing a great power ally squarely in Warsaw's rear. Though not acknowledged as such, Rapallo made the maintenance of a balance of power in Europe one of the premises of Soviet security.[19] *Izvestiia*'s chief editor Iurii Steklov described it in this vein, as "the first breach in the system of French hegemony in the European continent."[20] The treaty's commercial arrangements proved to be effective, and during the 1920s Germany became the Soviet Union's leading trading partner.[21] Finally, its secret protocols launched an interaction between the German national army, the Reichswehr, hemmed in by the provisions of the treaty of Versailles, and the RKKA. Collaboration grew in stages and eventually gave rise to cooperative projects for the production of aircraft and munitions, regular high-level consultations between the respective commands, the

17. France felt particularly threatened by German-Soviet collaboration, and concern for the consequences of such collaboration conditioned French security policy throughout the interwar period. See Renata Bournazel, *Rapallo: Naissance d'un mythe: La politique de la peur dans la France du bloc national* (Paris, 1974). Chicherin sought to assuage French concerns in a letter to Foreign Minister Louis Barthou on 29 April. *DVP,* 5:278–79.

18. For Lenin's remark, see Lenin, *PSS,* 45:193. The reference to Rapallo as a "model" is from Wolfgang Eichwede, *Revolution und internationale Politik: Zur kommunistischen Interpretation der kapitalistischen Welt 1921–1925* (Cologne, 1971), p. 151.

19. Carr, *The Bolshevik Revolution,* 3:381.

20. Iu. Steklov, "Kto zhe otvetit na provokatsiiu," *Izvestiia,* 26 April 1922, p. 1.

21. A. A. Akhtamzian, "Sovetsko-germanskie ekonomicheskie otnosheniia v 1922–1932 gg.," *Novaia i noveishaia istoriia* 4 (1988): 42–56.

establishment on Soviet territory of training facilities for tank commanders, pilots, and chemical warfare specialists, and the conduct of joint training exercises.[22] Rapallo made it clear that the horizons of the Soviet approach to security were broadening. At the 4th world congress of the Comintern in November 1922, the former Left Communist Bukharin could surprise his audience by remarking that under certain circumstances outright military pacts with bourgeois states might be justifiable.[23]

The implications of the Rapallo link were tested almost immediately. On 11 January 1923, seeking to enforce delinquent payment of reparations, French troops occupied the Ruhr Valley, Germany's exposed industrial heartland. The Soviet Union praised the Germans' desperate resort to passive resistance as a means of opposition, though Moscow's simultaneous effort to use the crisis to spark a German revolution caused many to question the sincerity or usefulness of such support. From the Soviet point of view a more immediate danger lurked behind the Ruhr crisis—the threat of a Polish attack against prostrate Germany, which would destroy the very foundation of the Rapallo line.[24] According to some sources, during December 1922 Radek offered German ambassador Count Ulrich Brockdorff-Rantzau Soviet military assistance against Poland in case of such an eventuality.[25] In May 1923, in the midst of the Ruhr controversy, a diplomatic clash with Great Britain concerning Soviet activities in Central Asia led to the issuance of an ultimatum by Lord Curzon and a brief war scare. The juxtaposition of events underlined the

22. Among western analysts, John Erickson places particularly strong emphasis upon the importance of Soviet-German military collaboration, the foundations for which were in place prior to the Rapallo treaty itself. See Erickson, *The Soviet High Command*, pp. 247–82. A contemporary account is provided by A. A. Akhtamzian, "Voennoe sotrudnichestvo SSSR i Germanii v 1920–1933 gg. (po novym dokumentam)," *Novaia i noveishaia istoriia* 5 (1990): 3–24.

23. *Protokoll des vierten Kongresses der Kommunistischen Internationale. Petrograd-Moskau vom 5. November bis 5. Dezember 1922* (Hamburg, 1923), p. 420. Bukharin conditioned the remark by noting that such combinations would be acceptable only (1) if they were undertaken in the interests of the entire world proletariat, and (2) when the proletarian state entering into the agreement was strong enough to avoid being manipulated by its bourgeois partner.

24. For Soviet reactions see Eichwede, *Revolution und internationale Politik*, pp. 154–56; Wolfgang Ruge, *Die Stellungnahme der Sowjetunion gegen die Besetzung des Ruhrgebietes: Zur Geschichte der Deutsch-Sowjetischen Beziehungen von Januar bis September 1923* (Berlin, 1962), pp. 28–85.

25. Rosenbaum, *Community of Fate*, pp. 52 and 55–56. Von Seeckt later claimed that Radek had requested German support for a preemptive strike against Poland in January 1922. Warren Lerner, *Karl Radek: The Last Internationalist* (Stanford, Calif., 1970), p. 113. Eventually Radek would openly threaten Poland with military retaliation. K. Radek, "Otvet gospodinu Foru i drugim sotsialisticheskim agentom Puankare," *Pravda*, 16 Oct. 1923, p. 1.

importance that Rapallo had assumed in conjunction with the menace posed by Poland's link to the Entente. Steklov editorialized in *Izvestiia* that the Soviet Union, in "its own vital interests, could not allow the final suppression and defeat of Germany."[26] In an address of 20 October 1923, Trotsky conjured up the prospect of a "gigantic coalition with the aim of crushing Germany and then, probably, attempting to run this roller over our spine ... a gigantic plan encompassing all of Europe," but also decried "fatalism" concerning war and urged that "all our strength, all the strength of our diplomacy must be directed and will be directed toward maintaining peace, peace to the end." Poland, suggested the war commissar, could choose to be "bridge or barrier," a barrier cutting off the Soviet Union from the West, or a bridge for positive interaction.[27] In either case Moscow's link with Berlin was vital.

The collapse of German passive resistance in the Ruhr at the end of 1923 meant a temporary vindication for France, but the crisis also reactivated the British and American diplomatic role on the continent and provoked a reconsideration of the Versailles order. Cautioned by Rapallo, the Entente powers launched an effort to regulate their differences with Germany and draw it away from an eastward orientation. The Soviet Union emerged from the crisis ever more disillusioned with the West and determined to maintain the Rapallo policy at all costs. Meanwhile, Berlin sought to play the two ends of the emerging diplomatic triangle against one another in order to broaden its own range of options.

In April 1923 an allied commission sponsored by the United States announced the Dawes Plan for managing the reparations problem and stabilizing the European economy. Soviet commentary described the plan as a "modernization" of Versailles intended further to hobble Germany.[28] In fact, however, the plan corresponded to an emerging strain in German foreign policy represented by Gustav Stresemann, which sought to rebalance international alignments by building links to the West. The implementation of the Dawes Plan began in August 1923 and initiated a process of reconciliation that culminated with the Locarno conference of October 1925. At Locarno, Germany, Great Britain, France, Italy, Czechoslovakia, and Poland came together to discuss European security and made some progress in regulating postwar territorial and military arrangements, in the process clearing the way for German membership in the League of Nations. In Moscow these events were regarded ominously. "Locarno is directed against the Soviet Union," claimed Grigorii

---

26. Iu. Steklov, "Tuchi sgushchaiutsia," *Izvestiia*, 24 Jan. 1923, p. 1.
27. *KVR*, 3, book 2: 141 and 143.
28. K. Radek, "Konferentsiia soiuznikov," *Izvestiia*, 9 July 1924, p. 1.

Zinoviev at the 14th party congress. "The main, the most important feature of Locarno is that its cutting edge is turned against the USSR."[29]

Zinoviev was right. By drawing Germany closer to the Entente, Locarno threatened to destabilize the foundation of the Soviet policy of accommodation. German policy makers were receiving divided council, however, and they took care not to burn all bridges to the east. On 12 October 1925, in the midst of the Locarno deliberations, Berlin pointedly signed a major commercial agreement with the USSR. Brockdorff-Rantzau and Chicherin remained outspoken proponents of German-Soviet friendship, and under their considerable influence, on 24 April 1926, a German-Soviet neutrality pact was signed that pledged noninvolvement if either party were the victim of unprovoked aggression. Despite the challenge of Locarno, the Rapallo link proved to be hardy. It worked to the advantage of both sides, and for Moscow it continued to represent the foundation for a long-term diplomatic strategy.[30]

The premises of accommodation were applied in crafting Soviet diplomacy outside of Europe as well. In August 1922 a mission headed by Ioffe arrived in Beijing, seeking to broaden the range of Soviet diplomatic contacts in Asia. Though unable to secure firm agreements, the Ioffe mission laid the foundation for a more active Soviet role in the Far East, which led to the establishment of full diplomatic relations with the Chinese regional government in Beijing on 31 May 1924, and with Japan on 20 January 1925.

The treaty of Sèvres of 10 August 1920 projected the Versailles system onto the Middle East, a region directly contiguous to the Soviet Union's exposed southern frontier. In response Moscow cultivated a relationship with Mustafa Kemal's Turkey, despite his bloody suppression of the Turkish communist movement. The Soviet-Turkish friendship treaty of March 1921 was followed by the dispatch of a military mission to Ankara headed by Mikhael Frunze, and arms supplies to assist Kemal in his war with Greece. Though the conference of Lausanne, convened during 1922–1923 to defuse conflict in the region, did not include a Soviet delegation, Moscow accepted an invitation to participate in the commission convened to discuss the problem of the Turkish straits. The Soviet

29. XIV s"ezd Vsesoiuznoi kommunisticheskoi partii (b). 18–31 dekabria 1925 g. Stenograficheskii otchet (Moscow, 1926), p. 652. See also the account in Di Biagio, Le origini dell'isolazionismo sovietico, pp. 156–72.

30. Traditional Soviet historiography touts the Rapallo policy as a prototype for peaceful coexistence with the capitalist world. In the words of a leading historian, "The Rapallo policy represents above all the first attempt in history to establish and strengthen normal, mutually beneficial relations between a socialist state and a capitalist power on the basis of mutual acknowledgment of the equality of rights of the two systems, the principles of peaceful coexistence and cooperation." A. A. Akhtamzian, Rapall'skaia politika: Sovetsko-germanskie diplomaticheskie otnosheniia v 1922–1932 godakh (Moscow, 1974), p. 8.

proposal to the commission revealed a defensive orientation by emphasizing the desire to close the straits to the warships of all nations except Turkey. It was more or less ignored in the final draft of the straits protocol, which the Soviet Union nonetheless ratified on 14 April 1923, in the process asserting its right to speak to the issue with the prerogatives of a great power.

Moscow's courtship of Turkey reached its peak with the conclusion of a treaty of friendship and neutrality on 17 December 1925, an achievement that *Pravda* hailed as "the foundation stone for a Soviet system of security," presumably free from the objectionable features of the Versailles order.[31] John Erickson similarly describes the treaty as the basis for a Soviet "security system" built upon close relations with key states in sensitive border zones—a "consistent strategic design" with the Turkish treaty as its "prototype," the neutrality pact of 1926 with Germany as its "heart," and "détente" with Japan as its vital component in the Far East.[32] To speak of a "security system" in these terms may be exaggerated, but the cultivation of stable relations with neighboring states in order to provide a buffer against aggression was certainly part of a diplomatic strategy intended to deter conflict at a moment of weakness. Accommodation was the watchword, and it was made even more urgent by the demobilization of the Red Army that followed the civil war.

The Politics of Defense

Accommodation in the realm of defense policy demanded an abandonment of provocative designs inspired by the doctrine of revolution from without. By 1921 the need to demobilize the swollen Red Army in order to reorient resources toward reconstruction was at any rate pressing. The army's peacetime role was perceived as low-key and commensurate with the regime's limited economic potential. The Soviet Republic could remain the first outpost of the world revolution with a defensive military orientation resting upon the ability rapidly to mobilize large manpower reserves. As Trotsky put it, the Soviet frontier was "the trench line beyond which counterrevolution shall not pass, and on which we shall remain at our posts until the reserves arrive."[33]

In his address to the 9th party congress in April 1920, Trotsky revived the classical socialist goal of a popular militia. While criticizing the

31. Cited in E. H. Carr and R. W. Davies, *Foundations of a Planned Economy*, 3 vols. (London, 1971–77), 3, part 2:642.
32. Erickson, *The Soviet High Command*, pp. 290–91. See also Carr, *The Bolshevik Revolution*, 3:469.
33. L. D. Trotskii, "4-i kongress Kominterna i perspektivy mirovoi revoliutsii," *Izvestiia*, 29 Dec. 1922, p. 2.

"petty bourgeois illusions" that he found attached to the idea in the work of Jean Jaurès and August Bebel, Trotsky sought to apply it to Soviet circumstances by emphasizing the contribution that territorial militia formations could make to economic recovery. Recruited according to the principle of "universal labor service," militia units would be attached to "territorial and production districts" capable of serving as nodal points for economic growth. "The essence of the militia system," he wrote, "consists in bringing the army closer, territorially and in the course of daily life, to the productive process."[34] Incorporated in a unanimously approved resolution at the 9th congress, these proposals came to characterize official attitudes toward conversion despite considerable opposition to them within the high command.

Though it was waged with some heat, the "militia controversy" of 1920–1921 has about it in retrospect an air of unreality. In January 1921 *Pravda* and *Izvestiia* published opposing theses from Nikolai Podvoiskii and Tukhachevskii which summed up the arguments on either side of the debate. Podvoiskii reiterated the case for an immediate transition to the territorial militia principle, mentioning concern for the "militarism" inherent in the institution of the standing army. Tukhachevskii insisted that militia formations were intrinsically defensive in nature, and not commensurate with the "current military task of spreading socialist revolution throughout the world."[35] At the 10th party congress a compromise of sorts was reached which approved the militia concept in principle but left the date of its introduction dependent upon the "external and internal situation."[36] Under Soviet conditions, territorial militia organization demanded a high degree of reliance upon the peasantry, a reliance that many did not believe was desirable. In practical terms, however, the Soviet Republic could ill afford to bear the costs of a large standing army. In the end, it was probably economic constraint that dictated at least a partial preference for the militia system.[37]

The 10th congress did not discuss matters relating to military strategy and doctrine, but it occurred against the background of controversy within the high command in this area as well. The spirit of the military opposition of 1919, temporarily stilled during the critical campaigns of the civil war, appeared again during 1920 on behalf of what became

34. Trotskii, *KVR*, 2, book 2:33–36.

35. Tukhachevskii, *Voina klassov*, p. 71; Benvenuti, *I bolscevichi e l'armata rossa*, p. 241.

36. *Desiatyi s"ezd RKP (b). Mart 1921 goda. Stenograficheskii otchet* (Moscow, 1963), pp. 708–9.

37. On the controversy see John Erickson, "Some Military and Political Aspects of the 'Militia Army' Controversy, 1919–1920," in C. Abramsky, ed., *Essays in Honor of E. H. Carr* (London, 1974), pp. 204–28; Benvenuti, *I bolscevichi e l'armata rossa*, pp. 236–44.

known as a "unified military doctrine." Support for unified doctrine emerged from a group of successful young revolutionary commanders led by Frunze and Sergei Gusev, who sought to codify the lessons of the civil war and apply them to the army's peacetime orientation. Two premises shaped the arguments of the Frunze group: (1) the importance of the RKKA's political mission and internationalist responsibilities, and (2) the need for a unified doctrinal and strategic orientation consciously grounded in Marxist analysis. In practical terms the revolutionary officers demanded a dynamic strategy steeped in the civil war tradition and informed by the spirit of the offensive, a stress upon mobility and maneuver as opposed to positional warfare, and an emphasis upon political agitation and party work within the RKKA.[38]

Opposition to unified doctrine was concentrated primarily among the "military specialists," with the irascible Aleksandr Svechin, formerly a major general in the Imperial Army and now a prestigious lecturer at the Red Army's new military academy, as their most effective spokesperson. In a series of brilliantly formulated rejoinders Svechin dismissed efforts to coordinate political principles with military strategy as pointless. The enemy, he never tired of explaining to his students, would not take time to consult *The ABCs of Communism;* military expediency must remain the decisive operational criterion.[39] The legacy of the civil war was repudiated as atypical, and in his classic *Strategy,* first published in 1923, Svechin directly assaulted the revolutionary officers' emphasis upon the offensive. Emphasizing the unprecedentedly large scale that modern war would assume and the need for an overall strategic design, he contrasted the alternatives of "destruction" (*sokrushenie*) achieved by resolute attack and "attrition" (*izmor*) achieved by strategic defense, and he argued that for a technically less-advanced adversary under specific operational circumstances, the latter could be a more appropriate choice. Svechin was a controversial but capable scholar, and his vivid categories, derived from the work of Carl von Clausewitz and Hans Delbrück, would provide a context for Soviet strategic dialogue for years to come.[40]

The discussion over unified doctrine came to a head at the 11th party congress in March 1922. Debate was less than coherent, reflecting the

38. See the discussion in Benvenuti, *I bolscevichi e l'armata rossa,* pp. 271–83. The original arguments are posed by M. V. Frunze, *Izbrannye proizvedeniia,* 2 vols. (Moscow, 1957), 2:4–26; S. I. Gusev, *Grazhdanskaia voina i Krasnaia Armiia: Sbornik statei* (Moscow, 1958), pp. 71–127, 132–36.

39. For a portrait of Svechin at work see Rapoport and Alexeev, *High Treason,* p. 175.

40. A. Svechin, *Strategiia* (Moscow, 1927), pp. 173–236. A. A. Kokoshin and V. N. Lobov, "Predvidenie (General Svechin ob evoliutsii voennogo iskusstva)," *Znamia* 2 (1990): 170–82, give a contemporary appreciation of Svechin's contributions that emphasizes the relevance of his thought to current strategic problems.

vagueness of the issues at stake. Trotsky supported Svechin's pragmatism as concerned the nature of military science but ridiculed his opposition to territorial militia formations.[41] Tukhachevskii, one of the most outspoken proponents of strategic innovation and a "proletarian" military doctrine, also supported a strong regular army.[42] A group of commanders once linked with the First Cavalry Army, including Voroshilov and Budennyi, sided with the Frunze faction on what were probably calculated political grounds. Trotsky retained sufficient prestige to secure a final resolution reflecting his priorities, but growing opposition within the command and his own increasing estrangement from military affairs (Trotsky had begun to concentrate his attention upon the problem of economic recovery) did not bode well for the future.

With Lenin at the head of the party, Trotsky's position was unassailable. Following the Bolshevik leader's incapacitating stroke in 1923, however, a triumvirate consisting of Zinoviev, Lev Kamenev, and Stalin took control with the specific purpose of blocking Trotsky's accession. By the time of Lenin's death in January 1924, drawing on the domination of the party apparatus that Stalin had begun to assert in his role as general secretary, they succeeded in isolating the war commissar, whose talents as a revolutionary firebrand and military administrator proved to be greater than his acumen in bureaucratic politics. The emergence of the triumvirs meant Trotsky's effective loss of control over military affairs. At the 13th party congress in January 1924 Frunze was made head of a new party commission for military reform, and in January 1925 he succeeded Trotsky as commissar of war. Frunze's appointment would seem to have signaled a victory across the board for the revolutionary officers. In fact, despite his sincere commitment to revolutionary principles, Frunze was also a responsible professional who could not blithely ignore the Soviet Union's drastically limited capacity to undertake a costly military restructuring. Beginning in 1922 the RKKA rapidly demobilized, and military affairs were relegated to secondary status. The theoretical disputations of the 11th congress and the emotional legacy of the civil war now ran head on into the prosaic realities of NEP Russia. The "Frunze reforms" of 1923–1925 (Frunze himself remained in office for only 278 days, between his appointment in January and death on the operating table in November 1925) represented much more a bow to

---

41. His biting critique is given in *KVR*, 2, book 1:115–21.

42. Carr characterizes his position as "anomalous" and describes him as "a slightly eccentric member of the Frunze group." E. H. Carr, *Socialism in One Country*, 3 vols. (London, 1958–64), 2:384.

necessity than the implementation of a consistent program based upon unified doctrine.[43]

In its transition to peacetime status the RKKA was reduced tenfold in size, from 5.3 million during 1921 to a permanent complement of 562,000. Military service was made compulsory for adult males, with the majority of recruits assigned to territorial militia formations located within the administrative district in which they resided for three months of active duty, followed by a reserve requirement of one-month service for each of the next five years. Of the Soviet Union's seventy-two infantry divisions in 1925, forty-six were territorial militia formations. The remaining regular army divisions were composed of officers and enlisted soldiers serving two-year terms of duty. A series of administrative reforms thinned out the officer cadre and streamlined the high command, and on 2 March 1925 a program to phase out the civil war legacy of "dual command" was announced. Likewise, efforts were made to improve the officer's status by granting pay hikes, higher housing allowances, and pensions.[44]

The military posture adopted with the reforms of 1923–1925 corresponded closely to the larger goal of accommodation and what Adam Ulam has called "diplomatic coexistence."[45] Standing army divisions provided a first line of defense, while reliance upon the territorial militia principle maintained a strategic reserve and kept military expenditures in line with competing priorities. A capacity to mobilize a force equal or superior to the combined armies of neighboring states in the western borderlands was considered sufficient to meet any challenge in Europe. Voroshilov, Frunze's successor as commissar of war, pointed out that an attempt to match the military potential of all its enemies would make of the Soviets "Don Quixotes." "We don't need this," he argued, "but to be on a common level with our immediate neighbors, with Romania, Poland, Lithuania, Latvia, Estonia, and Finland . . . this we must achieve

43. Frunze's death remains the subject of speculation. In 1927 the writer Boris Pil'niak published (in Sofia, after all issues of the Soviet journal in which it originally appeared had been confiscated by Soviet censors) "The Story of the Unextinguished Moon," in which he fictionally develops the thesis that Frunze was the victim of a medical murder with political implications. For an account of the episode and the text of Pil'niak's story see Vera T. Reck, *Boris Pil'niak: A Soviet Writer in Conflict with the State* (Montreal, 1975), pp. 13–53.

44. The classic source for these reforms remains I. B. Berkhin, *Voennaia reforma v SSSR, 1924–1925* (Moscow, 1958). Mark von Hagen, *Soldiers in the Proletarian Dictatorship: The Red Army and the Soviet Socialist State, 1917–1930* (Ithaca, N.Y., 1990), pp. 181–267, gives an interesting account of their social consequences.

45. Ulam, *Expansion and Coexistence*, p. 162.

come what may."[46] In the Far East, with China in the throes of revolution and Japan temporarily immobilized by the catastrophic earthquake of 1923, no serious threat was seen as imminent. The Soviet regime's military capacity rested squarely upon manpower, and it was acknowledged that the army's technical level was markedly inferior to that of potential rivals. Significant ocean-going naval forces were also rejected as too costly and inconsistent with a "proletarian" mission.[47] For the time being, revolutionary operational innovations such as those foreseen in the premises of "unified doctrine" remained in the realm of theory. This was an eminently unthreatening military posture, reflective of Soviet weakness and highlighting the importance of a flexible security strategy emphasizing diplomatic maneuver.

The Politics of Revolution

On 19 July 1924 a political cartoon in *Pravda,* famous in its day, depicted Zinoviev in his role as the chair of the Comintern delivering a fiery harangue while Commissar of Foreign Affairs Chicherin covers his head and anguishes in the background. Called into being to serve as the coordinating center for the world revolution, the Comintern, by its very nature, seemed directly to contradict the Soviet Union's new emphasis upon accommodation. In formal pronouncements the Soviet government tried hard to disassociate itself from an organization that was technically composed of autonomous Communist parties, and Chicherin tirelessly emphasized that "state policy and party policy are strictly separated."[48] Such protestations to the contrary, it required no great insight to note that with the vastly greater resources and prestige at its disposal, the Soviet party was bound to dominate the international communist movement. Though the Comintern could not abandon the goal of world revolution, it too was required to adjust to the new realities of the NEP era.

The Comintern's 2nd world congress in March 1920 marked a high point for intransigent revolutionary internationalism. When the 3rd world congress convened in June 1921, militant extremism had already begun to be tempered. An unsuccessful left-wing coup in Germany during March 1921 made clear the dangers of insurrectionary pretensions

46. K. E. Voroshilov, *Stat'i i rechi* (Moscow, 1937), p. 251.

47. Bryan Ranft and Geoffrey Till, *The Sea in Soviet Strategy* (Annapolis, Md., 1983), p. 86.

48. Chicherin, *Stat'i i rechi,* p. 233.

lacking an objectively revolutionary situation, and Moscow's turn toward a policy of accommodation clashed with an undiluted strategy of the revolutionary offensive. These trends were carefully registered by the international movement, and the 3rd world congress became a turning point in its development. The key initiative was to redefine the leading task of affiliated parties, away from organizing for a revolutionary seizure of power and toward a new emphasis upon party building, revealed by the 3rd world congress's slogan, "to the masses." In December 1921 the Comintern's executive committee (ECCI) issued a set of twenty-four theses entitled "Directives on the United Workers' Front," in which the new strategy was codified, and at the 4th world congress in November–December 1922 it received official sanction.[49]

The Comintern's united front strategy was built upon the assumption that international capitalism had achieved a temporary "stabilization" after the crisis provoked by the world war. The movement's theorists argued over the nature and extent of stabilization, but they were in accord about its political implications. At the 4th world congress, which opened four days after Mussolini's seizure of power in Italy, Radek spoke coldly of the "retreat" of the proletariat, which had "not yet come to an end."[50] The theme of the congress became the "offensive of capital," reflected by a falling off in working-class militancy and the decline of revolutionary prospects. Under these circumstances the radicalism that had been the hallmark of the international communist movement might become counterproductive. The united-front line called upon communists to escape from isolation by joining with other labor parties and mass organizations in a bloc of the left in order more effectively to engage them in popular struggles.

From the outset a distinction was drawn between two ways to apply the new strategy. The united front "from above" urged formal alliances with social democratic and other noncommunist organizations and aspired to the creation of a "workers' and peasants' government." The united front "from below" abjured such alliances in favor of agitation at the base within mass organizations. Originally the two variants of the united front were not considered to be mutually exclusive, but taken to their respective extremes, they represented conflicting strategies that soon came to characterize right- and left-wing currents within the movement as a whole. At the Comintern's 5th world congress in June–July 1924 the line of the united front from below prevailed, and the goal of a workers'-peasants' government was reinterpreted as being synonymous

49. Jane Degras, ed., *The Communist International 1919–1943: Documents*, 3 vols. (London, 1956–65), 1:307–16.

50. *Protokoll des vierten Kongresses*, p. 390.

with the dictatorship of the proletariat. This shift to the left reflected personal and bureaucratic rivalry more than a major reorientation, however, and the foundation of the united front approach remained in place. Revolutionary seizures of power in Europe were now presumed to be unlikely, the world revolution was redefined as an open-ended process extending over decades, and a retreat from the revolutionary offensive to a phase of party building was conceded to be in order. The united front, in the words of Wolfgang Eichwede, was an "accommodation to West European realities," just as the NEP was an "accommodation to Russian realities."[51]

The united front was accompanied by the increasingly undisguised subordination of the Comintern to Soviet direction. At its 2nd world congress, the famous "21 Conditions for Admission to the Communist International" imposed a highly centralized organizational model upon the movement, but its spirit remained that of collective struggle and genuine internationalism.[52] By the 3rd world congress this emphasis had begun to change in favor of a tutelary role for the Bolshevik party and an assertion of the universal relevance of the Russian revolutionary experience. Such an evolution was to some extent inevitable for an organization like the Comintern, one of whose members was the ruling party in a major state while the remainder were struggling revolutionary factions. Nonetheless, with the inauguration of a campaign for the "Bolshevization" of member parties at the 5th enlarged plenum of the ECCI in March 1921, Soviet domination began seriously to distort the movement's original purpose. Preservation of the world's first socialist state had been claimed by Lenin as a legitimate priority, but never as the entire raison d'être for the international movement. Bolshevization implied precisely such an emphasis, a transformation of the Comintern into an arm of Soviet foreign policy with the goal of world revolution subordinated to Soviet security concerns. The history of the Comintern after its 4th world congress, writes E. H. Carr, was "a long and sometimes embarrassing epilogue to its original revolutionary aspirations."[53]

Bolshevization became a leitmotif for the Comintern during the 1920s, but it is important to distinguish between the movement's central apparatus, which the Bolsheviks dominated, and the communist mass movement, which could never entirely be controlled. The promulgation of the united front as a general line did not prevent occasional outbursts of revolutionary enthusiasm, which more often than not resulted in failed insurrections followed by White terror. The crisis provoked by the

51. Eichwede, Revolution und internationale Politik, p. 19.
52. Degras, The Communist International, 1:166–72.
53. Carr, The Bolshevik Revolution, 3:442.

Ruhr occupation and runaway inflation in Germany during 1923 briefly revived hopes for revolution, culminating in the fiasco of the "German October," a confused and unsuccessful bid for power by the left. During the summer and autumn of 1923 a peasant uprising in Bulgaria attracted reluctant communist support before being unceremoniously put down, and in December 1924 a communist-inspired workers' uprising in the Estonian capital of Tallinn was crushed. These salutary lessons served to reinforce the saliency of the united-front approach, but they did not extinguish militancy at the base. Nor was the united front an unqualified success in its own terms. It bore little relevance for communist organizations working in conditions of illegality, which meant the bulk of the movement's affiliates, and in those instances where it could be applied consistently, it often produced ambiguous results or worse. Individual Communist parties continued to produce a dizzying succession of left and right "deviations" that posed a constant problem of discipline for the Comintern's executive organs. The united front as a general strategic orientation should be differentiated from the diverse tactical variants adopted by individual communist organizations in response to specific national circumstances.

The united front represented the Comintern's adjustment to the Soviet policy of accommodation. It was accompanied by a campaign for Bolshevization and a tightening Soviet hold upon the administrative apparatus of the international communist movement. The dynamic of world revolution did not disappear, but the Bolsheviks, and particularly the emerging leadership linked to Stalin, no longer necessarily perceived it to be a vital force. In general, the shift away from revolutionary internationalism and toward a policy of accommodation made the Comintern a less significant component of Soviet security strategy. Voroshilov summed up the altered perspective in a speech during 1928. The international proletariat, he repeated ritualistically, was still the Soviet Union's "best ally," but "at present it is still not even in a condition to cope with its own bourgeoisie. . . . Therefore, first of all, we must count on ourselves."[54]

Socialism in One Country

Underlying the evolution of policy throughout the 1920s was the post-Lenin power struggle and the rise of Stalin. At the 13th party congress in May 1924 the triumvirs' victory over Trotsky was crowned.

54. Voroshilov, *Stat'i i rechi*, pp. 250–51.

Nonetheless, with his immense prestige and polemical talent, Trotsky continued to organize opposition and launch sallies against the new leadership. With Lenin gone, the Bolsheviks found themselves caught up in a swirling mass of political, bureaucratic, and personal rivalry, the logic of which remains difficult to sort out. The power struggle was waged around vital issues such as inner-party democracy and industrial policy, but it included more crass and personal motives as well. The common assumption that it was Stalin's unprincipled manipulation of the party apparatus for individual advantage which proved to be the key to his success certainly contains an element of truth, but it may be challenged on the ground that it neglects the extent to which the general secretary's ability to embrace classic Bolshevik causes and place them in the context of an appealing political consensus contributed to his ability to garner bureaucratic support.[55]

At stake in the power struggle, in addition to personal destinies, was the future course of the Russian revolution. In regard to this larger issue, after 1924 two distinct currents of opinion could be identified within the party hierarchy. In 1925 Stalin broke with his fellow triumvirs and allied with the party's right wing, now led by Bukharin, trade union leader Mikhail Tomskii, and Sovnarkom chair Aleksei Rykov. As the group's leading theorist, Bukharin had emerged as a champion of the NEP and a balanced, incremental approach to the problems of development and industrialization. On the left, Zinoviev and Kamenev realigned with Trotsky in a "United" or "Left" Opposition, which based its program upon the economist Evgenii Preobrazhenskii's call for "primitive socialist accumulation," implying the gradual collectivization of agriculture and a forced pace of industrial growth. The party confronted a choice between continuing efforts to manage the NEP, now conceived as a long-term context for a gradual transition to socialism, and a turn to the left demanding a fundamental reordering of agricultural and industrial policy. Against the background of bitter inner-party feuding, increasing economic instability, and a worsening international conjuncture, the confrontation came to a head at the 15th party congress in December 1927 with what appeared to be a victory for the Bukharin-Stalin line of moderation.

The struggle against Trotsky and the Left Opposition, in one important particular, directly touched upon evolving Soviet perceptions of security. After his humiliation at the 13th party congress, Trotsky attached

55. See the discussions in Jerry F. Hough and Merle Fainsod, *How the Soviet Union Is Governed* (Cambridge, Mass., 1979), pp. 143–46; Isaac Deutscher, *Stalin: A Political Biography* (New York, 1967), pp. 317–40; Robert H. McNeal, *Stalin: Man and Ruler* (London, 1988), pp. 85–111.

an essay entitled "The Lessons of October," an uninhibited attack against his political opponents, to a forthcoming volume of his collected works.[56] With the gauntlet thrown down, Stalin responded in a series of polemical rejoinders in which he attempted to rebut Trotsky's arguments and, in the process, to assert his own credentials as a Marxist theorist. The result may be described as Stalin's most ambitious sally into the domain of political theory, the famous doctrine of socialism in one country.[57]

International affairs, as Jonathan Haslam notes, was not Stalin's métier.[58] By trade a revolutionary conspirator, he spoke no non-Soviet languages, had limited experience abroad, and displayed little interest in international matters. Stalin's doctrine of socialism in one country was devised first and foremost as a thrust against Trotsky in the power struggle, and as such it was calculated to win support among the party's bureaucratic elite. In formulating his views, Stalin set up Trotsky's "theory of permanent revolution" as a straw man. According to Stalin's rendition of this theory, its essence was the denial that a proletarian revolution in backward Russia could survive and build socialism in isolation. Trotsky's pessimism was said to contradict Lenin's emphasis upon the union (*smychka*) of proletariat and peasantry under the aegis of the dictatorship of the proletariat, to ignore the revolution's indigenous sources of strength, and to undervalue the contradictions working to weaken imperialism. Trotsky, Stalin charged, "does not feel the inner strength of our revolution . . . does not understand the inestimable importance of the moral support which is provided to our revolution by the workers of Europe and the peasants of the East . . . does not notice the weakness which is corroding imperialism from within."[59]

Against this morass of negativism, Stalin posed the "Leninist theory of building socialism in one country" as an alternative. His description of this alternative, presented in painfully nuanced language and in the didactic manner characteristic of the author's personal style, deserves to be cited at length.

There is no question that for the *complete* victory of socialism, for a *complete* guarantee against a restoration of the old order, the combined strengths of the proletariat of many countries is needed. There is no

56. L. Trotskii, *Sochineniia,* 12 vols. [incomplete, numbered nonconsecutively] (Moscow, 1924–27), 3, part 1:xi–lxvii.

57. See Stalin, *Sochineniia,* 6:324–401.

58. Jonathan Haslam, *Soviet Foreign Policy, 1930–33: The Impact of the Depression* (New York, 1983), pp. 18–19.

59. Stalin, *Sochineniia,* 6:375.

question that without support for our revolution on the part of the European proletariat Russia cannot stand against universal opposition, just as without support for the revolutionary movement in the West on the part of our revolution this movement cannot develop at the tempo that has characterized it since the proletarian dictatorship was established in Russia. There is no question that we need support. But what does support for our revolution on the part of the western European proletariat mean? The sympathy of the European workers for our revolution, their readiness to frustrate the plans of the imperialists concerning intervention . . . is this true support, that is, meaningful assistance? Without question it is. . . . Up to now has it sufficed, this sympathy and support, combined with the power of our Red Army and the readiness of our workers and peasants to defend socialist society with their own breasts. . . . will it suffice in order to beat back the attacks of the imperialists and to win for ourselves the necessary conditions for the work of serious construction? Yes, it will suffice. Will this sympathy continue to grow, or die out? Without question it will grow. Do we possess, therefore, auspicious circumstances, not only to move forward the task of organizing a socialist economy, but also, in turn, to offer support to the workers of Western Europe and the oppressed peoples of the East? Yes, we do.[60]

Stalin's approach curiously blended allegiance to the rudiments of Leninism with audacious theoretical innovations. The theory of socialism in one country asserted that the Soviet regime's dependency upon the progress of the world revolution was real but also conditional, that the Soviet Union could proceed independently to construct socialism despite its weakness, and that in so doing it would contribute to the eventual success of revolutionary movements elsewhere.

Regarded with a cold eye, Stalin's arguments appeared to be riddled with inconsistencies. Trotsky's theory of permanent revolution, which was first outlined in 1906, addressed the problem of *making* the socialist revolution in a "mixed" social environment such as that of tsarist Russia. It had little or nothing to say about the problem of *building* socialism, and in answering Stalin, Trotsky rather distractedly dismissed the entire issue as irrelevant to the matter at hand. In no way could Trotsky or his supporters be described as indifferent toward "the task of organizing a socialist economy" in Soviet Russia. Rather, their entire line was built around a critique of the NEP's adequacy for that purpose. Nor was the power of the Red Army entirely unattributable to the work of its commissar of war. What Stalin really polemicized against, but of course could not name as such, was Lenin's own visionary conception of the world revolution. Personally unconvinced of the relevance of the

60. Ibid., pp. 374–75.

international movement, Stalin did not need to exert any effort of will or follow any tortured intellectual odyssey to relegate it abruptly to the status of a provider of "sympathy and support" for the Soviet state. With self-effacing gestures toward the icon of the dead leader, Stalin proceeded to reverse Lenin's internationalist priorities. Revolutionary internationalism defined world revolution as the key to the survival of Soviet power in Russia. Socialism in one country came close to defining Soviet power as the key to the progress of the world revolution, and Stalin spoke confidently of the Soviet peoples' ability to build socialism and to "defend with their own breasts" the revolution's achievements.[61]

Despite their harshly polemical character, Stalin's conclusions merely summarized perceptions developed by Bukharin and others in support of the NEP.[62] The failure of the world revolution needed to be faced squarely, and it was the great strength of the doctrine of socialism in one country that it undertook to do so. Imprisoned by intellectual vanity, Trotsky continued dogmatically to insist that the original premises of revolutionary internationalism remained valid and hence left himself exposed on the issue. For it was Stalin's theory that most closely approximated Soviet reality in the year 1924. Lenin had urged a policy of accommodation as a temporary expedient in order to carry the revolution over a period of isolation. Socialism in one country described the consequences of accommodation more hopefully, by openly accepting a strategic deferral of world revolution and asserting the revolution's ability to prosper by drawing upon its indigenous strengths.

Socialism in one country provided reinforcement for certain trends in Soviet security policy that had emerged from the search for accommodation: the need for a flexible diplomacy geared to the avoidance of international conflicts, an emphasis upon the defensive capacity of the RKKA as an ultimate guarantor against external aggression, and a reduced role for the Comintern. It was also "Stalin's theory," and, inextricably attached to the persona of the future "great teacher," it pointed toward a new conception of security more conscious of Soviet potential and less troubled by the need to identify the world revolution with Soviet state interests. In its willingness to accept the national form as a legitimate legacy of the revolution, Stalin's theory represented a diminished

61. See Franz Marek, "Socialismo Sovietico e rivoluzione mondiale in Stalin," *Annali* (Milan, 1973), pp. 964–79. Robert C. Tucker, *Stalin in Power: The Revolution from Above, 1928–1941* (New York, 1990), p. 46, suggests that Stalin did believe in world revolution, but in "a decidedly un-Leninist way." According to Tucker's artful reconstruction of Stalin's thought process, his redefinition of the world revolution made the concept identical with an outward expansion of Soviet power.

62. The phrase itself is reported to have been coined by Rykov. See Tucker, *Stalin in Power*, p. 37; Cohen, *Bukharin*, pp. 147–48.

conception of security when compared with the more aspiring premises of revolutionary internationalism.[63] For that very reason it captured the essence of the Soviet state's real aspirations and as such would provide a rough conceptual foundation for Soviet security policy throughout the Stalin era and beyond.

The Third Period

The travail of the Left Opposition occurred against the background of a relative disintegration in the Soviet Union's international situation. The Locarno Pact weakened confidence in the Rapallo policy as an anchor for security in Europe. During 1926 and 1927 a series of setbacks aggravated the Soviets' sense of exposure and gave rise to a sharp though short-lived war scare. In May 1926 a coup in Poland brought Russia's archenemy Pilsudski back to power, and on 7 June 1927 the Soviet plenipotentiary representative (*polpred,* the equivalent to an ambassador) Petr Voikov was assassinated in Warsaw. Meanwhile, during the winter of 1926–1927 the German social democrats launched a public attack upon secret German-Soviet military cooperation. Anglo-Soviet relations deteriorated during the British general strike of 1926, as Soviet trade unions openly proffered support to the strikers. On 12 May 1927 the premises of the Anglo-Russian Cooperative Society in London were raided by the British constabulary, and on 27 May London canceled trade agreements and broke off diplomatic relations. On 6 April 1927, with hopes for the progress of the Chinese revolution collapsing, the Soviet embassy in Beijing was raided by soldiers of the local warlord Zhang Zuolin, a step that Moscow interpreted as a British-inspired provocation.[64] In part as a consequence of these events, the theme of the increasing danger of war became the foundation for a mass campaign. In January 1927 the Osoaviakhim (Society for Cooperation with Aviation and Chemical Defense) was created as an umbrella organization to coordinate military preparedness among the public at large.[65] A Central Committee appeal for "greater vigilance" was published in *Pravda* on 1 June, and a semi-hysterical atmosphere of threat provoked, including dire imprecations against the "enemy within." In this environment a

---

63. This is the sense of the remark by Allen Lynch, *The Soviet Study of International Relations* (Cambridge, 1988), p. 18, that Stalin's doctrine "in effect laid the foundation for the eventual development of international relations as a self-conscious area of study in the Soviet Union."

64. See Litvinov's protest in *DVP,* 10:149–52.

65. Erickson, *The Soviet High Command,* pp. 307–8.

premonition of terror occurred when, in early 1928, a group of fifty-three engineers working in the coal-mining region of Shakhty were charged with industrial sabotage (referred to as "wrecking") and in most cases condemned to harsh penalties including, in eleven instances, the death sentence.[66] "Wrecking," Stalin later wrote, was "a sure sign that capitalist elements . . . are gathering their forces for new offensives against Soviet power."[67]

In retrospect, the war scare of 1927 seems to have been grossly exaggerated.[68] The climate of fear was real, but it was also encouraged in order to strengthen the hand of the leadership in its confrontation with the Left Opposition. In an article entitled "On the Threat of War," which appeared in *Pravda* on 28 July 1927, Stalin made the connection crystal clear. In view of the "real and actual *threat* of a new war in general, and war against the USSR in particular," he asked, "what can be said . . . about our ill-stared opposition, which chooses to launch new attacks on the party in the face of the threat of a new war? . . . Can it be that the opposition is opposed to the victory of the USSR in its approaching battles with imperialism, against an increase in the defensive capacity of the Soviet Union, against a strengthening of our rear areas?"[69] The vulgarity of such insinuations was shocking, but in seeking to tar the opposition with the charge of insufficient loyalty, Stalin played off of real anxieties. Encirclement was a fact, the bourgeoisie was unremittingly hostile, the threat of war was constant, and the Red Army was poorly equipped and ill prepared. The Soviet Union's precarious security environment contributed its share to the inflated concerns of the war scare.

A heightened concern for the possibility of war was also reflected in a turn to the left by the Comintern. During the 1920s two themes came to dominate the movement's public forums. The first was "Bolshevization," which by 1927 was shamelessly propagated as a solution for all political ills. The theme exposed the loss of real autonomy by most national parties, and it was enforced by a long and demoralizing sequence of expulsions and disciplinary actions. At the 6th enlarged plenum of the ECCI in February 1926 the Italian Amadeo Bordiga made a last stand for

66. Robert Conquest, *The Great Terror: Stalin's Purge of the Thirties* (New York, 1968), pp. 730–33; Roy A. Medvedev, *Let History Judge: The Origins and Consequences of Stalinism* (New York, 1971), pp. 111–13; Tucker, *Stalin in Power*, pp. 76–80, describe the Shakhty process. Five of the death sentences were carried out.

67. Stalin, *Sochineniia*, 12:14.

68. See John P. Sontag, "The Soviet War Scare of 1926–27," *Russian Review* 1 (1975): 66–77; A. G. Meyer, "The War Scare of 1927," *Soviet Union/Union Soviétique* 5 (1979): 1–25; Louis Fischer, *Russia's Road from Peace to War: Soviet Foreign Relations, 1917–1941* (New York, 1969), pp. 165–79.

69. Stalin, *Sochineniia*, 9:322 and 330.

proponents of a truly cooperative movement in an eloquent address that denounced the sacrifice of revolutionary priorities on the altar of socialism in one country.[70] But Bordiga was by this point an isolated individual, respected for his integrity but without real influence. The second leading theme was the "stabilization of world capitalism," now defined as an extended phase during which the prospects for successful revolutionary challenges would be greatly reduced. Up until 1927, on the basis of the assumption that no major crisis was on the horizon, Comintern theorists recommended a gradualist perspective informed by concern for organizational integrity and growth. Against the foil of the war scare, however, their underlying assumptions began to unravel.

The stabilization achieved by world capitalism after the *Sturm und Drang* period of the world war was never regarded as permanent. Jenö Varga, the communist movement's leading economist during the 1920s, emphasized that the exacerbation of uneven and unequal development, the further progress of monopolization, recurrent overproduction crises, and the departure of the USSR from the world capitalist system all contributed to an ongoing general crisis of the capitalist mode of production. Varga rejected catastrophic crisis theories but confidently predicted "waves" of instability with potentially revolutionary consequences. Capitalism would not self-destruct overnight, but it would decline. Occasional phases of equilibrium and even real prosperity might occur, but eventually growing inequities, declining living standards for the working masses, and breakdown would prevail. The thesis of the general crisis of capitalism is sometimes dismissed as a rhetorical slogan devoid of real content. To the contrary, it represents a highly influential perception that has been integral to the Soviet theory of world politics. The capitalist world system, whatever its accomplishments, was portrayed by Varga as inherently unstable, a perpetual source of crisis and war.[71]

A link between the Soviet Union's increased sense of exposure and an approaching wave of capitalist crisis was asserted by the 7th enlarged plenum of the ECCI in November 1926 on the eve of the war scare. In

70. See Paolo Spriano, *Storia del Partito communista italiano,* 5 vols. (Turin, 1967–75), 2:3–17; Carr, *Socialism in One Country,* 3, part 1:522–23. Franz Borkenau, *World Communism: A History of the Communist International* (Ann Arbor, Mich., 1962), provides a classic account of Bolshevization.

71. The concept of the "general crisis" was fundamental to the Comintern's analysis, and Varga was probably its most cogent exponent. For a useful compilation of his writings, see E. Varga, *Die Krise des Kapitalismus und ihre politischen Folgen* (Frankfurt am Main/Vienna, 1969), and his *Die Wirtschaft der Niedergangsperiode des Kapitalismus nach der Stabilisierung* (Hamburg/Berlin, 1928). Ia. Pevzner, "Zhizn' i trudy E. S. Vargi v svete sovremennosti (k 110-letiiu so dnia rozhdeniia i 25-letiiu smerti)," *Mirovaia ekonomika i mezhdunarodnye otnosheniia* 10 (1989): 16–33, offers a recent Soviet appreciation.

his opening address Bukharin (who had replaced the disgraced Zinoviev as ECCI chair) turned to the theme of the postwar evolution of capitalism and identified a "new, third period, a period in which the progress of the stabilization of capitalism will reveal in ever sharper form its own internal contradictions."[72] By introducing the concept of the third period, the Comintern suggested that these "internal contradictions" were coming increasingly to the fore. The phases of crisis following the world war and of stabilization during the years 1922–1927 were now to be replaced by a new phase of "unstable stabilization" (as it was inelegantly phrased) that would place prospects for revolutionary change back onto the agenda. "The crisis of capitalism and preparation for its collapse," explained Stalin, "grow out of stabilization."[73] The forms that "collapse" might assume were varied: a new imperialist war, an attack upon the USSR, the eruption of national liberation struggles against colonialism, or an intensification of the class struggle within the developed world were all listed as possibilities. The consequences of such events would be the radicalization of the masses and the emergence of new revolutionary conjunctures. From the Soviet perspective, however, it was the danger of war that was most preoccupying. In his keynote address to the Comintern's highly stage-managed 6th world congress in July 1928, Bukharin summarized the new perspective by referring to war as "the central problem of our time" and noting ominously that although war against the USSR would not break out tomorrow, "I must say that we have very little time."[74]

The Comintern's third-period line was also related to the power struggle within the Kremlin. The defeat of the Left Opposition during 1927, culminating in the internal exile of Trotsky and thousands of his supporters, seemed to indicate a victory for Bukharin's pro-NEP orientation. Simultaneously, however, the NEP itself began to unravel, as peasant reluctance to deliver grain at fixed prices led to empty granaries and a threat of hunger in urban areas. This was not the first crisis in the stormy history of the NEP and the situation was certainly not insurmountable, but it provoked a confrontation between Stalin and Bukharin over whether or not to resort to forced requisitioning as a response.

72. Protokoll, Erweiterte Exekutive der Kommunistischen Internationale. Moskau, 17. Februar bis 15. März 1926 (Hamburg/Berlin, 1926), p. 37; Di Biagio, Le origini dell'isolazionismo sovietico, pp. 198–202.

73. Stalin, Sochineniia, 10:48.

74. Cited in von Boetticher, Industrialisierungspolitik und Verteidigungskonzeption, p. 73. See also the congress's theses on the international situation in Degras, The Communist International, 2:455–57.

Simultaneously, differences between the two leaders over international policy surfaced. Bukharin's response to the third-period scenario was to call for a more actively accommodationist Soviet diplomacy built upon the premise of what David Riazanov called "proletarian pacifism," for a "peace policy" that would include a reduced reliance upon the Rapallo link, a more pronounced opening to the Versailles powers, and overtures to Europe's social democratic left. Bukharin was now coming to view Stalin as a threat to all that the revolution stood for, and his international program, linked to an image of the NEP as a gradualist approach to building socialism, was intended to suggest an alternative to the increasingly belligerent and isolationist approach of the Stalin group.[75] By the summer of 1928, however, Bukharin and his allies, like the Left Opposition before them, had been defeated. Confronting an ever more severe crisis due in part to his own strong-armed requisitioning tactics, Stalin prepared to turn the revolution in a radical new direction with massive forced collectivization and the industrialization drives of the five-year plans.

The immediate goal of the domestic turn to the left in 1928–1929 and of Stalin's entire "second revolution" was to break the regime's dependency upon the peasantry once and for all. By promising to construct an industrial foundation for national strength, it also offered a solution to the problems of Soviet weakness and overexposure. Many former Trotskyites misperceived it as a vindication for their program and on that basis made a precarious peace with the Stalin leadership. It is still not entirely clear whether Stalin's program in 1928–1929 represented a carefully thought-through strategic design; during 1928 a real crisis of procurement had set in which demanded resolution.[76] The implications of Stalin's "revolution from above" as regards security policy were nonetheless consistent with the general secretary's clearly articulated preferences and priorities.

The theory of socialism in one country emphasized the importance of national strength, a point that was reinforced by the foreign policy

75. The controversy between Bukharin and Stalin within the Comintern is described in F. I. Firsov, "Stalin i Komintern," *Voprosy istorii* 8 and 9 (1989): 3–23 and 3–19, esp. 8:18–23. Attempts to trace the contours of an alternative approach to international relations in Bukharin's analysis during the 1920s appear in Dmitrii Volkogonov, *Triumf i tragediia: Politicheskii portret I. V. Stalina*, 2 vols. (Moscow, 1989), 1, part 1:193–211; V. Sirotkin, "Ot grazhdanskoi voiny ko grazhdanskomu miru," in Iu. V. Afanas'ev, ed., *Inogo ne dano* (Moscow, 1988), pp. 370–91; esp. Di Biagio, *Le origini dell'isolazionismo sovietico*.

76. One recent Soviet account suggests that Stalin intentionally provoked the crisis in order to prepare the ground for a confrontation with his political rivals. V. Tikhonov, "Chtoby narod prokormil sebia," *Literaturnaia gazeta*, 3 Aug. 1988, p. 10.

shocks of the late 1920s and the bleak prognoses of the third period. In practical terms, strengthening the Soviet Republic meant expanding its indigenous arms industry and modernizing the RKKA so as to make it better prepared technically and less dependent upon mobilizing the peasant masses—a program actively championed by an influential group within the high command. An official Soviet history of World War II states the problem clearly, although in retrospect.

> The question was posed as follows; either the Soviet people would create in the shortest possible time a heavy industrial base and a strong defense industry, or the Soviet state, which found itself in the position of a besieged fortress, would be destroyed by a new intervention on the part of the imperialist aggressors. Therefore it was necessary for the party . . . to support a forced pace of planned production, and to reduce the production of consumer goods and the provisioning of many factories and enterprises of secondary importance with commodities and raw materials in deficit supply.[77]

According to such logic, building socialism in one country under conditions of capitalist encirclement demanded more than the expedient of accommodation. It demanded the positive goal of security through strength, of "catching up with and overtaking" the leading imperialist powers. It would be an exaggeration to argue that the roots of the turn to the left of the late 1920s lay primarily in an altered perception of the prerequisites for security, but the connection should not be overlooked.[78] In August 1931, with the first five-year plan well under way, Stalin made the point in what is with good reason one of his most commonly cited observations.

> It is sometimes asked whether it is not possible to slow down the tempo somewhat? No, comrades, it is not possible! . . . To slacken the tempo would mean falling behind. And those who fall behind are beaten. . . . The history of old Russia consisted, by the way, of continuous beatings due to her backwardness. She was beaten by the Mongol Khans. She was beaten by the Turkish beys. She was beaten by the Swedish feudal lords. She was beaten by the Polish and Lithuanian gentry. She was beaten by the British and French capitalists. She was beaten by the Japanese barons. All beat her—because of her backwardness. . . . Such is the law of the exploiters—to beat the backward and weak. It is the jungle law of capitalism. . . . Do you want our socialist fatherland to be beaten and lose its independence? But if

77. A. A. Grechko et al., eds., *Istoriia vtoroi mirovoi voiny 1939–1945*, 12 vols. (Moscow, 1973–82), 1:10.
78. The thesis is most effectively presented by von Boetticher, *Industrialisierungspolitik und Verteidigungskonzeption*.

you do not want this, you must liquidate its backwardness in the shortest possible time and develop genuine Bolshevik tempo in the matter of constructing its socialist system of economy. There is no other way. . . . We are fifty or a hundred years behind the advanced countries. We must make good the distance in ten years. Either we do it, or they crush us.[79]

Overcoming backwardness was equated with the throttling of the peasantry and the rapid construction of an industrial base, and herein lay the essential thrust of Stalin's program—a heavy-handed application of "primitive socialist accumulation" undertaken in defiance of a resentful and resistant population. Stalin's break with Bukharin, a decisive turning point in the history of the Soviet state, implied a fundamental choice of orientation in security policy.

The search for security through strength left its mark upon the RKKA. Despite its emphasis upon industrialization, the first five-year plan did not abandon the conviction that military spending must be fixed in relation to the overall capacity of the national economy. In preliminary planning it was assumed that the health of the military sector depended upon the general level of economic performance, and that an overemphasis upon defense could do real harm. "It must never be forgotten," remarked Boris Shaposhnikov in his influential study of the Soviet general staff concept, "that military art does not dictate to politics, and that the military budget is not a purely military affair, but also a political and above all an economic one."[80] It was presumed that while it was engaged in building the foundations for an industrial economy, the Soviet Union would maintain the defensive orientation in military policy defined by the Frunze reforms.

During the 1920s the Soviet Union possessed no "official" military doctrine. It would be fairer to speak of a set of dominant assumptions, which were often challenged in a highly polemical specialized literature.[81] It was in this context that, beginning in 1926, a group of commanders inspired by the ever-vibrant personality of Tukhachevskii launched a challenge to the regime's predominantly defensive strategic outlook. Tukhachevskii remained sensitive to the Red Army's revolutionary heritage, to which concern he added a highly professional awareness of the changing nature of modern war and its ever more exacting

79. Stalin, *Sochineniia*, 13:38–39.

80. Cited in A. B. Kadishev, ed., *Voprosy strategii i operativnogo iskusstva v sovetskikh voennykh trudakh, 1917–1940 gg.: Sbornik* (Moscow, 1965), p. 202.

81. For an appreciation and survey of this literature that emphasizes the insights generated by a plurality of viewpoints, see V. N. Lobov, "Aktual'nye voprosy razvitiia sovetskoi teorii voennoi strategii 20-kh—serediny 30-kh godov," *Voenno-istoricheskii zhurnal* 2 (1989): 41–50.

standards. At the core of his arguments was a desire to revive the offensive as a component of Soviet strategy. By carrying the battle to the enemy, he proposed somewhat fancifully, the Red Army could provoke political unrest in the rear of capitalist armies, establish Soviets in occupied territories, and draw strength from its role as an army of liberation. More concretely, offensive operations allowed a fuller exploitation of modern military technology, which meant above all increased firepower and mobility. "The forms of war develop in complete harmony with the growth of productive forces," he wrote, paraphrasing Engels. Under contemporary circumstances, propelled by technology, a "primacy of the offensive" was emerging that was capable of reinforcing the RKKA's revolutionary mission.[82]

In essence, Tukhachevskii argued on behalf of Svechin's strategy of destruction, an orientation that Svechin himself discouraged because of its costs. "Preparation for a war of destruction [na sokrushenie]," Svechin wrote, "may lead to so extraordinary a strain upon the military budget as to stop in place or even ruin prospects for the balanced development of the state's productive forces. . . . Preparation for a war of attrition [na izmor], on the other hand, must be concerned above all with a general, proportional development, because a sickly economy is naturally not able to withstand the severe trials which attrition brings."[83] According to Soviet data, in 1928 the RKKA counted ninety-two "obsolete" tanks. A rifle division possessed forty-eight artillery pieces, compared with sixty and ninety-eight for its French and British equivalents. Supply vehicles were predominantly horse drawn—rear services operated with a total of 1,200 heavy trucks.[84] The RKKA was an army of infantrymen and cavalry, quite unprepared for the type of operations that Tukhachevskii and his supporters were recommending. Preparation for a war of destruction demanded, at a minimum, the mass production of tanks, a new emphasis upon military aviation, the thoroughgoing motorization of military transport, the development of new weapons systems, and a considerable extension of the national rail net. When Stalin received these proposals during 1929, he is said to have dismissed them as an argument for "red militarism."[85] But Tukhachevskii's star was temporarily on the

82. See Tukhachevskii's essays "Voina kak problema vooruzhennoi bor'by," in M. N. Tukhachevskii, *Izbrannye proizvedeniia*, 2 vols. (Moscow, 1964), 2:3–22, and "Voprosy sovremennoi strategii," in *Voprosy strategii i operativnogo iskusstva*, pp. 90–101.

83. Svechin, *Strategiia*, p. 42.

84. S. A. Tyushkevich et al., *The Soviet Armed Forces: A History of Their Organizational Development* (Washington, D.C., 1978), p. 163.

85. The remark, attributed to Stalin by Marshal Sergei Biriuzov in his introduction to the republication of Tukhachevskii's collected works in 1964, may be apocryphal. Tukhachevskii, *Izbrannye proizvedeniia*, 1:12.

rise. The issuance of new field service regulations in 1929 refocused attention upon offensive operations. A Central Committee decision of 15 July 1929 opened the door to military reforms, a *Revvoensovet* statement of 13 June 1930 unveiled plans for motorization and the development of new weapons types, and at the 16th party congress in 1930 underfunding of the military sector was criticized from the floor.[86] With Tukhachevskii's appointment in June 1931 to the posts of people's commissar for the army and navy and chief of armaments, the victory of his policies seemed to be assured.

In conjunction with the turn to the left of the late 1920s the Soviet Union moved toward a new strategic orientation that placed offensive operations in the foreground. The prerequisites for such an orientation were the systematic mechanization of the RKKA, the complementary development of its air arm, and a buildup of its regular army component—costly commitments that would radically alter Soviet economic priorities in the years ahead. It was a strategy that emphasized operations in depth capable of effecting decisive strategic breakthroughs and exploiting them by striking into the enemy's rear areas, of carrying war onto the enemy's territory and waging it to the complete annihilation of opposing forces. To enunciate such intentions was a far cry from creating the means to realize them, but by 1931 the general direction had been established.

The World Economic Crisis

There is some irony in the fact that Stalin's option for security through strength, because of the brutality with which it was pursued, should have led to a dramatic decline in the Soviet Union's defensive capacity, and that at a time when a real threat to Soviet power was emerging that transcended anything seen since the civil war.

The onset of the world depression with the American stock market crash of 1929 seemed to bear out the radical vision of the third-period scenario. Viewed from Moscow, the implications of the depression were especially disturbing. Economic instability increased the likelihood of war and disrupted patterns of exchange with the West considered to be important to the success of the five-year plan. In 1930 a sharp protest against the "dumping" of Soviet commodities onto depressed world markets led to the imposition of economic sanctions against the USSR by

---

86. von Boetticher, *Industrialisierungspolitik und Verteidigungskonzeption*, pp. 288–99; for an account of the debate over operations in depth, M. V. Zakharov, *General'nyi shtab v predvoennye gody* (Moscow, 1989), pp. 87–94.

France. Under the strains of the depression the hard-won gains of a decade of accommodation suddenly seemed to be at risk.[87]

Such concerns were aggravated by the short-term consequences of Stalin's turn to the left. Forced collectivization led to a state of virtual civil war in the countryside, while the hasty reordering of industrial priorities created chaos in transport and supply. With the Red Army still dependent upon its cavalry arm, the nation's stock of horses, as a direct result of resistance to collectivization, was more than cut in half.[88] Confusion in rail transport seriously affected the capacity for rapid mobilization. In July 1928 Sovnarkom chair Rykov argued in support of the NEP that "the first priority necessary for defense of the USSR is naturally grain,"[89] but the first years of collectivization saw a disastrous drop in agricultural output, which by 1932 brought famine to large areas of the fertile Ukraine. General disruption and disaffection among the peasantry created the worst possible context for waging war. A new trial of wreckers was held late in 1930 with a so-called industrial party brought before the dock, and the accusations did not fail to place the blame for difficulties upon "spies and saboteurs." In the end, however, the greatest wrecking seems to have been wrought by the regime's own insistence upon an unrealistic tempo of growth.

Stalin's disastrous miscalculation concerning the effects of collectivization was paralleled by a similarly misguided evaluation of the rise of European fascism. The Mussolini phenomenon was discussed and condemned at the Comintern's 4th world congress, but this did not prevent Soviet relations with fascist Italy from flowering during the 1920s. At the 5th world congress a resolution introduced by Bordiga established a context for future interpretations by deemphasizing the extent to which fascism and other forms of right-wing extremism represented a distinct threat independent of the general crisis of capitalism, which was presumed to be their source.[90] It was capitalism, not fascism, that was the real enemy, and it was the social democratic center, not the far right, that served as the most important political foundation for capitalism. The analysis reached a logical extreme at the 6th world congress in 1928 when, in conjunction with the Comintern's turn to the left, the menace of right-wing extremism was downplayed, the term "social fascism" coined to characterize the role of social democracy as the

---

87. See Haslam, *Soviet Foreign Policy, 1930–33*, pp. 21–45.

88. V. Nifontov, *Produktsiia zhivotnovodstva v SSSR* (Moscow, 1937), p. 11. The text notes a drop from 34.6 to 16.6 million.

89. A. I. Rykov, *Tekushchii moment i zadachi partii. Doklad ob itogakh iiul'skogo plenuma TsK VKP(b). 13.VII.1928 goda* (Moscow-Leningrad, 1928), p. 6.

90. Degras, *The Communist International*, 2:137–40.

essential prop for bourgeois hegemony, and an intransigent line of confrontation with reformism adopted with the rhetorical designation "class against class."[91]

So long as fascism was identified primarily with Mussolini's movement, it could comfortably be dismissed. Italy was of marginal importance in the larger spectrum of European affairs, and it was a state with which the Soviet Union enjoyed positive relations. Germany was another story, but even after its electoral breakthrough of 1930 Hitler's National Socialist German Labor party (NSDAP) continued to be regarded as a flash in the pan. If in retrospect the judgment seems to be incredibly deluded, it should be noted that it was by no means unique to the communist left. Before the autumn of 1930 no one regarded the Nazis as more than fringe-group extremists. Some Soviet commentary, assuming that the Nazis' prospects were limited, even implied that the Hitler phenomenon might serve to strengthen the Rapallo link. Since Radek had floated his famous "Schlageter Line" during 1920, suggesting that German communists seek to coopt the national reaction against the Versailles humiliation, German nationalism had been viewed from Moscow as a force that encouraged an eastward orientation in Berlin.[92] It was, after all, the social democrats who were the most insistent supporters of a foreign policy realignment toward the Entente, and the traditional conservative parties and Reichswehr that provided the backbone for Rapallo. While Hitler's brown-shirted storm troopers marched in the streets, the Comintern clung to the verities of social fascism and class against class, underestimated the Nazi threat, and encouraged division on the left.

The true character of German fascism remained to be revealed when on 18 September 1931, in part motivated by a depression-induced desire to secure access to a region of great economic and strategic importance, Japanese armies swept into Chinese Manchuria. During the 1920s, though it had been intimately involved in the affairs of China through the agency of the Chinese Communist party, the Soviet Union did not regard the Far East as an area of primary security concern. It was now confronted by the menace of a hostile army emplaced directly upon its far eastern frontier.

Since the creation of the Far Eastern Red Banner Army in August 1928, an effort had been made to develop the far eastern region, which

91. See the analysis in Helmut Gruber, ed., *Soviet Russia Masters the Comintern: International Communism in the Era of Stalin's Ascendancy* (New York, 1974), pp. 175–200.

92. Leo Schlageter was a right-wing extremist, executed by French occupation authorities in the Ruhr and hailed thereafter as a national martyr. On the "Schlageter Line" see Lerner, *Karl Radek*, pp. 120–23.

was tied to European Russia only by the slender thread of the single-track Trans-Siberian railway, as a self-sufficient strategic zone. Between July and September 1931 Voroshilov visited the region, awarded local commander Bliukher the General Order of Lenin and the Order of the Red Star, and in general emphasized the strategic importance of the Far East. But once the Japanese occupation had begun, the Soviets were careful to moderate their response. The Comintern urged China's communists to revive their united front with the nationalist regime on behalf of all-national resistance to the aggressor, and a substantial reinforcement of the Red Banner Army was undertaken. In an address of 22 December 1931, however, the new chair of the Central Executive Committee Viacheslav Molotov struck a more conciliatory tone. While reciting the ritualistic formula "we do not want others' land, but we will never surrender our own," Molotov underlined the Soviet Union's intention to answer provocations with a "policy of peace."[93] In practice this quickly evolved into a full-fledged policy of appeasement. Moscow turned to Japan with the offer of a nonaggression pact (which remained unanswered) and made major concessions in order to defuse points of conflict, including the surrender of control over the Chinese Eastern Railway and the offer of recognition for Japan's new Manchurian puppet state of Manchukuo. Though the regime's very existence was not at stake in the Far East as it was in Europe, fear of the consequences of war channeled Soviet policy toward acquiescence.

The Japanese military presence in the Far East revived fear of encirclement and simultaneous attack from east and west. Concern for the use of Poland as a staging area for aggression masterminded in Paris or London inevitably grew greater and stimulated new diplomatic overtures toward the Entente powers that culminated in nonaggression pacts with the Baltic states, Poland, and France during 1932. The obligations which these pacts entailed were limited, however, and despite political instability inside Germany, the Rapallo line remained the anchor for Soviet security policy in Europe. Electoral setbacks for the NSDAP in November 1932 gave rise to hopes that the Nazi phenomenon was at last in decline, but the scope for such illusions was about to run out. On 30 January 1933 Hitler was appointed chancellor. Several weeks later a fire gutted the Reichstag building in Berlin. The conflagration may intentionally have been set by Nazi agents, or it may merely have been the work of a deranged arsonist. In the event, it was seized upon as a pretext for the declaration of a state of emergency and a wave of executive decrees concentrating almost absolute power in Hitler's hands. In a

93. *DVP,* 14:725–28.

matter of months the NSDAP systematically crushed the communist and social democratic opposition and built the foundations for a dictatorship of terror.

A revanchist Germany pledged to rearmament and ruled by outspoken anticommunists and an expansionist Japan poised on the far eastern frontier confronted the Soviet Union with a completely transformed security environment. The promised benefits of industrialization still lay in the future, while the disruptions caused by collectivization and the five-year plan were massive and real. Suddenly, Moscow confronted the possibility of a two-front war that it was ill prepared to fight.

Between 1921 and 1933 the premises of Soviet security policy altered gradually but significantly. The stabilization of world capitalism identified in 1921 was originally presumed to be a brief process, the need for a policy of accommodation was justified as a temporary expedient, the ultimate dependence of Soviet power upon the progress of the world revolution was still assumed. By the time of Stalin's emergence as the Soviet Union's dominant leader in 1928–1929 these premises were no longer in place. The Comintern, always given pride of place in Lenin's scheme of things, had been reduced to a tame instrument of Soviet foreign policy. The diplomacy of accommodation had become virtually indistinguishable from an attempt to maintain a classical balance of power. A defensive orientation in military policy had begun to be displaced by a new emphasis upon security through strength.

The approach to security adopted in 1921 on the basis of the paradigm of accommodation and retreat was built upon several underlying assumptions. The stabilization of capitalism and failure of the revolution to expand necessitated a diplomatic strategy of maneuver designed to exploit the contradictions of imperialism and create a stake in peaceful relations with the USSR. For the Comintern, the postwar wave of revolutionary offensives would be replaced by a period of party building under the aegis of the united front. The world revolutionary process, now defined as extending over decades, would meanwhile be furthered by the growth of Soviet power, pursued in a gradual and proportional manner through the mechanisms of the NEP.

Stalin's theory of socialism in one country almost imperceptibly turned the premises of accommodation upon their head. The notion of retreat was abandoned altogether, and a new, more positive emphasis upon building an autonomous foundation for Soviet power was put in its place. The Soviet Union's dependence upon the progress of the international movement was replaced by the movement's reliance upon the "base" of Soviet support. Weakness and exposure, formerly assumed to be the unavoidable consequences of encirclement, now became intolerable. The shift in priorities was at least partially reflected in the decision to abandon the NEP and to launch into the trials of primitive socialist accumulation.

The confusion and violence attendant upon collectivization and the five-year plan, however, meant a short-term decline in the Soviet capacity for defense. Almost simultaneously the Soviet security environment disintegrated dramatically, as the ramifications of the world economic crisis led Japanese armies into Manchuria and brought Hitler to power in Berlin. In 1933, with the logic of accommodation undermined but the alternative of security through strength as yet unattainable, Soviet leaders were required to rethink the premises of their policy in the face of a major external threat.

CHAPTER THREE

From Collective Security to Separate Peace, 1928–1939

The Soviet government, which is alien to chauvinism, nationalism, racial or national prejudice, considers its national responsibilities to lie, not in conquests, not in expansionism, not in an extension of territory; it considers the honor of its people to lie, not in their education in a spirit of militarism and blood-thirstiness; but only in bringing to life those ideals for the sake of which it came into being, and in which it sees the entire meaning of its existence; namely, in the construction of socialist society, and this constitutes the inexhaustible wellspring of its policy of peace.

—Maksim Litvinov, 4 April 1934

The rapid changes of the 1930s traumatized Soviet society. Never had the regime been less prepared to withstand the shock of war, and yet never had war seemed to be more likely. The threat posed by imperialist crisis containing the seeds of confrontation was a familiar theme in Soviet analysis, but now it took on a new immediacy. In the wake of Hitler's accession to power Stalin must have concluded that a new imperialist war on the scale of 1914–1918 was in the making. The overriding dilemma for Soviet security policy became how most effectively to position the regime for an inexorably approaching conflict.

Preparation for war placed severe demands upon what was still an impoverished and administratively chaotic society. First, it required a strengthening of domestic controls in order to ensure loyalty. The orgy of political terror into which the Soviet Union was thrown during the years 1936–1939 certainly had sources other than those derived from the exigencies of the security environment, but fear of the consequences of an impending war and spy-scare witch-hunting cannot entirely be dismissed as contributing elements. Second, it called for increased military capacity. The direction to be pursued was indicated by the Tukhachevskii group and reflected in the military emphasis of the second five-year plan. Higher military spending contributed to real force improvements, but it also placed new burdens upon an already overtaxed economic mechanism. Finally, it demanded a diplomatic strategy crafted to ensure that the Soviet Union would not confront the worst of all possible contingencies, an anti-Soviet coalition among the leading imperialist powers and a simultaneous attack from east and west. Security through strength was still an unattainable goal. A diplomacy of accommodation remained essential, and with the Rapallo line in apparent ruin, only the Entente powers presented themselves as viable partners. But the stakes had grown higher, the terms for accommodation more demanding, and the outcome less predictable.

From 1933 onward Soviet security strategy was calculated in the shadow of war. Its primary goal, through intelligent diplomacy and the cultivation of intimidating strength, was to prevent war if at all possible, and if not, to ensure that the USSR would not become directly involved. Peace, defined as a necessary prerequisite for socialist construction, became the watchword of the decade. In a tremendously dynamic and confused international environment efforts to build a "peace front," while simultaneously preparing to fight should all else fail, represented the broad lines of policy. *Collective security,* based upon agreements linking the Soviet Union more closely to the bourgeois democracies of the West, with opposition to fascist aggression as its foundation, became the dominant security paradigm of a deeply troubled polity that could ill afford risky international engagements.

Indivisible Peace

Soviet foreign policy during the 1930s was represented by the personality of Maksim Litvinov. Already effectively in charge of the People's Commissariat of Foreign Affairs (NKID) from 1928 onward because of Chicherin's declining health, he was formally named commissar of foreign affairs in July 1930. Upon assuming the post, Litvinov announced that his appointment "did not signify even the slightest alteration in the foreign policy of the [Soviet] Union," which "fully corresponds to the will of the worker and peasant masses, and finds expression in the decisions of the Soviet government."[1] In fact, Litvinov's priorities had often clashed with those of Chicherin, and the Soviet

1. M. M. Litvinov, *Vneshniaia politika SSSR: Rechi i zaiavleniia 1927–1935* (Moscow, 1935), pp. 51–52.

government was by no means united over policy options. Litvinov did not share Chicherin's personal commitment to the Rapallo line, nor his special aversion for Great Britain. What is more, beginning in 1931 Moscow confronted an altered international situation that demanded new approaches. Gradually, under Litvinov's tutelage, the contours of Soviet international policy began to be reshaped.[2]

Historians continue to debate Litvinov's relative importance as an architect of Soviet policy. His tenure as commissar of foreign affairs corresponded with a period when the consequences of Stalin's personal dictatorship reached truly monstrous proportions. Litvinov never became a Politburo member and was not attached to Stalin's immediate entourage, he was not able to protect his commissariat during the terror, and he could not prevent his own ouster and the collapse of his policies in 1939. But Stalin's absolute control over the mechanisms of Soviet power was not fully in place until 1937, and despite his preeminence, disagreements over policy continued to exist beneath the surface within the Soviet elite. Given Stalin's personal lack of expertise in foreign affairs, it is possible that Litvinov exercised at least some degree of autonomy in implementing policy within broad lines approved by the leadership.[3]

Litvinov was not a theorist, and indeed with the onset of Stalinism the intense theoretical disputations that served as the context for policy formation during the first decade of Soviet power all but disappeared. Differences of opinion remained, but they were expressed bureaucratically rather than in a public contest of ideas and in the end could always be resolved by Stalin's personal intervention. The contours of Litvinov's approach to international relations may nonetheless be distilled from his many public statements as a representative of the Soviet state. His views were marked by a good deal of consistency, and they represent an approach to the Soviet security dilemma that is significantly distinct from those that had preceded him.

War, Litvinov repeatedly stressed and apparently sincerely believed, was the primary threat to the progress of Soviet industrialization and hence to the stability of Soviet power. In Asia the presence of Japanese armies along the far eastern frontier was an immediate danger that had to be neutralized at all costs. In Europe after 1933 Hitler's Germany

2. A biographical sketch of Litvinov is provided by Henry L. Roberts, "Maxim Litvinov," in Gordon A. Craig and Felix Gilbert, eds. *The Diplomats, 1919–1939* (New York, 1965), pp. 344–77.
3. Adam Ulam, *Expansion and Coexistence*, p. 215, calls him "a faithful executor of decisions laid down by Stalin and the Politburo." For Jonathan Haslam, *The Soviet Union and the Struggle for Collective Security in Europe, 1933–1939* (New York, 1984), p. 5, Litvinov functioned as "acting director, but only on Stalin's sufferance."

posed an even greater long-term menace.[4] These harsh realities demanded an unambiguous peace policy. The distinction drawn by the Comintern's 6th world congress in 1928 between wars among imperialist powers and war waged against a proletarian state, and the possibility of pitting the imperialist powers against one another in a fratricidal conflict from which the USSR might hope to stay removed, were given little credence. Peace, Litvinov constantly asserted, was "indivisible." "The Soviet delegation," he explained in his opening address to the League of Nations conference on disarmament during 1932,

> summarizes the problem which confronts us with the words: "security from war." In this regard, perhaps, our conception of security differs from the conception of other delegations, many of whom, in speaking here about security, have in mind to maximize possibilities to secure victory for this or that government when it is threatened by attack. The Soviet delegation, for its part, proposes that we strive to make war itself impossible.[5]

In pursuit of this lofty goal Litvinov championed a long list of devices. Nonaggression treaties, regional security pacts, pledges to abjure war as a means to resolve interstate disputes, universal disarmament, and the much-maligned League of Nations were among the concepts embraced as the foundation for a collective security regime resting upon mutually accepted principles and obligations. "Security from war" would be achieved by intimidating aggression through moral pressure, diplomatic cooperation, and if necessary the joint imposition of sanctions.[6]

The premises of collective security were not identical to those of the Leninist policy of accommodation. Like the Rapallo line, the new orientation encompassed a diplomatic strategy tying the Soviet Union to one side of a divided imperialist camp—in this case, to the Entente powers in opposition to revanchist Germany. Stalin justified the potential change of partners with the logic of crude *Realpolitik*. "We never oriented ourselves toward Germany just as we are not now oriented toward France and Britain," he told the 17th party congress in January 1934. "We have been oriented in the past and will remain oriented in the

4. See his confidential evaluation in "O podgotovke Germanii k voine. Zapiska M. M. Litvinova I. V. Stalinu, 3 dekabria 1935 g.," *Izvestiia TsK KPSS* 2 (1990): 211–12. Litvinov argues: "Enmity toward the USSR . . . constitutes the foundation for his [Hitler's] tactical line in the realm of foreign policy."

5. Litvinov, *Vneshniaia politika*, p. 197.

6. Robert Jervis, "Security Regimes," *International Organization* 2 (1982): 357–58, attempts to define the concept formally. The work of V. K. Sobakin, *Kollektivnaia bezopasnost'-garantiia mirnogo sosushchestvovaniia* (Moscow, 1962), and *Kollektivnaia bezopasnost' v Evrope* (Moscow, 1956), makes use of a similarly broad definition.

future toward the USSR and only the USSR."[7] For Litvinov, however, the degree of engagement that collective security demanded was qualitatively distinct from anything that had been offered in the past. Denunciations of the Versailles system and the League of Nations were staples for those who spoke for Soviet foreign policy in the Chicherin tradition. Now, Litvinov urged policies intended to strengthen the European status quo in opposition to Hitlerite revisionism and called for a positive orientation toward the League. The tactic of maneuver favored by Lenin and Chicherin demanded that the Soviet state retain a degree of flexibility to exploit intercapitalist rivalry. Now, Litvinov called for the conclusion of "entangling alliances" that would commit the Soviet armed forces to far-reaching obligations on behalf of the western democracies. The assumption of an essential equivalence among all capitalist states ran deep and militated against drawing qualitative distinctions between benign and aggressive rivals, but this was precisely the distinction that Litvinov proposed to make. The very concept of world revolution became anathema as Litvinov argued in speech after speech that building socialism in one country meant an indefinite postponement of efforts to achieve communism on a global scale. The Bolshevik tradition scorned "bourgeois pacifism" as a hypocritical illusion that ignored the sources of conflict built into the imperialist world order. Now, Litvinov launched a Soviet peace campaign that would put the bourgeois pacifists to shame. With its passionate commitment to avoiding war and attachment to coalition building as the foundation for security, Litvinov's collective security approach represented a virtual revolution in Soviet diplomacy.

Litvinov's project was not unopposed. The turn toward collective security was accompanied by a continued pursuit of security through strength via industrialization and a buildup of the RKKA. Taken to their respective extremes, these two options represented contrasting security paradigms that coexisted uncomfortably. An important body of opinion within the party hierarchy, including leaders closely linked to Stalin such as Viacheslav Molotov, Andrei Zhdanov, and Lazar Kaganovich, never accepted the legitimacy of Litvinov's program, which they felt placed too much reliance upon the good will of the bourgeois democracies, and they worked to replace it with a semi-isolationist, "fortress Russia" alternative. For this group the Rapallo line remained alive, and even with Germany in the hands of fanatic anticommunists, hopes for some kind of rapprochement constantly resurfaced. "I can say plainly that the Soviet government would like to establish better relations with Germany than

7. Stalin, *Sochineniia*, 13:302.

those that exist now," intoned Molotov on 10 June 1930 in a speech that summarized the priorities of those opposed to Litvinov. "We, toilers of the Soviet Union, must count on our own efforts in defending our affairs and in defense of our Motherland, and about all on our Red Army."[8] Stalin apparently did not wish to resolve the muted dispute among his lieutenants. His own preference probably leaned toward some kind of arrangement with Germany, but the Germans themselves were not cooperative, and for the time being contrasting options were kept open.

Did the Soviet Union enter sincerely into the collective security era? To the extent that Litvinov was able to guide policy, it most certainly did. But he was required to wage the struggle for collective security within the party apparatus as well as in the face of international mistrust and ill will. Nor did Soviet overtures toward the West ever imply an abandonment of freedom of maneuver—a freedom that would-be allies certainly retained for themselves. The collective security approach was a probe in the direction of an alternative security model, honestly pursued but also bitterly resisted, and in the end tragically unsuccessful.

The Diplomacy of Peace

Moscow could not help but be aware of the danger posed by Hitler, but in 1933 Germany was not yet in a position to contemplate aggression. In the Far East, by way of contrast, the leaders of Japan's Kwantung Army, emplaced on the Soviet border in Manchuria, openly supported a "continental orientation" and urged an attack upon the USSR. The Soviet Far East was a tempting target. It was sparsely populated (total population did not exceed 3 million in 1934), and Vladivostok and the Maritime Province represented valuable potential additions to Japanese possessions. Beginning in 1933 a succession of border incidents kept the strategic climate in the region on edge. The uncertain political balance in Tokyo, where the "war party" was strong but not dominant, left Soviet leaders wary. "Among the Japanese imperialists a struggle is in progress over the question of whether or not to go to war with the Soviet Union for the Far Eastern region," remarked Leningrad party secretary Kirov in January 1934. "In the face of a growing danger of war we must give the question of defense the most serious, the most concentrated attention."[9]

In order to bolster defenses the Soviets pursued several complementary approaches. The policy of appeasement begun in 1931 was moderated

8. DVP, 19:697 and 704.
9. S. M. Kirov, Izbrannye stat'i i rechi 1912–1934 (Moscow, 1939), p. 603.

but not abandoned. In 1935, after much wrangling, it led to an agreement to sell the Chinese Eastern Railway (which Soviet forces had intervened to defend against Chinese encroachment in 1928) to Japanese Manchukuo. Beginning in 1933 the Far Eastern Red Banner Army was dramatically expanded and investment in the region was increased, heavy economic burdens that the impoverished nation, with its resources already strained to the limit, could ill afford. "Russia was wasted with misery," wrote *New York Times* correspondent Walter Duranty, "but the Red Army had restored its food reserves and its reserves of gasoline, and cloth, and leather for uniforms and boots. And Japan did not attack."[10] Finally, a two-pronged diplomacy kept open the offer to Tokyo of a non-aggression pact while simultaneously pursuing closer ties with Japan's regional rivals. In December 1932 the Soviet Union restored diplomatic relations with the Chinese national government of Nanjing after a five-year hiatus. In 1936 it signed a mutual assistance protocol with the Mongolian People's Republic.[11] Appeasement was thus linked to calls for resistance to Japanese expansionism, accompanied by tacit offers of Soviet support.

In November 1936 Japan signed the Anti-Comintern Pact with Germany. This highly rhetorical document, eventually adhered to by Italy, Hungary, Spain, and Manchukuo as well, pledged its signatories to share intelligence data concerning Comintern activities and to collaborate in undertaking preventive measures. Despite the conceit that it concerned only the ideological threat of world communism, the pact had obvious anti-Soviet connotations. Closer German-Japanese collaboration encouraged Moscow's worst fears, but on 7 July 1937, following the so-called Marco Polo Bridge incident, Japan launched a full-scale invasion of China. Though it was not yet clear, a turning point in Soviet fortunes had arrived. Japan's choice of victims drew it into a protracted war on the Asian mainland and lowered enthusiasm for a simultaneous confrontation with the USSR.

10. Cited in David J. Dallin, *Soviet Russia and the Far East* (New Haven, Conn., 1948), p. 16. The Far Eastern Red Banner Army was expanded from six divisions in 1931 to twenty divisions in 1936. In 1935 the Trans-Baikal Military District command was created, and in 1938 the Far Eastern Army was broken into two special Red Banner armies, making a total of three military commands in the region. Japanese reactions to the Soviet military buildup are discussed in Jacob Kovalia, "Japan's Perception of Stalinist Foreign Policy in the Early 1930s," *Journal of Contemporary History* 2 (April 1984): 313–35.

11. In an interview granted to U.S. journalist Roy Howard on 1 March 1936, Stalin stated unambiguously, "In the event that Japan decides to attack the Mongolian People's Republic, we will be required to assist the Mongolian People's Republic. . . . We will aid the MPR in the same way we aided them in 1921." Stalin, *Sochineniia,* 1 [XIV]: 116–17.

Moscow's hope now became to keep Japan embroiled in China. With the national government of Jiang Jieshi (Chiang Kai-shek) under siege, the united-front line that had been pressed upon the Chinese Communisty Party (CCP) since 1935 began to bear fruit. In the name of national unity the CCP was legalized and its key leaders, Mao Zedong, Zhou Enlai, and Zhu De, were invited to participate in an All-National Defense Council. On 21 August 1937 a Sino-Soviet nonaggression pact was signed in Nanjing. The pact itself was a minimal gesture, but it was accompanied by Soviet military aid for the Chinese resistance. Friction along the Soviet-Manchurian border intensified as a result, but with Japan's best forces drawn into central China, the Soviet position became much stronger. In the summers of 1938 and 1939 border incidents erupted into pitched battles between Soviet and Japanese armed forces, first in the area of Lake Khasan near Vladivostok, and a year later along the Khalkhin Gol River on the border with Mongolia. In each case, with an overwhelming advantage in armor, motorized vehicles, and mobility, the Red Army won smashing victories. Khalkhin Gol developed into a major encounter where the rising star of the Red Army, Army Commander Georgii Zhukov, demonstrated his capacity by presiding over a near encirclement of opposing forces.[12]

The threat of fascism in Europe was less imminent than that posed by the Kwantung Army, but it was more dangerous in the long run. Germany was an imposing power, its new leaders were articulating deeply felt popular grievances, and the collapse of the Rapallo link left a void in Soviet European policy. The possible emergence of a German-led anti-Soviet front could not be excluded. Not surprisingly, it was within Europe that Litvinov's collective security regime achieved its fullest definition.

One dimension of the new approach was a "peace offensive" spearheaded by an outspoken disarmament campaign. In December 1925 the League of Nations convened a disarmament commission in Geneva composed of the representatives of twenty-one nations, including the USSR. Moscow welcomed the opportunity to participate, though it was only at the commission's forth session in November 1927, after a dispute with Switzerland concerning the assassination of a Soviet diplomat had been resolved, that a Soviet delegation led by Litvinov took up its place. Litvinov immediately caused a stir by calling for the total elimination of standing armies and military stocks, and he challenged the League to

12. See Amnon Sella, "Khalkhin-Gol: The Forgotten War," *Journal of Contemporary History* 4 (Oct. 1983): 651–87; A. A. Koshkin, "Kak gotovilsia Khalkhin-Gol," *Novaia i noveishaia istoriia* 4 (1989): 42–55.

approve a disarmament convention.[13] On 29 August 1928, two days after it was ratified by the fifteen original signatories, the Soviet Union approved the Kellogg-Briand Pact, a utopian pledge eventually approved by fifty-four states that solemnly renounced war as a means of resolving international disputes. Litvinov was a champion of the project, and on 9 February 1929 the Soviet Union, Poland, Romania, and Latvia (later joined by Lithuania, Iran, and Turkey) signed a similar agreement, dubbed the "Litvinov protocol," to govern their mutual relations.[14]

Within the League commission Litvinov earned worldwide repute as a tireless advocate of peace and disarmament. After the rejection, at the commission's sixth session in August 1929, of a comprehensive Soviet disarmament plan, he changed tracks and began to call for a disarmament conference to give greater visibility to the cause. The conference was eventually convened in February 1932, and in his opening address Litvinov again stole the show by demanding "the exclusion of war as a means of conducting national policy" and citing "full and complete disarmament as the only means for the destruction of war."[15] These visionary appeals were accompanied by more practical proposals for arms reductions, but in the end nothing came of them. Opinion among the great powers was too divided, France and Britain remained unbendingly negative, and initiatives were constantly submerged by problems of definition and technicalities. There was unquestionably an element of propaganda attached to the Soviet Union's maximalist positions, but they were not crafted idly. Litvinov's efforts as a champion of peace reinforced the Soviet collective security line, and some constraint upon German rearmament might well have emerged from a more effective disarmament regime.[16]

A new Soviet attitude toward the League grew out of Litvinov's work within the disarmament commission. Despite its formal exclusion from

13. Litvinov, *Vneshniaia politika*, pp. 106–13.
14. For the text and a comment by Litvinov see *DVP*, 12:66–70.
15. Litvinov, *Vneshniaia politika*, p. 195
16. Soviet disarmament efforts are carefully chronicled in a large and highly partisan literature. See L. Grigor'ev and S. Olenev, *Bor'ba za mir i bezopasnost' v Evrope (1925–1933 gg.)* (Moscow, 1956), pp. 132–43; V. M. Khaitsman, *SSSR i problema razorusheniia (mezhdu pervoi i vtoroi mirovymi voinami)* (Moscow, 1959), pp. 254–384. Vladimir Zubok and Andrei Kokoshin, "Opportunities Missed in 1932?" *International Affairs* 2 (1989): 112–21, criticize Soviet negotiating strategy at the world disarmament conference of 1932–34 for an excessive emphasis upon "propaganda-exposé" techniques and for a preoccupation with purely quantitative reductions, but also admit that Litvinov's dramatizations were "useful initially" as a means of calling attention to the issue. To the extent that the Soviet Union's public commitment to disarmament was intended to bolster the regime's image, it might be compared with the formally democratic character of the "Stalin constitution" of 1936.

the organization, since 1923 the Soviet Union had been active within a variety of League committees, and a kind of creeping engagement in League affairs had emerged as a trend.[17] The withdrawal from the League of Germany and Japan during 1933 cleared the way for a change of attitude, and on 25 December 1933 Stalin offered the novel opinion that the Soviet position was not "always and under all circumstances hostile," and that "the League can become a factor working to impede or prevent an outbreak of military activities."[18] On 18 September 1934, after accepting an invitation sponsored by the French, the USSR formally took up a seat at the League Council. Thereafter the League became the most significant forum from which Litvinov propagated his program. During the 1930s, as Europe was rocked by one crisis after another, the Soviet commissar of foreign affairs was consistent, though uniformly unsuccessful, in calling for League sanctions in response to acts of aggression.[19]

Another foundation for the Soviet collective security regime became a series of neutrality, nonaggression, and mutual assistance treaties. The neutrality pact with Turkey of December 1925 provided a prototype for the nonaggression concept, and it was followed by a string of similar agreements, culminating in the years 1931–1933 when treaties were signed with Finland, Latvia, Estonia, Poland, France, and even Italy. The agreements were commonly for three or five years' duration, with provisions for automatic extension. Their essence was a commitment to renounce the use of force in regulating differences, and a pledge of neutrality in the event that one of the signatories became involved in hostilities with a third party. Nonaggression meant a pledge of restraint; it did not provide for mechanisms to intimidate calculated expansionism. Following Hitler's seizure of power, with his announced intent to "revise" the Versailles order, stronger measures seemed to be in order. Radek made the point in a series of articles appearing in *Pravda* and *Izvestiia* during May 1933. "The word 'revision,' " he wrote, "is only another name for a new world war."[20]

The first Soviet reactions to the establishment of the Third Reich were cautious. Moscow did its best to keep open channels of communication, but a disintegration of bilateral relations set in inexorably. By December 1933 the Rapallo connection seemed to have become a thing of the past; Litvinov could speak of having reached the "junction of two diplomatic

17. See Carr, *Socialism in One Country*, 3, part 1:450–62.
18. Stalin, *Sochineniia*, 13:280.
19. Maxim Litvinov, *Against Aggression* (New York, 1939), chronicles Litvinov's activities within League forums from 1934 through 1939.
20. K. Radek, "Reviziia versal'skogo dogovora," *Pravda*, 10 May 1933, p. 2.

eras."[21] Peace must be guaranteed, it now began to be argued, by mutual
assistance agreements linking the Soviet Union with the European democracies in an antifascist front committed to resist, by force if necessary, any untoward act of aggression. The mutual assistance treaty,
which in distinction from the nonaggression pact defined active measures to intimidate aggression, henceforward became a key goal of Soviet
diplomacy. At the 17th party congress in January 1934, Litvinov was
coopted into the Central Committee, and Stalin spoke ominously of
events "clearly moving toward a new war."[22]

France was the major power most directly threatened by German re-
vanchism, and it was from a Franco-Soviet dialogue that Moscow's first
and most significant mutual assistance pact emerged. Negotiations began
in 1933, but they proceeded slowly; French opinion was divided concerning the propriety of a security link with the USSR, and Litvinov's
project was resisted within his own party. The purge of Erich Röhm's
paramilitary Sturmabteilung (Storm Trooper, or SA) organization during the 30 June 1934 "Night of the Long Knives" raised hopes for some
that the Nazis' star was waning, with traditional conservative elements
in the armed forces, in the past supportive of a positive relationship with
Moscow, reasserting their prerogatives.[23] Meanwhile a new setback for
collective security arrived with the assassination on 9 October 1934 of
French foreign minister Louis Barthou, a key architect of Franco-Soviet
rapprochement. Barthou's successor Pierre Laval was much less convinced of the value of an accord and worked to limit the extent of French
commitments.

Despite a host of obstacles, on 2 May 1935 a Franco-Soviet mutual
assistance pact was concluded, followed by a Czechoslovak-Soviet pact
on 16 May. The agreements were significant in their own right as well as
for what they revealed about Soviet priorities. As originally conceived by
Litvinov and Barthou, the goal was a comprehensive regional security
accord covering eastern and central Europe, an "eastern Locarno"

---

21. Litvinov's remark, in a speech delivered to the Central Executive Committee on 29
Dec., is given in *DVP*, 16:782. On Soviet efforts to keep relations with Germany open, see
Karlheinz Niclauss, *Die Sowjetunion und Hitlers Machtergreifung: Eine Studie über die
deutsch-russischen Beziehungen der Jahre 1929 bis 1935* (Bonn, 1966), pp. 171–72.

22. Stalin, *Sochineniia*, 13:291–306. Carr writes of this important speech: "Throughout the past year fear of Germany, and the desire to maintain good relations with Germany,
had been evenly balanced in Soviet policy and in Stalin's mind. Now the former factor had
begun to predominate." E. H. Carr, *Twilight of the Comintern, 1930–1935* (New York,
1982), p. 118.

23. Karl Radek, "Deux sous la cloche," *Le Journal de Moscou*, 7 July 1934, p. 1.

intended to intimidate German aggression.[24] The final treaties represented something considerably less ambitious, although the hope that they might become the foundation for more far-reaching accords remained alive. The texts of the treaties referred to the principles of the League of Nations Charter in citing national security, territorial inviolability, and political sovereignty as guiding principles. If either party were threatened by attack, mutual consultations were required, to be followed by military assistance in the event of "unprovoked aggression."[25] By committing itself in principle to provide military aid to what had long been considered its leading European rival, the Soviet Union was taking a step in an uncharted direction.

The quest for collective security also resulted in a shift in strategy on the part of the Comintern. At the ECCI's 12th enlarged plenum in August 1932 the "class against class" line was restated despite the rise of German fascism. Familiar themes such as the end of capitalist stabilization, the impending revolutionary upsurge of the masses, the approach of a new era of war and revolution, and the danger of imperialist aggression against the USSR were loyally repeated and continued to dictate a policy of radical exclusiveness.[26] In the German election of 6 November 1932, the last free election before the Nazi takeover, the combined tally of seats won by the Social Democratic party (SPD) (121) and the Communist party (KPD) (100) comfortably outweighed the 196 allotted to the NSDAP. But to no avail. Right up to the eleventh hour the Comintern continued to define the SPD as the main enemy.

A turning point arrived with the return to Moscow of the Bulgarian communist leader Georgi Dimitrov in February 1934. Dimitrov was the most prominent among the defendants charged with plotting the Reichstag fire, and from the dock in Leipzig he had succeeded in electrifying world opinion with a dramatic defiance of his accusers. Eventually released for lack of evidence, Dimitrov found himself transformed from an obscure functionary into a charismatic symbol of resistance to fascism. He used his new-found prestige to champion a "revolutionary united

24. See William Evans Scott, *Alliance against Hitler: The Origins of the Franco-Soviet Pact* (Durham, N.C., 1962), pp. 176–202. Molotov was especially insistent about the need to include Germany in a collective security regime. See his speech to the 7th Congress of Soviets on 28 Jan. 1935 in *DVP,* 18:39–52.

25. For the texts see *DVP,* 18:309–12 and 333–36. A clause in the treaty made the Soviet commitment to offer military assistance to Czechoslovakia conditional upon the provision of assistance by France.

26. Degras, *The Communist International,* 2:210–30, gives the theses on the international situation.

front" strategy that emphasized the potential for wide-ranging cooperation between communist and other mass-based antifascist movements,
including the social democrats.[27] Dimitrov encountered resistance within
the Comintern's old guard, but he also found influential supporters, including such powerful national leaders as Maurice Thorez of France and
Palmiro Togliatti of Italy. Not least, the "revolutionary united front"
corresponded to a trend that was emerging spontaneously from the
movement's rank and file.[28] On 27 July 1934 the French Socialist and
Communist parties signed a united-front agreement. In a speech on 1
November, Thorez gave the policy a name that would stick—the "popular front."[29] The new line was belatedly endorsed by the Comintern's
secretariat on 16 January 1935, seconded by Stalin, and promulgated by
the Comintern's 7th world congress during July and August.[30] In scenes
of enthusiasm the delegates endorsed Dimitrov's call for a "broad antifascist popular front" and directed communists to join with all popular
movements with an antifascist character. In line with Moscow's priorities the congress also emphasized the danger of a new imperialist war,
expressed support for the Soviet "policy of peace," approved the mutual
assistance pacts with France and Czechoslovakia, and even encouraged a
military buildup on the part of capitalist countries threatened by German expansionism. The turn to the left of the third period was implicitly
rejected, and the gap that had opened up in 1931–1935 between Litvinov's collective security approach and the class-against-class line was
closed. As Haslam notes, "collective security and the Popular Front were
twins."[31]

27. See Georgi Dimitrov, *Suchineniia*, 14 vols. (Sofia, 1953–55), 9:292–355; Alfred
Kurella, ed., *Dimitroff's Letters from Prison* (London, 1935), for his Leipzig speech and
public statements. An account of Dimitrov's defense of the popular front within the Comintern's executive is given in "K 70-letiiu Kominterna. Vystuplenie G. Dimitrova pri
podgotovke VII kongressa Kominterna,' *Izvestiia TsK KPSS* 3 (1989): 122–27.
28. The degree to which the popular front was a product of the communist mass movement is emphasized in K. K. Shiriniia, *Strategiia i taktika Kominterna v bor'be protiv fashizma i voiny (1934–1939 gg.)* (Moscow, 1979), pp. 90–106. See also Jiri Hochman, *The
Soviet Union and the Failure of Collective Security, 1934–1938* (Ithaca, N.Y., 1984), pp.
78–94. Hochman calls the popular front "a short-lived tactical variant, which was primarily a Soviet concession to the grass roots of the memberships of the national sections of the
Comintern" (p. 94).
29. Maurice Thorez, *Oeuvres de Maurice Thorez*, 22 vols. (Paris, 1950–64), 7:52–89.
This speech was delivered to the party's Central Committee and released as a pamphlet
with the title "Les communistes et le front populaire."
30. See Degras, *The Communist International*, 3:359–70, and the boastful account in
B. M. Leibzon and K. K. Shiriniia, *Povorot v politike Kominterna: Istoricheskoe znachenie
VII kongressa Kominterna* (Moscow, 1975), pp. 136–350.
31. Haslam, *The Soviet Union and the Struggle for Collective Security*, p. 59.

After the disasters wrought by revolutionary exclusiveness the popular front unleashed new energies within the communist mass movement. Still, the 7th world congress did not represent a new beginning for the Comintern so much as the culmination of its evolution away from the fighting, revolutionary organization that Lenin had originally envisioned. No subsequent world congress or ECCI enlarged plenum was even convened. The Soviet leadership had long since ceased to place any confidence in the international communist movement, and national parties were disorganized by factional rivalry and repeated Moscow-dictated changes in tactics. Soviet attention was now fixed upon the ruling elites of fascist Germany and the bourgeois democracies, not the communist opposition. The popular front swept away a self-destructive policy of radical extremism and was greeted with optimism, but its main impact was to add a new element to the edifice of collective security. In the dangerous world of the 1930s, revolutionary internationalism was a luxury that the Soviet state could not afford.

Ezhovshchina

The collective security project did not deflect efforts to build a foundation for security through strength—its goal was precisely to ward off war so that economic modernization and military preparation could go forward. Beginning in 1932, in the context of the second five-year plan, a significant expansion of the Soviet armed forces was begun. The Frunze reforms of 1923–1925 had reduced the RKKA to a level that conformed with the economic priorities of the NEP. After the 1927 war scare, defense expenditures began to rise, and in July 1930 the 16th party congress described an increase in defensive capacity as "a problem of the very greatest importance."[32] A buildup of the armaments industry was one of the goals of the first five-year plan, but it was not until after Japan's occupation of Manchuria that the defense sector began to be expanded radically.[33] Increased funding was accompanied by

---

32. *Kommunisticheskaia partiia Sovetskogo Soiuza v rezoliutsiiakh i resheniiakh s"ezdov, konferentsii i plenumov TsK*, 10 vols. (Moscow, 1970–72), 4:440.

33. See Alec Nove, *An Economic History of the U.S.S.R.* (London, 1969), pp. 224–55. According to Soviet sources, the defense component of the state budget grew progressively throughout the prewar period. Defense expenditures represented 5.4% of the state budget during the first five-year plan; 12.6% during the second five-year plan; 26.4% during the first three years of the third five-year plan; and 43.3% during 1941. A. M. Nekrich, *1941, 22 iiunia* (Moscow, 1965), p. 73.

organizational reforms and strategic innovations that transformed the character of Soviet military policy.[34]

The most immediate effect of the military buildup was a dramatic increase in the size of the army. Manpower organized in cadre divisions leaped to 940,000 in 1934 and by the end of 1938 stood at nearly 2 million. To increase the pool of eligible recruits, the authorities lowered the draft age to 19 and abandoned the restriction, inherited from the revolution, limiting armed service to citizens classified by social origin as "workers or peasants." Between 1936 and 1938 territorial militia formations were phased out altogether. The RKKA was becoming a mass army, conventionally organized and with fewer and fewer traces of its "people's war" heritage.

Beginning in 1934 a reorganization of the high command was attempted with the goal of increasing the efficiency of central control. The Revvoensovet was abolished, with a people's commissariat for defense headed by Voroshilov as defense commissar, a modest military council, and a new general staff assuming responsibility for coordinating the military function.[35] The technical revolution championed by Tukhachevskii was continued, though not without some second thoughts. This meant a strong emphasis upon mechanization and motorization, development of the tank weapon and reconsideration of its combat mission, the creation of mechanized corps and airborne units, and enhanced firepower attained through higher armaments norms and improved artillery. The role of other service branches was also expanded, with a threefold increase in the size of the air force, including the creation of a long-range bombing fleet and a modernization of tactical air support, the creation of a submarine flotilla, and a strengthening of coastal defenses. Eventually Stalin would opt to build a "balanced" Soviet fleet, including large battleships and cruisers in addition to submarines and coastal patrol boats.[36] The modernization of communications was begun, though not completed, with the goal of introducing wireless systems on the company, battery, and squadron levels. During 1935 Soviet forces were repositioned in European Russia in conjunction with the construction of a "Stalin Line" of permanent defensive fortifications. Soviet military planning by no means found refuge in a Maginot Line syndrome, however. The "spirit of the offensive" remained dominant. A course toward creating the capacity

34. Summaries of the reforms are attempted in Gosztony, *Die Rote Armee*, pp. 117–24; Erickson, *The Soviet High Command*, pp. 366–403.

35. Zakharov, *General'nyi shtab*, pp. 38–49.

36. See Sergei Gorshkov, *The Sea Power of the State* (Annapolis, Md., 1976), p. 137. Gorshkov emphasizes that "the view that the fleet should be used for defensive purposes predominated and the fleet itself was regarded as defensive factor."

for a war of destruction had been set, though its completion, as Tukha-chevskii noted somewhat ruefully, was "not so easy."[37]

Cumulatively, the military buildup of the 1930s had the effect of tight-ening central command and control, increasing the size and diversifying the capacity of the armed forces, moving toward a capacity of operations in depth, and restructuring the RKKA in a manner more closely approx-imating that of other leading European armies. The changes turned away from the army's revolutionary origins and placed a tremendous strain upon an economy already groaning under nearly impossible burdens. Erickson speaks of the army's being "conventionalized to the point where militarism seemed to be triumphant over socialism."[38] The army's standards were becoming higher, but its fighting ability was doubtlessly exaggerated by the endlessly repeated dogmas of official security pol-icy—the aphorism "we do not want others' land, but we will never sur-render our own," the assumption that in the event of war the "spirit of the offensive" would carry the battle onto foreign territory, and the con-viction that in the rear of an aggressor the RKKA would find support in an uprising of workers and peasant.

Through the 1930s the RKKA maintained a stability of leading per-sonnel that was unique among Soviet institutions. The revolutionary officers of the civil war dominated the high command, which demon-strated a strongly multi-ethnic character in addition to notably high lev-els of professional commitment and accomplishment.[39] In view of these qualities, and with preparations for war under way, the wave of political violence that swept through the officer corps during the terror of 1937–1939 seems illogical and perverse. The dangers inherent in the interna-tional situation were evident to all. Nothing was more important than military readiness. In such an environment Stalin saw fit to launch a campaign of bloody reprisals against the backbone of his army.

The Ezhovshchina (the "time of Ezhov," as the terror of 1937–1939 has been referred to in the Soviet Union, after N. I. Ezhov, director of the People's Commissariat of Internal Affairs [NKVD] beginning in Septem-ber 1936) emerged in part from the atmosphere of fear and exposure cre-ated by external threats.[40] In 1928 and again in 1930 the trials of "wreckers" widely publicized tales of conspiracy and subversion, and they left Soviet society overflowing with suspicion and intrigue. The

37. Cited in Erickson, *The Soviet High Command*, p. 323.

38. Ibid., p. 387.

39. Morozow, *Die Falken des Kreml*, p. 85, notes that thirty-seven of seventy-four com-manders were non–Great Russians in 1930, including two Estonians, eight Latvians, three Lithuanians, ten Poles, seven Jews, five Ukrainians, and two Germans.

40. Isaac Deutscher perceived the essence of the great purge to lie in an attempt by Stalin to ensure loyalty in view of an approaching war. Deutscher, *Stalin*, pp. 376–77.

mania for security that resulted was taken to the extreme of a systematic falsification of all maps of the USSR, with rivers, highways, and entire villages purposefully misplaced.[41] It was in such an environment that the murder of Leningrad party secretary Kirov on 1 December 1934 set the spark to what would gradually become a veritable witch-hunt after the "enemy within."

It is probable that Kirov was murdered at Stalin's behest in order to provide a pretext for his purge of the old Bolshevik party apparatus. Whether or not Stalin personally gave the order, the act set the stage for what Robert Tucker has referred to as the "Quiet Terror," a wave of mass arrests on charges of treason beginning in 1934–1935. An ominous plateau was reached in August 1936 when a public "show trial" of Bolshevik oppositionists, including former pillars of the regime such as Zinoviev and Lev Kamenev, was conducted in the Kremlin's October Hall. Complicity with "fascist and Trotskyist" circles abroad with the aim of undermining Soviet power was the featured charge. All the defendants were convicted and sentenced to death on the basis of their own confessions, extracted by torture, false promises of clemency, and threats of reprisals against family members. If treason lurked in such high places, one might well have wondered who was above suspicion. What followed in 1936–1939 was an unprecedentedly destructive terror, including two additional show trials of old Bolsheviks, the likes of Radek, Iurii Piatakov, Bukharin, and Rykov, and a tidal wave of denunciations, arrests, and executions reaching deep into society at large.

The arrest of the military leaders Witowit Putna and Vitalii Primakov soon after the first show trial made clear that the high command was not immune from persecution. During the second show trial in January 1937, while under interrogation Radek almost casually mentioned Tukhachevskii's name in conjunction with a conspiratorial encounter.[42] Though he was quick to assert that the Red Marshal was unaware of the intrigue surrounding him, Radek's "slip of the tongue" had obvious implications. On 1 April Tukhachevskii's scheduled visit to London to attend the coronation of King George VI was suddenly canceled at the last moment. In May he was reassigned to the command of the minor Volga military district at Kuibyshev and arrested upon arriving to assume his post. Further arrests of top commanders followed. The annihilation of the high command commenced with the suicide of Ian Gamarnik, former head of the Red Army's Political Administration, on 31 May 1937. On

41. "Les cartes Soviétiques étaient faussées," *Le Monde*, 4–5 Sept. 1988, p. 3.

42. Radek's remarks give the misleading impression of spontaneity. *Report of Court Proceedings in the Case of the Anti-Trotskyite Centre, Moscow, January 23–30, 1937* (Moscow, 1937), pp. 99–105.

11 June a group of eight commanders, including Tukhachevskii, Iona Iakir, and Putna, some of the leading names in Soviet arms, was tried before a special tribunal appointed by Stalin and including several of their peers (most of whom would themselves perish during the coming year) and, again on the basis of confessions extracted by torture, condemned to death for treason.[43]

What followed was an unparalleled bloodletting. According to Soviet statistics, by the time the terror had run its course up to 20 percent of the RKKA's officer corps had "undergone repression" in the form of dismissal, incarceration in labor camps, or execution.[44] The terror was most severe at the top; between May 1937 and September 1938, 3 of the 5 Soviet marshals (Tukhachevskii, Bliukher, and Aleksandr Egorov), 13 of 15 army commanders, 50 of 57 corp commanders, 154 of 186 division commanders, and 401 of 456 colonels were struck down.[45] The Soviet high command, at a moment of grave international peril, had been beheaded at a stroke.

The key to the terror was Stalin's merciless determination to root out any threat to his position from real or potential rivals. But the extent of the purge process and its disastrous impact upon Soviet society calls into question the extent to which it may be understood as an act of "delicate surgery" with rational political motivation.[46] J. Arch Getty has argued that a careful chronicle of the events between 1933 and 1938 does not necessarily reveal a "crescendo" of terror implying premeditation. Rather,

43. Tukhachevskii and his associates (Iona Iakir, Ieronim Uborevich, Vitalii Primakov, Witowt Putna, Robert Eideman, B. M. Fel'dman, and August Kork) were rehabilitated juridically on 31 Jan. 1957. The Politburo's special commission for rehabilitation reconfirmed their innocence on 26 March 1988. The trumped-up nature of the entire process is well documented in "Delo o tak nazyvaemoi 'antisovetskoi trotskistskoi voennoi organizatsii' v Krasnoi Armii," *Izvestiia TsK KPSS* 4 (1989): 42–61. Marshal Bliukher, who participated in the tribunal as a judge, is reported to have remarked immediately afterward that the same fate was in store for him. A. I. Kartunova, "V. K. Bliukher: Slavnaia i tragicheskaia sud'ba kommunista i polkovodtsa," *Voprosy istorii KPSS* 2 (1991): 126.

44. *Istoriia Velikoi Otechestvennoi voiny Sovetskogo Soiuza 1941–1945*, 6 vols. (Moscow, 1960–65) [hereinafter cited as *IVOVSS*], 6:124–25; Medvedev, *Let History Judge*, p. 213. V. D. Danilov, "Sovetskoe glavnoe komandovanie v preddverii Velikoi Otechestvennoi voiny," *Novaia i noveishaia istoriia* 6 (1988): 4–5, cites a remarks by Voroshilov according to which the military purge claimed "more than 40,000 victims." According to the historian G. Kumanev, "22-go, na rassvete," *Pravda*, 22 June 1989, p. 3, the number of executions alone probably numbered nearly 50,000. For a general summary of the process see Robert Conquest, *The Great Terror: A Reassessment* (Oxford, 1990), pp. 182–213.

45. According to the often-referenced count of General A. I. Todorskii, cited from Vasilii Polikarpov, "Fedor Raskol'nikov," *Ogonek* 26 (June 1987): 6. See also O. F. Suvenirov, "Vsearmeiskaia tragediia," *Voenno-istoricheskii zhurnal* 3 (1989): 39–47. The purge struck with equal force against the Red Army's political officers.

46. The phrase "delicate surgery" is used (though also qualified) by Erickson, *The Soviet High Command*, p. 473.

the terror may be perceived to have grown from an inner-party struggle that proceeded irregularly before spinning out of control. Stalin clearly initiated the purge for his own purposes, but he was actively abetted by a group of leaders (including Molotov, Zhdanov, Georgii Malenkov, and Lazar Kaganovich) who defended a "populist" program demanding higher planning tempos, a reduced role for the technical intelligentsia in the industrial sector, an isolationist foreign policy, and reprisals against "enemies."[47] The cumulative extent of the Ezhovshchina must in part be accounted for by the self-perpetuating wave of recriminations, the paroxysm of denunciation and vendetta, that Stalin's ambitions provoked and that his lieutenants urged forward.

The number of those victimized by Stalin's purges has been fixed by Soviet sources at nearly 4 million, including 786,098 executions.[48] In the realm of security policy the terror struck a particularly cruel blow. No rational purpose could have justified so massive an elimination of loyal, trained commanders. Stalin may well have feared "Bonapartism" within the command or have been concerned about the potential for opposition to grow out of local satraps among the military districts, such as those presided over for many years by Bliukher in the Far East, Iakir in the Ukraine, or Ieronim Uborevich in Belorussia. The cult of Stalin as military leader, launched with the publication of Voroshilov's sycophantic article "Stalin and the Red Army" in 1927, never sat well with the high command, many of whose leaders had first-hand awareness of Stalin's less than distinguished contributions during the civil war.[49] Since his association with the Tsaritsyn group during 1918, Stalin had supported tight political control over the professional military, an emphasis that many commanders resented. The popular film version of Dmitrii Furmanov's civil war novel *Chapaev*, released in 1934, idealized the role of the commissar, and on 8 May 1937, as the assault against the high command began, dual command was reinstated in the RKKA.

Disagreements over foreign policy may also have played a more direct role in some cases. "Whatever other significance could be read into Stalin's purge of the generals in June 1937," writes E. H. Carr, "it indicated a deep unease in foreign policy; Tukhachevskii had been a conspicuous

47. J. Arch Getty, *Origins of the Great Purges: The Soviet Communist Party Reconsidered, 1933–1938* (Cambridge, 1985).

48. A TASS release of 13 Feb. 1990, citing KGB sources and covering the years 1930–50, fixes the number of persons condemned by tribunals or other institutions at 3,778,234, including 786,098 executions.

49. Voroshilov, *Stat'i i rechi*, pp. 346–64.

protagonist of the anti-Fascist front."[50] German intelligence went so far as to compromise Tukhachevskii by channeling incriminating disinformation to Soviet authorities, but it is unlikely that Stalin was taken in; the materials in question were not cited as evidence against Tukhachevskii in his mock trial. Stalin's suspicions were boundless, but in the end none of the possible goals that may be adduced required a slaughter of the extent that occurred. Like the collectivization campaign, the terror seems to have been carried away by its own momentum and to have produced unintended consequences that partially contradicted its original intent.[51] The price was a sudden decline in the operational capacity of the Soviet armed forces that could not soon be made good.

The Rapallo Temptation

The commissariat of foreign affairs was another prominent target of the Ezhovshchina. Although Litvinov himself managed to survive, his subordinates were mercilessly eliminated and his policies came increasingly under attack.[52] Meanwhile, the Soviet collective security orientation encountered increasing difficulties in the international arena.

The most basic reality working to undermine support for collective security in Moscow was the unwillingness of the western powers and their

50. E. H. Carr, *The Comintern and the Spanish Civil War* (New York, 1984), p. 51. A concise summary of Tukhachevskii's evaluation of the German military threat, with editorial remarks by Stalin, is given in "Rukopis' stat'i M. N. Tukhachevskogo 'Voennye plany Gitlera' s pravkoi I. V. Stalina," *Izvestiia TsK KPSS* 1 (1990): 161–72. G. Alimurzaev, "Shchit ili mech? K istorii sovetskoi voennoi doktriny," *Mezhdunarodnaia zhizn'* 4 (1989): 120–21, poses the argument that the purge of Tukhachevskii and other commanders associated with an offensive orientation in military planning was intended as a gesture of appeasement to Hitler.

51. The conclusion does not conflict with the remark by Robert McNeal, *Stalin*, p. 200, that Stalin himself must be assigned responsibility for the "design" of the terror. At issue is its extent and cumulative impact. Volkogonov, *Triumf i tragediia*, 1, part 2:193–308, argues on the basis of considerable documentary evidence that Stalin possessed a realistic awareness of the extent of the purges, but he acknowledges, "At some point at the end of 1937 the repression does indeed seem to have spun out of control" (p. 220). Tucker calls Stalin the "general director" of the terror but also concludes, "As in collectivization, when Stalin deliberately started a process that got out of hand . . . so now his carefully prepared and precipitated reign of terror took on a spontaneous momentum of its own, with results that he probably had failed to foresee." Tucker, *Stalin in Power*, pp. 444 and 473.

52. Teddy J. Uldricks, "The Impact of the Great Purges on the People's Commissariat of Foreign Affairs," *Slavic Review* 36 (1977): 187–204, details the extent of the terror within the NKID (People's Commissariat of Foreign Affairs). According to Nikita Khrushchev, *Khrushchev Remembers* (Boston, 1970), p. 278, the NKVD also planned to murder Litvinov by staging a traffic accident.

eastern European allies to engage themselves unambiguously. The mutual assistance treaties with France and Czechoslovakia were real achievements, but their value was limited by the ambiguity of the provisions for collective action, the fact that French forces were not prepared to undertake an offensive of the type envisioned, and a lack of geographical contiguity between the signatories. The premises of cooperation were also called into question by the unresolved issue of right-of-passage for Soviet forces across eastern Europe in the event of a conflict. Poland and Romania stood outside the collective security system and adopted an obstructionist attitude concerning military collaboration with Moscow. British overtures toward Berlin were noted with concern in Moscow, and the Soviets could take no comfort in the failure of the League of Nations to approve collective sanctions in response to a series of German and Italian aggressions. Britain and France stood by passively as Hitler restored compulsory military service on 16 March 1935 in defiance of Versailles. The League refused to react to Italy's invasion of Abyssinia (Ethiopia) in October 1935, despite Litvinov's urging. It was also Britain that played the leading role within the League Council in opposing a strong response to the German reoccupation of the Rhineland in March 1936. Clearly, a significant body of opinion within British ruling circles favored some sort of accommodation with Germany, if need be at Soviet expense.

An additional cause for disillusionment were the modest achievements of the Comintern's popular-front orientation. The election of a popular-front government in France on 3 May 1936 led by the socialist Leon Blum and supported, though not participated in, by the French communists (PCF) raised some hopes, but the Blum government was weak and short-lived. Nor was the PCF an entirely disciplined organization. True to its antimilitarist inclinations, it continued to agitate against increased military spending at the same time that Moscow urged more decisive resistance to Hitler upon the Quai d'Orsay.

Electoral advances for the popular front in Spain on 16 February became the prelude to another disappointment. The revolt of the Spanish military led by General Francisco Franco during July sparked a full-fledged civil war in which a democratic republic, with strong left-wing representation, confronted an assault by forces openly sympathetic to fascism and supported militarily by Italy and Germany. Once again Britain and France adopted a policy of nonengagement. A Francist victory represented a particularly undesirable outcome for the latter, but the Blum government could not muster the will to act independently. Striving to maintain some continuity of policy with its would-be allies, on 27 August the USSR accepted a nonintervention pledge prepared, under

British sponsorship, by the League's newly created Non-Intervention Committee. Preoccupied with the Zinoviev-Kamenev process, which opened on 23 August in Moscow, Stalin and his coterie must have been hard-pressed to give the problem sufficient attention. Despite a desire to cater to allied priorities, however, there were strong forces pulling the USSR toward a more active role in Spain. The struggle of the embattled Spanish republicans gripped the international community. Within Spain the communist left was fully engaged, and on 4 September two members of the Spanish Communist party (PCE), with Comintern endorsement, joined the republican government. The consequences of defeat for collective security in Europe were less than palatable, even if it was not the Soviet Union that would be most immediately threatened.

By October, Soviet arms shipments to the republican armies through the agency of the PCE were arriving en masse. The PCE's role as an arms supplier enhanced its political stature, and, after a series of purges and factional encounters, it eventually came nearly to dominate the Republic's institutions.[53] Soviet planes and tanks played a conspicuous role in the defense of Madrid during November, accompanied by the first contingent of Soviet military advisors, some 3,000 of whom would eventually see service in Spain. The Soviets directed their attention toward the Republic's regular army. The famous international brigades received no public support from the Soviet government, though they were sponsored by the Comintern and contained many communist volunteers.

By gradually breaking with the strictures of the nonintervention committee, the Soviet Union reinforced the German-Italian axis and risked alienating Britain and France. Moreover, in the course of 1937 the fact that the contest in Spain was unwinnable began to dawn upon Soviet observers. By the summer of 1937, with the Ezhovshchina in full course, Moscow's commitment was already beginning to wane. Neither the Soviets nor the Comintern disengaged from the battle, but after the ill-fated republican offensives at Tereul (December 1937) and on the Ebro (July 1938), only a massive intervention could have turned the tide, an intervention that neither the western powers nor Moscow was willing to provide. The Spanish Civil War was a *cause célèbre* for progressive opinion worldwide, and an opportunity, after a series of setbacks and withdrawals, to confront the threat of fascism with arms in hand. The premises of collective security cried out for some kind of coordinated action, but it was not forthcoming, and the limited, unilateral Soviet engagement merely served to protract the republic's agony. With Franco's triumphant

53. See Burnett Bolloten, *The Spanish Revolution: The Left and the Struggle for Power during the Civil War* (Chapel Hill, N.C., 1978), pp. 361–448.

entry into Barcelona in January 1939 and the final surrender of Madrid on 29 March, the popular front in Spain, and the collective security regime in Europe, had suffered catastrophic defeats.[54]

The defeat added force to the arguments of those opposing Litvinov within the Soviet hierarchy. Immediately after Hitler's seizure of power no alternative to Litvinov's policy seemed feasible, but a new optimism concerning the prospects for a revival of German-Soviet relations could be detected beginning in 1935. Despite Hitler's virulent anticommunism, his repeatedly expressed desire to extend German hegemony eastward, and his apparent lack of interest in communicating with Moscow, Soviet leaders never burned all their bridges to Berlin. In March 1934 the Soviet government unsuccessfully offered the Germans a bilateral protocol guaranteeing the independence of the Baltic states. Mutually advantageous economic exchange was perceived as a means for stabilizing political relations, and the negotiation in April 1935 of a five-year German-Soviet credit arrangement signaled the intent to move in that direction.[55] On 26 October 1936, Tukhachevskii, then deputy commissar of military affairs, expressed to the new German military attaché in Moscow, General Ernst Köstring, the hope that Germany and the Soviet Union "can find themselves again."[56] So long as Hitler remained intransigent, no breakthrough was forthcoming, but the Rapallo temptation was never abandoned. The real value of collective security accords was called into question in crisis after crisis, and Litvinov's total dependence upon Stalin's good will was made clear by the fate of the NKID during the terror. The reincarnation of Rapallo awaited its moment, a moment that the events of 1938 would bring considerably closer.

A Toast to the Führer

In March 1938 Germany affected an *Anschluss* (union) with Austria in defiance of international protests. Czechoslovakia was now the logical next target for German expansionism, as Hitler assumed the

---

54. General accounts are provided by ibid.; Carr, *The Comintern and the Spanish Civil War*; Hugh Thomas, *The Spanish Civil War* (New York, 1961). Soviet interpretations have consistently emphasized the degree to which the complexities of the international situation placed constraints upon Moscow's ability to offer meaningful assistance. See M. T. Meshcheriakov, "Sovetskii Soiuz i antifashistskaia voina ispanskogo naroda (1936–1939)," *Istoriia SSSR* 1 (1988): 22–40.

55. Litvinov emphasized the importance of economic ties as a means of warding off a disintegration of political relations. "O podgotovke Germanii k voine," pp. 211–12.

56. Cited in Erickson, *The Soviet High Command*, p. 395. The remark was doubtlessly made at the behest of the Soviet government.

pose of "protector" for its German minority. Attached to both France and the USSR by the mutual assistance pacts of 1935, the government of Edvard Beneš sought reassurance from its great power allies. Viewed from Moscow, German demands against Prague had to be taken seriously, but the ability to provide military support was contingent upon the Soviets' obtaining a corridor of access for Soviet forces across Poland or Romania.

The necessary degree of cooperation was not forthcoming. Soviet relations with Romania were frozen because of Moscow's refusal to recognize Bucharest's seizure of the Bessarabia district during the civil war, and Soviet-Polish relations moved in a kind of permanent limbo conditioned by a history of animosity.[57] Only decisive pressure from London or Paris could have unblocked the situation, but by the autumn of 1938, with the conservative governments of Neville Chamberlain (since May 1938) and Edouard Daladier (since April 1938) in power, the leading western powers were looking in new directions. Chamberlain's hope was to build an Anglo-German rapprochement and to channel Hitler's aggression eastward, a preference conditioned by his long-standing and deeply rooted abhorrence for Soviet institutions. As the Czechoslovak crisis peaked in the autumn of 1938, Moscow took steps to prepare for military action, regrouping the Belorussian and Kiev military districts into a unified command and calling its forces along the border to a state of alert during September. In response to a direct query from Beneš, the Soviet *polpred* to Prague, S. S. Aleksandrovskii, stated on 21 September that the Soviet Union would fulfill its obligation to provide military support if France did likewise.[58] These gestures may well have been intended primarily as a bluff. If so, the bluff was not called. On 15 September Chamberlain consulted with Hitler in the Berghof at Berchtesgaden. The German dictator impressed him, as he confided to his wife, as "a man who could be relied upon when he had given his word."[59] One week later a second visit set the stage for the Munich pact of 30 September, where Chamberlain and Daladier, in the absence of representatives from both Czechoslovakia and the USSR, agreed to Hitler's demand for the

---

57. Described in Bohdan Budurowycz, *Polish-Soviet Relations, 1932–1939* (New York, 1963), pp. 73–96; A. A. Sheviakov, *Sovetsko-rumynskie otnosheniia i problema evropeiskoi bezopasnosti, 1932–1939* (Moscow, 1977), pp. 135–208; I. V. Mikhutina, *Sovetsko-pol'skie otnosheniia, 1931–1935* (Moscow, 1977), pp. 180–271.

58. See Morozow, *Die Falken des Kreml,* pp. 192–93; Hochman, *The Soviet Union and the Failure of Collective Security,* p. 121; G. Jukes, "Red Army and the Munich Crisis," *Journal of Contemporary History* 2 (April 1991): 195–214. The account by Zakharov, *General'nyi shtab,* pp. 111–17, makes it clear that Soviet forces undertook serious preparations for military action.

59. Haslam, *The Soviet Union and the Struggle for Collective Security,* p. 185.

annexation of the Czech Sudetenland. As a result of the Munich pact, Czechoslovakia was dismembered, with its natural defensive perimeter stripped away. The heart of Litvinov's collective security regime had turned out to be hollow.

So long as Hitler's intentions remained unclear, Moscow had little choice but to hold open channels of communication to London and Paris, but it was with scant hope. In September and December 1938 France and Britain concluded nonaggression declarations with Berlin. On 15 March 1939 Germany invaded the defenseless rump of Czechoslovakia, and on 23 March it seized Memel (Klaipéda) from Lithuania. Czechoslovakia's Carpatho-Ukrainian district, populated mainly by Ukrainians, was established as an autonomous "federal" unit and briefly became a center for anti-Soviet nationalist agitation. Soviet territory was now directly exposed to a German attack bypassing Poland through the Baltic states. Chamberlain's announcement on 31 March of a unilateral guarantee for the independence of Romania and Poland therefore did little to calm Soviet fears. Litvinov fired proposals at the Entente powers to guarantee the territorial integrity of the Baltic states, but there was no response. On 17 April he proposed a set of comprehensive security guarantees to Paris and received a reply described as "humiliating."[60] Collective security, for all intents and purposes, had unraveled.

Meanwhile, the signs of a new orientation became unmistakable. In a major address to the 18th party congress on 10 March 1939, on the eve of the fall of Prague, Stalin stated bluntly that a "new imperialist war had become a fact" because of the disruption of the postwar security system by three "aggressor states" (Japan, Italy, and Germany) and the failure of the international community to produce an adequate response. The reason for the failure "consists in the refusal of the majority of nonaggressive nations, and above all England and France, to participate in the policy of collective security, in the policy of collective repulse to aggression, in their transition to a position of noninterference, a pattern of neutrality."[61] The Soviet Union, Stalin admonished, should "maintain vigilance and not allow those who would provoke war to draw our country into a conflict, not to pull others' chestnuts out of the fire."[62] Pulling others' chestnuts out of the fire was unfortunately the essence of collective security.

Stalin probably intended his remarks at the 18th congress primarily as a warning to the West. At the time his speech was delivered Soviet policy

60. Ibid., pp. 211–12. Haslam describes this gesture as Litvinov's "last throw."
61. Stalin, Sochineniia, 1 [XIV]: 335 and 338.
62. Ibid., p. 345. Stalin's actual phrase (zagrabat' zhar chuzhimi rukami) makes no reference to "chestnuts," but the idiomatic translation is appropriate.

was in disarray, torn between conflicting and ambiguous alternatives. But German interest in a deal with Moscow was now becoming more evident. The Third Reich was preparing for the decisive confrontation that Hitler had always sought. Poland had been selected as the next target, and an attack on Poland meant the possibility (though not the certainty) of war with Britain and France. In such an event, in order to avoid a two-front war, Germany had every reason to be attracted by an arrangement with Stalin.

Between April and August 1939 negotiations among the Soviet Union, Britain, and France continued, but they proceeded at a snail's pace. The Soviets were now demanding a three-power mutual assistance treaty, security guarantees that would encompass the Baltic states and Finland, and a military convention spelling out the terms of mutual aid—substantial commitments from which Paris and London shied away. Meanwhile, during the spring and summer communication with Germany intensified. The writing on the wall became visible when on 4 May Litvinov was replaced as commissar of foreign affairs by his long-time nemesis Molotov. Litvinov was the living symbol of collective security, and as a Jew he could be presumed to be unpopular with the rabidly anti-Semitic Hitlerites. Even with Molotov in charge, however, talks with both sides went on, and there is no reason to conclude that any particular outcome was foreordained. It appears, rather, that Moscow continued to hold its options open to the last moment.[63]

The dilatoriness of the western powers culminated on 5 August when, in response to Moscow's urgent invitation to conclude a military convention, they dispatched low-level delegations without plenipotentiary authority, traveling via ship and requiring a full week to reach their destination. Once arrived, the delegates were unable to produce any commitment from Warsaw concerning the right of passage for Soviet troops across Poland in the event of hostilities.[64] It was Germany's urgency that now turned the tide. In the early morning hours of 24 August, after a round of last-minute negotiations in the Kremlin, Molotov and his counterpart German foreign minister Joachim von Ribbentrop signed a non-aggression treaty. On the same day a *Pravda* editorial compared the agreement to Rapallo and the 1926 neutrality pact, and described it as an "instrument of peace" that would "lessen international tension." But

---

63. Discussed in Reinhold W. Weber, *Die Entstehungsgeschichte des Hitler-Stalin-Paktes, 1939* (Frankfurt am Main, 1980), pp. 115–221; Donald Cameron Watts, *How War Came: The Immediate Origins of the Second World War, 1938–1939* (New York, 1989), pp. 361–84. The point concerning open options is corroborated by V. S. Parsadanova, "Tragediia Pol'shi v 1939 g.," *Novaia i noveishaia istoriia* 5 (1989): 11–27.

64. On the difficulties with Poland see Budurowycz, *Polish-Soviet Relations*, pp. 157–60.

no one was fooled. The Nazi-Soviet bargain was a diplomatic revolution of the first order, and it became the immediate prelude to war in Europe.

The terms of the Molotov-Ribbentrop pact were similar to those of the many nonaggression treaties negotiated by Litvinov earlier in the decade. More revealing than the treaty itself was a secret protocol defining a sphere of influence in eastern Europe that placed most of eastern Poland, Latvia, Estonia, and Finland into the Soviet zone.[65] The Soviets also asserted an "interest" in the Bessarabia region. Whatever the aspirations of its signatories, the pact was not a new Rapallo, but rather a narrowly calculated bargain concluded for limited ends by two wary opponents. Germany had temporarily secured its eastern front, and the USSR, or so it thought, had bought its way out of the approaching war. In so doing it gained access to the strategic territories in the western borderlands considered to be vital to an effective defense. But there was a price attached. The pact's most immediate effect was to strengthen Hitler's hand, certainly not the Soviets' first priority. Its enforcement required a considerable amount of reliance upon the Führer's good will. Most important, a deal with Berlin meant the abandonment of the collective security project. The extent of the turnabout was revealed by the famous toast offered by Stalin to Ribbentrop during the social hour following the signing of the treaty. "Knowing how much the German Nation loves its Führer," spoke the great leader of the international communist movement, "I should like to drink his health."[66]

Why had collective security failed? The question has commonly been answered by attempts to place blame. On one side of the issue, the Soviet Union is castigated for insincerity in its pursuit of collective security and accused of preferring a rapprochement with Hitler in the Rapallo tradition. A cynical disdain for the "bourgeois democracies" and shortsighted calculations of narrow self-interest are said to have encouraged Stalin to "unleash" fascist aggression against the West. For Jiri Hochman, the underlying problem was that "its membership in the [collective security] system and obligations following thereof notwithstanding, the Soviet government was striving for a political agreement with Germany, the main adversary of collective security."[67] More extreme views have

65. The text of the treaty and attached protocol is given in Jane Degras, ed., *Soviet Documents on Foreign Policy*, 3 vols. (London, 1951–53), 3:359–61. The existence of the secret protocol was finally acknowledged in the USSR during 1989. The Russian text, based upon a photocopy of the lost original preserved in the German archives, appears in " 'Kruglyi stol': Vtoraia mirovaia voina—istoki i prichiny," *Voprosy istorii* 6 (1989): 20.

66. Described in V. Berezhkov, "Proschet Stalina," *Mezhdunarodnaia zhizn'* 8 (Aug. 1989): 20; Volkogonov, *Triumf i tragediia*, 2, part 1:107.

67. Hochman, *The Soviet Union and the Failure of Collective Security*, p. 122. Hochman's work as a whole emphasizes the Soviet Union's responsibility for the failure of the collective security project.

accused Stalin of callously instigating a world war in pursuit of a "rational power strategy" tied to hegemonic designs.[68] Alternatively, the western democracies, and particularly Britain, have been excoriated for their own shortsighted lack of interest in collective security mechanisms. Fascism is seen to have been perceived as a lesser evil when compared with the contagion of communism: Haslam speaks of "the common thread which bound the Fascist Powers to the bourgeois democracies of the West, and separated both from the Soviet Union."[69] For its part, Soviet historiography has traditionally accused the western powers of maneuvering toward an understanding with Hitler that would channel German aggression eastward.[70]

None of these explanations seems satisfactory taken by itself. As defined by Litvinov, collective security represented a new approach to the Soviet security dilemma, but also a problematic one. Conspiracy theories claiming a conscious Soviet desire to provoke war make little sense, but there were leaders within the hierarchy with Stalin's sympathy pushing for an alignment with Germany in the Rapallo tradition. Moreover, like all states, the Soviet Union refused to commit itself to any single policy irrevocably, and it attempted to retain a range of options. Unfortunately, the brutality of the Stalin regime and the Ezhovshchina provided the worst imaginable context for efforts to overcome long-standing mutual distrust.[71] The massacre of the command undermined confidence in Soviet military capacity and caused the regime to appear much less desirable as a strategic ally. It left the RKKA in a state of confusion at the

---

68. For example, Ernst Topitsch, *Stalins Krieg: Die sowjetische Langzeitstrategie gegen den Westen als rationale Machtstrategie* (Munich, 1985), and in a more temperate but in my opinion no more convincing vein, R. C. Raack, "Stalin's Plans for World War II," *Journal of Contemporary History* 2 (April 1991): 215–27.

69. Haslam, *The Soviet Union and the Struggle for Collective Security*, p. 231.

70. E.g., V. Ia. Sipols, *Sovetskii Soiuz v bor'be za mir i bezopasnost', 1933–1939* (Moscow, 1974), pp. 286–419. These conclusions did not lose their force in the era of *glasnost'*. See "K istorii zakliucheniia sovetsko-germanskogo dogovora o nenapadenii 23 avgusta 1939 g. (dokumental'nyi obzor)," *Novaia i noveishaia istoriia* 6 (1989): 3–21, and Vsevolod Ezhov, "Antigitlerovskaia koalitsiia do voiny? Vozmozhnosti i real'nosti," *Literaturnaia gazeta*, 26 April 1989, p. 4, where collective security is described as a "strategic rather than a conjunctural" line on the part of the Soviet government and its failure is attributed to the primacy of anti-Soviet over anti-fascist motivation in western policy. There has been, however, some room for dissent. Mikhail Semiriaga, in "23 avgusta 1939 goda. Sovetsko-germanskii dogovor o nenapadenii: Byla li alternativa?" *Literaturnaia gazeta,* 5 Oct. 1989, p. 14, and "Sovetskii Soiuz i predvoennyi krizis," *Voprosy istorii* 9 (1990): 49–64, develops a revisionist argument condemning the pact and asserting that Moscow had not exhausted all options before turning to Hitler. The closest to an "official" interpretation reflecting the dominant viewpoint of the late 1980s appears in O. A. Rzheshevskii, ed., *1939 god: Uroki istorii* (Moscow, 1990).

71. The conclusion is stated powerfully by George F. Kennan, *Russia and the West under Lenin and Stalin* (Boston, 1961), pp. 312–13.

very moment when it was most needed. A decision for the western powers in 1938 meant the likelihood of war, a prospect before which, for good reason, Soviet leaders blanched. Such a decision might yet have been made, however, were it not for the hesitancy and hostility of London and Paris. Collective security provided a real opportunity to reintegrate the USSR into a pan-European security system, an opportunity that the leading European powers failed to seize. Given the prejudices and priorities of western elites, a state such as the USSR, officially committed to the cause of social revolution, could not but remain suspect. In the end, the crimes of the Ezhovshchina, Stalin's refusal to abandon the Rapallo temptation, and western irresolution and duplicity all interacted to frustrate the collective security project. Not least, all parties to some extent underestimated the ambition and power of Hitler's terrifying thousand-year Reich. Collective security may well have been the only alternative to a war waged on German terms. It was never an easy choice, and both sides bear some responsibility for its unfulfilled promise.

The Second Imperialist War

Within a week of the Molotov-Ribbentrop pact, on 1 September Germany launched its *Blitzkrieg* into Poland. Two days later France and Britain declared war against Germany. The overwhelming force of the German advance was unsettling to more than a few observers and prompted an intensification of Soviet efforts to stabilize relations with Berlin. On 17 September, the day after a truce was signed with Japan following the fighting at Khalkhin Gol, the RKKA marched into eastern Poland, with the purported goal of protecting the Ukrainian and Belorussian populations.[72] On 28 September Molotov and Ribbentrop concluded a Treaty of Friendship and Border Alignment that formalized their earlier, secret agreement on spheres of influence. A joint communiqué urged an immediate end to hostilities, charged Britain and France with the responsibility for continued loss of life, and vaguely promised "mutual consultation in regard to necessary measures" should the war go on.[73] The USSR also promised to supply Germany with strategic raw materials and to allow Soviet territory to be used for the transshipment

72. "Protection" included mass deportations that, according to one historian, affected up to 10% of the populations of the occupied territories. V. S. Parsadanova, "Deportatsiia naseleniia iz Zapadnoi Ukrainy i Zapadnoi Belorussii v 1939–1941 gg.," *Novaia i noveishaia istoriia* 2 (1989): 26–44.

73. Degras, *Soviet Documents on Foreign Policy*, 3:377–79. Soviet analysis in the age of *glasnost'*, though still predominantly supportive of the 24 Aug. nonaggression treaty, leveled devastating criticism at the accord of 28 Sept. See " 'Kruglyi stol'," p. 7.

of supplies purchased from third parties. The modest terms of the 24 August nonaggression pact were now being extended to a permanent alliance, with a confident Germany well placed to extract concessions. Stalin certainly had no intention of joining the war against the western powers, but his willingness to threaten to do so worked to Hitler's advantage. The terms of economic agreements disproportionately favored Germany and helped to bolster the very power that the Soviets wished to neutralize. Only mortal fear of a war for which it was ill prepared could have pushed Moscow to such dangerous commitments.

The classic justification for the Molotov-Ribbentrop pact was provided by Stalin on 3 July 1941 in his first address to the nation after the German surprise attack. "How was it possible," he asked,

> that the Soviet government could come to conclude a nonaggression pact with such treacherous people, such monsters as Hitler and Ribbentrop? Wasn't this a mistake on the part of the Soviet government? Of course not! A nonaggression pact is a pact of peace between two states. . . . Could the Soviet Union have refused such a proposition? I think that there is not a single peace-loving state which could refuse such a peaceful agreement with a neighboring power, when at the head of such a power we find such monsters and cannibals as Hitler and Ribbentrop. . . . What did we gain by concluding a nonaggression pact with Germany? We obtained a period of peace of one and a half years for our country and the possibility to prepare its forces for a rebuff if fascist Germany risked an attack against our country despite the pact. This was a definite gain for us, and a loss for fascist Germany.[74]

Under the circumstances Stalin had no choice but to justify his past decisions; the logic of "buying time" nonetheless did help to explain Soviet motivation.[75] During 1937 in the Far East and again during 1939 in Europe, peace was purchased by a policy of appeasement that had the undesirable effect of strengthening Moscow's most threatening rivals. These consequences were regrettable, but there was a crying need for time to overcome the effects of the Ezhovshchina and prepare for a

74. Stalin, *Sochineniia*, 2 [XV]: 3–4.

75. According to Gromyko and Ponomarev, *Istoriia vneshnei politiki SSSR*, 1:384, a bargain with Germany was the "only correct decision." The pact "freed the USSR for a period of time from the threat of a war waged without allies on two fronts (against Germany in the west and Japan in the east), and allowed time for strengthening the country's defenses." V. Ia. Sipols, *Vneshniaia politika Sovetskogo Soiuza, 1936–1939 gg.* (Moscow, 1987), p. 328, calls it "the only reasonable way out" for a government facing imminent threats on all sides. See also the pithy justification offered by Khrushchev in Jerrold L. Schecter and Vyacheslav V. Luchkov, eds., *Khrushchev Remembers: The Glasnost Tapes* (Boston, 1990), pp. 45–49.

confrontation that few could doubt was now approaching. On at least one occasion, in an address to military academy graduates in the Kremlin on 3 May 1941, Stalin is reported to have spoken of the inevitability of war with Germany, expressed hope that it could be put off until 1942, and even hinted at the possibility of a preemptive attack.[76] In the interim, a tactical alliance with Germany served to engage it in what it was presumed would be a long and difficult military struggle in the west. In the spirit of socialism in one country, defense of the USSR was justified as the highest goal, and if this meant standing aside while the imperialist powers waged war against one another, then a plague on both their houses. "It is out duty," remarked Molotov in justifying the pact before the Supreme Soviet on 31 August 1939, "to think of the interests of the Soviet people, the interests of the Union of Soviet Socialist Republics . . . all the more because we are firmly convinced that the interests of the U.S.S.R. coincide with the fundamental interests of the people of other countries."[77]

Between 1939 and June 1941, during the twenty-two months duration of German-Soviet collaboration, Soviet security policy ran along the parallel tracks of appeasement and preparation for war. Stunning demonstrations of German power left little room for maneuver. To avoid involvement in the European war for as long as possible remained a consuming goal, but the search for peace had now become reactive and at times almost desperate. The Soviet Union was no longer in control of events.

Soviet policy was most successful in the Far East. The Molotov-Ribbentrop pact and the defeat of the Kwantung Army at Khalkhin Gol discouraged any lingering aspirations in Tokyo of pursuing a "northern strategy" into the Soviet Maritime Province and Siberia. Germany's victories over the Netherlands and France in May–June 1940 provided encouragement for a turn southward by opening access to the colonial domains of Indochina and Indonesia. A more confrontational posture on the part of the United States added to the factors pulling Japan toward the Pacific and contributed to interest in a less contentious relationship with the USSR.[78] An agreement of 28 October 1939 began a process of rapprochement by resolving a series of fishing incidents. On 31 December

76. Described by Alexander Werth, *Russia at War, 1941–1945* (New York, 1964), pp. 135–36. Werth's account of the speech is based upon hearsay related after 22 June 1941. A more reliable rendering is provided by Volkogonov, *Triumf i tragediia*, 2, part 1:55–58.

77. V. Molotov, *Soviet Peace Policy* (London, 1941), p. 14.

78. L. N. Kutakov, *Istoriia sovetsko-iaponskikh diplomaticheskikh otnoshenii* (Moscow, 1962), p. 263, notes the important role that this perception played in Soviet calculations. See also S. L. Tikhrinskii, "Zakliuchenie sovetsko-iaponskogo pakta o neitralitete 1941 g.," *Novaia i noveishaia istoriia* 1 (1990): 21–34.

the sale to Manchukuo of the Chinese Eastern Railway, negotiated as long ago as 1935, was at last finalized. The Konoye cabinet, which came to power in July 1940, expressed interest in a tripartite pact with Germany and Italy but also supported an arrangement with Moscow. At this point, with Hitler's armies triumphant in Europe, Stalin confronted a potent and confident axis with which the USSR might well have to coexist permanently. The result was the Japanese-Soviet Neutrality Pact signed in April 1941, which included mutual recognition of the territorial integrity and right to exist of Japanese Manchukuo and the pro-Soviet Mongolian People's Republic. Japan's hands were freed for expansionist designs in the Pacific, but the long-standing threat to the Soviet Far East was contained.

The Comintern reacted to the outbreak of war in Europe by tearing a page from Lenin's notebook, denouncing the "new imperialist war" and asserting indifference to its outcome. The movement now launched a "peace offensive" with the limited goal of disassociating the Soviet government from the battle against fascism. "The second imperialist war," wrote Dimitrov in November 1939, "is, on the part of both warring sides, an imperialist, unjust war, despite the fraudulent slogans being employed by the ruling classes of the warring capitalist states in their endeavors to hide their real aims from the masses of the people."[79] In China the united front between the CCP and Jiang Jeishi's nationalist government remained in effect, but in Europe, according to an ECCI manifesto of 11 November 1939, "There can be neither a United Workers' Front, nor a People's Front . . . with the leaders of the other petty-bourgeois parties that are supporting the war."[80] "Revolutionary defeatism," in a travesty of the 1914 original, became the Comintern's general line, a line enforced upon communist organizations despite the fact that it permanently alienated some of their best cadre.[81] All this was of course quite insincere. It was Stalin's best hope that Germany would find itself embroiled in a military stalemate on the new western front. In the meantime, however, the Soviet Union bent over backward to avoid provocative behavior. By 1939 the sacrifice of the international communist movement was considered to be a small price to pay to that end.

The Soviet Union's own initiatives were more assertive and led to friction with its incongruous German ally. In September and October 1939, with an eye to the defense of the Leningrad region and the Baltic fleet,

79. Degras, *The Communist International,* 3:449.
80. Ibid., p. 447.
81. Stalin intervened personally in order to enforce this line upon a resistant Comintern. In April 1941, desperate to appease Hitler, he proposed to dissolve the organization altogether. "Komintern i sovetsko-germanskii dogovor o nenapadenii," *Izvestiia TsK KPSS* 12 (1989): 202–15.

Moscow concluded mutual assistance pacts with Estonia, Latvia, and Lithuania that included permission for the stationing of troops and the establishment of air and naval stations. Requests for similar concessions were directed to Finland, and on 11 October negotiations between the two states began in Moscow. With the Soviet-Finnish border passing within 32 kilometers of Leningrad, the Soviet requests had a legitimate foundation. In the Finnish case, however, a cultivated hostility toward Soviet power prevailed over sensitivity to Soviet security concerns. Negotiations broke down, and on 30 November Soviet forces attacked Finland at intervals along the entire length of the common border. The decision to resolve the Finnish problem by force represented a risk, motivated by a combination of arrogance and desperation, and the "Winter War" that followed became a bitter revelation.[82]

Despite overwhelming physical superiority, the Soviet offensive was ill conceived and poorly executed. Repeated mass assaults along the "Mannerheim Line," a sequence of lakes and fortified areas north of Leningrad, were turned back with heavy losses. Five hundred kilometers to the north, in the central region of the front near the village of Suomussalmi, a military debacle of the first order developed as attacking Soviet forces were cut off and destroyed in the midst of pitiless nordic terrain. As a final indignity, on 29 November the USSR was expelled from the League of Nations. It was hard to escape the conclusion that the effects of the destruction of the high command were being felt, and that the fighting capacity of the RKKA, if pitted against a major adversary, could very well prove to be minimal. According to a German general staff evaluation of late December 1939, prepared after the failed Soviet offensive, the Red Army was "in quantity a gigantic military instrument. . . . leadership itself, however, too young and inexperienced. . . . The Russian 'mass' is *no* match for an army with modern equipment and superior leadership."[83] Here was precisely the impression that Stalin needed to

82. The numerous available accounts of the war include Väinö Alfred Tanner, *The Winter War: Finland against Russia, 1939–1940* (Stanford, Calif., 1957); Eloise Katherine Engle and Lauri Paananen, *The Winter War: The Russo-Finnish Conflict, 1939–1940* (New York, 1972); Richard W. Condon, *The Winter War: Russia against Finland* (New York, 1972). D. W. Spring, "The Soviet Decision for War against Finland," *Soviet Studies* 2 (1986): 207–26, suggests that the desire to demonstrate Soviet power was an important motive for the decision to invade. The revisionist argument by A. G. Dongarov, "Voina, kotoroi moglo ne byt'," *Voprosy istorii* 5 (1990): 28–45, faults Stalin's crude diplomacy for the choice to use force but also notes the "complexities" of the international situation that legitimized Soviet concern.

83. Cited in Seweryn Bialer, ed., *Stalin and His Generals: Soviet Military Memoirs of World War II* (New York, p. 1969), p. 130. Similar conclusions were drawn by U.S. military attachés observing from eastern Europe. See David M. Glantz, "Observing the Soviets: U.S. Army Attachés in Eastern Europe during the 1930s," *Journal of Military*

avoid imparting. In February 1940 Soviet forces regrouped and overwhelmed the outnumbered Finns, but the damage had already been
done. In a peace treaty of 12 March, Finland acquiesced to all Soviet territorial demands, though contrary to original intention the Finnish political regime was left intact.

It was now Germany's turn to be concerned about Soviet maneuvers in
the east. When on 9 April 1940 the Wehrmacht put an end to the
"Phony War" by attacking Norway and Denmark, the Soviet leadership
was no doubt pleased. By extending his commitments, Hitler seemed to
be playing into Stalin's hands. Once again, however, German forces
quickly overran opposition. The decisive moment arrived with the attack
upon France on 10 May. The collapse of French defenses and the desperate withdrawal of the British expeditionary force from the continent
at Dunkerque after a six-week campaign shattered whatever illusions remained concerning the potency of German arms. Germany would not be
involved in a protracted war of attrition on the western front. Astride
central Europe, allied to Italy, and with the sympathy of Francist Spain,
Germany faced only beleaguered Britain and the USSR. The attempt to
buy time through the instrumentality of the Nazi-Soviet pact had ship-
wrecked.

On 17 June 1940 Molotov swallowed hard and congratulated Germany upon its "splendid successes."[84] Simultaneously the USSR hurried
to bolster its defenses. During June and July the Baltic states were
abruptly annexed. On 23 June Molotov informed Berlin of the Soviet intention to annex Bessarabia and the adjacent region of northern Bukov-
ina, and, despite German and Romanian protests, an occupation was
carried out during July. Perhaps most importantly, a major reorganization of the RKKA was begun. The Finnish war had brought manifold
deficiencies to light, and in its wake a high-level commission led by
Zhdanov and Andrei Voznesenskii was appointed to supervise reform.
On 7 May, Semen Timoshenko replaced the discredited Voroshilov as
people's commissar of defense, and an effort to rebuild the high command was begun.[85] The shortage of trained officers was addressed by
rehabilitating surviving victims of the Ezhovshchina, by instituting

---

History 2 (1991): 176–83. N. I. Baryshnikov, "Sovetsko-finlandskaia voina 1939–1940
gg.," *Novaia i noveishaia istoriia* 4 (1989): 29–41, unambiguously blames the disaster
upon the effects of the military purges and Stalin's faulty assessment of the situation.

84. Cited in Gerhard L. Weinberg, *Germany and the Soviet Union, 1939–1941* (Leiden,
1954), p. 101.

85. According to A. M. Vasilevskii, *Delo vsei zhizni* (Moscow, 1975), p. 102, Stalin was
preoccupied with taking the lessons of Finland into account in such a way as "to give our
enemies the right impression." On the various preparations see John Erickson, *Stalin's War
with Germany,* vol. 1: *The Road to Stalingrad* (New York, 1975), pp. 13–49.

special training programs for staff officers, and by a wave of promotions. Infantry manuals were repeatedly redrawn with an emphasis upon the provision of realistic training for combat operations. The fall of France provided a vivid lesson in the power of independent armored formations, and as a result the mechanized corps assembled by Tukhachevskii but disbanded during the terror began to be rebuilt. Discipline and morale, not always sterling in Finland, were tightened by a more severe disciplinary code promulgated in October 1940. As a symbol of the increasing emphasis upon strict hierarchical discipline, the ranks of general and admiral were rehabilitated and more rigid lines of separation established between commander and soldier. During the 18th party congress of March 1941, thirteen military officers were coopted into the Central Committee, an unprecedented step that one historian describes as "the first signal of preparation for the approaching war."[86] On 12 April 1940 the status of commander was further enhanced by the reintroduction of unitary command. New, Draconian labor laws were promulgated on 26 June 1940, establishing a seven-day-on, one-day-off work schedule and an eight-hour workday (seven had been the norm), forbidding internal labor migration, and defining severe measures to combat absenteeism. A major forward deployment of Soviet forces along the western border was begun in conjunction with the occupation of new territories, and in January 1941 a large-scale maneuver simulating defense against a German attack was conducted. These were sweeping measures, but they were only the first steps toward an adequate level of preparedness. In his speech for Red Army Day on 23 February 1941, Zhukov called 1941 "the year of the great restructuring" of the RKKA but emphasized that "much still remains to be done."[87]

The "great restructuring" that Zhukov invoked would not be completed in time. As early as 31 July 1940, in a meeting at the Berghof, Hitler announced to a select group of planners his intention to call off Operation Sea Lion, the plan for an amphibious assault against Britain, and to turn instead against the USSR. It was a fateful decision that the Soviet government had done all in its power to prevent. In the end, Hitler's choice was probably not motivated by any specific Soviet action, but rather by his own irrational hatreds and megalomaniac strategic designs. By the time that Molotov arrived in Berlin for consultations during November, planning for the invasion, eventually codenamed Operation Barbarossa, was already far advanced. During the talks Ribbentrop attempted to distract his guest with alluring images of a future Soviet sphere of influence "in the direction of the Persian Gulf," but Molotov

86. Morozow, *Die Falken des Kreml*, p. 241.
87. G. Zhukov, "Pod perestroiki," *Pravda*, 23 Feb. 1941, p. 2.

was not to be turned around and repeatedly expressed Soviet preoccupation with German troop movements in the western borderlands. His inquiries did not receive an adequate response, but at this point the Soviets had few viable options left to them. Moscow persisted in its dogged attempts to appease Hitler, continued to prepare its defenses, and hoped for the best.

In the months before Hitler's attack, Soviet appeasement reached new and sometimes shocking levels. Economic cooperation was expanded as the Germans systematically filled their strategic reserves. At the expense of their own military preparations, the Soviets assigned trains to haul rubber to Germany from Asia.[88] Moscow did not protest against the conclusion of the Tripartite Pact in September 1940 or its extension to include Bulgaria in February 1941, and made do with a mild note of caution when German forces entered Bulgaria during May. When the Japanese emissary Yosuke Matsuoko departed Moscow on 13 April after signing the Soviet-Japanese neutrality pact, Stalin saw him off at the station, where he pointedly sought out the German Ambassador Werner von der Schulenburg, publicly embraced him, and slavishly urged, "We must remain friends and you must now do everything to that end."[89] After Germany invaded Yugoslavia and Greece, Moscow expelled the Yugoslav ambassador (with whose defiantly antifascist government, arrived in power via a coup on 27 March, it had briefly concluded a friendship treaty on 5 April), and withdrew recognition from the Greek, Norwegian, and Belgian governments in exile. On 6 May 1941 Stalin assumed the chair of the Sovnarkom from Molotov, a gesture that may be interpreted as a signal to Berlin that Soviet policy was being guided by a strong hand and in a consistent direction. A TASS release of 14 June, soon to become infamous, lashed out at "rumors spread by forces hostile to the Soviet Union and Germany" predicting that war was imminent. The text, according to the understated judgment of the Soviet official history of World War II, "reflected I. V. Stalin's incorrect assessment of the political and military circumstances at the time."[90]

The depths of Soviet appeasement were never plumbed. Operation Barbarossa was originally scheduled to begin in May, but the defeats suffered by Mussolini's armies in Greece forced a German diversion into the Balkans during April, where Yugoslav and Greek resistance was crushed.

88. G. M. Ivanitskii, "Sovetsko-germanskie torgovo-ekonomicheskie otnosheniia v 1939–1941 gg.," *Novaia i noveishaia istoriia* 5 (1989): 28–39; Wolfgang W. Birkenfeld, "Stalin als Wirtschaftspartner Hitlers," *Vierteljahreschrift für Sozial- und Wirtschaftsgeschichte* 53 (1966): 492–99.

89. Described in Ulam, *Expansion and Coexistence*, p. 309.

90. *IVOVSS*, 1:404.

The attack against the Soviet Union finally came at 3:30 A.M. on 22 June 1941, without any declaration of war or prior warning, along the entire length of the western frontier stretching over 1,500 kilometers on a line from Vyborg to Kaunas, Bialystok, Brest, L'vov, and Kishinev. A total of 148 German divisions encompassing more than 3.2 million soldiers (of the Reich's total 3.8 million men at arms), 29 divisions and 16 brigades drawn from allied armies, 3,500 tanks, 7,184 artillery pieces, and some 2,000 aircraft were thrown against the Soviet Union in what remains the largest coordinated military operation ever attempted.[91] When Ambassador Schulenburg informed Molotov of the attack, Stalin's lieutenant could only exclaim in horror, "this means war . . . surely we have not deserved that."[92] A sensitive observer might have provided an explanation, but no matter. For more than twenty years, since the first day of Soviet power, Soviet security policy had been preoccupied by an awareness of weakness and exposure and predicated upon the need to avoid a major war. Now all efforts had failed, and the fate of the Soviet experiment was left to be decided by the gods of battle.

The shift in emphasis from a policy of accommodation toward security through strength coincided with the shocks of the world economic crisis, the Japanese occupation of Manchuria, and Hitler's rise to power. The exaggerated war scares of the 1920s had now been replaced by real danger. Simultaneously the short-term consequences of collectivization and Stalin's entire "revolution from above" lowered the Soviet capacity for defense. After 1933 the inevitability of an approaching conflict conditioned all Soviet perceptions of the international situation. Security policy was conceived in terms of positioning the regime to withstand such a conflict, by building an intimidating military posture while engaging in a diplomatic strategy of coalition building in the name of collective security.

The collective security project presided over by Litvinov demanded a degree of commitment and trust that was unique in the Soviet experience. Litvinov's liberal internationalism was opposed by isolationists within the power elite, but between 1934 and 1938, with Stalin's forbearance, it defined the substance of official policy. On one level,

91. Erickson, *The Road to Stalingrad*, p. 98. See also "Barbarossa," *Sovetskaia voennaia entsiklopediia*, 8 vols. (Moscow, 1976–80), 1:392–94, and the slightly revised accounting in "Barbarossa," *Sovetskaia voennaia entsiklopediia*, 2d ed., vol. 1 (Moscow, 1990), pp. 324–25. The Soviet accounts lists 190 divisions, including 19 tank and 14 motorized divisions, massed on the Soviet frontier, a total of 5.5 million soldiers, 4,300 tanks, and 5,000 military aircraft.

92. Cited in Gustav Hilger and Alfred Meyer, *The Incompatible Allies: A Memoir-History of German-Soviet Relations, 1918–1941* (New York, 1953), p. 336.

collective security was very much imbedded in the canons of traditional statecraft, with the goal of reestablishing a European balance of power by shifting Soviet support toward the Entente in opposition to a revitalized Germany. At the same time it encompassed a larger, hopeful vision, which Litvinov defined as a commitment to peace on behalf of development and social justice. Collective security did not mean a sudden conversion of Stalinist Russia to the values of the western democracies; it did not mean a renunication of all freedom of maneuver; and it did not mean the acceptance of a code of conduct that the Soviet Union's rivals were themselves quite willing to disregard. It did represent an earnest plea for a collegial approach to the problem of European security that focused upon the threat of fascism and demanded compromises on behalf of a common goal.

The failure of collective security, symbolized by the exclusion of the Soviet Union from the Munich pact and accompanied by the blow to Soviet preparedness wrought by the military purge, forced Stalin to reconsider his options. When Hitler's response to Soviet probing became more positive in the summer of 1939, the ground was prepared for a diplomatic revolution. The Soviet leadership did not feel ready to wage a major war and feared its consequences. Standing up to Germany in August 1939 meant a fight, and Stalin was not confident that in the event of a confrontation, London and Paris would not stand aside. The result was the Molotov-Ribbentrop pact, the German *Blitzkrieg* against Poland, and a general war.

The Nazi-Soviet bargain had none of the substance of earlier Soviet approaches to security. It was undertaken by both parties distrustfully and for narrowly instrumental ends—on the German side to clear the way for provoking a war, and on the Soviet side to avoid war at all costs. Revolutionary internationalism, accommodation, and collective security had all aspired to represent positive values. Under the terms of the Molotov-Ribbentrop pact the point of Soviet policy became little more than an abject attempt to appease the German colossus by whatever means necessary. Stalin's toast to the Führer, so beloved by the "German Nation," was damning. Trotsky's fiery internationalism, Radek's acerbic intelligence, Chicherin's cautious consistency, Litvinov's high principle, all had been replaced by a cynical and ugly *raison d'état*, the very antithesis of the principles to which Soviet power had originally aspired.

Even in its own calculated terms, the logic of a deal with Hitler proved to be flawed. In 1938 and 1939 the Soviet Union turned its back on what was at least the possibility of resisting German aggression together with powerful European allies. When Hitler moved to attack the Soviets in 1941, they stood alone against the entire German army, with the

CHAPTER FOUR

The Great Fatherland War, 1941–1945

> The water of the Volga! He drank water from the Volga and at the same time he was at war. These two concepts—war and the Volga—for all their obviousness never joined. Since childhood, since his schooldays, all his life the Volga had been for him something so profound, so endlessly Russian, that now the fact that he stood on the banks of the Volga, and drank its water, and that on those banks were the Germans, seemed to him unbelievable and wild.
>
> —Konstantin Simonov, *Days and Nights*, 1943

In 1941, for all the achievements of the five-year plans, the USSR was still an impoverished, developing nation. The majority of its citizens lived in simple wooden cottages, amidst extended families, in a timeless rural environment where attachments to place and community were strong. Hard work and meager reward were the lot of the "dark people," whose hardiness and endurance reflected age-old strengths of Russian civilization. Nor were the Soviet people strangers to political storms; World War I, the revolution, the civil war, collectivization, the Ezhovshchina, all had broken over the long-suffering nation in the span of a generation.

On 23 June 1941, in announcing the German surprise attack, and again in an editorial of 26 June, *Pravda* described the new trial that had burst from the blue as a "fatherland war" (*otechestvennaia voina*), a national struggle pitting the Soviet peoples against a ruthless invader. At stake were the most basic of values, not the political abstractions of the civil war but the integrity of hearth and home, the fate of the "country roads where our ancestors passed, with the simple crosses on their Russian graves."[1]

---

1. As expressed by Konstantin Simonov in a much beloved poem. Konstantin Simonov, *Sobranie sochinenii*, 6 vols. (Moscow, 1966), 1: 70. See "Nashe delo pravoe, vrag budet razbit," *Pravda*, 26 June 1941, p. 1, for the "fatherland war" characterization.

European Russia, 1990. From *Maps on File*. Copyright © 1990 by Martin Greenwald Associates. Reprinted with permission of Facts on File Inc., New York.

So it would be for the war's duration, and so it has remained. The contest with Germany of 1941–1945, by far the most deadly armed confrontation in history, is officially remembered as the Great Fatherland War and honored, above all, as a war for national survival. Hitler's Thousand-Year Reich was a formidable opponent, but with its long history of resilience in adversity and immense human and material resources, the Soviet Union was well placed to prevail. In his address to the nation of 23 June, Molotov made explicit reference to these virtues by invoking the legacy of 1812. His concluding words proved to be prophetic: "Our cause is just, the enemy will be beaten, victory will be ours."[2]

Hitler declared the war in the east to be a "total war." Stalin, in his address of 6 November 1941 delivered to representatives of the Moscow City Soviet in the Maiakovskii metro station with German armies less than 100 kilometers away, defiantly reciprocated: "if the Germans want a total war, they will get it."[3] Under these circumstances the concept of "security policy" had little meaning. After its early, catastrophic reversals, the Soviet regime's security goals were perforce reduced to sheer *survival,* and on several occasions the state tottered on the brink of an abyss. Given the pathological nature of Nazi racial doctrine, which declared the peoples of eastern Europe *Untermenschen* ("subhumans") fit only for enslavement or extermination, "survival" quickly assumed literal as well as figurative dimensions. The biological survival of entire ethnic groups; the institutional survival of the Soviet state, Soviet power, and the "achievements of October"; and the political survival of the Stalinist order were all at risk. In every case the issue would be decided by a titanic clash of arms, pitting Hitler's Wehrmacht, with its Finnish, Hungarian, Italian, Romanian, and Slovak allies, against a battered but relentless Red Army. Security policy was reduced to the business of mobilization and the art of war.[4]

2. "Vystuplenie po radio zamestitelia predsedatelia Soveta Narodnykh Komissarov soiuza SSR i Narodnogo komissara inostrannykh del tov. V. M. Molotova," *Pravda,* 23 June 1941, p. 1.

3. Stalin, *Sochineniia,* 2 [XV]: 24.

4. Of the many excellent histories of the Soviet-German war, I am particularly indebted to John Erickson's magisterial *The Road to Stalingrad* and its companion volume *The Road to Berlin: Continuing the History of Stalin's War with Germany* (Boulder, Colo., 1983), a comprehensive narrative of military operations and a powerful epoch of war itself. Erickson's bibliography is an excellent guide to source materials. Alexander Werth, *Russia at War,* is unsurpassed as a portrait of Soviet society at war. See also Albert Seaton, *The Russo-German War, 1941–1945* (New York, 1970); Alan Clark, *Barbarossa: The Russo-German Conflict, 1941–1945* (New York, 1965); Paul Carell [pseud.], *Unternehmen Barbarossa: Der Marsch nach Russland* (Frankfurt am Main, 1961), and *Verbrannte Erde: Schlacht zwischen Wolga und Weichsel* (Frankfurt am Main, 1966). A new official history of the war is currently being prepared in the former Soviet Union.

"Esli zavtra voina"

"If war comes tomorrow" (*esli zavtra voina*) was the title of a popular Russian film and song in the spring of 1941, relating the story of a putative German attack against the USSR. In the best heroic tradition German forces are given a swift repulse, culminating with a proletarian uprising in Berlin. The themes of readiness and invincibility were echoed in Sergei Eisenstein's film classic *Aleksandr Nevskii,* where the thirteenth-century Teutonic knights, portrayed with eerie parodies of Nazi ritual, march to their doom against stalwart Russian defenders. They appeared in popular fiction as well, in works such as Nikolai Shpanov's *First Strike: The Story of a Future War,* where a German air attack is totally repulsed within a single hour. Such fantasies were encouraged by the rhetoric of Soviet officialdom, filled with swaggering references to the might of the Red Army. Despite the rhetoric, however, when war finally came, the Soviets proved to be woefully unprepared. Before the shocks administered by Hitler's Ostheer ("Eastern Army"), the USSR's entire western defensive perimeter caved in, exposing the country's heartland to a savage occupation. The collapse of the front was a monumental disaster, and explaining why it occurred has become one of the most contentious issues in Soviet history.

The effort of Soviet historians to come to terms with the problem is a story unto itself. As long as Stalin remained alive, the issue was ignored. Hitler's treachery and the element of surprise were the standard explanations for early defeats, with even the fallback to Moscow justified as "active defense." Beginning with Khrushchev's attack upon Stalin at the 20th party congress in 1956, more critical evaluations became possible, and in 1960 the first volume of the official Soviet history of the Great Fatherland War published an extensive and often uninhibited analysis of the problem.[5] A special target was the "cult of personality of I. V. Stalin," which "especially after 1937 . . . led to dogmatism and doctrinairism, impeding the initiative of military researchers."[6] The culmination of such evaluations came in 1967 with the publication of Aleksandr Nekrich's *1941, 22 June,* an almost unbroken polemic against Stalin, whose "scarcely believable" actions and "schematic understanding of

---

5. *IVOVSS,* 1:395–481. P. Maslov, "Literatura o voennykh deistviiakh letom 1941 goda," *Voenno-istoricheskii zhurnal* 9 (1966): 88–95, reviews the relevant Soviet literature through the Khrushchev period. In his 1956 "secret speech" Khrushchev used unpreparedness in 1941 as a major item in his bill of indictment against Stalin. See "O kul'te lichnosti," *Izvestiia TsK KPSS* 1(1989): 145–51.

6. *IVOVSS,* 1:439.

the external world" the author decries.[7] Nekrich's book became a watershed. In the aftermath of its publication an official campaign was launched to tone down criticisms of Stalin, which by implication tarred the entire Soviet regime.[8]

Subsequently, though Soviet historians continued to fault Stalin for errors and misjudgments, greater emphasis began to be placed upon the intractable nature of the problems he confronted. In the words of a leading chronicler, "Much was done in order to confront the aggressor fully armed. But . . . several important measures, which in one or two years would have assured the Motherland first-class, well-equipped, and brilliantly prepared armed forces, remained unaccomplished at the start of the Second World War. Unfortunately, history provided us with too little time in order to fulfill them."[9] Such accounts, accurate as far as they went, left the most difficult questions unanswered. The lament "too little time" harked back to Stalin's original rationalization for the disaster, and the culpability assigned to "history" conveniently depersonalized the matter of responsibility. Under the impetus of the reform movement launched by Mikhail Gorbachev, the tide shifted yet again; Stalin's brutality and the "leadership principle" (vozhdizm) that characterized his reign were now unambiguously blamed for Soviet unpreparedness. According to the revisionist biography of Stalin by Dmitrii Volkogonov, "it is difficult to find in history a precedent where one of two adversaries did so much to weaken itself on the eve of a mortal combat."[10] The issue strikes at the very source of the regime's legitimacy; Stalin himself stated in 1933 that "no people can respect its government if it sees the danger of attack and does not prepare for self-defense."[11]

Viewed dispassionately, the debacle of June 1941 may be explained with reference to both long-term and immediate causes. Many of the

<hr />

7. Nekrich, 1941, 22 iiunia, pp. 131–32.

8. An account of the controversy, with translations of the most important texts, is provided by Vladimir Petrov, June 22, 1941: Soviet Historians and the German Invasion (Columbia, S.C., 1968).

9. V. V. Anfilov, Proval 'Blitskriga' (Moscow, 1974), pp. 213–14. Anfilov states what amounts to the official line of the Brezhnev period. A. M. Samsonov, ed., Sovetskii Soiuz v gody Velikoi Otechestvennoi voiny, 2d ed. (Moscow, 1985), p. 31, argues similarly that "the period of peace was not sufficient to allow for the rearmament and reorganization of the Armed Forces of the USSR to be completed prior to the war."

10. Volkogonov, Triumf i tragediia, 2, part 1:61, and the entire discussion on pp. 154–75. The remark quoted refers specifically to the consequences of the military purges. Danilov, "Sovetskoe glavnoe komandovanie," p. 4, reflects the dominant contemporary interpretation when he speaks of the "mistakes, severe miscalculations, and in a number of cases criminal actions of I. V. Stalin, V. M. Molotov, K. E. Voroshilov, and other high-ranking political leaders."

11. Stalin, Sochineniia, 13:279.

former revolve around the effects of the Ezhovshchina. The disruption of the command occasioned by arrests and executions speaks for itself and is widely acknowledged in Soviet accounts. A less referenced side effect was the temporary reversal of the modernization program associated with Tukhachevskii. Bombastic propaganda was no substitute for the latter's uncompromising professionalism, and the Red Army would pay dearly for the loss. After 1937 dogmatic faith in the priority of the offensive and insistence that war would be carried onto the enemy's territory and won at "little cost in blood" (*maloi krov'iu*) blinded planners to strategic realities.[12] Failure to consider the possibility of a surprise attack or to plan for the contingency of a strategic withdrawal proved to be devastatingly shortsighted.[13]

Compared with its German rival, the Red Army displayed markedly lower standards of professionalism. Its training procedures, constantly redrawn, were often ineffective, and following the military purge a shortage of commanders was acute. The army's raw recruits lacked any experience of war comparable to that of the Wehrmacht's battle-hardened veterans, and Red Army commanders, only 7 percent of whom had received higher military education and 75 percent of whom had occupied their posts for less than a year, lacked the acquaintance with mobile operations in depth demonstrated by their German counterparts.[14] Germany was an advanced industrial society that stood upon a level of development to which the USSR still only aspired. Despite prodigious achievements during the 1930s, the Soviet economic profile remained unbalanced and technological standards were often unacceptably low. As a result, in 1941 the Red Army was not yet a well-equipped modern fighting force on a par with its enemy. A modernization of equipment

12. The Soviet official history makes special reference to the failure to absorb the lessons of military engagements waged during the 1930s (the Spanish Civil War, the battles of Lake Khasan and Khalkhin Gol, and the Winter War). It deals gingerly with matters of doctrine. The field regulations (*polevoi ustav*) of 1939 are cited as a definitive outline of Soviet operational doctrine prior to the war, with their emphasis upon the priority of the offensive and the need rapidly to carry the war onto enemy territory (it is here that the reference to victory at "little cost" appears). These priorities are described as "correct in principle." The fault, it is claimed, lay not with doctrine, but with "insufficient practical and theoretical preparation." *IVOVSS*, 1:439–40. V. N. Lobov, "Strategiia pobedy," *Voenno-istoricheskii zhurnal* 5 (1988): 6, is less inhibited in condemning Stalin's "deformation of military doctrine" during the 1930s.

13. In his memoirs Zhukov faults Stalin directly for these errors (thereby providing a convenient scapegoat for the high command). "I. V. Stalin," he writes, "was for all of us the highest authority; no one at that time even thought to doubt his judgments and evaluation of the situation. However, though they had their grounds, I. V. Stalin's assumptions did not take into account the adversary's plans for a *Blitzkrieg* against the USSR." G. K. Zhukov, *Vospominaniia i razmyshleniia* (Moscow, 1969), pp. 267–68.

14. Bialer, *Stalin and His Generals*, p. 63.

design begun under the supervision of Nikolai Voznesenskii in 1940 was only partially completed when war struck. The Soviet tank park counted considerably more machines than those of its rivals, but the majority were outdated and often worse than useless.[15] The KV (Kliment Voroshilov) and T-34 heavy and medium tanks, accepted by the army in 1940, were excellently designed, but they were not available in significant numbers during the campaign of 1941. The carrying capacity of railways on the Soviet side of the frontier was three to four times less than corresponding capacity on the German side. The Soviet Union's auto industry was rudimentary, and as a result the war effort would suffer from a chronic shortage of trucks. Communications remained primitive, rear services underdeveloped—the list of deficiencies is long.

These long-term problems, some of which no leadership could entirely have made good, were compounded by short-term blunders. The abandonment of the carefully fortified Stalin line and redeployment forward into the newly occupied territories during 1940–1941 proved to be a disastrous mistake. Elaborate plans to secure new frontier defenses were not completed in time. Troops were too often multiplied in linear fashion within the frontier defense zone, without properly echeloned defense in depth or adequate strategic reserves. At the same time, border defense positions were often undermanned, or merely patrolled by NKVD border guards. On 22 June, along major lines of advance and particularly on the crucial Western Front, the Germans were able to assemble four- and five-to-one advantages in manpower. Supply dumps and mobilization stores, also relocated during 1940–1941, were quickly overrun. The Soviet air force was caught in the midst of a major deployment (supervised by Lavrentii Beria's NKVD), with the majority of its planes massed on a limited number of easily targetable airfields. On Aviation Day, 18 August 1939, *Pravda* covered its front page with a pompous sketch of Stalin and Voroshilov looking contentedly over line after line of fighters piloted by the "Stalin Falcons." In the first day of the war the majority of these machines were destroyed on the ground by German air raids. In sum, in the words of Malcolm Mackintosh, the Soviet armed forces were "caught between two types of organization and two types of armament," with catastrophic consequences.[16]

Equally damaging was a willful refusal to make use of excellent intelligence data and to acknowledge the likelihood of a German attack.

15. V. V. Shlykova, "I tanki nashi bystry," *Mezhdunarodnaia zhizn'* 9 (1988): 117–24. Shlykova's accounting concerning the Soviet tank park is challenged by V. P. Krikunov, " 'Prostaia arifmetika' V. V. Shlykova," *Voenno-istoricheskii zhurnal* 4 (1989): 41–44.
16. Malcolm Mackintosh, *Juggernaut: A History of the Soviet Armed Forces* (New York, 1967), p. 133.

Preparation for an undertaking on the scale of Operation Barbarossa could not go undetected, and the Soviets received adequate advanced warning from the famous spy Richard Sorge in Tokyo, from British and American sources, and, in the days preceding the attack, from German defectors.[17] Throughout May and June border friction and violations of Soviet air space occurred with increasing frequency, but all was dismissed as an elaborate "provocation." Stalin's fear of war had become paralyzing and created an irrational refusal to recognize the obvious.[18] The TASS statement of 14 June, dismissing the possibility of war, was not calculated to enhance vigilance. It was accompanied by the rejection of requests from front commanders to bring their units up to full strength. Only at 0:30 hours on 22 June, three hours before the German attack, was a full state of combat readiness declared.

More errors and misjudgments followed the assault. On 22 June the Wehrmacht's Army Group North struck from East Prussia and northern Poland across the Nieman River toward Kaunas and Grodno. Army Group Center moved from central Poland across the Bug at Brest-Litovsk. To the south of the Pripiat' marshes Army Group South advanced from southern Poland toward L'vov. Farther to the south Romanian armies prepared to seize Odessa, while in the far north sixteen Finnish divisions were mobilized to regain the territories lost in 1940. Almost immediately gaping holes were punched in Soviet defenses. Beleaguered troops fought heroically in place (the famous garrison of the Brest fortress holding out under siege until late July), but German encircling maneuvers left them isolated. The Soviet middle and high command fell into a state of confusion, with divisional commanders out of

17. The conclusion has been confirmed on the basis of archival data. See A. Baidakov, "Po dannym razvedki . . . ," *Pravda*, 8 May 1989, p. 4. Some of these archival materials, with an accompanying evaluation that damns the state authorities, appear in "O podgotovke Germanii k napadeniiu na SSSR," *Izvestiia TsK KPSS* 4 (1990): 198–222. Ribbentrop himself is reported to have betrayed Hitler by announcing the decision to attack to the Soviet *polpred* (ambassadorial representative) V. G. Dekazonov and naming 22 June 1941 as the date, a revelation that Stalin dismissed with the remark that "disorientation has now spread to the level of ambassadors"! Reported on the basis of a conversation with Anastas Mikoian in Kumanev, "22-go, na rassvete." Bialer concludes that the Kremlin "received more and better information on the approaching general danger, even on specific details of date and hour of invasion, than has any other leadership of an attacked country in the history of modern warfare." Bialer, *Stalin and His Generals*, p. 180.

18. According to Mikoian, to the very end Stalin clung to the belief that Hitler would avoid a two-front war by attacking Great Britain rather than turning against the USSR. See Kumanev, "22-go, na rassvete." Khrushchev insists that everyone knew the attack was coming but speaks of Stalin on the eve of war as being transfixed by the collapse of his calculations, in "a state of confusion, anxiety, demoralization, even paralysis. This was criminal inactivity on the part of Stalin and the other people who were directly responsible for the defense of our country." *Khrushchev Remembers: The Glasnost Tapes*, p. 56.

touch with their units and the defense commissariat in Moscow poorly informed of developments at the front. Stalin's reaction to word of the attack was disbelief, and defense commissar Timoshenko's first command directives, issued on the morning and evening of 22 June, contained the completely unrealistic instructions to "destroy" invading forces by launching "active offensive operations" but not to violate the German frontier in pursuit. A series of uncoordinated counterattacks followed, which only added to the momentum of the rout. When the extent of the catastrophe was made unmistakably clear, Stalin virtually withdrew from state affairs and for more than a week participated only passively and sporadically in military planning.[19] On 23 June it fell to Commissar of Foreign Affairs Molotov to read the announcement that war had come to an unsuspecting nation.

Regardless of how one chooses to allocate responsibility, the stark fact was that within days the Soviet front had been blasted apart. On 28 June, along the central axis, the German Second and Third Panzer Groups under generals Hermann Hoth and Heinz Guderian joined at Minsk, encircling a large concentration of Soviet divisions in the Bialystok-Minsk area and virtually eliminating the Soviet western front. On 29 June Front Commander Dmitrii Pavlov (subsequently shot as a "traitor") was replaced by General Andrei Eremenko, who strove unsuccessfully to rebuild a defensive line along the Berezina. To the north, on 30 June the German Fourth Panzer Group forced the Dvina. Pskov fell on 9 July, and Soviet forces scrambled to build a "Luga line" between the Gulf of Finland and Lake Il'men blocking the approaches to Leningrad. Army Group South made slower progress, in part because of the skillful use of fortified districts and armor by southwest front commander Mikhail Kirponos, who conducted a fighting retreat to the old Stalin line between Zhitomir and Berdichev. With the Germans still pressing forward, these accomplishments provided scant solace. Tomorrow had come, and the Soviet Union confronted a mortal peril.

19. Stalin's comportment during the first days of the war remains the subject of some controversy. According to Ivan M. Maiskii, "Dni ispytanii," *Novyi mir* 12 (1964): 163, Stalin withdrew to his study and remained incommunicado for three full days, muttering "all that Lenin bequeathed us we have lost." In his memoir Khrushchev describes him in the first days of the invasion as "a bag of bones in a grey tunic." *Khrushchev Remembers: The Glasnost Tapes*, p. 65. Commander Nikolai Voronov speaks of Stalin as being active but "depressed, nervous, and of uneven disposition." Cited in Bialer, *Stalin and His Generals*, p. 210. Zhukov's censored memoirs, on the other hand, relate Stalin's activity somewhat more positively. Zhukov, *Vospominaniia*, pp. 267–68. There seems little doubt that Stalin was at a minimum badly shocked and temporarily incapable of providing decisive leadership, particularly during the critical days 28–30 June. For more on the issue see Roy A. Medvedev, *On Stalin and Stalinism* (Oxford, 1979), p. 123; Volkogonov, *Triumf i tragediia*, 2, part 1:157–63.

The Sacred War

Not until 3 July did Stalin recover from his trauma sufficiently to address the Soviet people. His radio message, read in a subdued tone, made a vivid impression.[20] It began with an unprecedentedly personal salutation: "Comrades! Citizens! Brothers and sisters! Fighters of our army and fleet! I am speaking to you, my friends." What followed was a description of the situation at the fronts, an attempt to justify the government's policies, and the outline of a strategy for resistance. No effort was made to disguise the extent of the catastrophe: "The enemy continues to thrust forward. . . . A serious danger hangs over our Motherland." But the overall tone was positive, conveying the impression that, although a difficult struggle lay ahead, in the end victory was certain. On the whole it was an impressive performance. From one day to the next Stalin reasserted his authority as leader and provided the Soviet war effort with an overall direction. The address was not just a morale booster—it had a programmatic character and spoke directly to the issue of how the Soviet Union planned to conduct the war. Perhaps most striking was the degree to which the facile optimism of the prewar years had disappeared. Stalin's program was inspired much more by a strategy of attrition than by the spirit of the offensive, and of victory won at "little cost in blood" there was nary a trace.

The war with Germany, Stalin asserted, "cannot be considered a normal war . . . between two armies." It was a "fatherland war" in which the Soviet people fought to avoid enslavement. Resistance would be total and engage all levels of Soviet society in a great cooperative effort. It was necessary "immediately to put our whole production on a war footing, and to place everything at the service of the front" and "to organize every kind of assistance for the Red Army." These recommendations would be acted upon with alacrity. On the home front an unrelenting labor regime was installed. In combat zones citizen volunteer battalions dug fortifications, performed a variety of services, and in the war's first months suffered terrifying casualties as combat units. Stalin's appeal for "merciless struggle" against "spies, panic-mongers, and deserters" was carried out to the letter by the NKVD and the military counterintelligence organ SMERSH (Death to Spies). The strains of total war opened up many divisions within Soviet society, which despite official legend produced its share of collaborators, shirkers, and grumblers. In most cases, however, burdens were willingly shouldered on behalf of a cause

20. Stalin, *Sochineniia*, 2 [XV]: 1–10. The following quotations are taken from the Russian text.

whose justice few could doubt. The spirit of national mobilization was powerfully expressed in A. V. Aleksandrov's and V. Lebedev-Kumach's patriotic hymn "Sacred War," which Alexander Werth describes as a "kind of semi-official anthem throughout the war years," with its exhortation to rise up against the invader's "dark horde."[21]

Ultimate responsibility for defense was placed in the hands of the armed forces. "The Red Army and Navy, and all Soviet citizens," Stalin intoned, "must defend every inch of Soviet earth, fight to the last drop of blood for our cities and villages." A stubborn refusal to allow withdrawal from exposed positions would cost the Red Army dearly, but the suicidal resistance demanded by Moscow also took a cumulative toll of the enemy. The Wehrmacht, Stalin went to some length to demonstrate, was not "invincible." His references to the fate of Napoleon and the kaiser made the point that early reversals did not mean inevitable defeat. They also placed the contest with Hitler firmly in the tradition of Russia's national wars.

What could not be defended must be destroyed. "The enemy must not be left a single steam engine, a single train car . . . a single kilogram of bread, a single liter of oil." This was a scorched-earth policy, to which a call for the creation of partisan detachments in occupied territories was affixed. "In the occupied zone it is necessary to create untenable conditions for the enemy and his accomplices, to hound and destroy them at every step." With large numbers of Red Army soldiers cut off behind German lines and populous regions overrun, the resources for partisan activity were at hand, but in other ways conditions were inauspicious. A first wave of partisan operations, often a desperate last resort for men at the end of their tether, was smothered in the avalanche of Soviet defeats. It was not until 30 May 1942 that the General Staff of the Partisan Movement was created and "partisan district commands" delineated. Only in 1943–1944 did partisan resistance grow into a meaningful military factor.[22]

The contest was not limited to Russia. "In this war of liberation," Stalin assured his people, "we will not be alone. In this great war we will have true allies in the peoples of Europe and America, and also among

21. Werth, *Russia at War*, p. 190.
22. For accounts of the first phase of the partisan struggle see John A. Armstrong, ed., *Soviet Partisans in World War II* (Madison, Wis., 1964), pp. 75–88; Erickson, *The Road to Stalingrad*, pp. 240–48; Lev Nikolaevich Bychkov, *Partisanskoe dvizhenie v gody Velikoi Otechestvennoi voiny 1941–1945: Kratkii ocherk* (Moscow, 1965), pp. 41–266; Matthew Cooper, *The Nazi War against Soviet Partisans* (New York, 1979), pp. 11–18. The first orders establishing the conditions for organized partisan struggle dated 18 and 19 July 1941 appear in the series "Iz istorii Velikoi Otechestvennoi voiny," *Izvestiia TsK KPSS* 7 and 8 (1990): 217–18 and 209–11.

German people, enslaved by Hitler's henchmen . . . this will be a united front of people standing for freedom against slavery." Already on 22 June, British prime minister Churchill declared his government's intent "to give whatever help we can to Russia and the Russian people," and on 13 July, Molotov and British ambassador Sir Stafford Cripps signed a formal alliance.[23] On 1 October, Lord Beaverbrook and Averell Harriman concluded an agreement in Moscow stipulating material aid for the Soviet war effort, and by mid-October American Lend-Lease assistance had begun to arrive. The Soviets were in desperate need of any and all support, and these gestures were much appreciated. On 3 July, Stalin spoke of "a feeling of gratitude in the hearts of the people of the Soviet Union." Only desperation can explain Stalin's request of 13 September for "active military assistance," including the landing of twenty-five to thirty British divisions at Murmansk. Such aid was not forthcoming, but the emergence of what Churchill would call the "Grand Alliance" provided a real boost to morale, and a positive political context for waging war.

Stalin also announced changes designed to put Soviet institutions on to a war footing. On 23 July a supreme command was designated, the Stavka, encompassing senior commanders and political leaders and operating from a "war room" in the Kremlin.[24] One week later the State Defense Committee (GKO) came into being as an organ of political authority. Its membership—originally Stalin, Molotov, Voroshilov, Georgii Malenkov, and Beria, later expanded to include Lazar Kaganovich, Anastas Mikoian, Nikolai Bulganin, and Nikolai Voznesenskii—consisted of a handful of the Soviet Union's most influential leaders. The GKO was granted extraordinary powers to issue decrees, and its members were accorded the right to sit with the Stavka. Centralization was the rule, and in every case ultimate authority rested with Stalin. On the eve of the war Stalin held the positions of general secretary of the Communist party and chair of the Sovnarkom. During June and July he

23. Winston L. S. Churchill, *The Grand Alliance* (London, 1950), pp. 371–73. For an investigation of British motives see Sheila Lawlor, "Britain and Russian Entry into the War," in Richard Langhorne, ed., *Diplomacy and Intelligence during the Second World War: Essays in Honor of F. H. Hinsley* (Cambridge, 1985), pp. 168–86.

24. The original members were Stalin (chair), Molotov, Timoshenko, Budennyi, Voroshilov, Shaposhnikov, and Zhukov. The Stavka was renamed several times during the first months of its existence—from Headquarters of the "High Command" (Stavka glavnogo komandirovaniia), to "Headquarters of the Supreme Command" (Stavka verkhovnogo komandirovaniia), to "Headquarters of the Supreme High Command" (Stavka verkhovnogo glavnokomandirovaniia)—without changing its essential functions. See Samsonov, *Sovetskii Soiuz*, p. 55. According to Zhukov, *Vospominaniia*, p. 292, the Stavka was more a concept than a working body, in that it seldom met formally and "possessed no administrative apparatus other than the General Staff."

became chief of the GKO, Stavka chair, commissar of defense, and on 8 August "Supreme Commander of the Soviet Armed Forces." Henceforward he would play the role of the iron-willed leader to the hilt, and not without effect. Werth reports that during the autumn of 1941, in darkened Moscow theaters, Stalin's appearance in newsreels never failed to occasion spontaneous cheering.[25]

During the war military strategy was worked out at the center by the Stavka, the General Operations Directorate of the General Staff, and the defense commissariat, overseen politically by the GKO and ultimately approved or disapproved by Stalin—a unification of political and military authority such as Shaposhnikov had recommended during the late 1920s.[26] In July a brief, unsuccessful experiment with "high commands" (*glavkomy*) combining several fronts was attempted but quickly abandoned. Thereafter the Stavka communicated directly with the individual front commands. The high command learned from experience, and over time the "Stavka-GKO system" would become an effective mechanism for military direction.

Communist party organs on the national level, with the exception of the Central Committee, continued to function during the war, and the Politburo is reported to have held joint sessions with the GKO and the Stavka.[27] Party membership swelled as millions of soldiers and citizens were coopted into the organization in an effort to boost morale.[28] In many ways, however, the party's role was effaced. At lower levels party organs sometimes ceased to function altogether, emphasis upon the theme of national resistance caused a lowering of the organization's ideological profile, and party leaders quickly fell into the shadow of the high command. As an almost reflexive reaction to disaster, on 16 July 1941 Stalin restored the system of dual command. Subsequent interference with command decisions by incompetent commissars did nothing to enhance the party's prestige. The exaggerated harping upon the party's "leading role" that is characteristic of almost all postwar Soviet accounts may be interpreted as an attempt to disguise a very different reality.

Several other administrative decisions reached in the war's first days and weeks would have an important bearing upon its eventual outcome.

---

25. Werth, *Russia at War*, p. 189.

26. Described in A. M. Vasilevskii, "K voprosu o rukovodstve vooruzhennoi bor'boi v Velikoi Otechestvennoi voine," in A. M. Samsonov, ed., *9 maia 1945 goda* (Moscow, 1970), pp. 42–65.

27. Iu. P. Petrov, "KPSS—organizator i rukovoditel' pobedy sovetskogo naroda v Velikoi Otechestvennoi voine," *Voprosy istorii* 5 (1970): 13–15. See also Bialer, *Stalin and His Generals*, pp. 339–41.

28. T. H. Rigby, *Communist Party Membership in the USSR, 1917–1967* (New York, 1968), pp. 250–71.

An Evacuation Council created on 24 June, chaired by Nikolai Shvernik with Aleksei Kosygin and Mikhail Pervukhin as deputies, made an essential contribution by supervising the evacuation of industrial equipment from regions threatened by occupation. As chair of the State Planning Commission (Gosplan), Nikolai Voznesenskii and his commissar of armaments Dmitrii Ustinov labored to convert the Soviet economy to a wartime basis. The establishment of the Rear Services Administration in July 1941 represented another step toward a more vigorous application of the officially propagated "all for the front" ethic.[29]

Total national mobilization, steadfast resistance by the Red Army, systematic sabotage by partisan detachments, close cooperation with new-found allies in an antifascist front, central coordination of the war effort under the charismatic leadership of Stalin, and a confident faith in victory—these were the elements of the program unveiled in Stalin's address of 3 July. It was a strategy for victory that would be followed almost to the letter. But first it was necessary to stop the Wehrmacht's drive on Moscow.

The War for Survival

Hitler's intent in Operation Barbarossa was to engage and destroy the Red Army in the field before the onset of winter.[30] Under the best of circumstances this was a high-stakes wager, and in preliminary planning the Germans made several fundamental miscalculations. The Balkan campaign delayed the launching of Barbarossa by a full month, German intelligence underestimated the size of the regular Red Army, and disagreement over strategic goals was allowed to affect coordination between the three German army groups. As a result Barbarossa was a stunning success in almost all terms but its own. The Red Army suffered crushing defeats, but fed by a seemingly inexhaustible supply of fresh units, it continued to resist. German time-tables were delayed, losses were higher than planned, and the Ostheer was forced into a winter campaign for which it was inadequately prepared. As long as the Red Army was still in the field, there was substance to Maurice Hindus's boast, made even while contemplating a retreat to the Urals, that "Hitler cannot conquer Russia." "The prophets of easy collapse and ready

29. See L. M. Volodarskii, "Sovetskii tyl v gody Velikoi Otechestvennoi voiny," *Voprosy istorii* 7 (1985): 14–34, and the documentation in E. F. Spoin et al., ed., *RSFSR—Frontu 1941–1945: Dokumenty i materialy* (Moscow, 1987).

30. For descriptions of Hitler's larger strategic design and its fate see Bryan I. Fugate, *Operation Barbarossa: Strategy and Tactics on the Eastern Front, 1941* (Novate, Calif., 1984), pp. 61–93; Anfilov, *Proval 'Blitskriga'*, pp. 41–59; V. A. Anfilov, *Krushenie pokhoda Gitlera na Moskvu 1941* (Moscow, 1989), pp. 271–339.

subjugation," he wrote, "have reckoned without the power of the Russian earth and Russian humanity."[31]

Hindus was correct, but philosophical reflection was of no use against Hitler's legions. On 2 July, Army Group Central forced the Berezina and struck at Smolensk, along the high road to Moscow. A long and difficult battle followed, but during August Smolensk was overrun. German armies on the Moscow axis now went onto the defensive, a controversial decision disputed by some field commanders, who urged a lightning strike against the Soviet capital. In what may have been a fateful misjudgment Hitler overrode them, electing to keep all three groups advancing simultaneously and giving priority to a breakthrough in the south.

With a pause in effect on the central axis, Army Groups North and South continued to advance. In the Leningrad region the Finns recaptured Vyborg, while in mid-August a German offensive pierced the Luga line at Kingisepp and swept into Novgorod and Krasnogvardeisk, only forty kilometers from the former imperial capital. On 30 August the capture of the Mga junction cut off the city's last rail link to the outside world. The citadel of the revolution, a city of more than 2 million souls, Leningrad was now completely isolated. Already on 20 August a "Military Soviet for the Defense of Leningrad" was established and a commitment made to defend the city by all possible means. The appointment of Zhukov, rapidly emerging as the Stavka's premier troubleshooter, to command the newly designated Leningrad Front on 12 September lent force to the effort. Almost simultaneously, however, Hitler made the decision not to attempt to take the city by storm. While Leningrad saw to its defenses, a new kind of struggle appeared on the horizon, against the medieval terrors of siege. The blockade of Leningrad, one of the most horrible in all wars, had begun.

Even more ominous news emerged from the south. A renewed German offensive in late July turned the flanks of Budennyi's southwestern front and broke into Kiev on 18 September. Five Soviet armies, left stranded in the Kiev salient as a result of Stalin's dogged refusal to approve a timely withdrawal, were cut to pieces. Front commander Kirponos was killed by mine splinters during an attempted breakout, and the Germans claimed a haul of 655,000 prisoners.[32] After the debacle what remained of the southwestern front withdrew to a line along the Donets River between Belgorod and Khar'kov. The southern front was also pushed eastward

---

31. Maurice Hindus, *Hitler Cannot Conquer Russia* (New York, 1942), p. 19. Hindus recommends a variant of Bukharin's "revolutionary war" as a strategy of resistance—a desperate expedient that might well have been considered had Moscow fallen.

32. The circumstances of Kirponos's death are related in "O gibeli komanduiushchego iugo-zapadnogo fronta, Geroia Sovetskogo Soiuza, general-polkovnika M. P. Kirponosa," *Izvestiia TsK KPSS* 11 (1990): 192–94.

to Rostov on the Don, opening the doorway to the Crimea. The Black Sea fleet evacuated Odessa in mid-October and drew back to Sebastopol, already under siege by General Erich von Manstein's First Panzer Group. On 24 October, Khar'kov, the Soviet Union's fourth-largest city, was surrendered. Soviet defenses in the Ukraine had crumbled, and German armies were poised to enter the industrial heartland of the Donbas.

Amidst this morass of defeat the Soviets prepared for the defense of their capital. At the end of September a new German offensive struck along the Moscow axis, with familiar results. Guderian's armor turned the left flank of Eremenko's Briansk front and entered Orel on 3 October. Breakthroughs were achieved north and south of the Moscow-Smolensk highway and a ring closed at Viaz'ma, encircling another five Soviet armies, the entirety of General Ivan Konev's western front. These were unprecedented calamities, and they brought the fall of Moscow well into the range of possibility.

Stalin now summoned an emergency session of the GKO, which elected to stabilize a rebuilt western front at the hastily established "Mozhaisk line" some sixty kilometers to the west of the capital. On 10 October a newly constituted Moscow reserve front was placed under the direct command of Zhukov. After Richard Sorge in Tokyo reported an "irrevocable" Japanese decision not to enter the conflict, the decision was made to draw approximately half of the twenty divisions attached to the far eastern armies back to the west. The Moscow Defense Zone was also created, pulling hundreds of thousands of civilians into the work of digging trenches and assembling antitank barriers. By 12 October, with the city under air attack, the evacuation of government offices to the provincial city of Kuibyshev on the Volga began. Within days, fed by rumor, a full-scale panic gripped the city, accompanied by mass flight and looting. The worse disorders were calmed by a radio message on 17 October announcing that Stalin was remaining in the Kremlin and that Moscow would be defended "to the last drop of blood."[33] Two days later martial law was imposed. The celebrated (though perhaps apocryphal) words of a certain company commander Klochkov now became the substance of security policy for the entire Soviet state: "Russia is large, but for us there is no retreat beyond Moscow."[34]

The outcome of the battle of Moscow was not preordained. In their drive on the capital the Germans threatened on several occasions to

33. *Kommunisticheskaia partiia v Velikoi Otechestvennoi voine (iiun' 1941 g.–1945 g.). Dokumenty i materialy* (Moscow, 1970), pp. 59 and 153. The document in this collection, typical for materials edited after Khrushchev's revelations, eliminates the personal references to Stalin.

34. Cited in *IVOVSS*, 2:261.

break through into the Soviet rear. Politruk Klochkov to the contrary, a transferal of the capital to Kuibyshev and pursuit of the war under considerably less auspicious circumstances was a real possibility. The German forces bearing in upon the city were exhausted after months of nearly unbroken campaigning. But Soviet forces were also severely reduced, with more than 3 million prisoners in German hands and the Red Army's manpower, having fallen from 4.7 million to 2.3 million between June and October, at its lowest ebb in the entire war. In October and November the Germans stormed through the Mozhaisk line and pushed to the outskirts of Moscow. There was high drama in Stalin's appearance on the Lenin Mausoleum in snow-covered Red Square on 7 November for the annual Revolution Day parade, under glowering skies, with gunfire audible in the distance, addressing troops about to depart for the front. In his brief remarks Stalin emphasized that the Red Army had absorbed Hitler's worst blow and survived; that the Soviet peoples were waging a "war of liberation, a just war" together with powerful allies; and that within "little more than a year" (*mozhet byt' godik*) the Soviet Union's superior material resources would decide the issue in its favor.[35] After exaggerated references to the first Soviet Revolution Day, celebrated during the civil war at a time when the situation was "much worse" than at present, Stalin concluded with an unabashedly patriotic appeal: "May you be inspired in this war by the heroic image of our great ancestors . . . Aleksandr Nevskii, Dimitri Donskoi, Kuzma Minin, Dimitri Pozharskii, Aleksandr Suvorov, Mikhail Kutuzov! May you be blessed by the victorious banner of great Lenin! . . . Death to the German occupiers! Long live our glorious Motherland, its freedom, its independence!" In this remarkable speech Lenin shared pride of place with feudal lords, tsarist generals, and a saint of the Russian Orthodox church.

The Germans never took Moscow. During November attacks directed north and south of the city failed to achieve breakthroughs. On 1 December, in ferocious cold, Field Marshal Günther von Kluge's Twentieth Corps made a final attempt to break into the city by storm, fighting to within thirty kilometers of the Kremlin but no farther. Three days later Zhukov gave the signal for a general Soviet counteroffensive across the entire central front, throwing three fresh armies held in reserve into the battle. For the first time in the war the Wehrmacht had been stopped and pushed backward.

The Soviets had warded off the worse, though just barely. Distance, severe weather conditions, and the profligate sacrifice of Red Army soldiers, pressed time and again into unequal contests and subject to

35. Stalin, *Sochineniia*, 2 [XV]: 32–35.

frightful losses, had combined to blunt the German drive on the threshold of success. But the situation remained catastrophic. In the grip of occupation lay the Baltic states, Belorussia, much of the Ukraine, the Crimea, and a large swath of European Russia. Kiev, Khar'kov, and Odessa were lost. In December the population of blockaded Leningrad began literally to starve.[36] The occupied regions contained more than 80 million people or more than 40 percent of the Soviet population, a third of the state's industrial capacity including more than 300 armaments factories, 63 percent of coal production, 58 percent of steel production, 70 percent of pig iron reserves, 60 percent of aluminum reserves, and 47 percent of the total land under cultivation.[37] Into these regions, behind the Ostheer, came the *Einsatzgruppen* ("special teams") of the Nazi SS and Hitler's New Order. On the eve of Barbarossa, Hitler's "Commissar Order" transformed the war into an ideological crusade by specifying that communists and military commissars be summarily executed.[38] The large Jewish population of the occupied regions was systematically massacred. A slave labor regime was foisted upon the cowed local population, and tens of thousands of laborers were shipped off to work in German war industries.[39]

There was in spite of all a ray of light in the darkness. For all the damage wrought, Operation Barbarossa had failed in its larger purpose. Leningrad remained in Soviet hands even as it suffered martyrdom. Moscow had held, and the Soviet winter counteroffensive revealed how badly Hitler's attempt to destroy the Red Army had misfired. On 7 December, as German armies fell back from Moscow, the Japanese attack on Pearl Harbor brought the United States into the war. Most of all, by surviving the initial blow the Soviet Union had won time to mobilize its resources. In his Army Day address on 23 February 1942 Stalin drew the requisite conclusion.[40] The *Blitzkrieg* had failed and the element of surprise would not be decisive. Now the "permanent operating factors" of war were left to determine the outcome. Stalin identified five: the strength of

36. The story of the Leningrad blockade is powerfully related in the popular history by Harrison Salisbury, *The 900 Days: The Siege of Leningrad* (New York, 1969).

37. The statistics are cited from *IVOVSS*, 2:148; Erickson, *The Road to Stalingrad*, p. 223; Ia. E. Chadaev, *Ekonomika SSSR v period Velikoi Otechestvennoi voiny 1941–1945 gg.* (Moscow, 1965), p. 65. According to Samsonov, *Sovetskii Soiuz*, p. 272, the Soviet tractor park was also reduced to 56 percent of its 1940 level.

38. See Helmut Krausnick, "Kommissarbefehl und 'Gerichtsbarkeitserlass Barbarossa' in neuer Sicht," *Vierteljahrsheft für Zeitgeschichte* 4 (1979): 682–738; Hans-Adolf Jacobsen, "Kommissarbefehl und Massenexekutionen sowjetischer Kriegsgefangener," in Hans Bucheim et al., eds., *Anatomie des SS-Staates*, vol. 2 (Olten, 1965), pp. 163–97.

39. The best study of German occupation policy remains Alexander Dallin, *German Rule in Russia 1941–1945: A Study of Occupation Policies*, 2d ed. (Boulder, Colo., 1981).

40. Stalin, *Sochineniia*, 2 [XV]: 39.

the rear, the morale of the army, the quality and quantity of divisions, armament, and the organizing ability of command personnel. Much would be made of these "permanent factors" at a later date, though in and of themselves they were unremarkable. In the context of February 1942 they pointed confidently to the Soviet Union's ability to prevail in a protracted war of attrition.

Flushed by his first measurable success, Stalin concocted plans for a winter campaign designed to drive the Germans from Soviet soil. The grandiose undertaking, approved over the opposition of key advisors such as Zhukov and Nikolai Voznesenskii, proved to be overambitious. Operations opened along a broad front on 7 January and scored some modest local successes, but no decisive strategic breakthrough. By March they had dissolved into a series of partial offensives that drained Soviet strength to no purpose. Leningrad remained blockaded, and Hitler's Army Group Center entrenched in the Rzhev-Viaz'ma-Smolensk bulge, within striking range of Moscow.

By refusing to concentrate his resources along a single axis, Stalin had underestimated the enemy. Moreover, in the Red Army's first attempt to conduct a large-scale strategic offensive manifold weaknesses were revealed that put the lie to hopes for a quick victory. Most telling was a chronic shortage of mechanized and armored formations. During the Moscow counteroffensive experiments with mobile group formations were attempted, but the results were disappointing. Tactics also left much to be desired; commanders continued to prefer battering away with costly frontal assaults. Willful interference with the work of the Stavka by political authorities led to major disasters, notably the encirclement and destruction of General Andrei Vlasov's Second Shock Army on the Volkhov front during March.[41] Though it was already in the process of rebuilding, the war industry was not yet in a position to satisfy the voracious appetite of a major offensive. In sum, the results were chastening. Much of the optimism accumulated after the stand at Moscow was dissipated, the Soviets suffered disproportionate losses, and it was made clear that the war was far from over.

As operations slogged to a halt with the arrival of the spring thaw, Hitler turned to plans for a new summer offensive. The Wehrmacht had

41. In German captivity Vlasov would earn notoriety as the commander of a German-sponsored "Russian Liberation Army." He has been portrayed by his supporters as an idealistic partisan of democratic principles. See Sven Steenburg [pseud.], *Vlasov* (New York, 1970), pp. 29–67; Wilfried Strik-Strikfeldt, *Against Hitler and Stalin: Memoir of the Russian Liberation Movement 1941–1945* (New York, 1973), pp. 69–81. A more analytical assessment is provided by Catherine Andreyev, *Vlasov and the Russian Liberation Movement: Soviet Realities and Emigre Theories* (Cambridge, 1987). Vlasov was returned to the Soviet authorities in 1945 and executed in 1946.

been battered, and an onslaught along the entire front in the image of Barbarossa was now beyond its power. Stalin expected a renewed drive against Moscow, but Hitler chose to strike southward, toward the lower Volga, the Caucasus, and the oil reserves of the Caspian Sea. Once again a misreading of German intentions set the stage for defeat.

The German offensive was preceded by new calamities. During May a local offensive launched by Timoshenko's southwest front against Khar'kov shattered upon General Friedrich von Paulus's Sixth Army. A German clearing operation in the Crimea backed Soviet defenders onto the narrow Kerch peninsula, where evacuation procedures broke down and a wild slaughter of the disorganized remnants of twenty-one Soviet divisions ensued. Sebastopol was now isolated, and in June the historic fortress was literally bombarded into rubble by German heavy artillery. The succession of defeats depleted and disorganized Soviet forces in the south. When on 28 June Operation Blue was unleashed by Army Group South (now subdivided into Groups A and B) in the Kursk-Voronezh sector, another massive breakthrough was achieved.

The Germans intended to drive south to the Caucasus mountain passes and east to the Volga at Stalingrad (Volgograd), and during July and August they made stunning progress. After the initial breakthrough Soviet armies fell back to the Don south of Voronezh, where a new Voronezh front was created under General Nikolai Vatutin, but farther south defenses in the region of the Don bend began to crumble. By the last week in July the Germans had reached the Don north and south of the bend, and Rostov on the Don had fallen amidst scenes of panic. Group A now began to fan out into the Kuban while Group B, led by Paulus's Sixth Army and assisted by Hoth's Fourth Panzer Army, pressed beyond the Don bend toward Stalingrad. By 23 August, Paulus's troops had broken through to the Volga north of the city.

After the fall of Rostov the Soviets pulled out all stops in an effort to halt the tidal wave that once again threatened to sweep them away. On 28 July Stalin issued his famous order number 277, categorically forbidding retreat or surrender. Ni shagu nazad ("not one step backward") now became the army's motto.[42] Calls for "ruthless" discipline apparently led to a wave of abuses such that on 9 August the army newspaper Krasnaia zvezda (Red Star) felt compelled to editorialize on behalf of restraint. But the Soviets were fighting with their backs to the Volga, from whose steep western embankment one could look out onto the steppe of

---

42. Stalin's order reads, "It is time to finish with retreat. Not one step backward! This must now become our main slogan. We must stubbornly defend to the last drop of blood every position, every meter of Soviet territory, cling to every patch of Soviet earth and hold it to the limit of possibility." Cited in *IVOVSS*, 2:430.

central Asia, at the easternmost boundary of the Russian heartland. The limits of retreat had indeed been reached.

The decision to stand and fight at Stalingrad was never in doubt. The importance of this booming industrial city, stretching for over fifty kilometers along the right bank of the Volga, was not merely symbolic. As it was the key to the lower Volga, its capture would place Soviet armies fighting in the Caucasus in an impossible position and expose Moscow from the south and rear. Soviet resolve was indicated by the dispatching on 26 August of Zhukov, recently appointed deputy supreme commander, as Stavka representative to the Stalingrad front. At this point Soviet lines had shrunk within the city limits, where embattled soldiers fought with their backs to the river along a twenty-kilometer "front" nowhere deeper than 2,000 meters. Within the city center the Sixty-second Army, commanded after 12 September by General Vasilii Chuikov, contested control of every street corner, wall, and ravine. In these dire circumstances, the product of defeat and accident rather than design, the Stavka began to develop a larger strategic concept for what had become the battle of Stalingrad.

The Soviet plan, which had emerged by mid-September, called for drawing Paulus into a protracted battle for the city (now reduced to rubble by constant bombardment) while simultaneously massing reserves for a counteroffensive against the weakly defended German flanks. The key to success would be Chuikov's ability to hold Stalingrad while the blow was being prepared. Through September and October nightmarish fighting swept across the ruined city. These battles, waged night and day, in a howling inferno of fire and smoke, without quarter or room for retreat, have given Stalingrad its unique and legendary stature, and made it an enduring symbol of Soviet resistance. On 14 October, Paulus opened what he hoped would be a decisive drive to the Volga. German units succeeded in overrunning the factory district in the north of the city and even seized a 2,000-meter swath of the river shore, thus splitting Chuikov's command in two. But the fighting took a brutal toll, and a breakthrough in strength proved to be beyond the Germans' power.

The Soviet counteroffensive, code-named Uranus, was meanwhile being assembled at bridgeheads on the Don at Kletskaia and Serafimovich in the north, and at the Beketovka "bell" at the great bend of the Volga to the south. In preparing for the strike, the Stavka placed an unprecedented emphasis upon the role of armored spearheads freed from an infantry support role, building new, better equipped mobile groups and tank corps (the forerunners of tank armies). On 19 and 20 November the offensive commenced, and by 23 November the two prongs of the pincers had joined at Sovetskaia, southwest of Kalach in Paulus's deep rear. Fourteen infantry divisions, three motorized and three panzer divisions, a quarter million of the Reich's best soldiers were caught in the Stalingrad *Kessel* ("cauldron"). A German attempt to break through to Paulus was abandoned in mid-December, as a Soviet counterstrike toward Rostov threatened to cut off Group A in the Caucasus. Through superior generalship the German commander Manstein was able to pull Army Group South intact into the Donbas, but only at the price of sacrificing the Sixth Army. On 10 January 1943 operation *Koltso* ("Ring") was launched against the Stalingrad garrison. By 31 January, his once mighty army reduced to a pitiful mob, Paulus, now a field marshal by Hitler's personal appointment, elected to surrender.

It is customary to speak of Stalingrad as a turning point in the war on the eastern front. This it was, and Stalin was correct to note in his Army Day address of 23 February 1943 that even though a "cruel struggle" still lay ahead, the "correlation of forces" had fundamentally altered to Soviet advantage.[43] The battle represented a turning point in another, more enduring sense as well. "If the battle of Poltava in 1709 turned Russia into a European power," writes John Erickson, "then Stalingrad set the Soviet Union on the road to being a world power."[44] After Stalingrad, it was clear that whatever the cost, the Soviet Union would win its war for survival. In the midst of fearsome battles the consequences of its triumph could already dimly be discerned.

Soviet Society at War

The victory at Stalingrad unveiled a new face of Soviet power. The Soviet counteroffensive was propelled by a clear material superiority that would continue to grow in the future. On 9 November, with the battle of Stalingrad at its height, large-scale Allied landings began in north Africa. This was not the "second front in Europe" that had become an insistent Soviet demand, and the Allies' task, pitted against a total of four German and eleven Italian divisions, was not comparable with what was transpiring on the eastern front. But the grand coalition had become a fighting alliance. Meanwhile, the Romanian and Italian divisions holding the flanks at Stalingrad demonstrated their unreliability by melting away under pressure. Il'ia Erenburg's earlier reference to them as "slave

---

43. Stalin, *Sochineniia*, 2 [XV]: 89 and 92–93.
44. Erickson, *The Road to Stalingrad*, p. 431.

armies" now seemed prophetic.[45] By 1943, despite inevitable frictions, a relatively harmonious relationship had emerged between Stalin, the Stavka, and the front commands. Stalin himself, for all his failings, had grown into a reasonably competent wartime leader.[46] In contrast, the German command was visibly strained and suffered from the increasingly irrational interventions of its Führer. In every relevant category— the war economy, morale, alliance support, quality of leadership—a Soviet advantage had been established.

The full impact of the war upon Soviet life and society could now begin to be measured. The nation was passing through an immense experience, searing and complex in its implications, whose effects upon Soviet perception can scarcely be overestimated. Though the institutional and ideological context of Stalinism proved a certain continuity, the war was also altering Soviet attitudes and priorities in significant ways.

The main institutional beneficiary of the Stalingrad victory was the Red Army. A trend toward more conventional organization, long evident in the development of the RKKA, now came to fruition. In efforts to bolster morale following the loss of Rostov, an entire series of new decorations for commanders only was introduced, significantly named for heroes of Russia's national past. On 9 October 1942, for the third time since 1917 and now irrevocably, the principle of unitary command was

45. Il'ya Erenburg and Konstantin Simonov, *In One Newspaper: A Chronicle of Unforgettable Years* (New York, 1985), pp. 51–53. This is a translation of Erenburg's article "Coalition of Freedom," which originally appeared on 20 July 1941.

46. Until his death, the image of Stalin as "military genius" was unchallengeable. In his 1956 secret speech Khrushchev provided a different picture—that of a military primitive who plotted operations "on a globe" and whose blunders led millions of Red Army soldiers to needless deaths. In the voluminous Soviet memoir literature a basically positive portrait emerges: that of a tyrannical but dedicated leader who worked hard to master the details of military operations, who carefully absorbed advice from subordinates, and whose judgment improved as the war went on. For a good discussion based upon this literature see Timothy J. Colton, *Commissars, Commanders, and Civilian Authority: The Structure of Soviet Military Politics* (Cambridge, Mass., 1979), pp. 157–65. Colton discerns a center-periphery split in Soviet perception, with commanders who collaborated with Stalin within the Stavka presenting a more positive image, and front commanders and political officers such as Khrushchev generally critical. Volkogonov, *Triumf i tragediia*, 2, part 1: 265–88, points out that the Soviet memoir literature has been distorted by censorship and offers a devastating portrait of Stalin's lack of technical military competence but nonetheless praises his willingness to defer to the council of the General Staff. Previously unpublished portions of Zhukov's memoirs make certain criticisms of Stalin's style of work and brutality but include the observation, "in my thinking about Stalin's personality the positive characteristics prevail over the negative sides." "Marshal pishet knigu: Vospominaniia o G. K. Zhukove," *Ogonek* 16 (April 1988): 13–14, and 18 (April 1988): 19. S. M. Spirin, "Stalin i voina," *Voprosy istorii KPSS* 5 (1990): 90–105, confirms Stalin's lack of technical competence and his total disregard for the human costs of victory but also notes his ability to listen and to learn.

restored. The introduction in January 1943 of gold-braid epaulets, a symbol once associated with the pomp of the Imperial Army, was a clear manifestation of new trends. In January, Stalin was appointed marshal, and a wave of promotions among the high command followed. By the summer of 1943 conventional ranks had been established from corporal through lieutenant colonel, formal rank insignia restored (in place of the Red Army tradition of geometrical collar badges), and the politically charged term "officer" (ofitser) brought back into usage. Later in 1943 a new officers' code of manners was promulgated that placed unprecedented emphasis upon protocol and the bearing attendant upon rank. The "smartening up" of appearances, the retirement of civil war relics and incompetents, the effacement of prestigious but ineffective leaders such as Voroshilov and Budennyi, the rapid promotion of young officers of proven merit, the cultivation of a more pronounced caste status for the Soviet officer—these developments foreshadowed a more dynamic institutional role for the armed forces in society.

The Red Army was also learning how to fight. During 1942 Soviet rifle divisions were reorganized and packed with increased firepower. Order number 325 of 16 October 1942 described a new, more dynamic role for mechanized formations, and after Stalingrad five tank armies were created. A long-range bomber force was constructed, followed by the establishment of air armies as front components and an independent air corp as a Stavka reserve. Improved supply, smaller and more potent divisions, a revised conception of the role of armor, the centralized allocation of air assets, an unparalleled artillery reorganized since 1941 under the capable direction of Marshal Nikolai Voronov, these achievements made the Red Army a true rival to (and in some ways a carbon copy of) the Wehrmacht.[47]

Achievements on the home front were equally prodigious. Exploiting to the full the potential for mobilization inherent in a planned economy, military production soared despite a dramatic fall-off in the number of workers available and the disruption caused by relocation.[48] The Soviet labor force, composed predominantly of women in the agricultural sector and well over 50 percent female in industry, assumed massive sacrifices to make these accomplishments possible. Workers in war-related industries were placed under paramilitary disciplinary regimes. Holidays were suspended, overtime was made compulsory, and forced labor, in

47. The combat-ready manpower of the Red Army remained relatively constant after 1943. More and better equipment and more capable leadership was the key to improved performance. IVOVSS, 5:467.

48. See Nove, An Economic History of the U.S.S.R., pp. 268–86; Samsonov, Sovetskii Soiuz, pp. 242–80 and 526–70. Mark Harrison, Soviet Planning in Peace and War (Cambridge, 1986), pp. 222–45, perceives the creation of a war economy to be a key to the subsequent evolution of the national economy as a whole.

the form of "mobilizations," was nearly institutionalized. Living conditions in the new industrial centers were poor, marked by overcrowding, rationing, and constant shortages. On collective and state farms the demands of the front cut deeply into what were already depressed living standards, with the recompense for a labor day in some cases reduced to one-third of the 1940 level.[49]

Russian nationalism was the key to maintaining civilian morale, though in official propaganda it was primarily *Soviet* patriotism that was touted. The venerable Soviet president Mikhail Kalinin gave the theme emotive definition in July 1941: "Soviet patriotism expresses itself now in the fact that . . . the whole of the Soviet people, the whole of Soviet society now placed in danger, becomes for the citizens of our country extremely dear, beloved, near, and the struggle for our Motherland, in all its complexity, becomes a feeling which directs all our thoughts and actions."[50] Such sentiments were often quite sincere, but in practice some surprising developments occurred. The creation during 1942 of an All-Slav Committee under General Aleksandr Gondorov seemed to revive a century-old pan-Slavic ideal.[51] Even more incongruous was a public reconciliation between the atheistic Stalin regime and the Russian Orthodox church. In September 1943, in exchange for its support for the war effort, the church was permitted to elect a patriarch of Moscow and reestablish a Holy Synod, institutions that had not existed since the time of Peter the Great. Antireligious propaganda was halted, and on occasion religious themes found their way into the state-controlled media. In Mark Donskoi's popular film *The Rainbow*, a partisan headquarters is adorned by a *krasnyi ugolok* (icon corner), before which fighters for Soviet power make the sign of the cross. No chaplains were ever attached to the Red Army, but religious conviction was strong among peasant conscripts, and an image of tolerance in matters of faith contributed to the populist appeal that underlay wartime patriotism.

Another manifestation of the national theme was the disbanding of the Comintern on 15 May 1943.[52] This step was intended as a gesture toward the Allies, from whom Stalin still hoped to extract a commitment

---

49. Samsonov, *Sovetskii Soiuz*, p. 278.

50. *Kommunisticheskaia partiia v Velikoi Otechestvennoi voine*, p. 171. See also Erenburg's article "On Patriotism" in Erenburg and Simonov, *In One Newspaper*, pp. 171–78. "Soviet patriotism," the author notes, "is a natural continuation of Russian patriotism" (p. 174).

51. Described in G. D. Komkov, "Politicheskaia propaganda i agitatsiia v gody Velikoi Otechestvennoi voiny," *Istoriia SSSR* 4 (1972): 102–4.

52. Degras, *The Communist International*, 3: 476–81. Though technically approved after "consultations" with affiliates, the Comintern's dissolution in fact represented a unilateral Soviet decision. Annie Kriegel, "La dissolution du 'Komintern'," *Revue d'histoire de la deuxième guerre mondiale* 68 (1967): 33–43.

to a second front in 1943, but it also underlined the "USSR first" ethic that the leadership now unabashedly embraced. After the German attack upon the Soviet Union the Comintern once again shifted its line to call for a "national front" of opposition to fascism.[53] By 1943 communist-led resistance movements were making a real contribution in the battle against Hitler's "new order" in Europe, but as an institution the Comintern had been totally effaced. The loss of the Comintern meant least of all to Stalin, who on occasion referred to the organization as the "little shop" (*lavochka*). It came as a slap in the face to idealistic communist resistance fighters, but this was not where the focus of Soviet attention lay. Lenin's vision of a unified international communist movement had ended ignominiously. To reiterate the point, in June 1943 a decision was made to select a new Soviet national anthem, approved in 1944 with a text that praised Stalin by name, to replace the hallowed "Internationale."

The nationalist wave of the war years had its dark sides. At its worst "Soviet patriotism" became vulgar, strident, and xenophobic. Wartime agitation, particularly the immensely popular columns of Erenburg, contained a distinct anti-German hate theme, a populist appeal that was left to conflict with the official line identifying "fascism" as the enemy.[54] During and after the war entire national communities accused of collaborating with the occupation or sympathizing with the enemy, including the Volga Germans, the Crimean Tatars, and a number of small Caucasian tribes (the Chechens, Ingushi, Karachai, Balkars, and Kalmyks) were subject to collective reprisals in the form of internal deportation.[55] Repatriated Red Army soldiers, escaped or liberated from captivity, fell into the hands of the NKVD to be purged of exposure to "bourgeois influences" by incarceration in labor camps. Such injustices, often scarcely commented upon at the time, were an integral part of Stalin's conduct of the war.

Many who lived through the war years have testified to the existence of a positive spirit of collective endeavor in a just cause, strikingly different from the paranoid atmosphere of the 1930s. The great, unspoken, and perhaps naive hope was that innovation in social policy would continue, and a better, more accommodating Soviet regime emerge from the

---

53. See E. Fisher, "Ot narodnogo fronta k obshche natsional'nomu frontu," *Kommunisticheskii internatsional* 8–9 (1942): 26–30.

54. Described in Werth, *Russia at War*, pp. 267–68, 385–88, and 390–92.

55. Robert Conquest, *The Soviet Deportation of Nationalities* (New York, 1960); Alexander Nekrich, *The Punished Peoples* (New York, 1978). In his secret speech Khrushchev raised the grotesque possibility that Stalin would have deported the Ukrainians as well, had they not been so numerous! "O kul'te lichnosti," p. 152.

great national trial.[56] These hopes hinged upon domestic liberalization, but they also included the prospect of a "Big Three peace" and a cooperative postwar international order built upon the wartime alliance that would bring an end to Soviet isolation.

Soviet relations with the United States and Great Britain during the first two years of war remained stable. Hitler was the common enemy, and his defeat was rightfully considered to be a first priority. In September 1941 the Soviets gave qualified assent to the general democratic principles of the Atlantic Charter, and the western democracies embraced the USSR and its leader "Uncle Joe" as a legitimate ally.[57] Communication among the Big Three was brisk, reflected by an active diplomatic correspondence and a succession of visits and consultations. Material aid to the Soviet war effort, particularly American Lend-Lease, which was substantially increased during 1943, made a real contribution.[58] After the north African landings and the leap to Sicily and southern Italy in July 1943, the Allies were also battling fascist armies in Europe. While the war continued, the grand coalition was firmly rooted, and a flurry of concern in the spring of 1943 over suspected Soviet plans for a separate peace were quite overblown. Stalin was not above exploiting such concerns as a means to pressure the Allies, but in its total war with Germany the USSR had not allowed itself room for disagreement. In his 1943 May Day address Stalin attempted to scotch such rumors, describing German peace feelers as the product of desperation and pledging to fight "to complete destruction of Hitler's armies and the unconditional surrender of Germany."[59]

Problems nonetheless intruded upon the Big Three relationship and served to reveal its limits. Gratitude for material assistance was tempered

56. According to Il'ya Erenburg, *The War* (London, 1964), pp. 132–33, the impression was consciously encouraged in official propaganda.

57. Ralph B. Levering, *American Opinion and the Russian Alliance* (Chapel Hill, N.C., 1976), pp. 97–145, describes the American effort to remake the image of its formerly maligned ally.

58. The terms of the formal agreement are provided in *Kommunisticheskaia partiia v Velikoi Otechestvennoi voine*, pp. 447–49. Soviet statistics generated immediately after the war refer to British and U.S. aid equivalent to 4% of Soviet industrial production—a not insignificant amount. N. Voznesenskii, *Voennaia ekonomika SSSR v period Otechestvennoi voiny* (Moscow, 1948), p. 74. See also George C. Herring, Jr., *Aid to Russia* (New York, 1973).

59. Stalin, *Sochineniia*, 2 [XV]: 98. Accounts of these contacts, which generally give credence to the possibility of a separate peace, are provided by Vojtech Mastny, *Russia's Road to the Cold War: Diplomacy, Warfare, and the Politics of Communism, 1941–1945* (New York, 1979), pp. 73–85; H. W. Koch, "The Spectre of a Separate Peace in the East: Russo-German 'Peace Feelers' 1942–1944," *Journal of Contemporary History* 3 (1975): 531–49. For a somewhat contrasting account see Alexander Fischer, *Sowjetische Deutschlandpolitik im Zweiten Weltkrieg 1941–1945* (Stuttgart, 1975), pp. 39–45.

in Moscow by the realization that it was the Soviet peoples who were bearing the brunt of the fighting. The really telling issue here was that of the second front. In June 1943, when Stalin was informed that a cross-channel invasion was once again being postponed, his measured reply revealed depths of resentment. The decision, he claimed, "leaves the Soviet Army, which is fighting not only for its country, but also for its allies, to do the job alone, almost single-handed."[60] The "disheartentingly negative impression" that Allied caution was said to create would prove to be enduring.

Another point of contention concerned the status of Poland's government in exile, set up in London under General Wladyslaw Sikorski in September 1939 and accorded diplomatic recognition by the Soviets on 30 July 1941. In December 1941 Sikorski visited Moscow, but difficulties already plagued the relationship. Differences were allowed to hang fire with the Soviets fighting with their backs to the wall, but after Stalingrad a new, more assertive Soviet Polish policy began to emerge. As originally outlined in *Pravda* on 20 February 1943, it rested upon two fundamental demands: (1) a Polish-Soviet frontier roughly equivalent to the "Curzon line" of 1919, that is, defining a Poland shrunk westward to areas where the Polish population was demographically dominant, and (2) the establishment of a "friendly" government in liberated Warsaw.[61] These demands brought the Kremlin into direct conflict with Poland's London government, and the establishment of a pro-Soviet Union of Polish Patriots in Moscow during February 1943 made it clear from what source "friendly" forces were likely to emerge.

The issue was complicated in April 1943 when Berlin announced that a mass grave of Polish officers had been uncovered at Katyn Forest in Belorussia, presumably the result of a mass execution perpetrated by the Soviet authorities during the duration of the Nazi-Soviet pact. TASS abruptly denied the allegation, which nonetheless gave rise to an international outcry, vocally supported by the London Poles.[62] The murder of

60. *Perepiska predsedatelia Soveta Ministrov SSSR s prezidentami SShA i prem'er-ministrami Velikobritanii vo vremia Velikoi Otechestvennoi voiny 1941–1945 gg.*, 2 vols. (Moscow, 1976), 1: 167; for a work that fairly represents Soviet resentment, V. M. Kulish, *Istoriia vtorogo fronta* (Moscow, 1971).

61. Aleksandr Korneichuk, "Vossoedinenie ukrainskogo naroda v nedrakh svoego gosudarstva," *Pravda*, 20 Feb. 1943, p. 2. Korneichuk's article, which originally appeared in the Ukrainian language *Radians'ka Ukraina* ("The Workers' Ukraine") on 19 Feb., was in essence an argument for the reunification of the Ukrainian peoples within the Soviet federation. It posed a strong case for the Soviet absorption of L'vov.

62. See J. K. Zawedny, *Death in the Forest* (South Bend, Ind., 1962), pp. 77–95; A. Kwiatkowski-Viatteu, *1940–1943, Katyn, l'armée polonaise assassinée* (Brussels, 1982); Allen Paul, *Katyń: The Untold Story of Stalin's Polish Massacre* (New York, 1991).

the Polish officers was an unpardonable atrocity, and the Soviets' disguised guilt probably encouraged them to assume an uncompromising hard line. On 27 August the Soviet government used the incident as a pretext for suspending relations with the London government, now headed by Stanislaw Mikolajczyk following Silorski's death in a plane crash one month earlier. Moscow's preference for a unilateral resolution of the Polish problem was already undisguised.

With eyes now beginning to turn to the shape of postwar Europe, the Polish question loomed as a major irritant to Big Three harmony. For the Soviets, however, the issue brooked no compromise. The Nazi invasion had set off, in the main, from Polish territory. That the Soviet Union would not allow itself to be so exposed in the future was self-evident. Nor was an independent, nonantagonistic, but western-oriented Poland considered an acceptable alternative. During the 1920s and 1930s Poland's fifty divisions and close ties to the western powers represented a constant threat. The choice between "bridge or barrier" that Trotsky invoked in 1923 had been made, and Poland was transformed into the keystone of a western-sponsored *cordon sanitaire*. For all the attention devoted to the Polish question during and after the war, the Soviet position remained remarkably consistent. Only a "friendly" government closely bound to Moscow would conform to minimal Soviet requirements.

Both Soviet and western historians, operating under the spell of the Cold War, have tended to dwell upon the frictions that plagued the grand alliance from the outset.[63] What was most striking during 1942 and 1943, however, was the extent of cooperation. Stalin made an effort to swallow his disappointment over the postponement of the second front and strove to mollify his allies. Both London and Washington urged compromise upon the London Poles and attempted to prevent the Polish question from becoming an impediment to collaboration. The Axis was not yet beaten, and the need for positive relations was strongly perceived on both sides. In the meantime, the wartime alliance

---

In April 1990 a joint Polish-Soviet historical commission resolved the question of responsibility by acknowledging that the officers had been executed by Beria's NKVD in the spring of 1940. See V. S. Parsadanova, "K istorii katynskogo dela," *Novaia i noveishaia istoriia* 3 (1990): 19–36, where it is concluded that more than 14,000 officers were executed.

63. Compare Robert Beizell, *The Uneasy Alliance: America, Britain, and Russia, 1941–1943* (New York, 1972), pp. 3–149; V. L. Israelian, *Diplomaticheskaia istoriia Velikoi Otechestvennoi voiny 1941–1945 gg.* (Moscow, 1959), pp. 3–175; William Taubman, *Stalin's American Policy: From Entente to Detente to Cold War* (New York, 1982), pp. 31–72.

had become a kind of collective security system in a miniature, held together by a sufficient amount of good-will to make ongoing cooperation possible.[64]

The Tigers Burn

After Stalingrad, Hitler's total defeat became the first goal of Soviet policy. The Soviet Union had been ravaged and humiliated by German armies, and the desire to turn the tables, to wreak vengeance, and to take Berlin where Hitler had failed to take Moscow were consuming motives. Independent of plans for a postwar European order, the long march westward across the smoking ruins of the occupied territories, past the cowed capitals of eastern Europe, and into the German Reich took on trappings of a crusade.

In January 1943, inspired by the destruction of Paulus's army, Stalin repeated his mistake of one year earlier by calling for an overambitious winter counteroffensive. Once again the operation's strategic goals were not achieved, and what gains were accumulated came at high cost. In the north a twelve-kilometer-wide corridor was cut through to Leningrad south of Lake Ladoga, at last bringing substantial relief to the Soviet Union's second city, where hundreds of thousands of Leningraders had died of starvation as a result of the blockade. On the Moscow axis the Germans were pushed out of their threatening positions in the Rzhev-Viaz'ma-Smolensk and Demiansk salients. In the south Soviet forces pushed across the Donbas and briefly seized Khar'kov, only to be driven back to the Donets by a German counteroffensive led by Manstein's Fourth Panzer Army. The German front remained intact, however, now running in an almost direct line from the Gulf of Finland to the Sea of Azov, with the exception of a large salient protruding westward around the city of Kursk.

March thaws brought a halt to the fighting and initiated the longest pause in the entire course of the war. The Germans used the time to prepare their third summer offensive, codenamed Citadel. Plans called for simultaneous attacks against the northern and southern faces of the Kursk salient, organized in classic *Blitzkrieg* fashion and led by a new generation of "Tiger" and "Ferdinand" tanks. The halcyon days of 1941 were now past, however. There would be no question of surprise; the Soviet command was well informed concerning German intentions.

---

64. It is so described by Gromyko and Ponomarev, *Istoriia vneshnei politiki SSSR*, 1: 494. "With the creation of the anti-Hitler coalition," they write, "the idea of collective repulse of aggression, which Soviet foreign policy and diplomacy had already diligently striven to achieve on the eve of the war, found practical expression."

Defensive positions were assiduously prepared under the personal supervision of Aleksandr Vasilevskii and Zhukov, and the huge Kursk salient, encompassing General Konstantin Rokossovskii's central front and Vatutin's Voronezh front, was transformed into a veritable fortress.

The battle of Kursk commenced on 5 July with a preemptive Soviet artillery barrage, followed by German offensives in the areas of Izmailova and Belgorod. The Wehrmacht was as formidable as ever, but against a well-prepared enemy with a clear superiority in equipment, no decisive breakthrough could be achieved. By 10 July the Germans had been forced onto the defensive in the north. The culmination of the battle on the southern face came on 12 July, with the German pincer still making slow progress, when a huge force of over 1,000 tanks clashed head on west and south of the village of Prokhorovka. The *Prokhorovskoe poboishche* ("great battle of Prokhorovka") was fought to a standoff, but for the Germans this did not suffice. "The Tigers are burning" came the laconic report from the front. By 15 July Operation Citadel had been brought to a halt. The Ostheer had suffered heavy, indeed irreparable, losses in men and material. For the first time the Red Army had absorbed a major German strategic offensive and asserted its superiority on the battlefield.

Soviet counterattacks followed, launched northward toward Orel and southward toward Belgorod. By August a general counteroffensive was in progress, along a front from Velikie Luki (north of Smolensk) to Taganrog. Orel was taken on 4 August and Khar'kov on 23 August, as the Soviets made effective use of their new tank armies in breakthrough operations. Hitler now opted for a strategic retreat to the so-called Ostwall (a line from Kerch, northward along the Molochnaia and Dnieper rivers, to Gomel' and Orsha), but the positions proved to be untenable. The Red Army's advance was delayed more by its own logistical shortcomings than by German resistance. In September, after a pause to regroup, Smolensk was retaken, and Soviet armies prepared to force the Dnieper. By November, Kiev was once again in Soviet hands, and the Ostwall's southern wing lay in ruins.

In its summer and winter offensives of 1943–1944 the Red Army coordinated operations with what had become significant partisan detachments in occupied territory.[65] As a measure of success, on 13 January 1944 the General Staff of the Partisan Movement was disbanded; detachments would henceforward be attached directly to individual front commands. The German occupation was crumbling, and the strategic initiative had passed permanently into the hands of the Soviet command. During the winter offensive begun in January 1944, Leningrad was

65. See Armstrong, *Soviet Partisans*, pp. 437–57 and 525–46; Bychkov, *Partizanskoe dvizhenie*, pp. 267–326.

completely deblockaded and the Crimea retaken in a reversal of the bloodbath of 1942. In the Ukraine, after the annihilation of ten German divisions in the Korsun-Shevchenkhovskii salient, the front was pushed forward to the Romanian frontier along the Prut River.

The next Soviet target became Army Group Center, an imposing force of more than fifty divisions entrenched in Belorussia where it covered the high road across Warsaw to Berlin. Revenge was an unmistakable motivation behind the Red Army's 1944 summer offensive, codenamed Bagration in honor of the Russian general mortally wounded at Borodino in 1812, and scheduled to begin on 22 June, three years to the day from the launching of Operation Barbarossa. The offensive was preceded by Operation Overlord, the long-awaited Allied landings at Normandy, and on 10 June by Soviet attacks against Finnish positions along the Karelian isthmus. On 20 June, Vyborg fell, and by August a new Finnish government headed by Field Marshal Mannerheim was suing for peace. The "correlation of forces" had shifted decisively; for the Germans there remained only a desperate attempt to stem the tide of defeat.

On 22 June, Operation Bagration went off on schedule. The offensive did not promise to be a walkover; the integrity of the Reich was now at stake, and during the summer of 1944 the Wehrmacht achieved its highest manpower totals of the entire war. The Red Army's material superiority was overwhelming, however, and it was now the Ostheer's turn to be caught unprepared; the main Soviet blow had been expected farther south.[66] The well-fortified German positions were shattered in costly and bitter fighting, a mass encirclement of five German divisions was accomplished at Bobruisk, and the Ostheer's elaborate defensive system was cracked wide open. What followed was a *raz de marée*, as Soviet armies swept through Vitebsk, Orsha, Mogilev, and into the ruins of Minsk by 3 July. The battle of Belorussia, described by Paul Carell as the "Cannae of Army Group Center," was the worst defeat ever inflicted upon German arms.[67]

The Red Army that pressed forward across the Bug into Poland in 1944 was very different from Tukhachevskii's tattered legions of 1920, but in a sense its historical destiny had come full circle. On 17 July, in a manner reminiscent of the triumphal processions of imperial Rome, the Red Army paraded 57,000 German prisoners, generals among them, through the streets of Moscow. From Karelia through the Baltic states, Poland, Romania, and into the Balkans, the Soviet war of liberation was about to become a war of vengeance and conquest. The attempt on Hitler's life at his field headquarters in East Prussia on 20 July raised

66. See Samsonov, *Sovetskii Soiuz*, p. 459.
67. Carell, *Verbrannte Erde*, p. 426.

concern in some circles that a negotiated peace might once again become an option, but such assessments misread Soviet motivation. The slogan "to slay the fascist beast in its lair," first enunciated in Stalin's 1944 May Day address, expressed a profound aspiration.[68] The desire for vengeance was visceral, though the political leverage that would result from the presence of Soviet armies in the German capital was not an insignificant consideration. What is more, the road to Berlin passed across the independent states of eastern and central Europe, now haunted by the specter of the revolution from without.

The Europe into which the Red Army prepared to advance had experienced years of Nazi misrule. Its puppet rulers and collaborationists confronted the ruin of their policies and swelling popular unrest. In the wake of Germany's defeat a political tabula rasa was bound to develop. Armed resistance movements varied in strength from region to region, but in some cases they represented a significant political force. The Soviet leadership approached this divided and complex region with caution, and without carefully defined intentions.

The thesis that ideologically motivated expansionism played a primary role in Soviet policy formation during 1944–1945 does not stand up to close examination.[69] Insofar as clearly defined war aims had come into being, security was the overriding concern. Stalin did not wish to pursue aggressive policies at the cost of undermining the grand alliance; the second front was making a real contribution to Hitler's defeat and sparing Soviet lives, and hopes had risen for attracting a U.S. loan to help rebuild the Soviet economy. Indigenous, pro-Soviet communist elements were preferred partners from the first, but the Soviet formula for interim regimes in liberated Europe was the "popular front," in which coalition governments, usually dominated by bourgeois parties, were assembled with Moscow's forbearance. For a generation Comintern theorists had looked forward to the wave of revolution that would follow a "Second Imperialist War," a perspective that Stalin now seemed to be abandoning. The very substantial Greek communist resistance, after its December 1944 rebellion against British occupation, was cast adrift in deference to London.[70] In Yugoslavia, where Josip Broz Tito's communist partisans had already established the foundation of a national government at the Bosnian town of Jajce in November 1943, Stalin was confronted with a

68. Stalin, *Sochineniia*, 2 [XV]: 147.

69. The thesis is presented by Zbigniew Brzezinski, *The Soviet Bloc: Unity and Conflict*, 3d ed. (Cambridge, Mass., 1971), pp. 22–25; Hélène Carrère d'Encausse, *Le grand frère: L'Union Soviétique et l'Europe soviétisée* (Paris, 1983), pp. 13–14.

70. Stalin's essentially disinterested relations with the Greek communist movement are described in Peter J. Stavrakis, *Moscow and Greek Communism, 1944–1949* (Ithaca, N.Y., 1989), pp. 203–15.

fait accompli that he was powerless to affect. The Soviets negotiated a treaty of friendship with the Czechoslovak government in exile of Edvard Beneš as early as December 1943. Perhaps most remarkable, the armistice with Finland of 19 September 1944 permitted the establishment of an autonomous national government. As regards the German question, the creation in Moscow during July 1943 of a National Committee for a Free Germany and an antifascist German Officer's League indicated a willingness to toy with unilateralist solutions, but Stalin was consistent in articulating his preference for a cooperative, three-power arrangement. The same priorities were applied in crafting a communist strategy for western Europe. On 6 April 1944 the powerful French Communist party agreed to enter Charles de Gaulle's conservative government in exile, making do with two minor cabinet posts and little real influence.[71] Cooperation rather than confrontation was the word of the day, and Stalin's vigorous pragmatism still made a priority of the advance toward Berlin.

Problems to come with the Red Army operating outside the confines of the USSR were signaled almost immediately. On 23 July, Lublin was taken, the first major city west of the Curzon line to be occupied by Soviet forces. Simultaneously, a procommunist Polish Committee of National Liberation (referred to as the "Lublin Committee") was installed as a de facto national government.[72] The Lublin Committee, backed by the full weight of the Red Army, was now a direct rival to Poland's London government in exile. Under these circumstances, with the Red Army bearing down upon Warsaw, the London Poles and their underground "Homeland Army" (Armija Krajowa) made the desperate decision to proceed with an armed insurrection.

The ensuing tragedy added a new chapter to the long history of Russian-Polish enmity. In the first days of August, Rokossovskii's First Belorussian Front attempted to take Warsaw by storm, only to be driven back by German armored concentrations at the Vistula. On 7 August the Homeland Army rose in Warsaw. In the following weeks the rebellion was put down by the Germans with appalling barbarity, culminating with the systematic destruction of the entire inner city. The Soviets have been accused of intentionally holding back their armies while the armed forces of their rival were annihilated, a charge for which considerable circumstantial evidence can be adduced. The Homeland Army was one of the largest and best organized antifascist resistance movements in Europe, and it stood in the way of Soviet political goals. Stalin seems

71. See Alfred Rieber, Stalin and the French Communist Party (New York, 1962), pp. 55–80.
72. Mastny, Russia's Road to the Cold War, pp. 167–82, points out that Moscow's search for "sympathetic forces" in Poland was not quite so easy as might be assumed.

particularly to have resented not being informed of plans for the up-rising and to have suspected a plot to rob the Red Army of its hard-won gains. His first reaction was to wash his hands of the undertaking which he branded a "reckless adventure" launched by "power-seeking criminals."[73] As the full extent of the disaster became clear, the Soviets began to cooperate with relief efforts, but belatedly and ineffectively. So-viet motivation was obviously less than high-principled, though in purely military terms the option of a rapidly organized drive into the city did not really exist.[74] Nor would more aggressive Soviet action have been a guarantee of success. An uprising organized by the Slovak resis-tance with considerable Soviet assistance was also crushed during Au-gust as breakthrough efforts fell short.

These events were more significant for their political implications than for their impact upon the larger course of the war. If anything, they re-inforced the conclusion that heroic popular resistance was no substitute for the brute force of the Red Army, now regrouping for the drive into Hitler's Reich. In August a renewed offensive broke across the Prut into Romania, where on 23 August, King Michael dismissed the collabora-tionist government of Ion Antonescu. Three days later Romania per-formed an about-face and declared war on Germany, undermining at a stroke Hitler's entire defensive posture in the Balkans. The Red Army en-tered Bucharest on 30 August and fanned out north and south into the Carpathian mountain passes and the Dobruja. It was now Bulgaria's turn to capitulate, as on 15 September the troops of the Third Ukrainian Front, greeted as liberators and unresisted, marched into Sofia. In a stage-managed coup d'état a freshly minted "Fatherland Front" with strong communist representation acceded to power. By late September, Soviet armies had crossed into northern Yugoslavia and linked up with Tito's victorious partisans for the liberation of Belgrade.

The road to Vienna, Prague, and Berlin led across the Hungarian plains, but passage was not to be easy. An attempt by the regency of Miklós Horthy to ward off surrender by negotiating an armistice col-lapsed in mid-October as the collaborationist Ferenc Szalasi seized power in Budapest with German connivance and prepared for a last-ditch defense. A communist-led provisional government was established under Soviet control in the provincial city of Szeged as an alternative, and dur-ing December the Provisional National Council (71 of whose 237 dele-gates were communists) was established in Debrecen. But first Budapest

---

73. Cited in Erickson, *The Road to Berlin*, p. 283.

74. For arguments to this effect see Jan M. Ciechanowski, *The Warsaw Uprising of 1944* (Cambridge, 1974), pp. 243–80, where considerable responsibility is assigned to the "political and ideological" motives of the London government; Erickson, *The Road to Ber-lin*, pp. 247–90; *IVOVSS*, 4:228–53.

had to be taken, and this proved to be one of the most difficult tasks of the war. By January the city was encircled, but fierce battles were required to reduce its determined garrison. Not until 13 February did the last organized resistance on the Buda heights come to an end.

Meanwhile the final advance along the Warsaw-Berlin axis had begun in the north. During September and October, Army Group North was forced out of the Baltic states, with its remnants pressed back onto the Courland peninsula, where they remained under siege until the end of the war. With the road to east Prussia cleared and Soviet territory entirely liberated, the Stavka was prepared to organize its decisive blow. The huge lunge forward was initiated on 12 January, prematurely in order to take pressure away from the western front, where Allied forces were tied down in the Battle of the Bulge. On 17 January the ruins of Warsaw were overrun, and German defenses along the Vistula staved in. The last line of defense for Hitler's *Festung Deutschland* ("Fortress Germany") was drawn back to the Oder, as Konev's First Ukrainian Front achieved the honor of leading the way across the Reich frontier. After another pause to regroup, during which Soviet soldiers gave atavistic vent to accumulated resentments by brutalizing the cringing local population, on 16 April attacks were pressed across the Oder and Neisse, with Konev's First Ukrainian Front and Zhukov's First Belorussian Front encouraged literally to race for the honor of taking the German capital. Desperate German resistance was no match for a decisive Soviet material advantage. U.S. and Soviet forces joined hands on 25 April at Torgau on the Elbe, with Soviet shock troops already fighting their way into the Berlin city limits. Three days later the Reichstag was taken by storm as Hitler died a suicide in the depths of his *Führerbunker*. The surrender of the shattered Berlin garrison followed on 2 May. One week later, on 7 May, in a hastily organized ceremony at Rheims, the Wehrmacht surrendered unconditionally to representatives of the Allied powers. When informed of the event, Stalin was greatly displeased and made haste to arrange for a separate capitulation, offered uniquely to Soviet authorities, on the following day in Berlin. The gesture was significant. The defeat of the Wehrmacht, Stalin wished to point out, was above all a triumph for the Soviet people and the Soviet state. And, he might have added, to the victor belonged the spoils.

The Anti-Hitler Coalition

It was the Red Army that had broken the back of Hitler's Wehrmacht, but responsibility for the shape of the postwar world did not rest with the Soviet Union alone. It depended to a considerable degree upon the ability of the Big Three to maintain the cooperation that had defined their relations during the war. From the outset, the existence of a common threat was the key to the integrity of what the Soviets have taken to calling the "Anti-Hitler Coalition." As the impending defeat of the Axis caused the perception of threat to decline, differences among the "incompatible allies" almost inevitably became more pronounced. So long as the war continued in Europe, however, Allied relations remained collegial. In 1944 and 1945 hopes for a cooperative, Big Three peace remained a part of the Soviet Union's emerging security strategy.

High-level interaction between the Big Three during the first two years of war was carried out primarily by emissaries; the era of summitry awaited a change of fortune at the fronts. By the time that the first wartime foreign ministers' conference met in Moscow 19–30 October 1943, to be followed a month later by a Big Three summit at Teheran, the Wehrmacht had essentially been defeated. Soviet armies were within 200 kilometers of the 1941 frontier, and the issue of a second front no longer seemed quite so essential. On the other hand, the Pacific war against Japan was far from having been decided. Militarily, the Soviets found themselves in a relatively strong position as efforts to plan a postwar settlement began. Stalin made it a point of honor that the summit be held on or close to Soviet territory, and he got his way. At Teheran, for the first time in its history, the Soviet Union stepped onto the world stage as a major diplomatic actor.

The Moscow foreign ministers' conference discussed Soviet proposals for a "war shortening" strategy and attempted to lay a foundation for a peace settlement.[75] In the first instance, the basic Soviet demand remained the call for the establishment of a second front in northern France, which the Allies now promised no later than the spring of 1944. In exchange, Molotov voiced a Soviet pledge to enter the Pacific war against Japan following Hitler's defeat. A four-power declaration (also approved by the Chinese nationalist government) called for the unconditional surrender of the Axis powers, and a joint communiqué specified that "the very first goal was to hasten the end of the war."[76]

75. Accounts of the Moscow and Teheran conferences are provided by Mastny, *Russia's Road to the Cold War*, pp. 103–33; William H. McNeill, *America, Britain and Russia: Their Cooperation and Conflict, 1941–1946* (London, 1953), pp. 328–37 and 340–68; John W. Wheeler-Bennett and Anthony Nicholls, *The Semblance of Peace* (New York, 1972), pp. 103–21 and 143–67; Israelian, *Diplomaticheskaia istoriia*, pp. 176–93. The Soviet protocols of the sessions and official documents are given in *Tegeran, Ialta, Potsdam: Sbornik dokumentov*, 2d ed. (Moscow, 1970), pp. 31–100.

76. *Sovetskii Soiuz na mezhdunarodnykh konferentsiiakh perioda Velikoi Otechestvennoi voiny 1941–1945 gg. Sbornik dokumentov*, 2 vols. (Moscow, 1976), 1:346–48.

The most important step toward postwar cooperation was the creation of the European Advisory Commission with its seat in London to manage Germany's capitulation. The collapse of the Mussolini regime during July 1943 had already posed the issue of dealing with a defeated fascist power, and the Moscow Conference approved a "Declaration on Italy" calling for the establishment of a democratic successor regime. Arrangements were to be enforced by the Italian Consultative Committee, including representatives of the Big Three plus France, Greece, and Yugoslavia. Other joint statements established the goal of a "free and independent" Austrian state and demanded retribution for German war crimes. Not all was sweetness and light, however. The Polish issue was sidestepped, but it remained a point of contention. The Italian Consultative Committee, established to placate Moscow's concern over its lack of influence, would never function effectively. Instead, Italy became a prototype for the principle that "whoever occupies a territory imposes on it his own social system," a prototype that the Soviets would recall one year later in Romania, Bulgaria, and Hungary.[77] The German question also provoked discord, though for the time being it remained latent. More significant than the inevitable disagreements, however, was the commitment to collaboration that inspired the sessions. This was the accomplishment that Stalin chose to highlight in his Revolution Day speech several weeks later, the most open-minded and conciliatory of all his wartime addresses.[78]

The Teheran summit of 28 November–1 December served mainly as a public relations forum. Operation Overlord was fixed for May, with the Soviets pledging a simultaneous offensive on the eastern front. Stalin repeated his promise to join the war with Japan after Germany's defeat. Troublesome issues such as Poland were dodged, though during informal exchanges some progress toward common positions was made. The conference's joint declaration expressed "full agreement" on military matters and vowed "to destroy Germany's army on the ground, its submarines on the seas, and its planes in the air." It concluded with a hopeful commitment "to work together both during the war and in the ensuing peace."[79]

In the course of 1944 Soviet objectives for a postwar settlement became more coherent. Security was the overriding issue: to protect the

77. Stalin voiced this sentiment to Milovan Djilas in April 1945. Milovan Djilas, *Conversations with Stalin* (New York, 1962), p. 114.

78. Stalin, *Sochineniia*, 2 [XV]: 107–27.

79. *Tegeran, Ialta, Potsdam*, pp. 97–100. For interesting though somewhat impressionistic accounts of the Teheran conference see Keith Eubank, *Summit at Teheran* (New York, 1985), and V. M. Berezhkov, *Tegeran, 1943: Na konferentsii bol'shoi troiki i kuluarakh* (Moscow, 1968).

Soviet state from any possible repetition of the nightmare through which it had just passed. A cooperative, Big Three peace that would recognize the Soviet Union's prerogatives as a great power, contain Germany, and facilitate economic assistance for Soviet reconstruction was perceived as the best possible outcome. Soviet war aims in eastern and central Europe represented a potential barrier to Allied harmony, but the problem still seemed amenable to a number of solutions.

One form that a workable bargain might take was revealed during Churchill's visit to Moscow on 9–18 October 1944. At his first meeting with Stalin the British prime minister presented a scheme for allotting influence in southeastern Europe according to crude percentages. In Greece, the United States and Britain would assume 90 percent "predominance," leaving 10 percent influence for the USSR. In Romania, these percentages would be exactly reversed. Hungary and Yugoslavia were divided 50 percent–50 percent, and Bulgaria 75 percent–25 percent to Soviet advantage.[80] Stalin is reported to have approved the curious arrangement by checking the paper upon which Churchill outlined it with a blue pencil; subsequently foreign ministers Eden and Molotov would spend some time haggling over its implications. What was at issue, however, was a very simple idea—an informal sphere-of-influence arrangement in southeastern Europe. Churchill staked a British claim to hegemony in Greece, to which the Soviets acquiesced by turning away from the communist-led Greek resistance. As a quid pro quo the Soviets were granted predominance in their own sensitive border areas. The implications of such an understanding obviously extended beyond the Balkans. As Soviet armies advanced into the heart of Europe, the sphere-of-influence concept became ever more attractive, even if the phrase itself remained anathema.[81]

The slow progress of western armies after Normandy did not improve the Allied governments' negotiating position. When Churchill and a terminally ill Roosevelt flew into the Crimea on 3 February 1945 for the second Big Three summit, the Soviet winter offensive had already broken through to the Oder. Stalin did not spare Soviet lives to provide assistance to his beleaguered allies during the Battle of the Bulge, and the Allied armies still confronted the formidable barrier of the Rhine. Though Stalin was aware that the disorganized and depleted Soviet fronts were in no position to launch a rapid strike at Berlin, the military situation once again seemed to favor the Soviets.

80. Winston L. S. Churchill, *Triumph and Tragedy* (London, 1953), pp. 194–95.

81. Mastny, *Russia's Road to the Cold War*, pp. 97–110, describes the evolution of the concept in Soviet perception. Traditional Soviet evaluations strictly deny any interest in a sphere-of-influence arrangement. See *IVOVSS*, 5:134.

In a week of talks at the Crimean resort of Yalta, amidst the faded elegance of Tsar Nikolai II's seaside Livadia Palace but surrounded by lands still scarred by the fighting that had raged through them less than a year before, the most productive diplomatic encounter of the entire war unfolded. Key problems were addressed in turn, and in most cases a process of diplomatic give and take led to a mutually acceptable solution. Yalta left many questions unanswered, but as an exercise in cooperative negotiation it was an impressive example of the viability of the wartime alliance.[82]

The Yalta negotiators confronted numerous conflicts of interest, but a mutual willingness to compromise ultimately allowed the vital concerns of all participants to be accommodated. A European Advisory Commission proposal to establish military occupation zones in defeated Germany was accepted as a first step toward dealing with the question of Germany. Stalin, seconded by Roosevelt, revived the demand for a permanent "dismemberment" of the Reich, but the concept was merely passed on to the foreign ministers for further discussion. At Churchill's insistence, France was invited into the great-power club and granted its own German occupation zone. The French National Liberation Committee's modest military contributions (it fielded ten divisions compared with twelve for Josip Broz Tito's partisans in Yugoslavia) had not necessarily merited such an honor, but at issue was the larger question of western Europe's postwar political orientation, a question Stalin was ready to resolve in the spirit of a sphere-of-influence understanding. Churchill expressed the concept clearly, if unintentionally, when he remarked that France was "as important to Great Britain as Poland was to the USSR." The most prominent Soviet request was for a fixed sum of reparations from Germany, but here Moscow's expectations were to be disappointed. A Reparations Committee was established to monitor the issue, but no Three Power accord concerning a fixed sum could be achieved.

The American delegation's priority was to gain approval for the United Nations as a new global collective security forum. The Dumbarton Oaks conference, which began on 21 August 1944, had already given the proposed organization its basic outline, to which the Soviets agreed in principle. But two major issues remained to be resolved—a voting formula for the Security Council and the composition of the General Assembly. At Yalta the Soviets came toward the American position,

82. On the Yalta sessions see Diane Clemens, *Yalta* (New York, 1970); *Tegeran, Ialta, Potsdam*, pp. 101–200. Clemens emphasizes a view of Yalta as an example of positive diplomatic interaction. Jean Laloy, *Yalta, hier, aujourd'hui, demain* (Paris, 1988), provides a more critical evaluation.

accepting the veto mechanism and reducing a demand that all fifteen of the Soviet socialist republics be granted General Assembly seats to three (for Russia, the Ukraine, and Belorussia). During the discussion Soviet fears of isolation inherited from the 1920s and 1930s were clearly revealed; at one point Stalin asked what mechanisms would prevent the Soviet Union from being expelled as it had been by the League of Nations during November 1939.

The most fractious issue, as ever, was Poland, but here Soviet intransigence left almost no room for bargaining. Stalin made an impassioned plea on behalf of the Soviet position, rising from his chair and citing security concerns as a matter of "life and death." Though some concessions to western sensibilities were forthcoming, the essential Soviet demand—for recognition of the Lublin Committee (now firmly emplaced in Warsaw) as the foundation for a new government—remained unshakable. The Warsaw government would be "expanded," further consultations and discussions were placed on the agenda, and Poland's western frontier was left negotiable, but that the new Poland would be dominated by the USSR was not in doubt. In what passed for a corresponding concession Stalin reiterated the Soviet intent to enter the war in the Far East, though here, too, territorial concessions (a restoration of the Soviet position in Manchuria, the Kuril Islands, and the southern half of Sakhalin Island) were part of the package.

The argument that the western powers "sold out" at Yalta is pervasive but unconvincing.[83] The Soviet Union appeared at the conference in a strong position; its armies bestrode half of Europe and were not about to be dislodged. What occurred at Yalta was a classical negotiating process characterized by hard bargaining and mutual concessions: "a diplomatic encounter in which all sides . . . struggled to achieve their aims, but an encounter in which they prized agreement by traditional negotiation as preferable to unilateral action which might undermine international stability."[84] The Soviet Union, whose wartime losses were ten times greater than those of its negotiating partners, signed the Declaration on Liberated Europe with its reference to "broadly representative democratic elements," accepted France's role as a great power, acquiesced in an informal European sphere-of-influence arrangement, accepted American proposals for a new world security forum, and temporarily backed

83. Sophisticated variants of this thesis are presented by Mastny, *Russia's Road to the Cold War*, which emphasizes the negative impact of wartime collusion, and Keith Sainsbury, *The Turning Point: Roosevelt, Stalin, Churchill, and Chiang-Kai-Shek, 1943. The Moscow, Cairo, and Teheran Conferences* (Oxford, 1985), where the moment of surrender to Soviet priorities is pushed back into 1943.

84. Clemens, *Yalta*, p. 288.

away from requests for reparations and the dismemberment of Germany. One may argue that these concessions were both inadequate and hypocritical, but they were at least the product of collective bargaining. Cruel compromises were demanded of the western powers, but the Soviets had made cruel sacrifices, and there were no ideal solutions.

Did the Soviet Union's demands constitute "striving for power and influence in excess of its reasonable security requirements."?[85] Certainly not, as viewed from Moscow. Nor was the underlying issue "the degree to which the Soviet Union under Stalin would or would not pursue a path of cooperation."[86] The Soviets were committed to cooperation, but on their own demanding terms. And Moscow was not the only party to the negotiations whose motives should be judged. Also at issue was the West's willingness to accept the consequences of the Soviet victory and to engage with good spirit in the kind of reciprocal diplomatic interaction for which Yalta provided a prototype. The Cold War had not yet arrived in February 1945, the flickering light of Allied cooperation had yet to be erased by the blinding flash of Hiroshima, and the prospect of a managed peace remained alive.

Milovan Djilas recounts a revealing incident during his meeting with Stalin in Moscow on the eve of the Normandy landings.

> In the hallway we stopped before a map of the world on which the Soviet Union was colored in red, which made it conspicuous and bigger than it would otherwise seem. Stalin waved his hand over the Soviet Union and, referring to what he had been saying just previously against the British and the Americans, he exclaimed, "They will never accept the idea that so great a space should be red, never, never."[87]

Stalin may well have made the remark with calculated intent to impress the idealistic young communist whom he was escorting, but it has the ring of truth. The perception was not new: that a war which had so damaged the USSR should have reinforced it was probably inevitable. For important forces within the Soviet leadership the external world remained inevitably hostile. In defense of its fundamental interests the Soviet Union must therefore count first of all upon its own strength.

Until the winter of 1942–1943 Soviet security policy was dominated by the short-term exigencies of survival. After Stalingrad, when some

85. Mastny, *Russia's Road to the Cold War,* p. 283.
86. Erickson, *The Road to Berlin,* p. 507.
87. Djilas, *Conversations,* p. 74.

leeway was achieved to develop a more permanent perspective, the impact of the war itself had become a factor decisively conditioning attitudes. In 1941 the Soviet regime had nearly collapsed. The Nazis justified their campaign in the east as a crusade against Bolshevism, and Hitler was accordingly perceived as a monstrous incarnation of the external threat to which the Soviets had always felt themselves subject. Stalin made the point as early as November 1941: "The party of the Hitlerites is the party of the imperialists, indeed the most predatory and marauding imperialists among all the imperialists of the world."[88] The USSR fought Hitler in alliance with the western powers, but the perception was deeply imbedded that it had been left to bear the brunt of the struggle alone. Erickson writes of a "mood of embattled isolation," of the Soviets' conviction "that they were fighting alone . . . for their own survival and for their way of life."[89] In the end it was not diplomacy, not the modest contributions of the Allies, not the international resistance that turned the tide, but the sacrifices of the Soviet people and the blows administered by the Red Army. The premises of socialism in one country seemed to have been vindicated and, with the final, overwhelming victory of Soviet arms, the potential of Soviet power was demonstrated as never before. By 1945 these conclusions had been burned into the consciousness of every Soviet citizen by ghastly and unparalleled losses: a toll of perhaps 27 million dead, 1,710 towns and 70,000 villages destroyed, and an enduring legacy of suffering.[90] When the question of a postwar settlement moved onto the agenda, the establishment of a security regime that would insulate the USSR against external military threats had become an understandable preoccupation.

There is no reason to doubt the sincerity of the Soviet Union's desire to maintain the spirit of the wartime alliance as the basis for a Big Three peace. The Red Army was enormously powerful by 1945, but its strength was the result of an extraordinary mobilization that could not

88. Stalin, *Sochineniia,* 2 [XV]: 21. The interpretation of fascism as a variety of imperialist aggression would subsequently become standard. See G. Filatov, "Voprosy fashizma i sovremennost'," *Kommunist* 13 (1976): 99–109.

89. Erickson, *The Road to Berlin,* p. 341.

90. The figure of 20 million dead, originally covered up, would eventually become standard. J. A. Newth, "The Soviet Population: The Wartime Losses and Postwar Recovery," *Soviet Studies* 15 (1964): 345–47, uses independent calculations to arrive at the figure of 20 million deaths. More recent Soviet estimates have ranged considerably higher. V. I. Kozlov, "O liudskikh poteriakh Sovetskogo Soiuza v Velikoi Otechestvennoi voine 1941–1945 godov," *Istoriia SSSR* 2 (1989): 132–39, arrives at the horrifying total of 40 million deaths, including 15–20 million members of the Soviet armed forces. Volkogonov, *Triumf i tragediia,* 2, part 1:369, uses what has become the new "standard" figure, between 26 and 27 million deaths.

be maintained indefinitely. The country was absolutely devastated and urgently needed a period of peace and stability to begin its recovery. Calculated self-interest dictated an effort to preserve a positive relationship with the western powers.

Unfortunately, the barriers to positive relations were substantial. The alliance had been created and held together by a common threat that ceased to exist in 1945. The controversies that emerged during the war rested atop decades of inveterate hostility. Most revealing from the Soviet perspective was the Allies' refusal to shoulder their fair share of the military burden; resentment at the failure to establish a second front prior to 1944 can hardly be exaggerated. "It must be stated," telegraphed the Soviet ambassador to London Ivan Maiskii during July 1942 after being informed by Churchill that no second front would be forthcoming in the course of the year, "that in our most critical moments we are in essence being abandoned to the will of fate by our allies. This is a very unpleasant fact, but there is no sense trying to soften it. It must be remembered in the future."[91] It would be remembered, and the memory would dictate that cooperation with the Allies could not come at the price of guarantees that addressed fundamental Soviet security concerns.

In attempting to combine these contradictory impulses, the Soviets could not draw directly upon their own past. The principles of revolutionary internationalism had long since been abandoned. Flushed by victory, Moscow felt no need to accommodate to the capitalist world on any terms other than its own. Nor was an attempt made to revive the idealistic premises of Litvinov-style collective security. What seemed to be emerging at the time of Yalta was a conception of security based upon a managed rivalry with the leading capitalist states, where inevitable differences would be resolved diplomatically in collective forums, a conception of security through strength tempered by a concert of the great powers. There were preconditions for such interaction, however—namely, the "minimal" security requirements that the Soviets perceived to be their good right in view of the outcome of the war.

In the course of 1944 and 1945 the nature of these preconditions became apparent: territorial acquisitions; secure frontiers guaranteed above all by the establishment of a tight sphere of influence in eastern Europe; significant reparations; a resolution of the German problem that would ensure that no threat could emerge from that quarter again; and, more ambiguously but absolutely vital, an acknowledgment of the USSR's transformed international stature. Stalin's approach was pragmatic, but his preconditions were highly inflexible. Soviet security

91. Cited in Gromyko and Ponomarev, *Istoriia vneshnei politiki SSSR*, 1:436.

would not again be left to rest upon the good-will of reluctant allies. In Djilas's words, "Stalin trusted nothing but what he held in his fist."[92]

The outcome of the war, ironically in view of Stalin's responsibility for the debacle of 1941, had strengthened the Stalinist order and increased Soviet self-confidence. Western accounts of the reasons for the Soviet victory, including the one presented here, tend to emphasize coincidental factors and assume that defeat was narrowly warded off. Barbarossa was delayed, Russia proved to be too vast to subdue, Hitler performed irrationally, Japan chose to turn south, and so on. The explanation preferred by the postwar generation of Soviet leaders was very different. In the words of A. M. Samsonov: "The victory of the Soviet Union in the Great Fatherland War was historically conditioned in conformity with objective laws [*zakonomerna*]. It revealed, in all its force, the essential superiority of the new Soviet society and governing system born of the October Revolution."[93] Such conclusions emerged from the wartime theme of "Soviet patriotism" and served to prolong and reinforce it. Their weight should not be discounted. The perception of a Soviet state fully capable of defending its own interests established limits to Stalin's willingness to concede to the West and made possible a turn to unilateralism during the post-Yalta crisis that produced the Cold War.

92. Djilas, *Conversations*, p. 82.
93. Samsonov, *Sovetskii Soiuz*, p. 675.

CHAPTER FIVE

La Guerre Manquée, 1945–1953

> The longer the period that separates us from the war's end, the more clearly delineated are the two main trends in postwar international politics, which correspond to the division of the political forces active in the world arena into two main camps: the imperialist and anti-democratic camp on one side and the anti-imperialist and democratic camp on the other side. The leading force of the imperialists is represented by the United States.
>
> —Andrei Zhdanov, September 1947

On the night of 25 February 1945, with German armies in full retreat, the British Royal Air Force (RAF) launched its infamous firebombing raid against the Saxon capital of Dresden. The magnificent city, one of the gems of European culture, of virtually no strategic importance and overflowing with refugees, was razed. "The goal is to disrupt the German rear," read an RAF evaluation, "and incidentally, to show the Russians what we can do."[1]

The exigencies of combat being what they are, it would be wrong to attribute Allied policy during the war's final months exclusively to a desire to "show the Russians." But the Dresden action hinted at what was an increasingly significant motive as the impending collapse of the Axis removed the impetus to cooperation provided by a common enemy. The big three were incongruous allies, committed to radically different sociopolitical ideals. Only an imminent threat had brought them together, and with the threat removed, the competitive edge of their relationship quickly reemerged.

Although it is a commonplace to describe the postwar international system as bipolar, the two great powers that presided over it were not

1. Cited from Alexander McKee, *Dresden, 1945: The Devil's Tinderbox* (London, 1982), p. 46.

equally matched. American casualties during the war were only a fraction of those borne by the Soviets, and the U.S. economy, still mired in depression on the eve of Pearl Harbor, received a tremendous boost. In comparison, the Soviet Union had been brutalized by war as had no nation before or since. Much of its infrastructure lay in ruins, and the task of rebuilding, reintegrating millions of demobilized soldiers into a civilian economy, and healing psychic wounds absorbed all available energies. Never was a society less well placed to launch into risky imperial ventures. All logical considerations pointed in one direction: Soviet national interest demanded a period of recuperation in the context of the grand alliance.

The possibility of binding the victorious USSR into a new structure of world order was the great lost opportunity of the postwar era. The failure was occasioned first of all by the breakdown of Soviet-American relations in what would become known as the "Cold War." The two states had collaborated to win the war, and they had no history of direct national rivalry. But after 1945 they were the most extreme embodiments of the conflicting political ideologies that have dominated twentieth-century history. The debate over responsibility for the disintegration of their relationship continues to generate a large and contentious literature.[2] Regardless of how one chooses to allocate guilt, it

2. A distinction is usually drawn between "orthodox" and "revisionist" schools of interpretation concerning the origins of the Cold War. Orthodox arguments, positing Soviet imperial ambitions as primarily responsible for the disintegration of the international climate after 1945, include John Lukacs, *A History of the Cold War* (Garden City, N.Y., 1961); Herbert Feis, *From Trust to Terror: The Onset of the Cold War* (New York, 1970); Hugh Thomas, *Armed Truce: The Beginnings of the Cold War, 1945–46* (New York, 1987). The revisionist school emphasizes the refusal of the United States to make the compromises necessary to achieve international cooperation. Key works include William Appleton Williams, *The Tragedy of American Diplomacy* (New York, 1959); Donna F. Fleming, *The Cold War and Its Origins, 1917–1960*, 2 vols. (Garden City, N.Y., 1961); David Horowitz, *The Free World Colossus: A Critique of American Foreign Policy in the Cold War* (New York, 1971); Joyce Kolko and Gabriel Kolko, *The Limits of Power: The World and United States Foreign Policy, 1945–1954* (New York, 1972). In addition, a "post-revisionist" school may be identified, which attempts to avoid the polemical quality of much of the above literature. For examples see André Fontaine, *Histoire de la guerre froide*, 2 vols. (Paris, 1965–1967); John L. Gaddis, *The United States and the Origins of the Cold War, 1941–1947* (New York, 1972); Walter LaFeber, *America, Russia, and the Cold War, 1945–1975*, 3d ed. (New York, 1976); Wilfried Loth, *Die Teilung der Welt: Geschichte des Kalten Krieges* (Munich, 1980); Daniel Yergin, *Shattered Peace: The Origins of the Cold War and the National Security State* (Boston, 1977). Much of the orthodox-revisionist controversy revolves around conflicting interpretations of American policy. The Soviet side of the equation is treated in William Taubman, *Stalin's American Policy: From Entente to Détente to Cold War* (New York, 1982); from a traditional Soviet perspective, in Iu. M. Mel'nikov, *Sila i bessilie: Vneshniaia politika Vashingtona 1945–1982 gg.* (Moscow, 1983), pp. 11–86.

seems obvious that hostility and mutual recrimination need not have reached the levels of intensity that they did. Roosevelt's policies were built around the quest for cooperation with Moscow, but his death in April 1945 marked the end of an era. Thereafter, the Truman administration's drift toward more assertive policies, coupled with Stalin's insistence upon an extremely ambitious definition of minimal security requirements, provided a recipe for confrontation. When efforts to preserve cooperation on terms that they considered to be acceptable broke down, the Soviets responded with a policy of *retrenchment,* rebuilding their military posture in Europe and manning the defenses of a territorial bloc extended to include the newly acquired eastern European "satellites." The choice reflected a "hedgehog" approach to the Soviet security dilemma and included the utter abandonment of the revolutionary aspirations of a resurgent world communist movement. The justification for Soviet security policy became an unapologetic Soviet nationalism—after 1945 the drift away from the internationalist precepts of Lenin that had begun in the early 1920s reached its apogee.

The policies of the late Stalin period were often distasteful, but not entirely ineffective. Despite the escalating Cold War, the Soviet Union went about the business of reconstruction. By dodging confrontations and accepting defeats when necessary, Stalin successfully steered through the shoals that threatened on all sides at a moment of great danger and exposure. The Soviet peoples were ruthlessly bent to the will of a tyrant, but the goal of "peaceful coexistence" was kept in place as a counterpoint to calls for vigilance. Indeed, Stalin's foreign and security policies demonstrated considerably more intelligence than many would care to admit. Between 1945 and 1953 his "cruel, clumsy, bureaucratized, fear-ridden despotism, preoccupied with reconstructing a war torn land,"[3] managed to fend off the American challenge, build a new foundation for Soviet power, and create the prerequisites for a more ambitious Soviet rule in world affairs.

From Cooperation to Confrontation

During the six months between the Yalta and Potsdam summits Big Three relations worsened measurably. The key agitant was Stalin's persistent effort to consolidate Soviet influence in the occupied territories of eastern Europe. In Bulgaria political forces hostile to the Soviet Union were purged from the Fatherland Front. The transitional Romanian government of General Nicolae Rădescu was dissolved in February

3. Yergin, *Shattered Peace,* pp. 286–87.

1945 in response to Soviet pressure and replaced on 6 March by the National Democratic Front led by Petru Groza. The arrest of sixteen prominent Polish oppositionists during March, despite prior offers of amnesty, and the creation on 14 March of four Polish administrative districts in the formerly German eastern territories revealed the contours of the Soviets' preferred solution to the Polish problem. A fait accompli of sorts was created on 21 April with the conclusion of a treaty of friendship between Moscow and the pro-Soviet government in Warsaw. Moscow's intention to establish a tight sphere of influence in the western borderlands was becoming increasingly clear.

Stalin might well have assumed that his policies would not provoke a strong reaction. Moscow's actions did not violate the letter of the Yalta understandings, which implicitly acknowledged the legitimacy of Moscow's security concerns in central Europe.[4] Much of the Yalta bargain rested upon Roosevelt's willingness to champion a conciliatory approach, however, and his death on 12 April removed an important prop for a policy of accommodation. Unversed in foreign affairs and never made a party to Roosevelt's personal diplomacy, the new U.S. president, Harry S. Truman, would eventually opt for a very different set of priorities.[5]

The tone had already been set by influential advisors horrified at the sight of Soviet armies pouring into the heart of Europe. As the war ground to a conclusion during 1945 the U.S. ambassador to Moscow, Averell Harriman, spoke ominously of a "barbarian invasion," General George Patton characterized Russians as a "scurvy race" of "Mongolian savages," and Secretary of War Henry Stimson described the comportment of Red Army soldiers as "oriental pillages."[6] Such atavisms revealed more about the perceptions of American elites than they did about the sources of Soviet conduct, but they reflected a strain of thought that was making its way to the fore. On 14 April, his second day in office, Truman wrote to Stalin and emphasized that the establishment of a "representative Polish government" would be "the symbol of the future development of international relations." During his first series of meetings with Molotov he launched into a lecture concerning Soviet "obligations," snapping at the abashed Soviet foreign minister with the

4. See Melvyn P. Leffler, "Adherence to Agreements: Yalta and the Experience of the Early Cold War," *International Security* 1 (Summer 1986): 88–123.

5. On the evolution of Truman's views concerning the Soviet Union see Fraser J. Harbutt, *The Iron Curtain: Churchill, America, and the Origins of the Cold War* (Oxford, 1986); pp. 99–110.

6. Cited from Ernst Nolte, *Deutschland und der Kalte Krieg* (Munich, 1974), pp. 174–76; Michael Sherry, *Preparing for the Next War: American Plans for Postwar Defense, 1941–1945* (New Haven, Conn., 1977), p. 189.

preemptory tone of a schoolmaster.[7] On 8 May, with the guns in Germany barely silenced and the Pacific war still in full swing, Truman abruptly ordered the curtailment of Lend-Lease shipments to the USSR. Whatever the logic of the gesture, it was certain to be a source of resentment in Moscow.

Despite tensions, both sides worked to keep the spirit of alliance alive. In a reply to Truman on 24 April, Stalin sought to place differences in context, noting that the Soviet Union requested no assurances as to the representative character of the regime in Greece and emphasizing that Soviet interests in Poland were dictated exclusively by the problem of security.[8] On 27 May, Harry Hopkins arrived in Moscow as Truman's personal envoy and succeeded in smoothing over several contentious issues. In his exchanges with Hopkins, however, Stalin made a point of outlining Soviet grievances. Poland was a case of special importance to the USSR, he insisted, and could not be described as a "test" of relations.[9]

The fragile edifice of the grand alliance received a more serious blow when on 16 July the United State's top-secret Manhattan Project concluded its work by successfully testing an atomic bomb. When the final wartime summit opened in Potsdam one day later, Truman was aware of the awesome result. It was not an incentive to cooperation. Not until 24 July, with Churchill looking on circumspectly, did Truman remark to Stalin that the Americans had developed "a new weapon of unusual destructive force." The Soviet leader's reply to the disingenuous subterfuge was stoic, remarking simply that he hoped the Americans would make "good use" of it against Japan. But there is no doubt that Stalin was fully aware of what it was that Truman alluded to, and of its implications.[10]

7. When Molotov remarked that he "had never been spoken to like that in his life," Truman replied: "Keep to your agreements and you won't be spoken to like that." Harry S. Truman, *Memoirs*, 2 vols. (Garden City, N.Y., 1955–1956), vol. 1: *Year of Decision*, pp. 79–82 and 99. Fontaine, *Histoire de la guerre froide*, 1:283, remarks; "If this was not yet the Cold War, it was already its language."

8. Lynn Etheridge Davis, *The Cold War Begins: Soviet-American Conflict over Eastern Europe* (Princeton, N.J., 1974), p. 229. Security was also the main theme of Stalin's remarks on 21 April on the occasion of the signing of a Polish-Soviet friendship treaty. Stalin, *Sochineniia*, 3 [XVI]: 184–87.

9. The meetings between Stalin and Hopkins are described in Robert E. Sherwood, *Roosevelt and Hopkins: An Intimate History*, 2d ed. (New York, 1950), pp. 883–912.

10. Truman, *Memoirs*, 1:458. Churchill later voiced the conviction that Stalin "had no idea of what he was being told." Churchill, *Triumph and Tragedy*, pp. 668–70. Zhukov, *Vospominaniia*, p. 713, tells a different story. According to his version, Stalin approached him immediately after the encounter and remarked that the Soviet Union would have to speed up its atomic energy program. If the recollections in *Khrushchev Remembers* (Boston, 1970), pp. 58–60, are to be believed, Stalin was "frightened to the point of cowardice." See also the account by Andrei Gromyko, *Pamiatnoe*, 2 vols. (Moscow, 1988), 1:220–22, which credits Stalin with a solid awareness of what was at issue.

The shadow of the atomic bomb hung over the Potsdam deliberations, conducted from 16 July to 1 August on the outskirts of ruined Berlin.[11] Appropriate to the setting, it was the "German question" that dominated the agenda. Both sides arrived with positions that left space for accommodation. In his speech of 9 May acknowledging the German capitulation, Stalin spoke against the "fractionalization or destruction" of Germany.[12] Meanwhile, the United States began to move away from the punitive "Morgenthau Plan" approved by the Quebec conference in September 1944, with its proposal for the "agrarianization" of the German economy. At Potsdam the creation of a unified, neutral, and demilitarized Germany administered under four-power control pending a formal peace treaty became the basis for a common policy.

The issues of Germany's borders and the reparations burden were handled via compromise. After considerable debate, the United States agreed to accept that Poland's territory could be "pushed westward." Regions east of the Curzon line, including the cities of Vilnius and L'vov, would be absorbed by the USSR, with Poland to be compensated by portions of Silesia and Brandenburg east of the rivers Oder and Lausitzer-Neisse. The detachment from the Soviet occupation zone of the cities of Stettin (Szczecin) and Breslau (Wroclaw), as well as the Silesian mining and manufacturing regions, made it clear that at this stage the USSR was not considering a "two Germanies" solution. The territorial adjustments were blessed by the western powers in exchange for Soviet concessions on reparations. The demand for a fixed sum was dropped in favor of the principle that payments could be extracted by the victorious powers from their own occupation zones. An additional proviso granted the Soviets 15 percent of "nonessential" industrial production from the western zones, but only in exchange for compensatory payments in the form of raw materials and foodstuffs. Soviet requests for an internationalization of the Ruhr that would open access to the region's industrial potential, for a formal condemnation of Francist Spain, and for a mandate in the former Italian colony of Tripolitania were left unfulfilled, as were insistent U.S. demands for liberalization in eastern Europe and an internationalization of inland waterways (a rather incongruous pet project of Truman's).

11. Contrasting interpretations are provided by Herbert Feis, *Between Peace and War: The Potsdam Conference* (Princeton, N.J., 1960); Charles E. Mee, *Meeting at Potsdam* (New York, 1973); Ernst Deuerlein, *Potsdam: Ende und Anfang* (Cologne, 1970). The Soviet side of the story is told by V. N. Vysotskii, *Meropriiatie "Terminal": Potsdam 1945* (Moscow, 1975), and V. J. Beletskii, *Potsdam 1945: Istoriia i sovremennost'*, 2d ed. (Moscow, 1987).

12. Stalin, *Sochineniia*, 2 [XV]: 197–99. Fischer, *Sowjetische Deutschlandpolitik*, pp. 68–75, emphasizes the evolution in Stalin's attitude toward the German question that had occurred since Teheran.

Soviet priorities during the first phase of postwar diplomacy were transparent. The annexation of Finnish territories adjacent to Leningrad, the Baltic states, and a portion of Pomerania including Königsberg (Kaliningrad), the western Ukraine, Bessarabia, and Moldavia created an unbroken strip of new Soviet territory along the western borderlands. Moscow's claim to predominant influence in eastern Europe was not allowed to be questioned, but a limited form of pluralism was sanctioned in the context of the national front. Germany would be subjected to four-power control and if possible made to pay significant reparations. Cooperation with the western allies remained the keystone of security policy, and in order to maintain a climate of good-will, the Soviets showed themselves ready to grant at least some concessions.

These concessions were not sufficient to calm the growing concerns of the western allies. As negotiations became more difficult, London came to view America's programmed disengagement from Europe with uneasiness. Pressured by the British and increasingly alienated by Soviet negotiating behavior, the Truman administration shifted toward a hard line. The first session of the new Council of Foreign Ministers (CFM) forum took place in London from 11 September to 2 October 1945 and resulted in a nearly complete check. Rather than responding to Soviet efforts to fix the terms of peace treaties for Bulgaria, Hungary, and Romania, U.S. Secretary of State James Byrnes returned to the Polish question and insisted upon the establishment of a representative government on the basis of free elections. The result was stalemate and adjournment sine die. An ad hoc meeting of foreign ministers representing the Big Three only, held in Moscow from 16 to 26 December, was to some degree successful in regaining lost ground. But from February 1946 onward an irreversible disintegration of Big Three relations set in.

In his first major postwar address, delivered in Moscow on the eve of elections to the Supreme Soviet on 9 February 1946, Stalin sounded a note of warning. The world war, he insisted, had been an inevitable product of "contemporary monopoly capitalism."[13] The Soviet Union continued to confront powerful rivals and could not afford to relax its vigilance. The most important priority was economic reconstruction, which Stalin proposed to accomplish by familiar command methods implying a high degree of social regimentation. Stalin's speech was received badly in the West, where the articulation of what was in many ways a classic isolationist perspective seemed contrary to the spirit of diplomatic accommodation. According to one overwrought

13. Stalin, *Sochineniia*, 2 [XV]: 1–23.

U.S. official, it amounted to nothing less than "a declaration of World War III."[14]

George Kennan's famous "long telegram," wired to Washington on 22 February 1946, was in part a reaction to Stalin's speech. This urgent message from a young State Department functionary in Moscow combined sweeping generalizations about Russian national character with a plea for the need to contain what was perceived as an emerging wave of Soviet expansionism. Although Kennan's analysis was hardly original, it conveniently summarized a perception that was coming to dominate official circles. Henceforward the "containment" of the Soviet Union would be a major theme of U.S. policy.[15]

At this critical juncture a harshly ideological tone began to be introduced into the debate over postwar world order. The clarion was sounded by Churchill's famous speech in Fulton, Kansas, on 5 March 1946, delivered in Truman's presence, characterizing the extension of Soviet power over eastern Europe as an "iron curtain" descending upon the continent.[16] Stalin responded with an interview in *Pravda* on 17 March in which he labeled the address a "dangerous act." As to eastern Europe, the essence of Soviet concerns was stated bluntly: "The Germans launched their attack upon the USSR from Finland, Poland, Romania, Bulgaria, and Hungary. The Germans were able to launch their attack from these countries because at that time the governments in power were hostile to the Soviet Union."[17] "Freedom versus tyranny" was not the issue in eastern Europe, Stalin insisted. At stake were the most fundamental security interests of the Soviet state.

A trial by fire arrived with the Iranian crisis of February and March 1946, the first postwar clash in which Soviet and American interests were defined in such a way as to make them seem incompatible. During

14. Cited from LaFeber, *America, Russia, and the Cold War*, pp. 39–40. Alexander Werth, *Russia: The Post-War Years* (London, 1971), p. 96, was perhaps closer to the truth when he remarked: "The last thing the Soviet people, with all this work on their hands, were interested in was conquering the world."

15. Text in George F. Kennan, *Memoirs: 1925–1950* (Boston, 1967), pp. 547–59. Kennan's conception of containment is more fully developed in the famous article published incognito as "X" [George F. Kennan], "The Sources of Soviet Conduct," *Foreign Affairs* 4 (July 1947): 566–82. See also John Lewis Gaddis, *Strategies of Containment: A Critical Appraisal of Postwar National Security Policy* (New York, 1982), pp. 23–53; Deborah Welch Larson, *Origins of Containment: A Psychological Explanation* (Princeton, N.J., 1985), pp. 252–57; for a taste of the continuing controversy over what containment "really meant," Ben C. Wright, "Mr. X and Containment," *Slavic Review* 1 (March 1976): 1–31, and "George F. Kennan Replies," ibid., pp. 32–33.

16. The full text appears in "Mr. Churchill's Address Calling for United Effort for World Peace," *New York Times*, 6 March 1946, p. 4. A detailed though somewhat eccentric account of the presentation is given by Thomas, *Armed Truce*, pp. 500–513.

17. Stalin, *Sochineniia*, 3 [XVI]: 35–38.

the war Iran served as a conduit for supplies to the USSR, and its territory was jointly occupied by Soviet and Allied forces. At the Teheran conference in 1943 all parties pledged to withdraw within six months of the cessation of hostilities. The London CFM in September 1945 established 2 March 1946 as the deadline. By the spring of 1946, however, the Soviets had decided that prolonging their military presence might provide a source of leverage in the quest for certain diplomatic goals. Stalin wished to obtain an oil concession as a foundation for economic interaction with a region whose natural wealth could greatly assist Soviet reconstruction. In addition, he chose to lend support to the autonomous Azeri government installed in Tabriz during December 1945 in defiance of Teheran, perhaps with the hope of establishing a buffer state in a sensitive border area. These goals were ambitious, but their logic was not difficult to grasp. The Soviet Union inherited Russia's long tradition of imperial rivalry with Britain in Iran, and it had good reason to be wary of Anglo-American hegemony in the region. The draw of an oil concession was real, and in both Tabriz and Teheran strongly pro-Soviet communist factions could assert ideological affinity as a means of attracting support.[18]

At U.S. insistence, the U.N. Security Council scheduled a debate on the problem during March. On 27 March, Andrei Gromyko announced his country's refusal to participate. It was an inauspicious commencement for the body that had been conceived as the centerpiece of a new global collective security system. On 5 April, however, the USSR backed down, signing a bilateral agreement with Iran in which it pledged to withdraw its forces in six weeks in exchange for the creation of a joint Soviet-Iranian oil company. The autonomous republic of Iranian Azerbaijan, up to this point shielded by the presence of Soviet troops, was coldly mentioned as a "purely internal problem."[19] By 6 May, Soviet forces had pulled out as agreed. During the following December, Iranian soldiers marched into autonomous Azerbaijan and massacred its supporters, leaving hanged bodies on display for weeks in admonition. In July 1947 the Majlis in Teheran dutifully reneged upon the promise of an oil concession. The shah of Iran, now firmly in power with U.S. backing,

18. The best account of the episode, in Bruce Robellet Kuniholm, *The Origins of the Cold War in the Near East: Great Power Conflict in Iran, Turkey, and Greece* (Princeton, N.J., 1980), p. 379, assigns the Soviets classical imperial motives. "They sought," writes Kuniholm, "to secure their southern flank, to rid that region of Anglo-American influence and at the same time acquire a springboard to the Eastern Mediterranean and the Middle East."

19. The relevant texts are available in *Vneshniaia politika Sovetskogo Soiuza: Dokumenty i materialy* [hereinafter cited as VPSS], *ianvar'-dekabr' 1946 goda* (Moscow, 1946), pp. 113 and 116.

described the events as the "Stalingrad of the western democracies."[20] They provided an enlightening commentary upon how the principles of "self-determination" and "representative government" could be interpreted when western interests were at stake. Viewed from Moscow, the results constituted a humiliating defeat, administered without the slightest concession to national self-esteem.

A clash of interests with Turkey, with a similarly negative outcome, reiterated the point that Moscow could not expect to gather the spoils of victory without confronting resistance. Since 1944 the Soviets had made repeated appeals for a revision of the Montreux Straits convention, including requests for a permanent naval facility in the Dardenelles and the restitution of the territories absorbed from Russia by the Turks after World War I. The Soviets posed their conditions in a note of 7 August 1946, accompanied by what appeared to some to be an attempt to intimidate Ankara with threatening troop movements in border zones.[21] Emboldened by the success of containment in Iran and operating from a position of strength, the United States responded with a show of force, including the dispatching of significant naval forces to the Mediterranean. Once again Moscow abandoned its demands in order to avoid a potential confrontation. From Washington's perspective, the diplomacy of counterpressure seemed to be bearing fruit.

In the tense atmosphere generated by the Iranian and Turkish crises, progress on other issues slowed to a snail's pace. At the second CFM, which opened in Paris on 25 April 1946, the Soviets renewed requests for a more exacting reparations regime, four-power control of the Ruhr, and a mandate in Tripolitania. All were refused point-blank, and the sessions concluded on 15 May in a deadlock. A second round from 15 June to 12 July, and a third CFM in New York from 15 October to 12 December 1946 managed to regulate several minor issues, but the long-awaited general peace conference that opened in Paris's Luxembourg Palace on 29 July ground on for two and one-half months before breaking off inconclusively. "In retrospect," writes William Taubman, "all this talking seems a tedious sideshow to the onrushing Cold War."[22]

20. Cited in Kuniholm, *The Origins of the Cold War*, p. 396.

21. The Soviet note of 7 Aug. made no territorial demands, but it did hold out the possibility of obtaining basing rights. It was renewed on 28 Sept. See the texts in *VPSS 1946 goda*, pp. 167–70 and 193–202. See also Harry Howard, *Turkey, the Straits and U.S. Policy* (Baltimore, Md., 1974), pp. 242–60; Melvyn P. Leffler, "Strategy, Diplomacy, and the Cold War: The United States, Turkey, and NATO 1945–1952," *Journal of American History* 4 (March 1985): 807–25. A. Sh. Rasizade, "Turetskii aspekt doktriny Trumena i nekotorye proschety stalinskoi diplomatii," *Narody Azii i Afriki* 4 (1989): 40–50, condemns Stalin for pressing the Turks with overly harsh demands.

22. Taubman, *Stalin's American Policy*, p. 159.

What was happening, and why? The preferred explanation in the West has always emphasized Stalin's calculated desire to pursue a policy of expansionism by probing into adjacent territories. It would be foolish to deny any such ambitions to the cynical master of the Kremlin, but Moscow's legitimate security concerns in sensitive border regions, as well as its severely limited capacity to pursue confrontational policies, should also be factored into the equation. An intelligence report commissioned by the U.S. Navy in January 1946 struck at the heart of the matter, portraying Russia as "exhausted," noting that her economy and transport were "in an advanced state of deterioration," and characterizing policy in Europe as designed "to establish a Soviet Monroe Doctrine for the area under her shadow, primarily and urgently for security."[23] It remains the case nonetheless that Stalin's foreign policy was at the least insensitive to the special demands of maintaining a climate of cooperation in the difficult postwar environment. Despite his repeated pleas for accommodation, Stalin refused to surrender an "enemy image" of the leading capitalist powers, useful as a tool of internal mobilization as well as a means for reinforcing ideological orthodoxy. With the situation in Europe in the process of stabilizing on something resembling Soviet terms, the harsh reassertion of a competitive ideological posture, rigorous domestic policies, and adventuristic thrusts toward Iran and Turkey conjured western worst-case scenarios back to life and contributed to a spiral of confrontation. Stalin seems almost to have willed the Cold War into being, reluctant to give up the besieged-fortress mentality that had served his purposes so well in the past.

By the summer of 1946 the focal point of the emerging U.S.-Soviet rivalry had become the atomic bomb. The thesis that America's monopoly of the weapon after 1945 "determined much of Truman's shift to a tough policy" and occasioned a resort to "atomic diplomacy" intended to intimidate the USSR has given rise to a tangled controversy.[24] If one accepts Greg Herkin's definition of atomic diplomacy as "using the bomb to gain a diplomatic advantage," however, there seems to be little ground for denying the concept's legitimacy.[25] Whether or not their conviction was well founded, the bomb gave American policy makers such as James Byrnes a sense of power that they were determined to exploit. Such determination, in turn, touched upon the most sensitive of Soviet security concerns.

23. Cited in Greg Herkin, *The Winning Weapon: The Atomic Bomb in the Cold War, 1945–1950* (New York, 1980), p. 138.
24. For the citation and the thesis in its most straightforward form see Gar Alperowitz, *Atomic Diplomacy: The Use of the Atomic Bomb and the American Confrontation with Soviet Power* (London, 1966), pp. 13–34.
25. Herkin, *The Winning Weapon*, p. 44.

The appointment of Bernard Baruch, a seventy-five-year-old Wall Street millionaire renowned for his vanity and lacking any technical competence in the matter at hand, as U.S. representative to the U.N. Atomic Energy Commission (AEC) in the spring of 1946 was a sign of things to come. The "Baruch Plan" for the international control of atomic energy, presented on 15 June 1946, seemed to have been designed to alienate Moscow. It envisioned a step-by-step process leading toward the eventual elimination of nuclear weapons on the basis of a managed international control regime. In step one Moscow would be required to submit to an unrestricted survey of its uranium and thorium resources. During step two U.N. commissions would be charged with indexing and storing all world reserves of fissionable materials. Penalties for noncompliance were foreseen, up to and including military action against violators. The process appeared feasible in principle, but in fact it contained critical flaws. Decisions were to be placed in the hands of a special U.N. Atomic Development Agency, where the United States was likely to enjoy majority support and where the Security Council veto would not apply. Only with a control system in place, a goal for which no time limit was fixed, would the United States cease to manufacture bombs and destroy existing stocks. In the meantime, the U.S. atomic monopoly would remain intact. Stripped of its idealistic trappings, the plan proposed to place decisions concerning the Soviet Union's most vital security problem into the hands of a multilateral agency controlled by its leading rival.

Gromyko responded on 19 June with a counterproposal that turned Baruch's concept upside down.[26] According to the "Gromyko Plan," the first step would be the destruction of all existing atomic weapons, followed by negotiations leading to the establishment of a control system. With its demand for what amounted to unilateral American disarmament, the plan was fully as unrealistic as Baruch's. On 24 July, Gromyko rejected the Baruch plan outright, and on 31 December the United States sponsored a vote on the plan in the Security Council, where its passage was blocked by Soviet and Polish abstentions. The result was the collapse of any hope for effective international control. In the following years, freed from constraint and confident that its advantage would last indefinitely, the United States went on to create a series of strategic contingency plans based upon an "air atomic" attack upon the Soviet Union.

The Soviets continued to pursue a dialogue within the various multilateral forums that had been assembled since Potsdam. When peripheral issues threatened to generate conflict, Stalin preferred to back down. In Iran and Turkey the results were Soviet humiliations. Instead of supporting Yugoslavia in its campaign to absorb Trieste, Stalin bowed to the

---

26. The text of Gromyko's proposal is in *VPSS 1946 goda*, pp. 630–37. See also his own account in Gromyko, *Pamiatnoe*, 1:288–90.

West, sending Tito a harsh letter condemning adventurism. The Soviets contented themselves with a token voice in peace arrangements for western Europe and Japan, their request for a mandate in Tripolitania was allowed to lapse, and in France and Italy they urged compromise upon dynamic and ambitious Communist parties. In interviews accorded to Charles Baily of the United Press and Elliot Roosevelt in October and December 1946, Stalin reiterated his desire to maintain the spirit of the Big Three.[27] But the Soviets failed to produce the kind of decisive concession or diplomatic gesture that might yet have reinvigorated the waning momentum of East-West cooperation.

Stalin's ambiguous priorities were mirrored in the Soviet military posture, which against the background of the U.S. atomic monopoly was crafted to remain intimidating without provoking confrontation. Aware of the Manhattan Project from early on, skeptical of prospects for international control, and with its own A-bomb project, under the direction of Igor Kurchatov, in existence since 1943, the Soviet Union made development of its own atomic weapon a priority goal after Hiroshima and Nagasaki.[28] The intensive research and development effort extended beyond nuclear energy to other areas of advanced military technology where the Soviet Union found itself at a disadvantage, including jet propulsion, long-range aircraft and rocketry, and radar.

To bridge the gap during which a U.S. atomic monopoly remained in place, Stalin relied upon public diplomacy. No hint that the bomb could become a potentially useful weapon of war was allowed to appear in Soviet sources; Raymond Garthoff notes that between 1945 and 1953 virtually no discussion of nuclear strategy appeared in the popular or specialized military press.[29] In response to questions posed by Alexander Werth on 17 September 1946, Stalin stated flatly, "I do not believe in a real danger of a 'new war'," and went on to disparage the bomb as a weapon intended "to intimidate the weak-nerved." The potential advantages occasioned by the U.S. monopoly, he suggested, would be neutralized by the facts that it could not last indefinitely, and that the bomb would soon be banned.[30] Stalin's remarks contained a good deal of

27. Stalin, *Sochineniia*, 3 [XVI]: 57–63 and 65–70.
28. David Holloway, *The Soviet Union and the Arms Race* (New Haven, Conn., 1983), pp. 15–28; David Holloway, "Entering the Nuclear Arms Race: The Soviet Decision to Build the Atomic Bomb, 1939–1945," *Social Studies of Science* 11 (1981): 159–97.
29. Raymond L. Garthoff, *Soviet Strategy in the Nuclear Age* (New York, 1958), p. 67.
30. Stalin, *Sochineniia*, 3 [XVI]: 53–56. S. A. Kiselev, "Iadernoe oruzhie i vneshnepoliticheskaia mysl' partii (1945–1955 gg.)," *Voprosy istorii KPSS* 8 (1990): 64–76, is critical of Stalin's inflexible and narrow approach to the problem as embodied by his remarks in this interview, but he nonetheless concludes that the effort to break the U.S. monopoly of atomic weapons was "historically necessary and correct" (p. 72).

bravado, but in some ways he was right. Overoptimistic U.S. estimates concerning the possibility of prolonging monopoly control by closing access to atomic raw materials proved to be unfounded. On 29 August 1949, much earlier than expected, the USSR successfully tested its own, advanced-design atomic weapon. The lack of proportion between the bomb's destructive force and the ambiguous choices that are the stock and trade of international politics, a dilemma that strategic theorists have never entirely resolved, considerably reduced its usefulness. The U.S. atomic monopoly, Stalin seems to have divined, was indeed a paper tiger.

In the United States the pursuit of an air atomic strategy was justified as a counter to the threat to Europe posed by Soviet conventional forces. Given their geographical proximity and demonstrated capacity, the Soviet armed forces could obviously look to certain advantages when contemplating war in the European theater. But estimations of Soviet conventional forces in the immediate postwar years were more often than not willfully inflated. From May 1945 onward the Soviet armed forces were rapidly demobilized. Stalin's postwar army, which western intelligence sources consistently listed as between 4 and 5 million soldiers, was in fact reduced to a manpower level of 2,874,000.[31] One of the primal fears of the Cold War became the threat of an overwhelming Soviet conventional offensive capable of conquering western Europe at a stroke, but in the immediate postwar years so grandiose an undertaking was the last thing the Soviet leadership desired to contemplate. Nor were the means for the implementation of a *Blitzkrieg* strategy put into place. Undermanned divisions, primitive transport, outmoded equipment, and low morale in a period of intense economic hardship all dulled the striking force of Soviet armies, which never approached the three-to-one ratio of superiority deemed necessary for the successful conduct of an offensive.[32] Prior to 1947 Stalin did not seek to offset the U.S. atomic monopoly by holding western Europe "hostage" to the Red Army. Rather, he adopted a deliberately nonprovocative military posture compatible with Soviet economic priorities, comparable to the posture that resulted from the Frunze reforms during the 1920s.

31. Thomas W. Wolfe, *Soviet Power and Europe, 1945–1970* (Baltimore, Md., 1970), pp. 9–12; "Demobilizatsiia," in *Bol'shaia sovetskaia entsiklopediia* 13 (Moscow, 1952): 652–53.

32. The point is argued by Matthew A. Evangelista, "Stalin's Postwar Army Reappraised," *International Security* 3 (Winter 1982–83): 110–38. It is reiterated in the commentary "Otkuda ugroze," *Voenno-istoricheskii zhurnal* 2 (1989): 16–31, which cites a 43% reduction in Soviet military spending during 1945 and blames the West for exaggerating the Soviet threat in order to justify an expanded U.S. role in Europe. The article includes the operational war plans for the Soviet Group of Forces in Germany for 1946, which rest upon strictly defensive assumptions. The evidence is not conclusive, but it is of interest.

No amount of restraint could halt the ongoing slide toward confrontation. On 10 February 1947 peace treaties with Bulgaria, Finland, Hungary, Italy, and Romania were finally concluded. But hopes to resolve the vital German question via negotiation were rapidly disappearing. By the summer of 1946 the United States had turned toward a new goal: the creation of a west German "partial state" (*Teilstaat*) that could be integrated into the U.S.-dominated west European bloc without encumbrances.[33] Implementation of the new U.S. orientation began with the merger of the British and American occupation zones into a "Bizonia" by 1 January 1947, and in May 1947 a preliminary West German government was established in Frankfurt on Main. These were unilateral steps to which the USSR was hard pressed to respond. Though the creation of an independent West Germany was temporarily blocked by French resistance, the writing was on the wall.

The edge of Soviet-American rivalry was sharpened even more when on 12 March 1947 Truman went before Congress to request emergency aid to support the governments of Greece and Turkey in their battles against communist subversion, in the process enunciating the Truman Doctrine pledging U.S. support to the "defense of freedom against tyranny" worldwide.[34] These sweeping commitments were accompanied by the promulgation of the Marshall Plan for the economic reconstruction of Europe, announced by Secretary of State George Marshall in a speech at Harvard University on 5 June 1947. After a moment of reflection *Pravda* denounced the project in an editorial of 16 June. One week later Molotov arrived at the Quai d'Orsay with a delegation of nearly one hundred technical advisors to explore its implications with the British and French. The Soviet foreign minister expressed a preference for bilateral aid without conditions rather than a collective enterprise that threatened to undermine the Soviet position in eastern Europe by encouraging reliance upon the United States. No concessions were forthcoming, and by the time of Molotov's departure from Paris on 2 July, TASS had definitively rejected the entire concept. Expressions of interest by Poland and Czechoslovakia were quickly withdrawn under Soviet pressure. The Marshall Plan could thus be launched in the form that its sponsors had always preferred as an infusion of aid aimed at heading off the west

33. The evolution of U.S. policy is described in Axel Frohn, *Deutschland zwischen Neutralisierung und Westintegration: Die deutschlandpolitischen Planungen der Vereinigten Staaten von Amerika 1945–1949* (Frankfurt am Main, 1985), pp. 18–100; John H. Backer, *The Decision to Divide Germany: American Foreign Policy in Transition* (Durham, N.C., 1978), pp. 69–72. The first Soviet reactions to the idea of division appear in Molotov's speech of 10 July 1946, in V. M Molotov, *Voprosy vneshnei politiki: Rechi i zaiavleniia aprel' 1945 g.-iiun' 1948 g.* (Moscow, 1948), pp. 60–66.

34. The full text is in Kuniholm, *The Origins of the Cold War*, pp. 434–39.

European left by stimulating economic development under conservative auspices, and as a means for tying Europe closer to the United States.[35]

The Truman Doctrine and the Marshall Plan brought a phase in Soviet-American relations to an end. A *Pravda* editorial on 15 March commented upon the Truman Doctrine by concluding that things could not go on as they were: "All this business of protecting 'free people' against totalitarianism goes far beyond Greece and Turkey. . . . This is a turning point in American foreign policy." In an interview with Harold Stassen on 9 April 1947, Stalin made yet another futile plea for accommodation.[36] Meanwhile, sessions of the CFM in Moscow from 10 March to 24 April, and in London from June to December, completely broke down as Molotov's insistent efforts to prevent the emergence of a West German partial state, to obtain reparations drawn from continuing production, and to resist the emergence of a west European bloc closely linked to Washington ran into a stone wall. The London sessions marked the demise of the CFM as a viable diplomatic forum. With the premises of accommodation disappearing one by one, an alternative approach to the Soviet security dilemma was urgently called for.

The Zhdanov Line

The Soviet reaction to the onset of the Cold War was a retreat from a policy of accommodation: an intellectual retreat toward the trusted homilies of Stalinism, and a physical retreat into the confines of the new Soviet "bloc" in eastern Europe. Domestically, the last vestiges of the relative liberalism of the war years disappeared beneath a wave of dogmatism and repression. Internationally, eastern Europe was transformed into a redoubt under the command of pro-Soviet Communist parties. The failure cooperatively to resolve the problem of postwar world order thereby resulted in a divided Europe, split into contending power blocs dominated by the ascendent "superpowers."

A hint of what was to come arrived in August 1945, as a crackdown swept over the Soviet intellectual community. Confronting the rigors of reconstruction and in the midst of a severe drought that briefly posed the threat of famine, the Soviets judged the ideological openness of the war period to be no longer acceptable. Dubbed the Zhdanovshchina after

35. For arguments broadly supportive of my own conclusion on this controversial point see Charles S. Maier, "Die konzeptuellen Grundlagen des Marshall-Plans," and Geir Lundestad, "Der Marshall-Plan und Osteuropa," both in Othmar Nikola Haberl and Lutz Niethammer, eds., *Der Marshall-Plan und die europäische Linke* (Frankfurt am Main, 1986), pp. 47–74.

36. Stalin, *Sochineniia*, 3 [XVI]: 75–92.

Stalin's current heir apparent Andrei Zhdanov, the campaign was launched with attacks against two paragons of the cultural establishment, the respected humorist Aleksandr Zoshchenko and the poet Anna Akhmatova. Purges in the name of "party spirit" (*partiinost'*) quickly spread through other scientific and cultural branches. Julian Huxley perceived the Soviet leadership to be "preparing the people of the USSR for a long struggle, possibly involving war, with the capitalist world in general and the USA in particular."[37] The years 1946 and 1947 saw the beginning of an officially sponsored campaign touting Soviet nationalism that soon became absurdly excessive. Family legislation outlawed marriages between Soviet citizens and non-Soviet nationals, and a new state secrets law radically inhibited contacts with foreigners on all levels. The Soviet leadership was seeking to reassert its monopoly of authority, to intimidate any and all dissent, and to portray the outside world as alien and threatening as a prelude to possible confrontations.

A response to the U.S. challenge in the foreign policy realm came on 22–27 September 1947 when the representatives of nine Communist parties met in the resort town of Szklarska Poreba, south of Jelenia Gora in upper Silesia, to create a new international communist organization dubbed the Communist Information Bureau (Cominform).[38] The keynote address, delivered by Zhdanov for the Communist Party of the Soviet Union (CPSU), sounded a note of defiance. The world order that had emerged since 1945, Zhdanov posited, was irrevocably divided between "two camps": a progressive socialist camp led by the USSR, and a reactionary imperialist camp led by the United States. Encouraged by the aggressive designs of a declining imperialism torn by unresolvable contradictions, the rivalry between these contending blocs contained the constant threat of a new world war, for which the Soviet Union must do all in its power to prepare. Stripped of their rhetorical trappings, Zhdanov's remarks did little more than summarize stock-in-trade Leninist chichés, but in the context of 1947 they conveyed a clear message. The "Zhdanov line" offered a mirror image of Truman's "freedom versus tyranny" rhetoric. It described the world in Manichean fashion, as strictly bipolar and potentially fated to an apocalyptic showdown.[39]

37. Julian Huxley, *Soviet Genetics and World Science: Lysenko and the Meaning of Heredity* (London, 1949), p. 153.

38. A good evaluation of the sessions is provided by Charles Gati, *Hungary and the Soviet Bloc* (Durham, N.C., 1986), pp. 108–15. See also the participant's account by Eugenio Reale, *Nascita del Kominform* (Milan, 1958).

39. The original text of Zhdanov's speech is available in *Informatsionnoe soveshchanie predstavitelei nekotorykh kompartii* (Moscow, 1948), pp. 13–49, and the English version in A. Zhdanov, "The International Situation," *For a Lasting Peace, For a People's Democracy*, 10 Nov. 1947, pp. 2–5. Volkogonov, *Triumf i tragediia*, 2, part 2: 95–97, points out that the content of the address was carefully monitored by Stalin.

Outspoken as they may have been, Zhdanov's remarks did not unambiguously commit the USSR to a foreign policy hinged upon confrontation. Stalin's lieutenant spent most of his time reiterating familiar
postwar themes, including the importance of peace, the struggle for national independence, and, somewhat incongruously, the need for a
"long-term coexistence of the two systems." The Zhdanov line certainly
represented a challenge. It is not necessarily correct to perceive it as what
one historian calls "a declaration of war against western civilization."[40]
Despite his stature, Zhdanov was still a secondary figure in a regime
where only Stalin's word truly carried weight. Speaking from a nongov-
ernmental forum, he was well placed to provide an ideological buttress
for the campaign of retrenchment without foreclosing policy options.

The Cominform was not intended to reincarnate the spirit of world
revolution. It represented the Communist parties of Bulgaria, Czechoslovakia, Hungary, Poland, Romania, Yugoslavia, the USSR, France,
and Italy, and was therefore exclusively European in character. Notably
absent were the Communist parties of Greece and China, both engaged
in armed struggles for state power. The founding congress was held out
of the public eye, and a summary of the proceedings was not released
until after its adjournment. Another manifestation of prudence was the
failure of the leading lights of the international movement, such as
Georgi Dimitrov of Bulgaria, Maurice Thorez of France, Togliatti of
Italy, Mátyás Rákosi of Hungary, Tito of Yugoslavia, or Klement
Gottwald of Czechoslovakia (not to mention Stalin himself) to appear.
Despite the two-camps rhetoric, support for a unified, demilitarized, and
neutral Germany was reiterated.

The Szklarska Poreba sessions approved a concluding declaration that
synthesized the main points of Zhdanov's keynote address. A joint communiqué and resolution announced the creation of a permanent Information Bureau, to be based in Belgrad and tasked with supervising
activities "on a basis of free consent." The Information Bureau was also
charged with editing a bimonthly (and after September 1949, weekly)
publication with a clumsy title reportedly chosen by Stalin: *For a Lasting
Peace, For a People's Democracy.* In the course of its existence up to
1956 the Cominform sponsored three "world congresses," maintained
the publication of *For a Lasting Peace, For a People's Democracy* as a
point of reference for communist militants, and presided over a highly
visible world peace movement. These activities were not insignificant,
but the organization's evident structural weakness (its leading historian
speaks of an institutional "quasi-nonexistence")[41] and its absolute

---

40. Fontaine, *Histoire de la guerre froide*, 1: 392.
41. Lilly Marcou, *Le Kominform: Le communisme de la guerre froide* (Paris, 1977), p. 10.

subservience to Soviet priorities make clear that a new version of Lenin's Comintern was never in question. The Cominform had a narrowly defensive character. Its first purpose was to unify the European communist movement around a general line supportive of Moscow in view of the climate of hostility engendered by the Cold War.

The creation of the Cominform was paralleled by the elimination of all traces of political pluralism in Soviet eastern Europe. The spirit of the "national front," which had promised space for a limited degree of opposition, was abandoned. In its place the individual eastern European polities were coercively transformed into miniature models of the Stalinist order in the USSR.

Eastern Europe in 1945 offered a daunting portrait of devastation and confusion. The only state in the region that had emerged from the war with a representative national government was Czechoslovakia, where free elections in 1946 made the Communist party a potent force with 37 percent of the national vote. The situation appeared propitious for the emergence of a state that would be both authentically democratic and securely pro-Soviet, the ideal toward which the Yalta accords had aspired. Elsewhere in the region the absence of democratic traditions, the crying need for land reform and other social changes, and the staunch resistance of traditional elites made the Yalta formula for representative government "too ambitious and prey to all possible misunderstandings."[42] Bulgaria, Hungary, and Romania were the defeated allies of fascist Germany. Finland had waged war against the USSR unrepentently and contributed in no small measure to the martyrdom of Leningrad. In Yugoslavia and Albania autonomous communist movements, loyal but not subservient to Moscow, had taken power on their own. Poland, Truman's "test case" for cooperation, was the most difficult instance of all. Ravaged by war, the country bore the burden of immense rural poverty, a ruined industrial sector, and intense social and communal strife. Poland's anti-Russian traditions and the political weight of a conservative Catholic establishment did not bode well for Moscow should the "free election" solution be applied.

Soviet policy toward the eastern European region after 1945 was neither uniform nor consistent.[43] The Baltic states were declared reattached to the USSR with little international reaction. Czechoslovakia could tout itself as a "third force" between East and West with Soviet blessing.

42. François Fejtö, *Histoire des démocraties populaires*, 2 vols. (Paris, 1952–69), 1:53.
43. Scholars who defend the thesis of a larger Soviet "masterplan" for expansion also usually take note of the contradictions plaguing the attempt. See, e.g., Brzezinski, *The Soviet Bloc*, pp. 4–9; Carrère d'Encausse, *Le grand frére*, 83–92; Hugh Seton-Watson, *The East European Revolution* (New York, 1951), pp. 167–230.

Finland, despite its status as a defeated belligerent, was reconstructed as a parliamentary democracy. The Czechoslovak and Finnish solutions, however, rested upon an intact national consensus and positive orientation toward the USSR that did not exist elsewhere. For the former German allies and Poland the Soviets favored the concept "national democracy," a formula for coalition governments with "progressive" orientations in which the communist left would be strongly represented but not necessarily in a position to rule by coercion.

A theoretical foundation for the concept of national democracy was offered in Varga's seminal postwar study *Changes in the Economy of Capitalism as a Result of the Second World War.* Varga's work emphasized the dynamism of a resurgent, U.S.-led world capitalism. The capitalist world order continued to pose the constant threat of crisis and war, he opined, but it also allowed space for a progressive democratic transition. The regimes emerging in eastern Europe, which Varga described as "state capitalist" formations supervised by "a democratic state resting upon the broad strata of the workers," were conceived as potential models for such a transition. Though they were phrased cautiously, Varga's theses seemed to grant a certain legitimacy to the revisionist argument on behalf of a peaceful, reformist path toward socialism.[44] Other theorists described the "popular democratic" revolutions in eastern Europe as a consequence of the weakening of capitalist imperialism occasioned by the war. They were "democratic and anti-imperialist revolutions of a special type," committed to building a "new socio-economic structure— the structure of a period of transition from capitalism to socialism."[45]

The hopes attached to the concept of national democracy could not survive Moscow's turn toward retrenchment. In 1947 the decision was made to eliminate the noncommunist agrarian opposition from national-front coalitions. A number of leaders were tried on flimsy charges and meted out ferocious sentences. Others, such as Ferenc Nagy of Hungary and Stanislaw Mikolajczyk of Poland, were pressured to resign. Soon the communist left was using its control of the police apparatus to intimidate opposition across the board. After the inauguration of the Marshall

44. E. Varga, *Izmeneniia v ekonomike kapitalizma v itoge vtoroi mirovoi voiny* (Moscow, 1946), p. 291. See also Laszlo Tikos, *E. Vargas Tätigkeit als Wirtschaftsanalytiker und Publizist* (Tübingen, 1965), pp. 65–79; the insightful study by Lynch, *Soviet Study of International Relations,* pp. 18–25, who expounds upon the larger theoretical implications of Varga's work.

45. I. P. Trainin, "Demokratiia osobogo tipa," *Sovetskoe gosudarstvo i pravo* 1 (1947): 5; A. Leont'ev, "o sotsial'no-ekonomicheskikh osnovakh novoi demokratii," *Partinaia zhizn'* 17 (1947): 42. Elsewhere, Varga spoke openly of a central European alternative to the Soviet model: "The old State apparatus will not be torn down, as in the Soviet Union, but be transformed." E. Varga, "Demokratie neuer Art," *Neue Welt* 11 (1947): 33.

Plan a series of bilateral economic agreements between the eastern European states were imposed, culminating in the creation of the Council for Mutual Economic Assistance (CMEA) in June 1949. The Soviet Union had begun to enforce conformity upon the region and to press for a monopoly of power by the communist left. The reforms of 1945–1947, often impressively successful and fairly described by François Fejto as "a national effort, accomplished with the more or less active support . . . of all democratic parties," were as a consequence distorted and discredited.[46] Against the background of the escalating Cold War, Moscow had concluded that its security interests would best be served, not by experiments with supervised reform, but by the undisguised imposition of Soviet hegemony over a homogenous "east bloc."

The final step in a first phase of retrenchment came in Czechoslovakia. With its developed industrial economy, powerful Communist party, Slavic attachment to the East, and cultural affinity with the West, that country had seemed ideally placed to succeed as a model for autonomous development. Such hopes shattered upon the increasing polarization of regional politics; by the spring of 1948 the national front government of Edvard Beneš and Thomas Masaryk was plagued by an increasingly bitter confrontation between the Czechoslovak communists and their rivals. After a series of protests against communist infiltration of the national security and police apparatus, on 20 February twelve members of the government representing three right-of-center parties sought to force a crisis by resigning. Their hope seems to have been that with support from the Socialist party and president Beneš a new government could be appointed in which communist influence would be reduced. In view of events elsewhere in the region, where in one country after another the communists were using coercion to subvert democratic procedures, concern with control over the national security organs was understandable. But the presumptions of the opposition proved to be unfounded. Faced with the fait accompli of demission, the Socialist party remained passive. The communists, correctly perceiving the maneuver as a challenge to their entire position, reacted by organizing a series of intimidating mass demonstrations. Beneš was left with no alternative other than to accept the resignations on 25 February and approve a new government submitted by the communist leader Gottwald. Dubious elections organized under its aegis on 30 May gave the new communist-dominated national front no less than 90 percent of the vote. The Czechoslovak opposition had overplayed its hand. The result was a rapid transition from an authentic coalition government to a communist monopoly of power.

46. Fejtö, *Histoire des démocraties populaires,* 1: 127.

Though commonly referred to as a "coup," the events of February 1948 were initiated by the noncommunist opposition and unfolded entirely within the parameters of constitutional legality. The hand of the USSR could be detected in the form of Soviet advisors in Prague and troops adjacent to the Czechoslovak border, but it was not decisive. It was the consequences that were telling. Taking advantage of the opposition's tactical blundering and no doubt with Moscow's encouragement, the Czechoslovak communists manipulated their nation into abandoning its democratic institutions and drew it into the Soviet Union's eastern European glacis.[47]

The subversion of Czechoslovakia was not intended as an offensive thrust toward the West. It was the final act in the consolidation of the Soviet bloc, a circling of the wagons in the face of U.S. pressure. The Zhdanov line was not an attempt to resurrect the ideals of the world revolution. It pointed backward toward a familiarly isolationist security posture, inspired by the kind of besieged-fortress mentality that Litvinov had sought to transcend a decade before. The "two camps" presumption that lay at the foundation of a policy of retrenchment was deeply rooted in the entire Soviet national experience. Hopes by liberal reformers to work around it in the changed conditions of the postwar world had come to naught. Enunciated almost reflexively in response to the new external threats created by the Cold War, it left no room for a Czechoslovak "third way."

Crisis and Defeat

The movement toward retrenchment was accelerated during 1948 by two parallel crises: the Berlin crisis of 1948–1949, and Stalin's simultaneous rupture with Tito's Yugoslavia. The outcome of these clashes, in both cases unfavorable to the USSR, exposed the fragility of the USSR's postwar international position and added momentum to the conservative reaction already under way.

The blockade of Berlin between June 1948 and May 1949 was the final act in a drama that had begun with the U.S. decision to work for the creation of a west German partial state. During the spring of 1947 the Communist parties of France and Italy were expelled from governing

47. Morton A. Kaplan, *The Communist Coup in Czechoslovakia* (Princeton, N.J., 1960), emphasizes the Soviet role behind the scenes. See also François Fejtö, *Le coup de Prague 1948* (Paris, 1976); Karel Kaplan, *Der Kurze Marsch: Kommunistische Machtübernahme in der Tschechoslovakai 1945–1948* (Munich, 1981).

coalitions. April 1948 elections in Italy, conducted under considerable U.S. pressure, swept the conservative Christian Democrats to an absolute majority. On 17 March 1948 the Brussels Pact was signed, uniting Great Britain, France, and the Benelux nations in a western European security alliance, nominally concerned with the threat of a revanchist Germany, but in fact directed against the Soviet Union.[48] The "bloc system" in Europe was being consolidated, and a two-Germanies solution was an important part of its logic.

During the first half of 1948 representatives of the United States, France, Great Britain, and the Benelux met in London to work out the terms of the London Protocols outlining procedures for the creation of an independent West Germany. Soviet diplomatic initiatives simultaneously strove to halt the project in its tracks. Diplomatic notes during February and March warned against international consultations on the German question to which the Soviet Union was not made a part. On 18 February the foreign ministers of Poland, Yugoslavia, and Czechoslovakia issued the Prague Declaration calling for a renewal of four-power consultation.[49] When U.S. General Lucius Clay refused to permit a discussion of the Prague Declaration in the Allied Control Commission for Berlin on 20 March, however, the Soviet delegates unceremoniously walked out. "The control commission," stated the delegation head Marshal Vasilii Sokolovskii, "for all practical purposes has ceased to exist."[50]

None of the Soviet gestures was to any avail. On 18 June a currency reform created a standardized *Deutschmark* for all three western occupation zones. Five days later the reform was extended to the western sectors of Berlin. There was no doubt about what was at stake. The installation of a liberal market economy in a west German partial state, the integration of that state into the western European bloc, and its eventual remilitarization as a bastion of containment were all in view. The Cold War, only three years since the defeat of Hitler's Reich, had led to the resurrection of a Germany declaredly hostile to the USSR.

The Soviets confronted the options of either accepting a fait accompli and limiting damage or defining means to reverse the situation. The first option would eventually be adopted, but not without a trial of strength. During the night of 23–24 June rail traffic between Berlin and Helmstadt was halted by Soviet authorities. A "blockade" of overland routes to the former capital was being implemented in the hope of exploiting its

48. Frohn, *Deutschland zwischen Neutralisierung und Westintegration*, p. 120.
49. *VPSS 1948 goda: Chast' pervaia, ianvar'-iiun' 1948 goda* (Moscow, 1950), pp. 124–25 and 136–47.
50. Ibid., pp. 383–86.

exposure as a means of exerting political leverage. Subsequent Soviet justifications for the action ranged from the absurd to the essential. They included the claims that technical problems required a "temporary suspension" of traffic; that the unilateral western currency reform threatened to flood the eastern sector with the obsolete *Reichsmark;* and that after the collapse of joint administration Berlin as a whole belonged to the Soviet zone of occupation. On 24 June the foreign ministers of the Soviet bloc states came closest to the heart of the matter by emphasizing the "unacceptable" situation created by the London Protocols.[51] In effect, the western sectors of Berlin were being held hostage in a desperate attempt to reverse movement toward the creation of an independent West Germany.

The Soviet action was a calculated risk. Berlin was regarded as a lever, not a prize, and a claim to sovereignty over the city was never posed as a demand.[52] Rather, emphasis was placed upon the fate of four-power cooperation. Soviet notes of 14 and 16 July justified the measures taken by citing western violations of the Yalta and Potsdam accords, especially the provisions concerning demilitarization and reparations. On 2 August, Stalin met with the foreign ministers of the United States, France, and Great Britain and proposed a suspension of the London Protocols and renewal of four-power consultations.[53] The blockade did not exclude residents of the western sectors from entering and making purchases in east Berlin, and it was carefully crafted to allow room for retreat should the western reaction create a real danger of armed confrontation.

The western powers responded with a U.S.-sponsored airlift designed to supply the city with essentials from exclusively western sources while avoiding even the slightest diplomatic concession. The airlift was an expensive proposition but also an impressive success. Voices calling for more confrontational actions such as that of General Lucius Clay, who on 10 July wrote to Omar Bradley recommending that armed convoys be used to reopen overland access, remained isolated.[54] The Soviets were left with the unpalatable choice between tolerating the airlift and

---

51. Ibid., pp. 237–48. See also the account in Hannes Adomeit, *Soviet Risk-Taking and Crisis Behavior: A Theoretical and Empirical Analysis* (London, 1982), pp. 93–96.

52. Walter Phillips Davidson, *The Berlin Blockade: A Study in Cold War Politics* (Princeton, N.J., 1958), p. 144, calls Berlin "both a lever and a prize."

53. *VPSS, 1948 goda: Chast' vtoraia, iiul'-dekabr' 1948 goda* (Moscow, 1951), pp. 16–29.

54. On Clay's option see Herkin, *The Winning Weapon,* pp. 258–59. An alternative program developed by George Kennan calling for concessions to defuse a dangerous confrontation received no more attention. The Kennan program is described in Frohn, *Deutschland zwischen Neutralisierung und Westintegration,* pp. 124–34.

using force to disrupt it. The latter option seems never seriously to have been considered.

Once the viability of the airlift was demonstrated, it was clear that the Soviets had lost their wager. On 9 September 1948 the Brussels Pact members plus the United States and Canada issued a joint statement in Washington describing peaceful coexistence with the Soviet Union as "impossible" and underlining the need for a common defense. The up-shot was the creation of the North Atlantic Treaty Organization (NATO) during April 1949. On 8 May 1949 a parliamentary council in Bonn adopted "fundamental law" for a newly christened Federal Repub-lic of Germany (FRG.) The blockade, it seemed, was accelerating the very actions it had been designed to prevent. All that remained was the possibility of a face-saving withdrawal, and Stalin made the necessary concession in an interview in January 1949, remarking that he saw no obstacle to lifting transport and trade restrictions providing that the western powers reciprocated. Soviet ambassador Iakob Malik carried the initiative into the United Nations, and on 5 May 1949 a four-power communiqué announced that the "blockade and counter blockade" would be ended.[55]

The Soviets had been administered a stinging defeat. The so-called starvation blockade cast them in the role of aggressor, while the attempt to block the creation of a west German state failed miserably. By way of recompense an independent German Democratic Republic (GDR) was constituted in the Soviet zone on 7 October 1949. But "socialism in one-half a country" was not an adequate balance for the security dilemma created by the existence of the FRG and NATO.[56] "Whether one wishes to accept it or not," editorialized Le Monde on 5 April 1949, "the re-arming of Germany is contained within the Atlantic Pact like the yoke within the egg."

In the midst of the Berlin crisis a clash between Stalin and Tito created a new source of tension in the midst of the Soviet Union's European se-curity zone. The Soviet-Yugoslav conflict caught the world by surprise in the summer of 1948, though in retrospect its roots are not difficult to trace. Tito's partisans, because of their achievements in combat as well as inspired leadership, emerged from the war as Yugoslavia's only viable

55. VPSS, ianvar'-dekabr' 1949 goda (Moscow, 1953), pp. 21–22 and 99.
56. Dietrich Staritz, Sozialismus in einem halben Land (Berlin, 1976), pp. 155–74, de-scribes the creation of the German Democratic Republic. Interpretations of the Berlin crisis are offered by Davidson, The Berlin Blockade; Adomeit, Soviet Risk-Taking; Hans Herzfeld, Berlin in der Weltpolitik, 1945–1970 (Berlin, 1973), pp. 212–86. For a sum-mary of the traditional Soviet perspective see V. N. Vysockij, "Die deutschen Angele-genheiten auf den internationalen Beratungen der Jahre 1948 und 1949," Zeitschrift für Geschichtswissenschaft 23 (1975): 384–402.

national force. The rapid consolidation of a new state structure placed Tito and his followers in a position of dominance that was the result of their own sacrifices and efforts. Totally, even fanatically, devoted to the Soviet Union and Stalin, Yugoslav communism was nonetheless an independent force whose hold on power did not rely upon Soviet sponsorship.[57]

Conflicts of interest between the Soviets and Yugoslavs were not long in appearing. The Red Army entered Yugoslavia in 1944 to assist in the liberation of Belgrad, an "assistance" that soon became undisguised competition to reach the prize first. Subsequent Yugoslav protests concerning the undisciplined comportment of Soviet soldiers provoked mutual resentments. During the Trieste controversy in 1945 Stalin made it clear that the Soviet search for accommodation with the western allies took precedence over Yugoslav national concerns. As the phase of postwar economic reconstruction began, Belgrad's dissatisfaction with the activities of Soviet-sponsored joint companies grew steadily. A personality clash between Stalin and Tito, both notoriously intolerant of challenges to their authority, added a more personal dimension of rivalry. Not least, a hint of ideological competition surfaced as the Yugoslavs began to describe their own revolution as a "model" distinct from the Soviet experience.[58]

An open quarrel was precipitated by the project announced by Tito and Dimitrov during a conference at Lake Bled (near Ljubljana) on 1 August 1947 for the creation of a confederation of Balkan states. Although it was a long-standing goal of Balkan socialism, Stalin's attitude toward the project was ambiguous from the first, and his concern with the independent comportment of his Balkan lieutenants was growing. At the Cominform session at Szklarska Poreba during September the Yugoslav delegation asserted itself as the leading militant force within the movement, and the location of the organization's permanent executive in Belgrad seemed to be a mark of respect. Appearances were deceiving, however, and it can be argued that the Yugoslavs were encouraged to isolate themselves at Szklarska Poreba in order to prepare the way for disciplinary action.[59]

The direct provocation for the crisis came from Stalin, convinced, if Khrushchev's 1956 "secret speech" is to be believed, that he had only to

---

57. Vladimir Dedijer, *The Battle Stalin Lost: Memoirs of Yugoslavia, 1948–1953* (New York, 1971), pp. 36–46, vividly evokes the Yugoslav communists' offended nationalism and disillusionment with their former hero during the crisis.

58. See Adam B. Ulam, *Titoism and the Cominform* (Cambridge, 1952), pp. 69–95; Marcou, *Le Kominform*, pp. 198–236; Carrère d'Encausse, *Le grand frére*, pp. 137–57.

59. The possibility is mentioned by Vladimir Dedijer, *Tito* (New York, 1953), p. 295.

"shake his little finger and Tito would disappear."[60] On 18 March 1948 all Soviet civilian and military advisors to Yugoslavia were precipitously withdrawn and aid programs frozen. Perhaps most threatening, a campaign of subversion directed against Tito's authority was initiated by pro-Soviet elements within the Yugoslav Communist party. A remarkable exchange of correspondence between Tito and Stalin followed, spanning several months and concluding in mutual defiance.[61]

Tito was certainly aware that the very existence of his regime, as well as his personal safety, had been placed at risk. His reaction was appropriately strong willed. A special session of the Yugoslav Central Committee on 2 April raised the call for resistance, and pro-Soviet elements within the hierarchy were arrested. Stalin upped the ante at the Cominform's 2nd world congress in Bucharest on 20 June, which unanimously approved a resolution that excommunicated Yugoslavia from the communist bloc and openly appealed for "healthy elements" within the Yugoslav party to rid themselves of the heretic.[62] The Yugoslavs' 5th party congress during July responded by organizing an impressive display of public support for the leadership. Stalin had shaken his finger and balled his fist, but Tito remained stubbornly in place.

At this point the Soviet-Yugoslav dispute reached a plateau. Admonitions, plotting, and solemn denunciations had not sufficed. Stalin now faced choices not dissimilar to those he confronted in Berlin. In the electric climate of 1948 any aggressive action directed against Yugoslavia could have sparked enormous repercussions. A Soviet military thrust toward the Adriatic would have been a provocation of the kind that Stalin always scrupulously sought to avoid. Nor was Yugoslavia's ability to resist a Soviet assault negligible. Efforts to isolate Tito, an economic boycott, the staging of small-scale incidents along the Yugoslav frontier, and constant vilification were not sufficient to set in motion a process of destabilization. And here the matter rested. Once again Stalin preferred to accept defeat rather than court the risk of an unpredictable confrontation.

In some ways Stalin was proven correct. Cast adrift, Tito was forced to seek a modus vivendi with the West that made his country a virtual protectorate whose maverick policies were tolerated in the name of

60. "O kul'te lichnosti," p. 154. Recent Soviet accounts have been sharply critical of Stalin's provocative comportment. See, e.g., Iu. C. Girenko, "SSSR-Iugoslaviia, 1948 god," *Novaia i noveishaia istoriia* 4 (1988): 19–41; V. K. Volkov and L. Ia. Gibianskii, "Otnosheniia mezhdu Sovetskim Soiuzom i sotsialisticheskoi Iugoslaviei: Opyt istorii i sovremennost'," *Voprosy istorii* 7 (1988): 3–18.

61. The correspondence has been published as *Tito contra Stalin: Der Streit der Diktatoren in ihrem Briefwechsel* (Hamburg, 1949), pp. 26–70.

62. Ibid., pp. 71–80.

geopolitical expediency. Attempts to create an alternative model for socialist development under the rubrics of nonalignment and Titoism followed after the break and were not an essential cause. Viewed from
Moscow, Titoism meant nothing more than independent national communism defiant of Soviet control. It was a sufficient menace. The intensifying military threat from the West, which the Berlin crisis and its
aftermath had reinforced, demanded a strengthening of the Soviet defensive glacis in eastern Europe. Titoism gave substance to the possibility of
a breakdown from within. The foundation of the Soviet Union's European security posture was at risk, and a strong reaction inevitable.

The Apotheosis of Stalinism

The crackdown that followed the confrontations in Berlin and
Belgrad also impacted upon the Soviet political hierarchy. After the
purges of the 1930s the Soviet power elite remained remarkably stable in
terms of its leading personalities. It was nonetheless consistently divided
among contending factions. The most visible opponents were Andrei
Zhdanov and Georgii Malenkov, based, respectively, in Leningrad and
Moscow. The tension between these two stalwart Stalinists is well documented, but the implications of their rivalry remain unclear. Though
Zhdanov has traditionally been portrayed as the hardliner par excel-
lence, there are some grounds for suggesting that the judgment may be
partly incorrect. An iconoclastic study by Werner Hahn attempts to turn
the tables by casting Zhdanov in the role of a "moderate" battling to
resist the pressures of a conservative opposition including Malenkov, police chief Beria, and the young Mikhail Suslov. Whatever the cogency of
these arguments may be, Hahn's point that Zhdanov's premature death
on 31 August 1948 corresponded to a "historic defeat of moderate elements in the Soviet political establishment" seems well taken.[63] The
worst abuses of the Zhdanovshchina and the intensification of retrenchment that followed the foreign policy defeats of 1948 came after the
death of their supposed protagonist.

In the wake of the Berlin and Yugoslav crises a policy of retrenchment
quickly became apparent. The grotesque personality cult of Stalin was
intensified, culminating with an orgy of sycophantic praise surrounding

63. Werner G. Hahn, *Postwar Soviet Politics: The Fall of Zhdanov and the Defeat of
Moderation* (Ithaca, N.Y., 1982), p.9. The account by Iu. S. Aksenov, "Apogei Stalinizma:
Poslevoennaia piramida vlasti," *Voprosy istorii KPSS* 11 (1990): 90–104, is broadly supportive of Hahn's interpretation, though it avoids the characterization of Zhdanov as a
"moderate."

his seventieth birthday in December 1949. Simultaneously, the destructive purge of Soviet science already in progress reached new lows with the official sanction granted to T. D. Lysenko's scientifically untenable "acquired traits" genetic theory. The postwar nationalist wave took on bizarre and malignant forms with a publicly sponsored campaign against "cosmopolitanism" that soon degenerated into undisguised anti-Semitism. In the "Leningrad Case" of February–October 1950, an attack upon Zhdanov's former bastian culminating in mass arrests and executions, the use of terror against political opponents was revived.[64] In March 1949 Molotov surrendered control of the foreign ministry to the infamous prosecutor of the 1930s show trials Andrei Vyshinskii, while his Jewish wife, Polina Zhemchuzhina, was arrested and sent into internal exile. Xenophobic nationalism, insitutionalized terror, harsh economic regimentation, and a mystified cult of the "great leader" became the substance of the Soviet domestic order.

Following Tito's defiance comparable horrors were exported into Soviet-controlled eastern Europe. The way was prepared by ideological revisions. A first step away from postwar liberalism came with the publication of Nikolai Voznesenskii's *The Military Economy of the USSR during the Period of the Fatherland War* in 1947.[65] The focus of Voznesenskii's important book was economic recovery in the USSR, but it included an analysis of the transition to peace in the capitalist world, which Voznesenskii predicted would be marked by a deep structural crisis. The thesis constituted a veiled attack upon Varga's contention that pluralistic "new democracies" with mixed economies could provide a viable context for a transition to socialism.

By 1948 the assault upon Varga had grown into an orchestrated campaign.[66] The theorist B. S. Mankovskii completely redefined the national democratic model by describing it as, "in terms of its class essence, a revolutionary socialist model."[67] For the old loyalist Dimitrov, in his keynote address to the 5th congress of the Bulgarian Worker's party in

64. See V. A. Kutuzov, "Tak nazyvaemoe 'Leningradskoe delo'," *Voprosy istorii KPSS* 3 (1989): 55–67, and the summary in "O tak nazyvaemom 'Leningradskom dele'," *Izvestiia TsK KPSS* 2 (1989): 126–37. On 26 Feb. 1988 nine victims (N. A. Voznesenskii, A. A. Kuznetsov, Ia. F. Kapustin, M. I. Rodionov, P. S. Popkov, P. G. Lazutin, I. M. Turko, T. V. Zakrzhevskaia, and F. E. Mikheev) had posthumous rehabilitations confirmed by the Politburo's Commission for Rehabilitations.

65. N. A. Voznesenskii, *Voennaia ekonomika SSSR v period Otechestvennoi voiny* (Moscow, 1947).

66. See the discussion in Heinrich Heiter, *Vom friedlichen Weg zum Sozialismus zur Diktatur des Proletariats: Wandlungen der sowjetischen Konzeption der Volksdemokratie 1945–1949* (Frankfurt am Main, 1977), pp. 78–82.

67. B. S. Mankovskii, "Klassovaia sushchnost' narodno-demokraticheskogo gosudarstva," *Sovetskoe gosudarstvo i pravo* 6 (1949): 7.

Sofia during December 1948, people's democracy placed the working class in a "leading" role. It demanded collaboration with the USSR in a "democratic, anti-imperialist bloc" and would exercise "the function of the dictatorship of the proletariat."[68] According to the new orthodoxy, the sine qua non of revolutionary change in eastern Europe was nothing less than the presence of the Soviet Army, which allowed progressive forces to establish themselves by preventing civil war and blocking foreign intervention.[69] Taken together, these "redefinitions" added up to a brutal rejection of even the most vaguely pluralistic model for social change. They asserted a rigid two-camps framework, elevated the Soviet experience to the status of a universal model, and demanded that the threat of Titoism be burned out root and branch.

From 1948 onward retrenchment and "Sovietization" were pushed forward relentlessly. One of the most significant changes came in the realm of military policy. Organizational reforms, new training programs, and an upgrading of equipment in 1948 and 1950 began to prepare Soviet forces in the European theater for a more assertive strategic role. More effective Soviet control was also established over eastern European national armies, and between 1948 and 1953 a series of overlapping bilateral security pacts bound the bloc more closely together as an informal regional security system. Officer corps were restaffed with a younger generation of commanders who had received some portion of their professional training in the USSR, and the thousands of Soviet advisors attached to military missions in east European capitals came to constitute something like a semi-official chain of command. The various changes made it clear that the era of postwar demobilizations was over. Soviet levels of preparedness leaped upward as Stalin strove to endow his theater forces with the capacity for an intimidating forward defense.[70]

The most dramatic manifestations of retrenchment became the eastern European show trials. These patented Stalinist devices for enforcing control struck most severely in Hungary, climaxed by the prosecution of László Rajk in September 1948. A veteran of the Spanish Civil War, a

---

68. Georgi Dimitrov, *Suchineniia*, 14 vols. (Sofia, 1953–55), 14: 292–99.

69. The point is developed by Stalin's "house philosopher" F. Iudin, "Na putakh perekhod k sotsializmu v strankakh narodnoi demokratii," *Voprosy filosofii* 1 (1947): 40–59.

70. Force improvements are detailed in A. A. Babakov, *Vooruzhennye sily SSSR posle voiny (1945–1986 gg.): Istoriia stroitel'stva* (Moscow, 1987), pp. 49–59; Wolfe, *Soviet Power and Europe*, pp. 32–49. The size of the Soviet armed forces nearly doubled from 1948 to 1953. The former chief of the Soviet General Staff, Sergei Akhromeev, described these measures retrospectively in 1989 as an attempt to create "in response to the threat from the United States a military threat to U.S. allies in western Europe," a situation that is perceived to have remained "frozen" up to 1985. S. Akhromeev, "SSSR—za dialog i sotrudnichestvo, a SShA?" *Pravda*, 30 Oct. 1989, p. 7.

resistance leader under the Horthy regime, and subsequently Hungarian interior and foreign minister, Rajk possessed impeccable credentials as a militant. His "trial" was preceded by a massive propaganda campaign and disfigured by the accused's abject confession to a list of absurd crimes. Rajk was executed immediately following the spectacle. In the following weeks, lest the point be missed, the Soviet Union and all of its eastern European allies broke diplomatic relations with Yugoslavia.

Similarly crude retribution was staged elsewhere. The major victim in Albania became Koci Xoxe, vice-president of the council of ministers and the most outspoken proponent of a pro-Yugoslav line in a party that had risen to power under Tito's tutelage. Outmaneuvered by emerging strongman Enver Hoxha, Xoxe and numerous associates were sentenced to death in June 1949. In Poland the main target was Wladyslaw Gomulka, leader of the communist underground during the war and subsequently general secretary of the Polish Communist party. Condemned by the Polish Politburo in July 1948, Gomulka managed to avoid execution, but he was ousted from his leadership posts in November and subsequently confined to a form of house arrest. These stage-managed exercises in vilification hit a snag with the show process of the Bulgarian communist Traicho Kostov in December 1949. Left crippled after leaping from a window to escape interrogation under the old regime, hardened by a life of struggle, Kostov astonished his inquisitors by publicly denying the legitimacy of his signed confession. The inconvenient comportment exposed the trials for the farce that they were, but it did not prevent Kostov from being sentenced to death.

The purges of 1948–1949 demonstrated a certain coherence. All of the major victims could be described as national communists with independent sources of authority, militants who had often spent the war years fighting from the underground. Tito, like Trotsky in the 1930s, was identified as the ringleader in absentia in every case, and treasonous collaboration with the Yugoslav leader was mentioned in almost all indictments. In addition to striking down leading personalities, the purge cut deeply into party organizations. General suspensions of recruitment were declared, and from 1948 to 1951 25 percent of eastern European party members were expelled, and 5–10 percent arrested.[71] The harsh logic informing these measures was not difficult to fathom. Accompanied by an acceleration of unpopular programs such as collectivization, they had the effect of intimidating dissent within communist organizations, detaching leaders from their national milieu, and strengthening their dependence upon Moscow.

71. Fejtö, *Histoire des démocraties populaires,* 1: 256.

A second wave of eastern European purges in 1951–1952 served different ends. The major trials now victimized "Moscow"communists who had spent the war years in the USSR and could hardly be suspected of Titoist inclinations. In Poland a trial of leading military officers in August 1951 decimated the high command. In Czechoslovakia a series of arrests during 1951 culminated with the trial of former secretary general Rudolf Slánský in November 1952, the last major show process in the eastern bloc. Factional rivalry within the leadership may well have been at the root of these events, with the Jewish Slánský targeted as a scapegoat for popular dissatisfaction. In Romania leading militants such as Ana Pauker, Teohari Georgescu, and Vasile Luca were dragged down during 1952 without the sanction of a public sentencing.

As a result of these brutal proceedings eastern European Communist parties were cut off from their mass base and transformed into cowed servants charged with presiding over a homogenized Soviet bloc. In its own terms, Soviet-inspired retrenchment had succeeded impressively. In the process, however, a long-term dilemma was created. The Soviet security posture now rested upon the integrity of an eastern European glacis that had been built entirely upon coercion. Herein lay the fatal shortsightedness of Stalin's reliance upon intimidation as a means of enforcing discipline. The bizarre cult of personality, social regimentation, and bloody reprisals against real or imagined rivals provided an impossible foundation for the cooperative European order that the USSR claimed to want and from which it most certainly would have benefited. Lacking indigenous sources of legitimacy, the people's democracies would soon become a permanent source of tension and instability.

The Cold War in Asia

Through 1949 the crucible of the Cold War was in Europe. From 1949 onward new foci of tension began to appear in Asia as well. Although the issues at stake were often quite different from those being disputed in Europe and the degree of Soviet exposure was much less, the premises of Soviet security policy remained consistent: to pursue advantage when achievable at low cost, but to avoid overexposure and risky confrontations.

Postwar Asia was rent by an array of conflicts that peace had not contributed to resolving. The war dealt a fatal blow to tottering colonial orders. In Malaya, Indochina, Indonesia, Burma, and the Philippines national liberation struggles were in full course. The British imperial system in the Indian subcontinent was approaching its final agony, and China had plunged into the concluding act of its protracted civil war.

Immense changes were emerging on all sides, but they were changes over which the Soviet Union had very little control. Moscow's support for national liberation movements was minimal.[72] Effectively excluded from the Japanese settlement, the Soviets made do with modest territorial acquisitions. Though it watched the course of the Chinese revolution apprehensively, Moscow was only marginally engaged. A forward role in Asia was not part of the Soviet game plan.

The best example of Moscow's caution was its ambiguous relationship with the Chinese Communist party (CCP). Despite their long association with the movement, during the war the Soviets preferred to bank upon a state-to-state link with the government of Jiang Jieshi and his nationalist party (Guomindang). When the Chinese civil war heated up during 1946, Moscow sought to maintain leverage over both parties. In Soviet-occupied Manchuria stocks of arms were turned over to the communist People's Liberation Army, but punitive expropriations were carried out by the Soviets unilaterally. Moscow's refusal to consider territorial adjustments in outer Mongolia and a short-lived attempt to build a sympathetic political movement in Manchuria around the personality of Gao Gang were not calculated to win the hearts of Chinese of any stripe.[73] During 1946 a primary concern became the presence of U.S. troops in northern China. Molotov requested their withdrawal at the Moscow CFM in the spring of 1947, but his priority was to eliminate a potential threat to the USSR rather than to assist the CCP. Doubtful of Mao's ability to hold southern China even after Jiang's armies had revealed their utter unreliability, the USSR continued to urge a compromise between the embittered rivals through 1948. When, after a series of defeats, the Guomindang moved its capital to Canton in February 1949, the Soviet Union became the only country in the world to assign a new ambassador. Indeed, Stalin clung to his alliance with Jiang right up to the latter's flight to Taiwan. Contemporaries regarded the creation of the People's Republic of China in October 1949, followed by the conclusion of a Sino-Soviet friendship treaty in February 1950, as a triumph for Soviet diplomacy. In retrospect it is clear that Stalin already feared the emergence of an "Asian Tito" in the person of Mao Zedong.[74]

The one Asian region where the Soviets were significantly engaged was Korea. Although it should properly have been considered as a liberated

---

72. See Mark N. Katz, "The Origins of the Vietnam War, 1945–1948," *Review of Politics* 2 (April 1980): 131–51.

73. Harry Schwartz, *Tsars, Mandarins, and Commissars* (Philadelphia, 1962), p. 147; James Harrison, *The Long March to Power* (New York, 1972), pp. 380–82.

74. Discussed in Robert R. Simmons, *The Strained Alliance: Peking, P'yongyang, Moscow and the Politics of the Korean Civil War* (New York, 1975), pp. 48–75; Max Beloff, *Soviet Policy in the Far East, 1944–1951* (London, 1951), pp. 56–57; David Floyd, *Mao against Khrushchev* (New York, 1964), p. 12.

nation rather than a defeated foe, Korea was divided by the Allies into zones of occupation. By 1946 the North Korean Communist party, led by Kim Il-sung, assumed authority in the Soviet zone. Stalin's motives in backing Kim were not all that different from those that determined Soviet policy in Poland. Directly contiguous to the important Soviet naval center of Vladivostok, located sixty kilometers to the north of a small common border, North Korea was a region that had to be denied to potential adversaries.[75]

Such adversaries did exist. On 15 August 1948 the outspoken anticommunist Syngman Rhee became president of South Korea. Rhee's use of terror to eliminate opponents, refusal to undertake necessary social legislation, and uninhibited calls for military action against the North marked him as a potentially dangerous aggressor. Nonetheless, on 1 January 1949 Soviet troops evacuated Korea. During 1949 and 1950 Rhee presided over a considerable expansion of the South Korean armed forces, which swelled from 60,000 early in 1948 to 181,000 by May 1950. The buildup was reciprocated by the North. An escalation of hostile rhetoric, an open arms race, and a proliferation of armed clashes along the border made it obvious that war was on the horizon.

The outbreak of war on 25 June 1950 was not so surprising as were its immediate consequences. Within days Kim Il-sung's armies swept across the frontier and routed their adversaries, forced to retreat in full flight toward the south. The first major armed clash of the Cold War seemed to be shaping up as a cake walk for the Reds. The situation was reversed at the eleventh hour by the intervention of American armed forces under the flag of the United Nations. Having withdrawn its representative from the Security Council in protest against the U.N. refusal to seat the People's Republic of China, the USSR was not able to block the decision with its veto. With American protection, Rhee's embattled armies could reassemble around the port of Pusan, at the Korean peninsula's extreme southern tip, and prepare for a counteroffensive.

The question of who was to blame for the Korean war might well seem pointless to a neutral observer. Each party to the conflict cultivated an oft-expressed hatred for its rival, and each was pledged to the reunification of Korea, divided by the fortunes of war against all cultural and historical logic, under its own banner. Khrushchev's memoir reports that a North Korean war plan was approved by Stalin during Kim's visit to Moscow in 1949, but he makes clear that the initiatives came from the Koreans themselves, and it is not certain whether the circumstances of

75. Erik van Ree, *Socialism in One Zone: Stalin's Policy in Korea, 1945–1947* (Oxford, 1989), pp. 267–77, provides a useful account of Stalin's postwar policy in Korea, suggesting that the consolidation of authority in the north rather than expansion remained the dominant Soviet motive.

the war's outbreak corresponded to Soviet presumptions or intentions.[76] To some extent both Kim and Rhee were imposing their own agendas, with Moscow and Washington forced to accommodate their errant behavior lest they lose all control over events.[77]

Moscow issued no public statements between the commencement of hostilities on 25 June and 4 July, at which time the vice-minister of foreign affairs, Gromyko, characterized the entire incident as a stage-managed pretext for U.S. intervention. A Radio Moscow statement of 7 July went further in broaching the "threat of attack upon Russia by imperialist powers."[78] Meanwhile, buoyed by a massive influx of U.S. forces, commander Douglas MacArthur was able to break out of Pusan during July and roll back the exhausted northern armies. On 15 September, MacArthur launched his famous amphibious assault upon Inchon, north of Seoul, and with official authorization pressed beyond the 38th parallel that had marked the original border between North and South. U.S. policy now became to reunify Korea by force under southern auspices, a direct challenge to the security interests of both the Soviet Union and China. The offensive was accompanied by a series of provocations directed against Moscow. On 13 July, Acheson posed the threat of an air atomic offensive; on 10 August the United States bombed Najin (Rashin), only seventeen kilometers from the Soviet border; on 4 September a Soviet warplane was shot down by U.S. fighters over the Yellow Sea; and on 8 October two U.S. F-80s attacked a Soviet aerodrome located twenty-nine kilometers south of Vladivostok on Soviet territory. The possibility of Soviet forces' entering Korea, or of a sudden U.S. thrust toward Vladivostok, could not totally be excluded. The Korean conflict had led the superpowers to the brink of a direct confrontation.

76. *Khrushchev Remembers: The Glasnost Tapes*, pp. 144–47. Khrushchev's account, which documents Soviet acquiescence rather than initiative, contradicts an image of the war as the product of "a Soviet war plan" (David Rees, *Korea: Limited War* [Baltimore, Md., 1964], p. 19), or as "planned, prepared, and initiated" by Stalin (David Dallin, *Soviet Foreign Policy after Stalin* [Philadelphia, 1961], p. 60).

77. The perception was recorded soon after the war's outbreak by Wilbur Hitchcock, "North Korea Jumps the Gun," *Current History* 115 (March 1951): 136–44. See also Simmons, *The Strained Alliance*, pp. 102–30; Robert A. Scalapino and Chang-sik Lee, *Communism in Korea: The Movement* (Berkeley, Calif., 1972), pp. 382–452; Pierre Devilliers, "La Chine et les origines de la guerre de Corée," *Revue française de science politique* 6 (1974): 1174–94. Kolko and Kolko, *Limits of Power*, pp. 578–85, make the provocative argument that Rhee intentionally pulled back to Pusan in order to encourage American intervention. The Kolkos' thesis is criticized by William Stueck, "The Soviet Union and the Origin of the Korean War," *World Politics* 4 (July 1976): 622–35. A good survey of these and other more current studies is provided by Philip West, "Interpreting the Korean War," *American Historical Review* 1 (Feb. 1989): 80–96.

78. *VPSS 1950 goda* (Moscow, 1953), pp. 195–205.

Once the tide of battle began to turn against the North, the primary motive shaping Soviet behavior became the desire to avoid engagement. Military assistance to the North was held to modest levels and included almost no heavy equipment such as tanks, howitzers, or artillery. The main contribution was air support, staged from Soviet territory and of limited usefulness. Soviet ground forces in the region were kept in a defensive posture in order to prevent them from being drawn into the fighting. Moscow refused Kim the kind of aid that could have made a decisive difference and made clear that it did not intend to intervene.[79] When MacArthur's counteroffensive placed Kim's government in peril, it was left to China to act unilaterally in order to ward off the worst. In October and November, Beijing repeatedly voiced its intention to attack should MacArthur's forces continue to approach the Chinese border along the Yalu. MacArthur turned a deaf ear. When China struck in force on 26 November, U.S. forces were strung out in indefensible positions and completely exposed. What followed was one of the worst defeats in the history of American arms. After a desperate U.S. retreat to the 38th parallel, the front was stabilized during the winter of 1950–1951 approximately where it had been before the war began. The Korean conflict had escalated to a clash between major world powers, but the Soviet Union was not among them.

In six months of constant fighting armies had marched up and down the length of the Korean peninsula and left it in ruins. By the time the war had run its course Korea's population was reduced by nearly a million. U.S. casualties numbered 142,091, with 33,629 killed. This was no longer a "cold" war, and in the heat of battle all sense of proportion threatened to disappear. Stung by defeat, MacArthur reacted with the demand for an attack with "thirty to fifty" atomic bombs against Manchuria and the establishment of a "radioactive cobalt barrier" along the Yalu. On 15 December Truman declared a state of emergency and blamed "the leaders of the Soviet Union" for the Korean impasse.[80] But it was not the Kremlin so much as overreaching on its own part that had mired Washington, contrary to original intentions, in a large-scale land war in Asia.

79. Simmons, *The Strained Alliance*, pp. 180–82; William Zimmerman, "The Korean and Vietnam Wars," in Stephen S. Kaplan et al., *Diplomacy of Power: Soviet Armed Forces as a Political Instrument* (Washington, D.C., 1981), pp. 314–56. Subsequent Soviet accounts such as that of Mikhail S. Kapitsa, *KNR: Dva desiatiletiia—dve politiki* (Moscow, 1969), pp. 36–38, emphasizing Soviet readiness to intervene, may be taken with a grain of salt as ex post facto bravado. Khrushchev confirms that Stalin absolutely rejected the very idea of a Soviet counterintervention. *Khrushchev Remembers: The Glasnost Tapes*, p. 147. Some Soviet pilots served as "volunteers" in Korea, but on a strictly unofficial basis.

80. Truman, *Memoirs*, 2: 134–35.

The door toward a compromise was finally opened by a Soviet initiative. On 23 June 1951 U.N. representative Malik, posing as a neutral party, proposed an armistice on the basis of a ceasefire and mutual disengagement at the 38th parallel. Several weeks later north and south Korean, Chinese, and U.S. military delegations began consultations at Panmunjom. A negotiated solution would prove elusive, and two years of costly military stalemate still lay ahead. Throughout the marathon the Soviet Union remained in the background, directly involved in neither the fighting nor the negotiations. From the outset the threat of escalation in Korea had been the Soviets' prime concern. The consequences of a northern collapse, which would have placed U.S. forces immediately south of critical Soviet military facilities, were unpalatable. Even so, all signs indicate that Moscow would have tolerated even so bitter a defeat rather than court the risk of war. Whether the war is best explained as an uncontrollable explosion or an adventure gone wrong, Soviet reactions to the course of events in Korea fit the logic of Stalin's larger security paradigm: to seize opportunity but to dodge confrontation, to avoid war at all costs, and to retrench around the Motherland when all else failed.

The consequences of the Korean conflict for the Soviet security posture in Asia were immense all the same. Though it saved the Soviet position in the short run, the Chinese intervention became a watershed in Moscow's relations with its Asian allies. The leaders of the North Korean Worker's party, after so many sacrifices, must have been embittered by Malik's conciliatory U.N. speech, which called for an armistice "without conditions." The Chinese, whose national interests were as much at stake as were Moscow's were left to bear the costs of a savage war with only the most parsimonious assistance from their "fraternal ally." The Soviet Union made clear that it would accept no major risk on behalf of its Korean and Chinese allies, ended by favoring a "two Koreas" solution, and appeared willing to accept the defeat of revolutionary forces rather than put its own interests on the line.[81] Preoccupied with the threat of war, Stalin sacrificed revolutionary solidarity with the peoples of Asia and betrayed the spirit of his newly crafted alliance with People's China. As in eastern Europe, short-term solutions carried the seeds of long-term dilemmas.

Defensive Coexistence

The Korean conflict added the final ingredient to the Cold War consensus growing up within the United States. With Americans dying in

81. See the analysis in Allen S. Whiting, *China Crosses the Yalu* (New York, 1960), pp. 72–91.

the fight against "Godless Communism," no barrier could contain a flood of right-wing extremism. Senator Joseph McCarthy's assault upon "subversion," begun in February 1950 in the wake of the panic set off by the successful Soviet A-bomb test, was transformed by the atmosphere of crisis into a witch-hunt reaching into every area of public life. McCarthy would eventually be destroyed by his own excesses, but he left a significant legacy. Henceforward the American ultra-right, unbendingly anti-communist and anti-Soviet, would be a force to be reckoned with.

The U.S. call to arms was summarized by the National Security Council's NSC-68 memorandum, a sweeping outline of international priorities drawn up in the spring of 1950.[82] The key author of NSC-68 was Paul Nitze, whose position at the State Department had come to resemble that formerly held by Kennan and who would remain an important architect of U.S. Soviet policy for decades to come. Nitze's image of a larger-than-life Soviet threat was entirely in the spirit of the time. NSC-68 sounded the tocsin, and propelled by the war in Korea, the United States responded by trebling military spending, approving massive force buildups in Europe, and vastly extending its global security commitments.

None of this should have surprised Stalin and his entourage, for whom the tenor of western policy had long since become clear. By 1950, however, the Soviet Union was no longer quite so exposed as it had been in the immediate postwar years. Crude but effective, the policy of retrenchment had begun to create the foundation for a more self-assured international policy. This awareness was summarized by Suslov in his report to the Cominform's third general plenum at Matra, Hungary, during November 1949.

> In the struggle against imperialism and war, the forces of peace, democracy, and socialism have grown and affirmed themselves. The continued development of the power of the Soviet Union, the political and economic consolidation of the countries of people's democracies and their entry onto the path of socialist construction, the victory of the German [Democratic] Republic, the consolidation of communist parties and the development of the democratic movement within the capitalist countries, the huge amplitude of the movement of champions of peace; all this marks an important extension and strengthening of the anti-imperialist and democratic camp.[83]

82. After being classified for over twenty years, NSC-68 was finally published in the *Naval War College Review* (May/June 1975): 51–108. See Samuel F. Wells, "Sounding the Tocsin: NSC 68 and the Soviet Threat," *International Security* 4 (Fall 1979): 116–38; Gaddis, *Strategies of Containment*, pp. 91–95.

83. M. A. Suslov, *Marksizm-leninizm i sovremennaia epokha: Izbrannye rechi i stat'i v trekh tomakh* 3 vols. (Moscow, 1982), 1: 188.

Suslov's optimism was not entirely off the mark. Though it still lacked the means to deliver atomic strikes against its adversary, the Soviet Union had overcome the U.S. monopoly of the atomic bomb. Conventional forces were being restructured commensurate with the new military challenge posed by NATO in Europe. The integrity of the east bloc was temporarily secured, and economic recovery programs were moving forward. By nurturing its strengths and avoiding unequal contests, the Soviet Union had placed itself in a position to reemerge as a competitive force in world politics. "The democratic forces," Suslov commented archly, "are growing more rapidly than the dark forces of the warmongers. The correlation of forces in the international arena is changing in a fundamental manner, in favor of the camp of peace, democracy, and socialism."[84]

Retrenchment had never been conceived as an end in itself, or as an alternative to a policy hinged upon coexistence, but rather as a prerequisite for the successful pursuit of such a policy. Suslov seemed to be suggesting that the necessary prerequisites were in place. From 1950 onward "inevitable conflict" rhetoric began to be toned down, and a "détente offensive" seeking to revive the themes of coexistence and cooperation was moved back to center stage. The contours of Soviet policy were not altered, but the change in emphasis revealed a revival in self-confidence.

The most visible manifestation of the coexistence line during the final years of the Stalin period became the communist-led world peace movement. The World Congress of Intellectuals for Peace held in Wroclaw from 25 to 28 August 1948, concluding with a harshly anti-American speech by the Soviet novelist Aleksandr Fadeev, was its starting point. Under the aegis of the Cominform the movement proceeded to organize the World Peace Congress, held simultaneously in Paris and Prague on 20–25 April 1949, in which representatives from seventy-two countries took part. The congress adopted a manifesto phrased in the Stalinist idiom calling for the banning of nuclear weapons and reductions in conventional force levels.[85] It also established the World Peace Committee in Paris as an executive organ. Affiliated sections, described as "national councils of partisans of peace," soon sprang into being worldwide. Tactically the movement was conceived as a popular front in which communists would play a leading but by no means exclusive role. Its official purpose was summarized by Stalin at the end of 1948; to resist the "new threat of war" posed by imperialism by staging demonstratory mass

84. Ibid., pp. 183–84.
85. "Manifesto, World Peace Congress," *For a Lasting Peace, For a People's Democracy,* 1 May 1949, p. 1.

mobilizations.[86] The movement's high-water mark was the World Peace Committee's second world congress, held in Stockholm 15–19 March 1950. The congress issued the famous Stockholm Appeal, a call for the banning and destruction of atomic weapons, which was eventually signed, after an intensive petition campaign, by more than 560 million people.[87] Subsequent world peace congresses in Warsaw (16–22 November 1950) and Vienna (12–19 December 1952), and the conferences of a rechristened World Peace Council in Berlin (21–27 February 1951), Vienna (1–7 March 1951), and Berlin (1–6 July 1952) carried on the tradition, albeit with diminishing effect.

The Soviet-sponsored world peace movement of the early 1950s is commonly dismissed as an exercise in propaganda. The two-camps image into which analysis was pressed and the primitive rhetoric used to castigate opponents no doubt served to vulgarize the issues at stake. The movement was nonetheless a meaningful pillar of Soviet policy. In addition to its propaganda value it had more calculated purposes, notably the attempt to neutralize the United States' air atomic strategy by placing an onus upon the contemplated use of atomic weapons.[88] The movement offered an interface between the international communist movement and progressive opinion worldwide and as such represented an opening toward the noncommunist left. Finally, with its implicit acknowledgment that war was neither inevitable nor desirable, the movement negated an important premise of the Zhdanov line and paved the way for Stalin's new emphasis upon coexistence.

The peace movement also overlapped with the Soviet Union's most important diplomatic effort during the early 1950s—a campaign to prevent the remilitarization of West Germany. The Korean conflict lent new urgency to the American push for the integration of a German military contingent into NATO. The main barrier blocking the way was not the USSR, but France, which had its own reasons to fear a resurgence of German power. The need to bring the French on board complicated U.S. plans, but it did not derail them. The first step was an attempt launched during 1950 to create a "European defense community" including West Germany. The project proved to be abortive, but it indicated the direction in which the Soviet Union's rivals were determined to move.

86. Stalin, *Sochineniia*, 3 [XVI]: 105–7. See also the sycophantic appreciation by B. Ponomarev, "Stalin—genial'nyi teoretik i vozhd' mezhdunarodnogo kommunisticheskogo dvizheniia," *Bol'shevik* 1 (1950): 56–74.

87. Text in "Session of Permanent Committee of World Peace Congress," *For a Lasting Peace, For a People's Democracy,* 24 March 1950, p. 1. A disproportionately large percentage of the signatures came from the socialist countries.

88. Good accounts are offered by Marcou, *Le Kominform,* pp. 289–310, and Marshall D. Shulman, *Stalin's Foreign Policy Reappraised* (Cambridge, Mass., 1963), pp. 199–237.

The Soviets responded with a series of proposals attempting to revive the principle of four-power cooperation. On 23 October 1950 the foreign ministers of the Soviet bloc states signed a statement in Prague calling for a German peace treaty including the principles of demilitarization and the evacuation of all occupation forces. At Soviet initiative, representatives of the Big Four met at Château de la Muette in France between March and June 1951, but the sessions adjourned without any substantial accomplishments to their credit. The most dramatic Soviet initiative was the issuance on 10 March 1952 of a diplomatic note, addressed to France, Great Britain, and the United States, which proposed the creation of a united and neutral Germany. The concept was similar to that which had been outlined by James Byrnes in September 1945 (and which the Soviets had at that time rejected), and included the important concession that an independent Germany would eventually be permitted a limited national defense force and military industry. Additional Soviet notes of 9 April, 24 May, and 23 June added facets to the original proposal, including a plan for elections to an all-German parliament to be supervised by the four occupation authorities.[89]

Orthodox interpretations in the West portray the Soviet March note of 1952 as a ploy, intended to slow progress toward the creation of a European defense community by tying the western powers into an open-ended process of negotiation. The argument would be easier to substantiate if these same western powers had in the slightest measure attempted to put Soviet intentions to the test. Rather than pursuing Stalin's initiative, the western allies sought to block negotiated options by establishing impossible preliminary conditions. What it was that Stalin meant when he spoke of an "independent, democratic, and peaceful state" was never explored. With the United States committed to a policy of strength, diplomatic channels for accommodation remained closed.[90]

Stalin's emphasis upon peaceful coexistence was not derailed. His last major theoretical work, a series of essays entitled *The Economic Problems of Socialism in the USSR*, included a review of Soviet international

89. The diplomatic process is described by Loth, *Die Teilung der Welt*, pp. 269–308; Fontaine, *Histoire de la guerre froide*, 2: 51–55. The texts of the various Soviet notes are assembled in Eberhard Jäckel, ed., *Die deutsche Frage 1952–1956: Notenwechsel und Konferenzdokumente der vier Mächte* (Frankfurt am Main, 1957).

90. For an interpretation critical of Soviet intentions see Gerhard Wettig, *Entmilitarisierung und Wiederbewaffnung in Deutschland 1943–1955* (Munich, 1967), pp. 497–522. Interpretations of the Soviet March note as a "missed opportunity" appear in Klaus Erdmenger, *Das folgen-schwere Missverständnis: Bonn und die sowjetische Deutschlandpolitik 1949–1955* (Freibrug, 1967), pp. 132–61; Gerd Meyer, *Die sowjetische Deutschland-Politik im Jahre 1952* (Tübingen, 1970); Rolf Steininger, *Die vertane Chance: Die Stalin-Note vom 10 März 1952 und die Wiedervereinigung* (Berlin, 1985).

policy that was notable for its accommodating spirit. The world war had weakened imperialism, the aging dictator explained, intensifying competition and making new wars between rival capitalist states unavoidable. But it had also greatly strengthened the socialist bloc. As a result, despite chronic saber rattling, no capitalist country could contemplate attacking the USSR without courting its own destruction. With Soviet power as a reliable deterrent to imperialist aggression, the active thrust of Soviet security policy would henceforward be "to rouse the masses of the people to fight for the preservation of peace and the prevention of another world war."[91] The Soviet Union was willing to coexist with the capitalist world on these terms; with the foundations for security through strength in place it expressed an openness to pragmatic cooperation. In fact, it was something very much like the status quo that Stalin was seeking to perpetuate. What he recommended was a strategy of defensive coexistence premised upon the avoidance of war, consolidation of the Soviet sphere of influence, a renewed great power concert, and patient work to build and extend the foundations of Soviet power.

The Economic Problems of Socialism in the USSR was published three days prior to the CPSU's 19th party congress, which met during October 1952. Although Stalin did not deliver the keynote address, his essays established the themes that would dominate the proceedings. In the report of the Central Committee, read by Malenkov in Stalin's place, a two-camps perspective was reaffirmed, but the "inevitable conflict" implication of the Zhdanov line was rejected. Though inter-capitalist contradictions remained the main threat to peace, the strength of the socialist bloc was now sufficient to neutralize them. "The Soviet policy of peace and security for all peoples," Malenkov stated, "proceeds from the assumption that the peaceful coexistence and cooperation of capitalism and communism is quite possible given a mutual desire to cooperate, readiness to carry out commitments undertaken, and observance of the principle of equality and non-interference in the internal affairs of other states."[92] In his brief closing remarks Stalin was equally straightforward. The continued progress of the world communist movement, he suggested, rested upon the ability of the Soviet Union and the People's democracies to preserve world peace. In his very last public statement, a brief interview with James Reston of the *New York Times* on 21 December 1952, Stalin remained true to his precepts. "I continue to believe," he reiterated, "that war between the United States of America and the

---

91. Stalin, *Sochineniia* 3 [XVI]: 188–245.
92. G. Malenkov, *Otchetnyi doklad XIX s"ezda partii o rabote Tsentral'nogo komiteta VKP (b)* (Moscow, 1952), p. 31.

Soviet Union cannot be considered inevitable, that our countries can continue in the future to live in peace."[93]

The message was without question tarnished by the *fin de régne* intrigue surrounding Stalin's last months in the Kremlin. In December 1952 a putative plot was uncovered among Kremlin doctors, most of them Jewish, charged with planning the medical murders of leading Soviet personalities at the behest of "Zionist and anti-Soviet organizations." The Byzantine accusation may well have been intended as the prelude to a new blood purge.[94] Whatever the case, events in train were cut short by Stalin's death on 5 March 1953. The Generalissimo had exercised virtually unlimited power for a quarter of a century. The backward, isolated nation whose leadership he had inherited was now a great world power. But it was weighed down by a bitterly oppressive domestic order, its citizens cowed and passive, its prisons gorged with millions of victims. The severity of the regime constructed in Stalin's name had always been and would remain a barrier to the achievement of the coexistence which he claimed to seek on the international level. Stalin's legacy in international affairs was at the least complex. There was some irony, but not necessarily incongruity, in the fact that the great tyrant should leave the stage as the world's most insistent proponent of a policy of peace.

There is a sense in which it may be argued that the Cold War was the West's greatest gift to Stalin. World War II and its outcome could have unleashed powerful forces for change within the USSR, but change was possible only in a cooperative and peaceful environment where the Soviet search for security had ceased to be a burning preoccupation. The West's insensitivity to the legacy of the war, its refusal to treat with Moscow on a foundation of collegiality and reciprocal advantage, and the polarized international system that resulted made it easy for Stalin to reassert the kind of rule by terror that he had patented during the 1930s. Almost any measures could be justified on behalf of the sacrosanct cause of defense from external threats. Xenophobic isolationism, the cult of personality, the forced Sovietization of central and eastern Europe, and the remilitarization of Soviet defense policy after 1947 all suited the exigencies of the Cold War as well as Stalin's personal proclivities.

93. Stalin, *Sochineniia* 3 [XVI]: 310–15 and 316–17.

94. Interviews with surviving relatives of the accused doctors (all of whom were pardoned in April 1953 immediately after Stalin's death) that shed some light on the affair have been published in the Soviet Yiddish publication *Sovietich Heimland* (June 1988). See *Le Monde*, 25 Nov. 1988, p. 4, for extracts. Of particular interest is the memoir by Yakov Rapoport, *The Doctors' Plot of 1953* (Cambridge, Mass., 1991).

As sharp as it may have been, the intensification of East-West rivalry that set in from 1945 onward never led Stalin to cross the threshold of provocation that might actually spark a direct confrontation with his new global rival; for the USSR, the Cold War was a *guerre manquée*. The common thread that linked Soviet security policy as it moved from the premises of accommodation, to retrenchment, to defensive coexistence was the desire to avoid costly external engagements, to prevent war with the United States at any price, and to rebuild the foundations of Soviet power. In these admittedly narrow terms Stalin's postwar security policy may be said to have succeeded in some measure.

Beginning in 1947 Stalinism renewed what had always been its essential historical character—the political regime of a revolutionary polity that considered itself to be permanently under siege, forced to lash its recalcitrant citizens toward their rendezvous with destiny, ready to sacrifice, because its entire existence was perceived to hang from a thread, almost any civilized norm on behalf of the "good of the cause." How long could the Soviet peoples bear up under the weight of the sequence of extraordinary mobilizations to which they were subjected without collapsing into lethargy and despair? This was not a question that interested the aged dictator, callous, calculating, and confident to the end. It was, however, a question that would have to interest his successors, for whom the cumulative strains of unrepentant Cold War rivalries raised the specter of new and unprecedented kinds of dislocations.

CHAPTER SIX

Paths of Coexistence,
1953–1964

Coexistence means the continuation of the struggle between two social systems, but of a struggle by peaceful means, without war, without the interference of a state in the domestic affairs of another state. One should not be afraid. We must struggle resolutely and consistently for our ideals, for our way of life, for our socialist system. The partisans of capitalism, too, will not, of course, abandon their way of life, their ideology; they will fight. We hold that the struggle must be economic, political, and ideological, but not military.

—Nikita S. Khrushchev, 10 October 1959

The post-Stalin era in Soviet politics was shaped by the ambitious, idealistic, and occasionally contradictory priorities of Nikita S. Khrushchev. After a brief transition following the death of the grim dictator the door was opened to a period of experiment and reform, which in retrospect appears to have been a dress rehearsal for the more substantial changes that would arrive a generation later. The result was a number of impressive reforms and a considerable amount of sound and fury, but not necessarily the kind of decisive redirection that the leadership desired.

Under Khrushchev the Soviet Union's security environment changed in important ways. Stalin passed on the legacy of defensive coexistence together with a bristling security posture resting upon budgetary priorities described by one scholar as "those of a war economy."[1] Once Khrushchev was safely installed in power, alternatives began to emerge. Soviet strategists received a green light to explore the new strategic realities of the nuclear age, and an attempt was made to reduce the military burden

1. George W. Breslauer, *Khrushchev and Brezhnev as Leaders: Building Authority in Soviet Politics* (London, 1982), p. 23.

by cutting conventional forces. Peaceful coexistence was declared to be the "general line" of Soviet foreign policy, and in general the ideological contours of the Cold War period were softened. But attempts to reduce Cold War confrontation were partially offset by an aggressive assertion of Soviet rights and prerogatives, including the emergence of an ambitious forward policy in the Third World. The paradigm underlying Khrushchev's security policy is therefore best characterized as *competitive coexistence.*[2] Less constrained by fear than Stalin, the new Soviet leadership sought to reinforce international cooperation without abandoning the effort to increase Soviet power.

The consequences of Khrushchev's policies were as contradictory as the aspirations that inspired them. The wave of domestic reforms over which he presided produced mixed results. The decision to accept the implications of a full-scale strategic rivalry with the United States pressed the USSR into the implacable logic of an arms race that it could scarcely afford. Efforts to achieve massive conventional force reductions were successfully warded off, and forward deployments in Europe continued to demand high levels of readiness. Although Khrushchev made the Soviet Union a force to be reckoned with in the Third World, many of his achievements proved to be transitory. Despite efforts to reduce the intensity of the Cold War, his belligerency occasioned some of the most dangerous confrontations of the postwar period. Not least, Khrushchev's tenure in office ended with his political defeat, launching a conservative reaction that would undo many of his positive accomplishments.[3]

Khrushchev succeeded in eliminating some of the worst abuses of Stalinism and in softening the Soviet Union's relations with its major rivals. His redefinition of peaceful coexistence provided a conceptual foundation for Soviet international policy that proved enduring. Under his leadership the USSR recovered from the ravages of the war and expanded its economy, and on balance its stature as a world power was enhanced. But in international as well as in domestic affairs Khrushchev's work was left incomplete. Ernst Neizvestnii's famous grave marker in honor of the fallen leader, with Khrushchev's bust poised against a background of black and white marble, captures the ambiguity of his legacy. Despite Khrushchev's best efforts, at the time of

2. Khrushchev used this phrase in an interview with Egyptian journalist Mohamed Heikal, speaking of the need to keep Soviet relations with the Arab world "within the limits of the broader policy of competitive but peaceful coexistence with the Western powers." Cited in Mohamed Heikal, *Sphinx and Commissar: The Rise and Fall of Soviet Influence in the Arab World* (London, 1978), p. 83.

3. See the analysis in F. Burlatskii, "Khrushchev (shtriki k politicheskomu portretu)," in Iu. N. Afanas'ev, ed., *Inogo ne dano* (Moscow, 1988), pp. 424–40, which attributes many of Khrushchev's political frustrations to his personal failings.

his political demise the Cold War system inherited from Stalin, with its tenacious logic of confrontation, continued to inform the Soviet quest for security.

Khrushchev and Coexistence

In the wake of Stalin's death his fearful lieutenants opted to concentrate authority by replacing the Enlarged Presidium created at the 19th party congress with a smaller body of ten members. Apparently at Beria's suggestion, Malenkov was appointed as the new chair of the Council of Ministers, which, combined with the post of Central Committee secretary, made him the dominant figure in the new government. But in fact the succession was only beginning. As head of the state security apparatus Beria had ambitions of his own, and Malenkov's position was far from secure.

Already on 21 March, Malenkov announced his withdrawal from the Secretariat, leaving Khrushchev as the only Presidium member who was simultaneously a Central Committee secretary. Strongly based in the party apparatus, with his ally Nikolai Bulganin as the new minister of defense, and with the prestige of having been chosen to head Stalin's funeral commission, Khrushchev rapidly emerged as Malenkov's leading contender. Before settling their own accounts, however, the two leaders moved to eliminate a common threat by plotting to bring Beria down. During July, with the help of the military command, Stalin's police chief was arrested and executed, and the arbitrary authority of his security police curbed.[4]

With Beria gone, the years 1953–1954 were dominated by the reforms of the "New Course" associated with Malenkov. Though his character remains to some extent obscure, it appears that from the early 1950s onward Malenkov was committed to a liberal program hinged upon a shift toward consumerist priorities in the economy and a more moderate foreign policy. His first statement on foreign affairs as head of state, a speech delivered to the Supreme Soviet on 15 March 1953, picked up the moderate tone of his keynote address to the 19th party congress one year earlier by asserting that "at the present time there is no disputed or unresolved question that cannot be settled peacefully by mutual agreement

4. In his memoirs Khrushchev names himself as the organizer of the plot against Beria. *Khrushchev Remembers*, pp. 322–41. Recent revelations concerning the plot and its motives are offered in F. Burlatskii, "Posle Stalina: Zametki o politicheskoi ottepeli," *Novyi mir* 10 (1988): 164; "Dokumenty general-leitenanta T. A. Strokacha o podgotovke Beriei zagavora v 1953 g.," *Novaia i noveishaia istoriia* 3 (1989): 166–76.

among the interested countries."[5] In the spirit of conciliation Moscow approved the appointment of Dag Hammerskjold as U.N. general secretary after having vetoed four prior candidates, offered to resume diplomatic relations with Yugoslavia, Greece, and Israel (the latter having been severed during the Doctors' Plot affair in 1952), and withdrew territorial claims against Turkey. During a four-power foreign ministers' conference in Berlin conducted from 25 January to 18 February 1954, Foreign Minister Molotov (who had returned to his old post after Stalin's death) renewed the proposal for a European collective security system. The Soviet Union also participated in the Geneva conference of April–July 1954 charged with regulating the regional conflicts in Indochina and Korea.

One of the most notable new foreign policy directions was a change of style in Soviet-dominated eastern Europe. Following police action to put down strike actions triggered by Stalin's death in Plzen, Czechoslovakia, and East Berlin during June 1953, the New Course began to change the face of the Soviet bloc. Amnesties of political prisoners were carried out, compromised Stalinist leaders were dismissed, an attempt was made to curb arbitrary police power, pressures to collectivize agriculture were eased, and most of the mixed companies widely resented as symbols of Soviet exploitation were abolished. Inside the USSR the first steps designed to shift economic priorities from the heavy industry and military sectors toward light industry, agriculture, and consumer goods were undertaken in August 1953. Malenkov engineered deep cuts in Soviet military spending in 1953–1954, and in 1955 a large-scale demobilization of active-duty military personnel began.

Malenkov's New Course revealed the contours of a more flexible security strategy, with reduced military spending and a less confrontational posture toward the West as its hallmarks. In practice, however, Malenkov never achieved sufficient authority to give his policies momentum. During 1954 Khrushchev won the succession struggle by aligning with powerful vested interests that felt threatened by radical reform. Khrushchev was able to upstage his rival's economic program by offering an alternative plan for agriculture that promised low-cost miracles in the vast "Virgin Lands" of Kazakhstan, the Volga region, and Siberia. He refused to sanction military cutbacks and catered to the high command by opposing Malenkov's dovish orientation concerning nuclear war. In a speech delivered on 12 March 1954 Malenkov attacked the pursuit of the Cold War as "a policy for the preparation of a new world holocaust which, with the present means of warfare, means the

5. G. M. Malenkov, "Rech' na piatoi sessii Verkhovnogo Soveta SSR," *Kommunist* 12 (Aug. 1953): 30.

destruction of world civilization."[6] Khrushchev responded during June, boasting that in view of Soviet achievements in nuclear technology a new war would mean "the defeat and destruction of capitalism."[7] By establishing his credentials as a moderate open to change but opposed to destabilizing extremism, Khrushchev successfully outmaneuvered his rivals. At a session of the Supreme Soviet in February 1955 Malenkov offered his resignation. Khrushchev's associate Bulganin replaced him as chair of the Council of Ministers, with Zhukov emerging from the netherworld to which Stalin had consigned him to take over the ministry of defense. The Soviet military was rewarded for its support in March, when eleven Soviet generals received the marshal's baton, and with a 12 percent hike in the military budget.

Malenkov's defeat did not mean the end of reform. Rather, with his "liberal" rival out of the way, Khrushchev was in a position to push a reformist agenda of his own. In foreign and defense policy Malenkov's New Course was, if anything, accelerated. A July 1955 Central Committee plenum set the tone, with Khrushchev and Mikoian now calling for a general review of priorities. Khrushchev's report proposed a number of audacious alternatives, including the adoption of a "strictly defensive" orientation toward the West, reconciliation with Tito, and a more active policy toward the less developed countries.[8]

During May 1955 Khrushchev, Bulganin, Anastas Mikoian, and Dmitrii Shepilov paid a visit to Tito in Belgrad, thereby implicitly acknowledging the injustice of the Cominform's actions in 1949. A Soviet demarche of 10 May came toward the West's positions in a plea for comprehensive disarmament, and on 15 May the Austrian State Treaty was concluded, providing for the creation of a neutral and nonaligned

6. "Rech' tovarishcha G. M. Malenkova na sobranii izbiratelei Leningradskogo izbiratel'nogo okruga," *Pravda*, 13 March 1954, p. 2.

7. "Rech' tovarishcha N. S. Khrushcheva na desiatom s"ezde Kommunisticheskoi partii Chekhoslovakii," *Izvestiia*, 13 June 1954, p. 3. Molotov was even more explicit, thundering before the Supreme Soviet that in a nuclear war "what will perish will not be 'world civilization,' no matter how it suffers as a consequence of aggression, but that decaying [capitalist] social system with its blood-soaked imperialist foundation which has outlived its time." V. M. Molotov, "O mezhdunarodnom polozhenii i vneshnei politiki pravitel'stva SSSR," *Pravda*, 9 Feb. 1955, p. 4. Malenkov was forced to back down, and on 26 April 1954 he delivered an address in which he spoke of "the collapse of the capitalist social system" as the inevitable result of a new world war. "Rech' predsedatelia Soveta Ministrov SSSR, deputata G. M. Malenkova," *Izvestiia*, 27 April 1954, p. 7.

8. The session is described in Dallin, *Soviet Foreign Policy after Stalin*, pp. 228–33. Myron Rush, *The Rise of Khrushchev* (Washington, D.C., 1958), p. 25, calls Khrushchev's victory at the plenum "a turning point in Soviet history."

Austrian state.[9] Meetings between the heads of state of the four wartime allies in Geneva during July 1955 were the first formal encounters on that level in more than five years, and though the summit produced few substantial accomplishments, the "spirit of Geneva" became a watchword for the fresh winds that seemed to be stirring up the fetid atmosphere of the Cold War. During August the USSR restored the Porkkala naval facility to Finland, assumed its seat at the U.S.-sponsored International Conference for Peaceful Use of the Atom, and announced a reduction of 600,000 military effectives. In September, West German chancellor Konrad Adenauer visited Moscow, paving the way for the establishment of diplomatic relations. The Third World also received new attention. During October Burma's U Thant appeared in Moscow, and in November, Khrushchev and Bulganin embarked on a highly publicized state visit to India. Rather than reversing the momentum of reform, Khrushchev was taking over significant aspects of Malenkov's international policy and attaching them to a program that bore his own distinctive stamp. The culmination of this transition from one new course to another, and an event of fundamental importance in Soviet history, became the 20th party congress of the CPSU held from 14 to 25 February 1956.

The 20th congress was Khrushchev's event, a gathering which the first secretary dominated by sheer physical energy, constantly visible, shaking hands and politicking in all directions. The key initiatives were the first secretary's report for the Central Committee, delivered as the keynote address on 14 February, and the famous "Secret Speech" read before a closed session on the congress's final day. Together, these presentations summarized much of the reform program that the Khrushchev leadership would attempt to pursue thereafter.[10]

Khrushchev's report on the international situation begins with a string of traditional Stalinist clichés. The main feature of the contemporary epoch is described as the emergence of socialism as a world system and its steady progress relative to capitalist imperialism. Fear of the socialist alternative is identified as the basic source of the Cold War, reflected in Washington's desire to "contain" the USSR by conducting its policy

9. Accounts are provided by Audrey Kurth Cronin, *Great Power Politics and the Struggle over Austria, 1945–1955* (Ithaca, N.Y., 1986); Deborah Welch Larson, "Crisis Prevention and the Austrian State Treaty," *International Organization* 1 (Winter 1987): 27–60; Vojtech Mastny, "Kremlin Politics and the Austrian Settlement," *Problems of Communism* 4 (July–Aug. 1982): 37–51.

10. Citations from Khrushchev's report for the Central Committee are drawn from the official protocol, *XX s"ezd Kommunisticheskoi partii Sovetskogo Soiuza, 14–25 fevralia 1956 goda: Stenograficheskii otchet*, 2 vols. (Moscow, 1956), 1: 9–120.

"from a position of strength." But Khrushchev strikes out independently by identifying new forces in the international arena with the potential to contain Cold War rivalries. Special emphasis is placed upon the breakdown of the European colonial empires, described as "a fundamental change in world politics." The emerging nations of the Third World are identified as "objective allies" of the socialist camp within a "zone of peace" capable of challenging the aggressive designs of imperialism. These were audacious conclusions that made clear Khrushchev's desire to move Soviet thinking away from the fixations of the past.

Khrushchev's analysis is built around what he calls the "three principles of contemporary international relations." The first and most important is the "Leninist principle of the peaceful coexistence of states with different social systems," now described as the "general line" of Soviet foreign policy. Khrushchev's peaceful coexistence no longer designates a temporary tactical expedient; it has become a basic principle of interstate relations applying specifically to relations between capitalist and socialist states. In the spirit of Jawaharlal Nehru, peaceful coexistence is said to rest upon five pillars: mutual respect for territorial integrity and sovereignty, nonaggression, noninterference in internal affairs, equality and mutuality, and the peaceful regulation of disputes. None of these "pillars" is foreign to the repertoire of traditional statecraft, and by describing them as a general line, Khrushchev takes a long step toward accommodation with the norms of international relations that the October revolution originally sought to transcend.

Khrushchev's second principle is "the possibility of preventing war in the contemporary epoch." A controversy over the inevitability of war had already erupted under Stalin and had been resolved on a theoretical level in favor of the orthodox assumption that so long as capitalism existed, war could not altogether disappear. Khrushchev's remarks cut through the debate by allowing that although so long as imperialism remained intact, a *threat* of war would exist, the growing strength of the forces working for peace ensured that war was no longer "fatalistically inevitable." At the beginning of his address Khrushchev walked around Malenkov's "destruction of world civilization" thesis by remarking that if war did occur, the defeat of capitalist imperialism was assured. But the spirit of his conclusions was much more dovish than it was deemed politic to admit. Khrushchev had undermined a basic premise of the Zhdanov line and in a few lapidary phrases discarded an assumption of Soviet international theory handed down intact from the classic texts of Leninism.

Khrushchev's third principle rejects by implication the priority traditionally accorded to the Soviet model of socioeconomic development by acknowledging the validity of diverse paths toward the common goal of communism. Khrushchev specifically sanctions peaceful, parliamentary tactics, embraces the concept of national communism as embodied by Tito, and seems to encourage an opening to the social democratic left. The submission of the international communist movement to the dictates of Soviet power was an important part of Stalin's legacy. The attempt to redress the balance by introducing the concept of "polycentrism" as the foundation for a more collegial movement thus represented another break with the past.

The first secretary's keynote address traditionally articulates the collective position of the entire Soviet leadership. Khrushchev's "Secret Speech," delivered ten days later, added a personal dimension with its passionate attack upon the legacy of Stalin. Far from being kept a secret, the gist of the address was widely publicized, thus linking the cause of "de-Stalinization" to the person of Khrushchev himself.[11] Debate still goes on concerning Khrushchev's motives in making the speech and the logic of its timing at the eleventh hour just prior to the congress's closure. The revelations struck a blow against conservative resistance to reform, but Khrushchev was also implicated in the crimes of the Stalin era, and it is difficult to see what narrowly political ends were served that could not have been accomplished by other, potentially less destabilizing measures. Given all that we know about Khrushchev, it is reasonable to assume that the decision to attack Stalin also reflected deep personal conviction.[12]

Despite the effort to distinguish between Stalin the Bolshevik prior to 1934 and Stalin the terrorist dictator thereafter, and the elimination of collectivization from the list of Stalin's crimes, Khrushchev's exposure of the abuses of authority and merciless vendettas presided over by the great tyrant is overwhelming. Stalin is portrayed as a man perverted by power, directly responsible for the massacre of thousands of loyal communists and military cadre during the great purge, for Soviet unpreparedness on the eve of Operation Barbarossa, for military blunders as supreme commander, and for the savage arbitrariness of the postwar regime. Stalin's crimes were hardly a well-kept secret, but to articulate them in such a manner before the assembled elite of Soviet communism was an act of courage and an essential first step toward a difficult process of redress

---

11. I cite from the Russian text in "O kul'te lichnosti," pp. 128–70. A good account of the origins and aftermath of the speech is given by Adriano Guerra, *Il giorno che Chruscev parlo: Dal XX congresso alla rivolta ungherese* (Rome, 1986).

12. Roy Medvedev, *Khrushchev* (Oxford, 1982), pp. 90–92. Medvedev calls the speech a "movement of the heart" and "the principle feat of his [Khrushchev's] life." Khrushchev gives his own version of the speech's genesis in *Khrushchev Remembers: The Glasnost Tapes*, pp. 38–44.

that has not been completed to this day. It also set the tone for the reform program that Khrushchev himself was about to implement. By raising the "Stalin question," the new first secretary cleared the way for wide-ranging revisions in almost every area of public policy.

In the aftermath of the congress Khrushchev had to ward off one final challenge. At a Presidium session on 18 June 1957 a bare majority rallied behind the leaders of the conservative opposition, including Molotov, Kaganovich, Voroshilov, and now Malenkov as well, as they read out an indictment of the first secretary's "voluntarism" and demanded his resignation. A dramatic confrontation within the Kremlin followed. With the support of the armed forces, which guaranteed access to the Kremlin and commandeered aircraft to bring supporters to Moscow, Khrushchev was able to resist and have the question of his replacement placed before the Central Committee.[13] In a rapidly convened Central Committee plenum conducted from 22 to 29 June, Khrushchev's primacy was reconfirmed. A press release on 4 July condemned the opposition as an "anti-Party group," and the incident was followed by a shake-up that restructured the Presidium to Khrushchev's advantage. The extraordinary 21st party congress in January 1959 ratified these outcomes and in fact came to represent something like a high-water mark for Khrushchev's personal authority. The first secretary's triumph in the post-Stalin power struggle was complete, and it was linked to a reform agenda with important implications for security affairs.

The Revolution in Military Affairs

As Stalin's successors argued among themselves, the Soviet Union's security environment was being transformed from without by assertive western policies designed to strengthen the foundations of containment. In 1953 the Eisenhower administration unveiled its New Look strategic concept, calling for greater emphasis upon the intimidating force of atomic weapons.[14] The role of the nuclear "big stick" was emphasized in a speech by Secretary of State John Foster Dulles on 12 January 1954 which stressed the deterrent effect of "massive retaliatory power."[15] The phrase "massive retaliation" would henceforward

13. On the military's role in the 1957 crisis see Roger Pethybridge, *A Key to Soviet Politics: The Crisis of the Anti-Party Group* (New York, 1962), pp. 128–32.

14. Michael Mandelbaum, *The Nuclear Question: The United States and Nuclear Weapons, 1946–1976* (Cambridge, 1979), pp. 46–54.

15. The text is given in Raymond O'Connor, ed., *American Defense Policy in Perspective: From Colonial Times to the Present Day* (New York, 1965), pp. 327–28.

summarize a declared U.S. intention to respond to aggression with a devastating nuclear strike.

The military doctrine that the Soviet Union inherited from Stalin was not adequate to meet the American challenge. In the postwar period the Generalissimo's 1941 address outlining the "five permanently operating principles of war" was exaggerated into the foundation for a comprehensive strategic doctrine. All Soviet military thought was said to rest upon the work of Stalin, the "extraordinary creator" of Soviet military science.[16] In the cold light of day, however, the "extraordinary" contributions appeared to be rather insubstantial. Stalin's theory rested upon the assumption, inherited from the writings of Frunze, that military doctrine reflected the class essence of a society. Because it possessed a higher form of social organization, the Soviet Union was presumed to be in a position to outlast its rivals in a war of attrition. The "permanently operating principles" were reinforced by official legend concerning the Great Patriotic War and assumed that future armed confrontations would be won or lost in the context of traditional conventional operations.

An immediate consequence of Stalin's passing was a revival of the Soviet strategic debate. A high-level exchange of views was opened by Major General Nikolai Talenskii in the pages of the classified journal of the Soviet General Staff *Voennaia mysl'* (Military Thought) during September 1953. Talenskii challenged the premises of "Stalinist military science" by positing the existence of laws of war with universal relevance, arguing that as a socialist society the Soviet Union could not assume an inherent military advantage and pointing out that in the age of nuclear weapons the importance of the element of surprise needed to be reevaluated. A wide-ranging debate followed, including ten major articles and over forty letters in *Voennaia mysl'* and numerous commentaries in the Army newspaper *Krasnaia zvezda* (Red Star). Ultimately, it was Talenskii's call for revisions that prevailed, and a *Voennaia mysl'* editorial statement of April 1955 drew preliminary conclusions that encouraged innovation. The essential attribute of war was judged to be "armed conflict" rather than "social phenomenon," and the existence of universally valid laws of warfare was therefore granted. It was acknowledged that the destructive force of nuclear weapons made the element of surprise more important than in the past, but also cautioned that the advantage obtained by surprise was not decisive. Many of the underlying assumptions upon which the concept of "permanently operating factors" had rested were in fact retained, though by 1956 the phrase itself had entirely

16. *Bol'shaia sovetskaia entsiklopediia,* 2d ed., 51 vols. (Moscow, 1949–58), 8 (1951): 408, 406–11, and 436–40.

disappeared from the Soviet military press. These were cautious reevaluations, but as a step away from the straitjacket of Stalinist dogma, they were of great significance.[17]

Between 1955 and 1960 the new directions in Soviet strategic thought were pursued to a logical conclusion. The debate was extended backward in time by the posthumous rehabilitation of Tukhachevskii and the republication of his most important theoretical writings, as well as a new edition of Svechin's text on strategy. It also spilled over into the domain of politics. Zhukov's dual appointment as minister of defense and Presidium member in 1955 demonstrated the enhanced institutional weight achieved by the armed forces during the power struggle and provided a propitious political context for a wide-ranging reconsideration of the fundaments of military doctrine. The ambitious war hero was forced to retire in October 1957 in favor of Khrushchev's wartime associate Marshal Rodion Malinovskii, but Zhukov's personal discomfiture did not represent a setback for the military as a whole.[18] Meanwhile, on 26 August 1957 the Soviets successfully tested their first ballistic missile and on 4 October surprised the world by launching the Sputnik space satellite. U.S. president Eisenhower attempted to save face by remarking disingenuously that the new technology possessed "no military value," but no one was deceived.[19] The Soviets had unveiled a "delivery system" with the potential exponentially to increase the nuclear threat to the United States.[20]

The new emphasis upon the centrality of nuclear arms only served to underline the inadequacy of the Soviet strategic arsenal. Beginning in 1953 the introduction of the turbojet Bison strategic bomber theoretically gave Moscow the means to attempt nuclear strikes against the United States, but it was a tenuous capacity at best. Although the July 1955 Moscow air show created some consternation in the West as squadrons of Bisons repeated circling overhead led to inflated counts of the Soviet inventory, few professional observers could have been taken

17. Raymond L. Garthoff, *The Soviet Image of Future War* (Washington, D.C., 1959), provides the best summation of the debate. See also H. S. Dinerstein, *War and the Soviet Union: Nuclear Weapons and the Revolution in Soviet Military and Political Thinking* (New York, 1959), pp. 28–64.

18. For accounts of the "Zhukov Affair" see Yosef Avidar, *The Party and the Army in the Soviet Union* (University Park, Pa., 1983), pp. 117–78; Colton, *Commissars, Commanders, and Civilian Authority*, pp. 175–95.

19. Cited in André Fontaine, *Histoire de la guerre froide*, Vol. 2: *De la guerre de Corée à la crise des alliances, 1950–1971* (Paris, 1967), p. 315.

20. Contemporary Soviet accounts emphasized the decisive nature of the breakthrough. According to N. Talenskii, "Voprosy voennoi strategii i vneshniaia politika," *Mezhdunarodnaia zhizn'* 3 (1958): 35, what had occurred was "not only a quantitative increase in the potential of military strategy, but a qualitative leap, fundamentally changing the methods and forms of armed conflict."

in.[21] The first generation SS-6 Soviet ICBM (intercontinental ballistic missile) was technically flawed, and in 1957 the decision was made not to undertake serial production.

Some analysts have argued that between 1957 and 1961 Khrushchev intentionally pursued a policy of "strategic deception" by exaggerating real Soviet capacity in order to intimidate the West.[22] Though Khrushchev's discourses may indeed have been intended to reinforce the deterrent effect of the modest Soviet strategic arsenal by raising doubts in the minds of adversaries, they need not be interpreted as part of a coherent policy linked to aggressive designs.[23] The Soviet first secretary was notoriously prone to overstatement, and his "rocket-rattling" quickly proved to be counterproductive, as U.S. planners compensated for uncertainties in their intelligence data with a series of assertive strategic initiatives.

The foundation for the "missile gap" scare and for the massive strategic deployments of the Kennedy years was the 1957 Gaither Report (named for H. Rowan Gaither, the initial head of the presidential committee that composed it), filled with dire warnings concerning the supposed vulnerability of the U.S. strategic arsenal to a surprise first strike. The report provided a convenient point of reference during the debate over purported U.S. inferiority that followed the Sputnik launch later in the year. In 1958 the decision was made to deploy liquid-fueled Jupiter and Thor missiles in Britain, Italy, and Turkey. Almost simultaneously these weapons were being programmed for replacement by the solid-fueled Minuteman ICBM and the submarine launched ballistic missiles (SLBMs) carried by the nuclear-powered Polaris submarine. Henceforward the Minuteman, Polaris, and the B-52 strategic bomber fleet would make up a U.S. strategic "triad" that far outmatched any Soviet equivalent.

The upgrading of U.S. nuclear forces was accompanied by doctrinal innovations. The first single integrated operations plan (SIOP—a nuclear targeting strategy) appeared in 1960 and emphasized "refined" targeting focused upon the adversary's command and control centers and strategic launchers. The United States had begun to flirt with a "counterforce" doctrine calling for strikes at the enemy's retaliatory capacity

21. Allen Dulles, *The Craft of Intelligence* (New York, 1963), p. 149, suggests that it was immediately surmised that the Bisons were flying circles.

22. Arnold L. Horelick and Myron Rush, *Strategic Power and Soviet Foreign Policy* (Chicago, 1963), p. 69. Horelick and Rush offer the classic version of the strategic-deception thesis.

23. Roman Kolkowicz, *The Soviet Military and the Communist Power* (Princeton, N.J., 1967), p. 284, comments that the purpose of Khrushchev's exaggerations was to contribute to "international stabilization" by raising doubts concerning America's margin of advantage.

in place of the "countervalue" or "city-busting" logic of massive retaliation. The trend was summarized by Secretary of Defense Robert Mc-Namara in a commencement address at the University of Michigan on 16 June 1962.[24] In a nuclear war, McNamara proposed, American nuclear warheads would not be released in a "spasm," but targeted selectively in order to reduce the enemy's ability to hit back. Increased counterforce capacity would make the threat of a preemptive first strike more real. The fact that the United States was articulating such a doctrine was therefore a destabilizing gesture of some significance.

The threat posed by the U.S. nuclear arsenal was the critical reality driving forward the Soviet strategic debate of the 1950s and early 1960s. A preliminary summary was offered by Khrushchev in an address to the Supreme Soviet in January 1960, during which he announced the creation of the Strategic Rocket Forces as a new armed service branch.[25] Debate continued and in fact intensified in a series of articles appearing in Voennaia mysl' during 1960–1961, culminating with the publication of the text Military Strategy in 1962 under the general editorship of Marshal Vasilii Sokolovskii.[26] The first high-level text on strategy to appear in the USSR since Svechin's work almost forty years before, the Sokolovskii collection is properly regarded as a landmark in the evolution of Soviet military thought.

Sokolovskii is careful to place his analysis into a Marxist-Leninist context. "It is apparent," he writes, "that the essence of war as a continuation of politics does not change as a consequence of changing technology and armaments."[27] This tip of the hat to orthodoxy does not disguise the author's preoccupation with the effects of technological change upon military operations, and specifically with the impact of nuclear weapons. Thomas Wolfe notes correctly that Sokolovskii's primary goal is to probe "what the limits of military power in the nuclear age are understood to be."[28]

24. Robert S. McNamara, "Defense Arrangements of the North Atlantic Community," Department of State Bulletin 47 (9 July 1962): 67–68.
25. N. S. Khrushchev, O vneshnei politike Sovetskogo Soiuza 1960 goda, 2 vols. (Moscow, 1961), 1: 5–64.
26. V. D. Sokolovskii, ed., Voennaia strategiia, 2d ed. (Moscow, 1963). I cite from the second edition, which includes amendments to the first edition issued one year earlier. Sokolovskii served as general editor for the text, which consists of articles by fifteen collaborators. A third edition was published in 1968 with important editorial changes reflecting a somewhat different strategic emphasis. A translation incorporating the texts of all three editions is offered by Harriet Fast Scott, ed., Soviet Military Strategy by V. D. Sokolovskii, Marshal of the Soviet Union (New York, 1968).
27. Sokolovskii, Voennaia strategiia, p. 25.
28. Thomas W. Wolfe, Soviet Strategy at the Crossroads (Cambridge, Mass., 1964), p. 77.

The most fundamental assertion of *Military Strategy* is that under contemporary circumstances any general war involving the two antagonistic systems led by the United States and the USSR would inevitably be both global and nuclear in character, a war for survival fought with unlimited means. This is so precisely because of the change in the essence of war affected by technology. The appearance of nuclear warheads, long-range delivery systems, and computerized command and control combine to create what is described as a "revolution in military affairs." Hallowed in Soviet social theory as a designation for fundamental and irreversible change, the term "revolution" is not used lightly. "The decisive means for waging contemporary war," it is stated unambiguously, "are strategic nuclear arms."[29]

Even if it is not "fatalistically inevitable," global nuclear war is possible. It is therefore the responsibility of military professionals to prepare for the eventuality. "Preparing" means taking the steps necessary to wage a nuclear confrontation at any level of intensity. Sokolovskii's assertion that nuclear war can be fought to a successful conclusion, ferocious by any standard, has become the focus of a good deal of merited criticism, but it should at least be understood in context. Sokolovskii insists that the consequences of a nuclear war would be absolutely catastrophic. In accordance with the terms of peaceful coexistence, he asserts that socialism can triumph worldwide without resort to war, but that in order to do so, the socialist countries must also be ready to defend themselves. In order to deter a war provoked by the imperialists, the USSR must be strong enough to absorb a surprise attack and launch a response capable of "destroying" the aggressor. Preparation for nuclear war is posed as a technical problem of military organization, global war is described as supremely undesirable, and calls for readiness are tempered by protestations of peaceful intentions.

The war that Sokolovskii evokes will begin, not with an invasion along the frontier, but with rocket strikes into the interior. The partial invalidation of the traditional concept of the front, combined with the destructive force of nuclear arms, gives a great advantage to the initiator and makes the element of surprise critically important. But the advantages implicit in surprise are not sufficient to ensure victory. The traditional service branches are called upon to perform complementary roles in a future war, and the concept of the combined arms offensive is retained. "It will be a theater offensive following after nuclear strikes by strategic systems," Sokolovskii writes, "to which will belong the decisive role in

29. Sokolovskii, *Voennaia strategiia*, p. 366.

the defeat of the enemy."[30] Although the nuclear battlefield poses all kinds of new demands, "contemporary war will be waged by mass armies" trained and equipped to occupy contaminated terrain and psychologically primed to withstand the effects of "massively destructive and devastating nuclear strikes."[31] The list of unpredictables grows longer as the narrative progresses, but Sokolovskii refuses to abandon the proposition that with proper preparation the Soviet Union can emerge victorious from a global nuclear war.

The Sokolovskii text has been seized upon in the West as proof of aggressive intentions and as an illustration of the inhumanity presumed to underlie the Soviet system.[32] Examined without preconceptions, its conclusions appear somewhat less baleful. First, in the early 1960s the Soviet Union was nowhere near to possessing the kind of arsenal that might actually have allowed it to fight a war such as Sokolovskii describes. During the early 1960s the Soviets devoted most of their energy to the deployment of the SS-4 and SS-5 intermediate range ballistic missiles (IRBMs), primarily relevant to the European theater where the real focus of Soviet military strategy continued to lie. Only four of the first-generation SS-6 ICBMs were ever deployed, and it was not until 1962 that deployment of the second-generation SS-7 and SS-8 was begun.[33] Meanwhile, the Kennedy administration had nearly completed a major expansion of the American arsenal. At any point through the late 1960s it was certainly not the USSR that would have prevailed in a global nuclear exchange.

Sokolovskii's conclusions are also ambiguous. The attempt to cater to the army by maintaining a commitment to large-scale combined arms operations sits uneasily alongside the emphasis placed upon surprise and the nuclear blitz. In the end it is not clear whether the Soviets have opted to prepare for a short war by accumulating nuclear strike forces or for a lengthy conflict including a significant conventional phase.[34] What is

30. Ibid., p. 372.

31. Ibid., p. 47.

32. See particularly Richard Pipes, "Why the Soviet Union Thinks It Could Fight and Win a Nuclear War," in Douglas J. Murray and Paul R. Viotti, eds., The Defense Policies of Nations: A Comparative Study (Baltimore, Md., 1982), pp. 134–46; for an alternative perspective Robert L. Arnett, "Soviet Attitudes toward Nuclear War: Do They Really Think They Can Win?" Journal of Strategic Studies 2 (Sept. 1979): 172–91. Sokolovskii's book was not widely interpreted as proof of aggressive intent at the time of its appearance; arguments such as those cited above are presented as contributions to the U.S. strategic debate of the late 1970s and the 1980s.

33. Holloway, The Soviet Union and the Arms Race, p. 43.

34. Wolfe, Soviet Strategy at the Crossroads, p. 225, remarks that this tension between two conflicting doctrines runs through the entire specialized military literature.

more, Sokolovskii leaves no doubt that a global nuclear war would be a universal disaster that could never be the result of rational choice. Allowing for differences of emphasis and phrasing that reflect traits distinct to Soviet military culture, what Sokolovskii really recommends is a nuclear strategy grounded upon a concept of deterrence comparable to that emerging simultaneously in the United States. As interpreted by the political leadership under Khrushchev, Sokolovskii's warfighting doctrine implied that the best way to prevent a nuclear confrontation was to make potential adversaries fear the consequences. Sokolovskii's exaggerations result partly from the intention to exhort an effort to close the gap separating the USSR from its American rival, partly from concern for the potential failure of deterrence, and partly from a desire to support the military's institutional goals in an ongoing debate over economic priorities. As the Soviet Union's first attempt to craft a military doctrine for the nuclear age, *Military Strategy* undoubtedly contains a number of grotesque misconceptions. Whether they are more egregious than similar misconceptions in the contemporary western literature is perhaps an open question.

It remains the case that the Soviet strategic debate of the 1950s did culminate in a decisive choice with far-reaching consequences. By accepting an aggressive definition of deterrence, the Soviet Union locked itself into a competitive strategic relationship with its American rival. Continued high levels of military spending, a constantly escalating nuclear arms race, a spiraling technological competition grossly distorting of social concerns, the heightened anxiety of societies whose very existence suddenly seemed to hang by a thread, and the inherently unstable foundation of any relationship resting upon the premise of mutual assured destruction all followed inexorably in the train of the Soviet choice. Was an alternative available? Without question, the harshness of the language chosen by editors such as Sokolovskii could have been softened and the emphasis shifted to a minimum-deterrence posture that avoided references to the chimera of "victory." But the Soviets were not calling the tune. The reality of massive U.S. deployments linked to a strategic doctrine increasingly tempted by counterforce scenarios virtually compelled Moscow to respond in kind.[35]

35. See Lawrence Freedman, *The Evolution of Nuclear Strategy* (New York, 1981), pp. 99–128, for a discussion of the U.S. flirtation with warfighting doctrine during the Kennedy administration. Matthew Evangelista, *Innovation and the Arms Race: How the United States and the Soviet Union Develop New Military Technologies* (Ithaca, N.Y., 1988), pp. 155–217 and 233–35, develops a sophisticated "action-reaction" model for tactical nuclear competition during the 1950s according to which: "the main impetus to the development of Soviet tactical nuclear weapons appears to have been . . .

The Warsaw Pact

The problem of conventional war was also broadly debated under Khrushchev. Stalin's security policy had resulted in a militarized Europe, including a significant American presence with the capacity, from 1952 onward, to launch nuclear attacks against Soviet territory from European bases. At the moment of Stalin's death a U.S.-led campaign urging the arming of the FRG within the western alliance was far advanced. Efforts to ward off West German militarization, to respond to the step once it had been taken, and to reassert an acceptable strategic balance along the Soviet Union's western flank by preparing to wage a European war if need be were preoccupations all through the Khrushchev years.

During 1954 and the first months of 1955 Moscow issued several proposals for a European collective security system, all of which seemed intended to block West German accession to NATO. At the Berlin foreign ministers' conference during January and February 1954 Molotov's proposal for a European collective security treaty inspired by the 1947 Rio Pact and excluding the United States was dismissed by Secretary of State Dulles as a "bad joke."[36] A Soviet note of 31 March 1954 suggested that NATO itself could serve as the foundation for a pan-European security order if it were restructured and broadened to include the Soviet bloc. On 22 October 1954, and again on 13 November, 15 January 1955, and 8 February, Moscow issued statements proposing a collective security framework to include a reunited and democratic Germany.[37] None of these offers evoked a positive response. Rather, in September 1954 a London conference endorsed the goals of full sovereignty and NATO membership for the FRG. On 9 May 1955 the FRG officially shed its status as an occupied power and joined the western alliance.

Moscow responded with a preemptory gesture on 7 May by annulling treaties with Great Britain and France dating to World War II. One week

---

the deployment of U.S. nuclear weapons in Europe, starting in 1952–53." Avidar, *The Party and the Army in the Soviet Union*, p. 249, characterizes Khrushchev's primary goal as the creation of a "minimal deterrent strategic force" to blunt the intimidating potential of U.S. superiority.

36. The remark is cited in Fontaine, *Histoire de la guerre froide*, 2: 91–92. For the text of the Soviet proposal see "Sovetskii Soiuz i obespechenie bezopasnosti v Evrope," *Pravda*, 11 Feb. 1954, pp. 3–4.

37. P. A. Nikolaev, *Politika Sovetskogo Soiuza v germanskom voprose, 1945–1964* (Moscow, 1966), pp. 211–18. Fontaine, *Histoire de la guerre froide*, 2: 144, comments on the 8 Feb. proposal that "it is difficult to avoid the impression that at this moment a unique opportunity to leave behind the Cold War for the better had perhaps been lost." On 29 Nov. 1954 the eight European socialist countries (alone among the twenty-three countries originally invited) convened a conference on European security in Moscow which went on to threaten countermeasures.

later, at a hastily convened conference in Warsaw, a "Treaty of Friendship, Cooperation, and Mutual Assistance" was signed by the Soviet Union, Poland, Czechoslovakia, Hungary, the GDR, Romania, Bulgaria, and Albania. As the institutional embodiment of Soviet military capacity, the Warsaw Pact would henceforward function as the keystone of the Moscow's security posture in Europe.

The Warsaw Pact was a consequence of the perceived need to react strongly to the integration of the FRG into NATO. The preamble to the Warsaw treaty made the connection explicit by citing the "threat to the national security of peace-loving states" created by the attachment of West Germany to the North Atlantic bloc. Apart from its symbolic function, however, the creation of the pact did not alter the balance of forces in the central European theater. The reductions in Soviet and east European national armed forces initiated by the New Course continued unabated, and the pact added little to the controls already exerted by Moscow since 1948 over the national military contingents of the bloc states. The Warsaw treaty may also be regarded as a complement to the Austrian State Treaty, formally ratified only twenty-four hours later on 15 May; the Soviet troop presence in Romania and Hungary was originally sanctioned in order to provide a corridor of access to occupied Austria, and a continued military presence could now be justified in the context of the Warsaw Pact. Likewise, the existence of the pact precluded an "Austrian option" for the other eastern European states. The pact was created to reinforce the status quo, not to enhance the threat to the West.

In some ways the Warsaw Pact corresponded to the more accommodating spirit of the New Course. Stalin's hold over eastern Europe was maintained by arbitrary coercion, applied with extraordinary insensitivity to national feeling. The Warsaw Pact provided a context for reform by basing the Soviet presence in the region upon a structured alliance including what were at least formally cooperative mechanisms for regulating differences. It likewise offered Moscow a kind of diplomatic parity with the West. By May 1955 the Geneva summit was on the diplomatic agenda. Khrushchev could now appear with his "own" European alliance as a counterpart to NATO.

The Warsaw Treaty, consisting of a preamble and eleven articles, was based very closely upon the North Atlantic treaty.[38] Although the People's Republic of China was represented at the Warsaw conference with observer status, article four clearly confined the scope of the treaty to Europe. The purpose of the alliance was specified as joint defense, and

38. The text and related documents are assembled in Alexander Uschakov and Dietrich Frenzke, eds., *Der Warschauer Pakt und seine bilateralen Bündnisverträge: Analyse und Texte* (Berlin, 1987).

it was stated unambiguously that the pact would disband automatically at such time as NATO went out of existence. The 1955 accords also endowed the pact with the rudiments of an organizational structure. The Political Consultative Committee was designated as an executive organ, consisting of the prime ministers and foreign ministers of the member states. Article five provided for the establishment of a unified military command, set up in Moscow during 1956 with the Soviet marshal Ivan Konev as its first commander in chief. At its origins, however, the pact was very loosely coordinated. Its primary purpose was to stand as a symbolic admonition to the West.[39]

Soon after its creation the Warsaw Pact was subjected to a severe test. During 1956 in both Poland and Hungary popular disaffection encouraged by liberalization and the revelations of Stalin's crimes spun out of control. An international trade fair in the Polish city of Poznan during June 1956 provided the background for a militant strike action that soon assumed the proportions of an urban insurrection. The decision to open fire on demonstrators, leaving fifty-three dead, inflamed the entire nation. Concessions now became the order of the day, and on 19 October the communist reformer Wladislaw Gomulka was brought back to the leadership with Moscow's blessing. By pledging his government to reform, Gomulka was able to dampen pressure for radical change. At the height of the crisis Soviet tanks ringed Warsaw and the threat of military intervention was aired, but in the end a compromise solution prevailed.[40]

In Hungary a similar train of events ended in confrontation and tragedy. After a promising beginning, the New Course in Budapest bogged down in factional strife between a reformist wing of the Hungarian Communist party led by Imre Nagy and the Stalinist leadership of Mátyás Rákosi. During the summer of 1956 popular pressure for change began to accumulate. On 17 July the uniformly unpopular Rákosi was forced to step down, but his replacement by the equally dogmatic Ernö Gerö gave the impression that nothing essential had changed. It was thus in a situation of standoff and frustration that the news of Gomulka's triumph arrived in mid-October.

39. There are a number of useful studies of the origins and development of the Warsaw Pact, including Robert W. Clawson and Lawrence S. Kaplan, eds., *The Warsaw Pact: Political Purposes and Military Means* (Wilmington, Del., 1982); Gerard Holden, *The Warsaw Pact: Soviet Security and Bloc Politics* (Oxford, 1989); David Holloway and Jane M. O. Sharp, eds., *The Warsaw Pact: Alliance in Transition?* (Ithaca, N.Y., 1984); Christopher D. Jones, *Soviet Influence in Eastern Europe: Political Autonomy and the Warsaw Pact* (New York, 1981); Stephan Tiedtke, *Die Warschauer Vertragsorganization: Zum Verhältnis von Militär- und Entspannungspolitik in Osteuropa* (Munich, 1978).

40. See the accounts in Konrad Syrop, *Spring in October: The Polish Revolution of 1956* (London, 1957); Brzezinski, *The Soviet Bloc*, pp. 237–68.

The Hungarian uprising began in Budapest on 23 October when a demonstration organized by students unexpectedly swelled to huge proportions and erupted into rioting. Armed forces sent in to quell the disturbances mutinied and distributed weapons to the crowd, and control over events slipped from the government's hands. In these dire straits Nagy, who had been in eclipse since his expulsion from the Communist party one year before by the Rákosi group, was installed as prime minister. A "Polish solution," with Nagy in the role of Gomulka, was probably envisioned, but first, order had to be restored in the streets. To that end, during the night of 23–24 October the Hungarian government requested that Soviet tanks be deployed in Budapest. Responsibility for the decision has remained a point of controversy, and with good reason. Rather than intimidating protestors, the Soviet behemoths only served to crystallize popular anger. Days of violence followed during which an enraged population, using hit-and-run guerrilla tactics and aided by breakaway units of the Hungarian armed forces, completely neutralized three Soviet mechanized divisions.

On 27 October, Nagy announced an impressive list of reforms, including the elimination of the one-party system, the abolition of censorship, and the disbanding of the security police. The Hungarian Communist party was abolished and a new Hungarian Socialist Worker's party created to replace it under the leadership of another victim of repression as a "Titoist," János Kádár. These were audacious measures, but they were to no avail. Armed, increasingly well organized, and inspired by a conflicting melange of motives, including destructive vengefulness as well as healthy patriotism, the uprising sputtered onward in waves of anarchic violence. A culmination of sorts came with the storming of the Communist party headquarters in Pest on 30 October and the brutal murder of its defenders.

Moscow reacted by announcing its acceptance of the reforms and pulling the ineffective tank units out of Budapest. Simultaneously, Soviet forces began to be massed in areas surrounding the capital. Under pressure from all sides and fearing the worst, Nagy called a press conference on 1 November to announce Hungary's unilateral withdrawal from the Warsaw Pact, declare neutrality, and appeal for United Nations assistance.

Although the decision to pull out of the Warsaw Pact is often interpreted as the trip wire that set off Soviet intervention, it is probable that at this point the decision to intervene had already been made. By 1 November the machinery of repression was in place, consultations were under way between Moscow and other east European capitals, and Kádár and Ferenc Münnich were being spirited away to the Kremlin, where they would strike a deal to inherit power.[41] Nagy's decision to withdraw from the pact was less an ultimate provocation than a desperate act of defiance by a leadership that could already see the writing on the wall. Seven months later Kádár explained his motives as those of a sincere communist horrified at the Nagy government's unwillingness to take the steps needed to contain a "counterrevolutionary mutiny."[42] Khrushchev emphasized the threat that a "counterrevolution" in Hungary would pose to Soviet security interests, and in a speech delivered in Hungary on 8 April 1958, he sought to justify Soviet actions with an early variant of what would later become known as the Brezhnev Doctrine. "We declare that if a new provocation is directed against any socialist country whatsoever," Khrushchev asserted, "then the provocateur will have to deal with all the countries of the socialist camp, and the Soviet Union is always ready to come to the assistance of its friends, to give the necessary rebuff to the enemies of socialism if they attempt to disturb the peaceful labor of the people of the socialist countries."[43]

The intervention itself, begun on 4 November, was a minor masterpiece of meticulous preparation and deception.[44] The new Hungarian defense minister Pál Maléter was arrested while engaged in negotiations with his Soviet counterparts, and the Nagy government never issued orders calling for military resistance. Confronted by overwhelming force, popular resistance was quickly snuffed out. Any hope of international aid was negated by the eruption of the Suez crisis during the last days of October, temporarily pitting the United States against its most important European and Middle Eastern allies. Nagy, Maléter, and a number of other partisans of reform were executed in 1958 in what can only be described as an act of cruel and immoderate vengeance. As for Hungary's unilateral withdrawal from the Warsaw Pact, it was quietly moved into the shadow world of Soviet nonhistory.

The Hungarian uprising of 1956 helped to clarify the nature of the post-Stalin European security order. André Fontaine describes the first

41. Veljko Micunovic, *Moscow Diary* (Garden City, N.Y., 1980), pp. 131–42 recounts Khrushchev's journey to consult with Tito on the Yugoslav island of Brioni on 2 Nov. In a speech delivered in Pula on 11 Nov., Tito sanctioned the intervention in Hungary as a "necessary evil." Stephen Chissold, ed., *Yugoslavia and the Soviet Union, 1939–1973: A Documentary Survey* (London, 1975), pp. 263–70.

42. *Vsevengerskaia konferentsiia Vengerskoi sotsialisticheskoi rabochei partii (Budapesht, 27–29 iiunia 1957 g.)* (Moscow, 1958), pp. 7–30.

43. N. S. Khrushchev, *K pobede v mirnom sorevnovanii s kapitalizmom* (Moscow, 1959), p. 225. Khrushchev made remarks to this effect on numerous occasions during his visit to Hungary, often referring to the events of 1956 as a "fascist mutiny."

44. P. A. Lashchenko, "Vengriia, 1956 goda," *Voenno-istoricheskii zhurnal* 9 (1989): 42–50, in an account that is unrepentantly supportive of the decision to use force, provides a good description of the operational side of the incursion.

week of November 1956 as the "week of truth" of the Cold War, a harsh demonstration of the permanence of Europe's division and of the hegemony of the superpowers within their respective camps.[45] The Soviets' goal in Hungary was not necessarily to block reform; Khrushchev was committed to pursuing the New Course, and Kádár would eventually preside over changes that in some ways went beyond the unrealized initiatives of 1956. The great threat was a wave of destabilizing mass actions motivated primarily by anti-Sovietism, with the potential to tear down Moscow's elaborately assembled eastern European security zone from below. Simultaneously, the ignominious retreat from Suez of Great Britain and France under U.S. pressure left no doubt as to who it was that established priorities for the western alliance. Agnes Heller and Ferenc Fehér interpret the Hungarian uprising as a revolt against the "cold war system" and its implications for lesser powers; whether or not they are correct, the net result was a reinforcement of Cold War structures.[46]

In order to calm eastern European national feeling in the wake of the repression, Moscow offered a number of concessions. In 1956–1957 status-of-forces agreements specifying the conditions attached to a permanent Soviet troop presence were signed between the USSR and Poland, Hungary, Romania, and the GDR. Traditional military insignia were reintroduced for eastern European national forces, the role of Soviet military advisors was deemphasized, and an upgrading of Soviet-issue equipment was approved. Not least, in early 1958 all Soviet armed forces were pulled out of Romania.

Khrushchev also attempted to proceed with Soviet conventional force reductions. Malenkov's program (which by opposing, Khrushchev had come to power) had already shrunk the 5-million-strong army inherited from Stalin to approximately 3.5 million men at arms by 1958—a unilateral reduction of nearly 40 percent. Speaking to the Supreme Soviet in January 1960, Khrushchev unveiled a plan for reducing manpower by an additional one-third, trimming the armed forces to a permanent complement of 2,423,000 over the next two years. Khrushchev's "firepower over manpower" philosophy intensified the debate in progress within Soviet military circles, to which Sokolovskii's *Military Strategy,* with its emphasis upon the role of mass armies, sought to make a partisan

45. Fontaine, *Histoire de la guerre froide,* 2: 281.
46. Ferenc Fehér and Agnes Heller, *Hungary 1956 Revisited: The Message of a Revolution a Quarter Century After* (London, 1983), pp. 76–77. There is a large literature concerning the events of 1956. See Bill Lomax, *Hungary 1956* (London, 1976), and Bill Lomax, *The Hungarian Revolution of 1956 and the Origins of the Kadar Regime* (Nottingham, 1985), plus the participant's account by Miklós Molnár, *Budapest 1956: A History of the Hungarian Revolution* (London, 1971). On 16 June 1989 the remains of Nagy and his executed associates were reburied in Budapest with full honors.

contribution.[47] The first secretary's own priorities were primarily budgetary, but the extent of the cuts that he proposed made it necessary to contemplate alternative scenarios for conventional defense.

Beginning in the early 1960s, as a dimension of its overall reconsideration of military and defense policies, the Soviet Union began to place more weight upon the Warsaw Pact's potential as a fighting alliance. The replacement of Konev as commander in chief by Andrei Grechko in April 1960 and the pronouncements of the March 1961 session of the Political Consultative Committee marked the beginning of a significant change in the pact's character, from the political instrument crafted in 1955 to a military organization operating on the basis of a doctrine of coalition warfare. Under Grechko's direction the pact's first multilateral training exercises were conducted in 1961. Modernization and standardization programs for armaments were initiated, including the introduction of T-54 and T-55 tanks and modern fighter and interceptor aircraft such as the MiG-21 and SU-7, and by the mid-1960s some eastern European units were being trained in the use of short-range ground-to-ground delivery systems for nuclear weapons. The increased discipline demanded of the eastern European member states occasioned some resistance, most notably from the Romanians, who from 1965 onward broke with the pact's coalition war doctrine and moved toward an independent national security policy based upon territorial defense. The Romanian case was exceptional, but it exposed a more general problem. Despite the attention devoted to the pact, its reliability in the event of war, given uniform popular resentment of the Soviet Union's hegemonic role, could never be guaranteed.

In the end Khrushchev's proposed conventional force reductions were successfully resisted; the international crises of the early 1960s, institutional opposition to measures that threatened premature retirement for hundreds of thousands of Soviet officers, and the continuing military buildup being undertaken by the United States created an impossible context for continuing unilateral reductions. On 8 July 1961, in the midst of the Berlin crisis, Khrushchev announced the suspension of the troop-reduction program, with only about one-half of the scheduled 1.2

47. Jutta Tiedtke, *Abrüstung in der Sowjetunion: Wirtschaftliche Bedingungen und soziale Folgen der Truppenreduzierung von 1960* (Frankfurt am Main, 1985), provides an excellent analysis of the decision to push ahead with conventional force reductions. Dale R. Herspring, *The Soviet High Command, 1967–1989* (Princeton, N.J., 1990), pp. 34–37, calls attention to the professional foundation for the military's resistance to what he calls Khrushchev's "single variant" reliance upon nuclear deterrence. The case against Khrushchev's program is made by V. Kurasov, "Voprosy sovetskoi voennoi nauki v proizvedeniiakh V. I. Lenina," *Voenno-istoricheskii zhurnal* 3 (March 1961): 3–14, and by Minister of Defense Rodion Malinovskii, "Programma KPSS i voprosy ukrepleniia vooruzhennykh sil SSSR," *Kommunist* 7 (May 1962): 11–22.

million man cutbacks having been completed. In the future it was the revival of conventional warfighting capacity as a component of Soviet strategy that would become the order of the day.

Relations with the Third World and China

An important new direction associated with Khrushchev's conduct of foreign policy was a more assertive role in the Third World. The Soviets were not the first to arrive, but the effort to establish themselves as a global power helped to project Cold War rivalry into the farthest reaches of Asia, Africa, and Latin America. It also contributed to a rift with the People's Republic of China (PRC) that would eventually develop into a major security problem.

Stalin had little real interest in the Third World, and under his direction Soviet policy remained passive. In his 1947 speech at the founding congress of the Cominform, Zhdanov revived the 1920s notion of a "crisis of colonialism," but his rigidly bipolar two-camps framework seemed to consign emerging nations not clearly aligned with the Soviet bloc to the camp of the enemy. The first steps beyond a policy of benign neglect were undertaken by Khrushchev. During 1955 Khrushchev and Bulganin staged a whirlwind tour of India, Burma, and Afghanistan; Moscow announced its intention to finance the construction of a large steel complex in Bhilai, India; and a significant arms deal with Gamal Abd al-Nasir's Egypt was negotiated via the intermediary of Czechoslovakia. Khrushchev's references at the 20th party congress to the "zone of peace" broke down the bipolar presumptions of the two-camps model, and Soviet ideologists were quick to respond with formal justifications for the extension of aid to progressive but noncommunist Third World allies. The existence of a socialist sector within the world economy and the disintegration of the colonial system were said to create the possibility of a noncapitalist path of development that made movement toward socialism possible without a protracted phase of neocolonialist dependency.[48]

48. The foundation for a noncapitalist path of development was identified as the "national-democratic revolution," a concept that was mentioned at the world conference of communist and workers' parties in Moscow during November 1960, and that appeared in the party program approved by the 22nd party congress of the CPSU in 1961. It is summarized and elaborated in A. S. Shin, *Natsional'no-demokraticheskie revoliutsii: Nekotorye voprosy teorii i praktiki* (Moscow, 1981), pp. 11–12. According to Shin: "By national democratic revolutions we understand anti-imperialist, anti-feudal, democratic revolutions in economically underdeveloped nations during the contemporary era, carried out by an alliance of national-democratic forces under the leadership of revolutionary democrats, in the course of which the possibility exists for the planned creation of the conditions of a gradual transition to socialism, by-passing capitalism or interrupting its development at the initial stages."

The self-serving nature of these arguments, which made alliance with Moscow the key to progressive social development, was obvious. The noncapitalist path scenario nonetheless provided Soviet Third World policy with a degree of nuance that under Stalin it had lacked.

Even with the benefit of hindsight it remains difficult to specify the motives that inspired Khrushchev's opening to the Third World. Although it had recovered from wartime damages, the USSR was still in some ways a developing nation itself. Khrushchev's Third World engagements were high-risk undertakings that demanded a considerable investment of resources and prestige. What aspirations led the Soviet leadership to so substantial a rupture with the Eurocentric foreign policy of the Stalin era?

Part of the explanation concerns the changing nature of world politics. By the mid-1950s, after an East-West dispute over conditions of admission had been resolved, a flood of nearly fifty states poured into the United Nations in less than a decade. Though prey to every sort of problem, these emerging nations represented a potential force that no one with aspirations to play a leading international role could afford to ignore.

There was also a defensive component to Soviet policy. The Eisenhower administration sought, as an aspect of its global containment posture, to ring the USSR with regional security pacts, a policy ridiculed by Soviet commentators as "pactomania" with the goal of "encirclement and constant military pressure upon the USSR."[49] In 1951 the Anzus alliance brought together the United States, Australia, and New Zealand. On 8 September 1954 the United States, France, the United Kingdom, Australia, New Zealand, Thailand, the Philippines, and Pakistan signed the Manila treaty creating a Southeast Asia Treaty Organization (SEATO). In the Middle East the Baghdad Pact was formed in February 1955 uniting Turkey, Pakistan, Iraq, the United Kingdom, and Iran (redesignated as the Central Treaty Organization or CENTO in 1958). These arrangements made it possible for the United States to project military power into the immediate vicinity of Soviet national territory. In response, Moscow sought to undermine the pacts by courting disgruntled regional powers that stood outside them.[50] That the Soviet Union's

49. Iu. M. Mel'nikov, *Sila i bessilie*, pp. 105 and 129.

50. A Ministry of Foreign Affairs statement of April 1955 described the threat posed by U.S.-sponsored security pacts in the Middle East as follows: "the Soviet Union cannot remain indifferent to the situation arising in the region of the Near and Middle East, since the formation of these blocs and the establishment of foreign military bases on the territory of the countries of the Near and Middle East have a direct bearing on the security of the U.S.S.R." Cited in Alvin Z. Rubinstein, *Red Star on the Nile* (Princeton, N.J., 1977), p. 4.

first important Third World allies became Nehru's India and Nasir's Egypt was due not only to the fact that their leaders seemed to be drawn toward noncapitalist development; India and Egypt were also the countries best placed to frustrate the logic of SEATO and the Baghdad Pact.

Finally, it is impossible entirely to overlook the personality of Khrushchev himself. The first secretary was committed to achieving the global power status that he felt to be the USSR's good right. He took the vocation of Marxist seriously and inherited from Lenin a political vision that emphasized the importance of the national liberation movement. Khrushchev was personally pledged to the goals of communism and convinced that the Soviet Union had a positive role to play in aiding the wretched of the earth in their struggle against injustice and exploitation.

The most persistent Soviet effort to penetrate the Third World came in the Middle East, where policy was hinged upon a calculated influence relationship with Egypt. Moscow's progress in establishing itself as a regional actor was not unimpressive, but the link to the volatile Nasir proved to be encumbering. During the Suez crisis of 1956 the Soviets were forced to guard their alliance by releasing a diplomatic note on 5 November (well after the most dangerous phase of the confrontation had passed) that blustered: "We are fully resolved to use force to crush the aggressor and to restore peace."[51] Though it was not backed by deeds, such intemperate language did nothing to assist in the quest for peaceful coexistence. Moscow was also required to bite its tongue and look on passively as Nasir and his Arab allies began large-scale persecutions of communists in 1958. With its entire regional policy built around the tie to Cairo, the Soviet Union found itself pressed into the Arab camp in the unfolding Arab-Israel drama, thereby contributing to polarization in a region that has never ceased to pose a major threat to international stability.

Comparable dilemmas plagued Soviet policy in other Third World regions. From 1955 onward a relationship with Nehru's India provided a useful counter to the U.S.-Pakistan defense treaty of 1954 and to SEATO. It also contributed to a worsening of Sino-Soviet relations, particularly after the 1962 Sino-Indian war. The Soviets were successful in using trade credits and financial aid as well as expressions of ideological support to secure close ties with the radical African regimes of Kwame Nkrumah in Ghana, Ahmed Sekou Toure in Guinea, and Modeiba Keita in Mali. Unfortunately such regimes often turned out to have been built on sand, and by the end of the 1960s little remained to show for a decade

51. "Poslanie predsedatelia Soveta Ministrov SSSR N. A. Bulganina," *Pravda*, 6 Nov. 1956, p. 2.

of effort. The Soviets chose to back Prime Minister Patrice Lumumba in the postindependence power struggle in the former Belgian Congo (Zaire) after July 1960, but they were incapable of placing forces on the ground in support of their client. By September, Lumumba had been unceremoniously murdered, and power was in the hands of the CIA-backed Colonel Joseph Mobuto. The flight of the Cuban dictator Fulgencia Batista on New Year's Day 1959 and the subsequent radicalization of the revolutionary government of Fidel Castro provided the Soviets with recompense in a region long considered to be the closed preserve of the United States. After some hesitation the Soviet Union concluded a trade agreement with Cuba in February 1960, formalized diplomatic relations in May, and during July came to Havana's rescue by agreeing to massive sugar purchases in order to make good on canceled U.S. contracts. Thereafter, Castro's regime became increasingly dependent upon Soviet financial assistance and security guarantees. The Soviet-Cuban relationship proved enduring, but it was very costly for Moscow in purely economic terms as well as posing a barrier to improved U.S.-Soviet relations.[52]

Activism in the Third World was one factor among many contributing to the disintegration of relations between Moscow and Beijing. In retrospect, it is clear that tensions had already begun to develop in the immediate aftermath of the 20th party congress, described by Donald Zagoria as "the major turning point in Sino-Soviet relations in the post-Stalin era."[53] Rivalry between the two communist giants, respectively the world's largest and most populous nations and divided by the world's longest common border, was an important new reality in international affairs. Khrushchev did not create the rivalry, but his policies served to aggravate it.

The Sino-Soviet rift rested first of all upon a cultural divide. One of the most deeply rooted Russian national images is that of Batu Khan and his Asiatic "hordes" descending upon the Slavic heartland during the thirteenth century, and the Christian civilization of medieval Muscovy was to a considerable extent defined in opposition to the "Mongol Yoke." China's rich ancient culture encouraged disdain for the "northern barbarians," and tsarist Russia's imperial role in the weakened China of the nineteenth century aggravated long-standing resentments.

52. Evaluations of Soviet policy initiatives in South Asia, Africa, and the Caribbean under Khrushchev are provided by Robert H. Donaldson, *Soviet Policy toward India: Ideology and Strategy* (Cambridge, Mass., 1974); Robert Legvold, *Soviet Policy in West Africa* (Cambridge, Mass., 1970); Jacques Levesque, *The USSR and the Cuban Revolution* (New York, 1979).
53. Donald S. Zagoria, *The Sino-Soviet Conflict, 1956–1961* (New York, 1969), p. 40.

During the Khrushchev period cultural rivalry became a subtle but potent factor reinforcing mutual ill-will.

A more recent heritage of mistrust emerged from the history of relations between the Communist parties of the Soviet Union and China. The Chinese Communist party (CCP) became a member of the Comintern in 1921 and, at the urging of Soviet advisors, committed itself to a united-front strategy in alliance with Jiang Jieshi's nationalists. The united front in China culminated in a catastrophe when in 1927 the victorious nationalists launched a bloody purge against their would-be communist supporters. During the years that followed the CCP was able to regroup under the leadership of Mao Zedong only by opting to pursue a rural-based strategy in defiance of Moscow's directives. After the Long March of 1936 led Mao and his People's Liberation Army into the distant reaches of China's northwest, the movement was operating completely independently of Moscow's influence. Stalin's preference for relations with the nationalist government during the world war must have been a source of resentment for Mao and his lieutenants. The same thing may be said about Soviet comportment during the Korean conflict. The Sino-Soviet friendship treaty of 1950 seemed to put everything in order, but it was negotiated with difficulty and left important issues unresolved. The CCP had come to power not only without significant Soviet assistance, but in direct defiance of Soviet directives and in the face of Soviet obstruction. Moscow had repeatedly demonstrated distrust for Mao, and the two sides expressed radically different attitudes toward basic problems such as development policy, military strategy, and the tasks of the international communist movement.[54]

Third World policy added a new dimension of rivalry. Zhou Enlai's appearance at the founding conference of the nonaligned movement in Bandung, Indonesia, during April 1955 was an act of Chinese self-assertion. It was accompanied by intensified Chinese diplomatic activity among the eastern European Soviet bloc states.[55] In both cases Beijing encouraged polycentrist tendencies by posing its own experience as an alternative point of orientation for anti-imperialist struggles and socialist construction. Khrushchev's anti-Stalin initiatives at the 20th party congress added a personal and ideological dimension to the budding conflict. The Soviet leader's attack upon the cult of personality could all too easily be applied to the burgeoning cult of Mao Zedong. Subsequently, as

54. Traditional Soviet interpretations cite Chinese extremism as the original source of tension. See O. B. Borisov and B. T. Koloskov, *Sovetsko-kitaiskie otnosheniia 1945–1970: Kratkii ocherk* (Moscow, 1971), pp. 45–63; B. N. Slavinskii, *Vneshniaia politika SSSR na Dal'nem Vostoke 1945–1986* (Moscow, 1986), pp. 89–99.

55. The Chinese initiatives are detailed in Zagoria, *The Sino-Soviet Conflict*, pp. 55–61.

Soviet reformism hit full stride, the Chinese revolution lurched to the left. Beijing's One Hundred Flowers campaign during 1957 became the prelude to the creation of the People's Communes and the radical voluntarism of the Great Leap Forward.

Sino-Soviet tensions also spilled over into the realm of security policy. During the Middle East crisis that followed the overthrow of Iraq's Hashemite monarchy in July 1958 and the Taiwan Straits crisis in the autumn of that same year, the Soviet Union refused to heed China's calls for strong reactions. Differences in policy toward India from 1958 onward became both a source and a consequence of worsening relations. These frictions were intensified by an arcane debate over nuclear weapons and class conflict. In the wake of the Taiwan Straits crisis (during which the use of nuclear weapons was considered by Washington) Beijing increased pressure upon Moscow for assistance in developing its own strategic arsenal. The Soviets turned the request down flat, going to the extreme of unilaterally abrogating the relevant terms of the Sino-Soviet military aid agreement.

In November 1957 a world conference with sixty-eight Communist parties represented convened in Moscow. The peace manifesto adopted unanimously by all participants and a separate "Declaration of Twelve" approved by the Communist parties in power (with the exception of Yugoslavia) supported the theme of peaceful coexistence. China lowered its voice and approved the declarations in public, but in the corridor Mao both enthralled and horrified his colleagues with bloodcurdling rhetoric about the potentially "progressive" consequences of a nuclear war.[56] In October 1958 Mao published a pamphlet in which he specified that the deterrent effect of nuclear weapons in the hands of the leading communist powers could allow revolutionary forces in the Third World to emerge victorious without confronting the risk of imperialist intervention. As to the threat of nuclear confrontation that might result:

The First World War was followed by the birth of the Soviet Union with a population of two-hundred million. The Second World War was followed by the emergence of the socialist camp with a combined population of

56. For an account of the Moscow conference see Lilly Marcou, *L'Internationale après Staline* (Paris, 1979), pp. 33–75. The event established the world conference as a new collective forum for the international communist movement, which had lacked any kind of executive since the disbanding of the Cominform on 17 April 1956. At the conference Mao replied to Togliatti's invocation of the horrors of nuclear war that "three hundred million Chinese will be left, and that will be enough for the human race to continue." Cited in Medvedev, *Khrushchev*, p. 122.

nine-hundred million. If the imperialists should insist on launching a third world war, it is certain that several hundred million more will turn to socialism.[57]

Such rhetoric constituted a challenge to which Moscow felt obligated to respond. A campaign of ideological sniping ensued, and Khrushchev's visit to Beijing in October 1959 was a complete fiasco, concluding without the issuance of a joint communiqué. The Soviet leader returned to Moscow to report to the Supreme Soviet on 31 October and delivered a speech that became one of his strongest assertions of the peaceful coexistence line.[58]

In the spring of 1960 Sino-Soviet polemics became undisguised. A pamphlet issued by the CCP in April 1960 entitled *Long Live Leninism* portrayed China as the sole representative of Lenin's legacy within the international communist movement and assailed the Soviets as "modern revisionists."[59] At the third congress of the Romanian Communist party at Bucharest in June, Khrushchev poured scorn upon the Albanian "dogmatists" in a transparent attack by proxy and announced the immediate withdrawal of Soviet economic advisors from China.[60] The latter decision was no doubt precipitous. Though it dealt a telling blow to the Chinese economy, already struggling with the consequences of its overreaching during the Great Leap Forward, Beijing was neither disciplined nor encouraged to return to the fold. At the world conference of Communist parties in Moscow during November 1960 the leader of the Chinese delegation, Deng Xiaoping, struck back with another attack by proxy aimed against the Yugoslav "revisionists." An open break arrived at the 22nd congress of the CPSU in 1961, when Soviet criticism directed against Albania motivated Zhou Enlai to walk out with the entire Chinese delegation in train.[61]

The antagonisms that surfaced during the early 1960s would prove to be enduring. The Chinese denounced Khrushchev's reform program as

57. Mao Tse-tung, *Imperialists and All Reactionaries are Paper Tigers* (Beijing, 1958), pp. 29–30. Mao made the point even more bluntly: "The atom bomb is a paper tiger with which the American reactionaries try to frighten the people." Cited in Alice Langley Hsieh, *Communist China's Strategy in the Nuclear Age* (Englewood Cliffs, N.J., 1962), p. 132.

58. N. S. Khrushchev, *Mir bez oruzhiia—mir bez voin*, 2 vols. (Moscow, 1960), 2: 343–78.

59. The text is in John Gittings, ed., *Survey of the Sino-Soviet Dispute: A Commentary and Extracts from the Recent Polemics, 1963–1967* (Oxford, 1968), pp. 334–45.

60. Khrushchev, *O vneshnei politike*, 1: 35–72.

61. These events are described in Borisov and Koloskov, *Sovetsko-kitaiskie otnosheniia*, pp. 225–29. A good contemporary summary of the sources of the Sino-Soviet dispute is offered by E. P. Bazhanov, "Sovetsko-kitaiskie otnosheniia: Uroki proshlogo i sovremennost'," *Novaia i noveishaia istoriia* 2 and 3 (1989): 3–25 and 43–59, esp. 2: 17–20.

an abandonment of socialism, accused the Soviets of discarding the principle of class struggle in search of accommodation with the West, and mocked Khrushchev personally as a "ridiculous buffoon." In response the Soviets reinforced their commitment to peaceful coexistence and worked to organize a new world communist conference with the intention of excommunicating the CCP.[62] During the spring of 1963 the schism took on direct implications for national security when the Chinese raised the issue of the "unequal treaties" imposed by Imperial Russia during the nineteenth century and posed an irredentist claim to nearly one million square kilometers of Soviet territory. In October 1964 the Chinese successfully tested an atomic bomb. Of all the consequences of the Khrushchev years, the breakdown of relations with China bore the most ominous implications for Soviet security. It was a loss that the modest gains attributable to a forward policy in the Third World could not make good.

"We Will Bury You"

Khrushchev's problems with the Chinese did not distract him from the attempt to transform Soviet society from within, or from the search for a more stable relationship with the West under the aegis of peaceful coexistence. With resistance to his project temporarily stilled after 1957, Khrushchev was able to undertake a series of unprecedented reform measures. The competitive edge of Khrushchev's coexistence did not, however, disappear. Liberal reforms were paralleled by an adventuristic striving for advantage that repeatedly threatened to provoke conflict.

In 1957 Khrushchev initiated a sweeping reform of economic administration, including the abolition of most ministries and the transfer of their functions to territorially defined People's Economic Councils. The Soviet educational system was revamped with a new emphasis placed upon polytechnical training, and a major purge of the state security apparatus was undertaken. In 1959 an ambitious seven-year plan was adopted, accompanied by further changes in the techniques of economic management. From 1960 onward the hasty nature of many reforms began to make itself felt, but the leadership persevered. Another series of agricultural reforms arrived in 1961, and in October of the same year, while presenting a new party program, Khrushchev made the extravagant claim that "our generation of Soviet people will live under

---

62. Raymond L. Garthoff, *Soviet Military Policy* (New York, 1966), pp. 191–206, provides a careful analysis of these polemics.

communism."[63] It was now the party's turn to feel the whip, in the form of reforms dictating three-year term limits for Presidium members, obligating 25 percent membership turnovers at each Central Committee election, and reorganizing basic administrative units into agricultural and industrial sectors. The 22nd party congress in October 1961 became the high point for de-Stalinization, culminating with the decision to remove Stalin's mummified corpse from its place of honor next to Lenin in the mausoleum on Red Square.

These waves of reform added up to an impressive but flawed effort to place the entire Soviet political and economic mechanism onto a new foundation. They were accompanied by an equally ambitious series of international initiatives. Khrushchev repeatedly insisted that although the Soviet system could ultimately defeat the West in peaceful economic competition, nothing could be achieved without a climate of trust sufficient to ensure peace. Speaking in the aftermath of the repression in Hungary at a Kremlin reception in November 1956, Khrushchev snarled at his interrogators the famous phrase "we will bury you." Though the sentiment was hostile enough, the idiomatic Russian actually conveyed the notion of outlasting one's opponent, of being present at the interment of a rival. Competitive coexistence was in principle nonconfrontational. It implied an effort to direct the ongoing struggle between capitalism and socialism into peaceful, evolutionary channels.

Khrushchev's coexistence offensive was pursued most insistently in the field of disarmament. Though it did not lead to a breakthrough, a 10 May 1955 proposal to the U.N. Disarmament Committee (created in 1954 and including the United States, United Kingdom, France, and Canada as well as the USSR) came toward western positions on several points.[64] A proposal to the same committee of 20 March 1957 offered a complete interdiction on nuclear testing. October saw the promulgation of a first variant of the Rapacki Plan, named for Poland's foreign minister Adam Rapacki and calling for the creation of a demilitarized zone in central Europe to include the two Germanies, Poland, and Czechoslovakia.[65] On 31 March 1958 the USSR unilaterally suspended nuclear

---

63. N. S. Khrushchev, *Kommunizm—mir i schast'e narodov,* 2 vols. (Moscow, 1961), 2: 307.

64. The text is given in *50 let bor'by SSSR za razoruzhenie: Sbornik dokumentov* (Moscow, 1967), pp. 287–98. See also Lincoln P. Bloomfield, Walter C. Clemens, Jr., and Franklyn Griffiths, *Khrushchev and the Arms Race: Soviet Interests in Arms Control and Disarmament* (Cambridge, 1966), pp. 22–25.

65. Gromyko and Ponomarev, *Istoriia vneshnei politiki, SSSR* 2: 247, note that the plan was developed "after consultation with the other members of the Warsaw Pact." It was refused by the West on the grounds that it did not provide for a resolution of the German question.

testing, setting into motion a process of consultations that would lead to the inauguration of a conference on the problem in Geneva during November.

A high point for the coexistence campaign arrived with Khrushchev's colorful tour of the United States in September 1959. Speaking before the U.N. General Assembly on 18 September, the Soviet leader presented a visionary program for general and complete disarmament.[66] The existence of antagonistic social systems organized in military blocs coupled with the nature of modern military technology, Khrushchev argued, made the concept of military superiority irrelevant and disarmament an objective necessity. To this end he urged the phased elimination of all conventional air, naval, and ground forces, with only "minimal contingents" retained to provide for domestic order. The plan called for the simultaneous liquidation of nuclear, chemical, and bacteriological weapons, monitored by an intrusive control regime to be supervised by a specially constituted international body. Despite the complexity of the undertaking, the entire project was to be completed in the space of four years. Blindly idealistic as they may have been, Khrushchev's suggestions were approved by the General Assembly unanimously and turned over to the special ten-nation U.N. Disarmament Conference just beginning its work in Geneva.

It is not difficult to highlight the self-serving aspects of Khrushchev's coexistence offensive. His proposals arrived at a time when the Soviet strategic arsenal remained greatly inferior to that of the United States. Offers such as the Rapacki Plan could easily be construed to be targeted at blocking the nuclear arming of NATO. The Soviet nuclear test moratorium was timed to Moscow's advantage, verification problems were never adequately addressed, and with its four-year time-table the plan for general disarmament appeared so wildly utopian as to court the charge of having been made exclusively for the ends of propaganda. It would nonetheless be unfair to ignore the extent to which Khrushchev's proposals were inspired by real ideals. As had been the case with Litvinov's campaign on behalf of collective security three decades before, Khrushchev sought to articulate a series of long-term aspirations as well as a practical program. In the spirit of peaceful coexistence, Moscow was signaling its interest in disarmament and commitment to dialogue.

Whether or not Khrushchev's efforts were well intentioned, the contradictions of competitive coexistence, as well as his own personal failings, worked against the progress of East-West détente. The first secretary could be a tremendously appealing public figure, but he was

66. The complete text of the speech is in Khrushchev, *Mir bez oruzhiia,* 2: 143–84. See also Bloomfield et al., *Khrushchev and the Arms Race,* pp. 138–45.

prone to rhetorical excess. In an interview during 1957 he emphasized the extent to which the United States would be exposed to Soviet rocket strikes in the event of war, and in his January 1960 Supreme Soviet speech he spoke of the ability "literally to wipe from the face of the earth the country or countries that attacked us."[67] Khrushchev's unconventional diplomatic style, while often refreshingly candid, occasionally degenerated into vulgarity.[68] The most famous incident occurred on 12 October 1960 in the U.N. General Assembly, when Khrushchev saw fit to protest against a speech by Britain's Harold MacMillan by rhythmically banging a shoe on his desk. Despite its humorous aspects, the incident only reinforced an image of the Soviet Union as coarse and dangerously volatile.

A series of foreign policy crises also worked to undermine the premises of coexistence. The most persistent among them was a new Berlin crisis, inaugurated by Khrushchev in a speech of 10 November 1958 in which he raised the possibility of eliminating four-power occupation and reconstituting Berlin as a demilitarized "free city." If these changes were not accomplished within a six-month interval, Khrushchev blustered, control over access routes to the western sectors would be transferred to the GDR.[69] The ultimatum was justified by references to the West's refusal to acknowledge the sovereignty of the GDR and to the misuse of West Berlin as a "NATO outpost," and with the argument that the arming of the FRG had invalidated the Potsdam accord upon which Berlin's four-power status rested. It may also be explained as a product of Soviet frustration over the failure to block the nuclear arming of NATO.[70] Tensions temporarily subsided when Khrushchev withdrew his ultimatum in March 1959, but the confrontation over Berlin had not yet been resolved.

The Soviet-American summit scheduled for May 1960 in Paris became the backdrop for yet another Cold War crisis. On 1 May 1960 an American U-2 high-altitude reconnaissance plane set out from its base in Pakistan to transit the USSR. U-2 flights had been staged for more than four years without incident, but luck was now about to run out. In the early morning hours the U-2 was shot down by a Soviet surface-to-air

67. Khrushchev, O vneshnei politike, 1: 37, and the interview in N. S. Khrushchev, Za prochnyi mir i mirnoe sosushchestvovanie (Moscow, 1958), pp. 299–300.

68. A quarter-century later Roy Medvedev, Khrushchev, p. 146, still recalled the disagreeable impression created by Khrushchev's use of the coarse idiomatic expression My pokazhem vam kuz'kinu mat'! ("We'll let you have it") in his televised "kitchen debate" with U.S. vice-president Richard M. Nixon during the summer of 1969.

69. Khrushchev, K pobede v mirnom sorevnovanii s kapitalizmom, pp. 552–66.

70. See the accounts in Nikolaev, Politika Sovetskogo Soiuza v germanskom voprose, pp. 268–95; James L. Richardson, Germany and the Atlantic Alliance: The Integration of Strategy and Politics (Cambridge, 1966), pp. 301–13.

missile in the vicinity of Sverdlovsk, and its pilot was captured after he managed to eject. By withholding the full extent of their knowledge, the Soviets lured the Eisenhower administration into a trap, and in a speech of 7 May, Khrushchev rubbed salt in the wound by exposing Washington's embarrassed explanations as bare-faced lies. On 9 May Moscow threatened military strikes against basing areas if the flights were continued. Khrushchev traveled to Paris for his scheduled meeting with Eisenhower, but it was only to announce that in the absence of a personal apology from the U.S. president the summit conference could not take place.[71]

The U-2 incident was followed by a second round of the Berlin crisis. In his speech to the November 1960 international communist conference in Moscow, Khrushchev returned to the idea of altering the city's four-power status and called for "decisive measures."[72] Speaking with the new U.S. president John F. Kennedy in Vienna during June 1961, the first secretary established the end of the year as a new deadline. A phase of reciprocal bluffing ensued, with both sides announcing increases in military spending and placing their forces in Europe on advanced alert status. It was during and immediately after these events that Moscow suspended its 1960 troop-reduction program and tested several fifty-megaton "superbombs," the largest nuclear warheads ever detonated. In the end, however, Soviet pressure proved to be nothing more than an elaborate preliminary for the East German decision to close its border by building a wall around West Berlin in August 1961. Once the GDR had restored domestic order by blocking emigration, Khrushchev's campaign for a revision of Berlin's status was allowed to peter out.[73]

The final foreign policy crisis of the Khrushchev period was also the most serious. As the only bona fide nuclear brinkmanship crisis of the postwar era, the Cuban missile crisis of October 1962 (known as the Caribbean crisis in Soviet parlance) has generated a large body of analysis seeking to fix the mechanism of international crisis behavior in the nuclear age. Much of the work has focused upon decision making within

71. Khrushchev gives an interesting version of the incident in Strobe Talbott, ed., *Khrushchev Remembers: The Last Testament* (Boston, 1974), pp. 443–46. He emphasizes the need for a strong response in order to make clear to the Americans that spy flights would not be tolerated. A good overall account is provided by Michel Tatu, *Power in the Kremlin: From Khrushchev to Kosygin* (New York, 1969), pp. 41–122.

72. Khrushchev's remarks appear in N. S. Khrushchev, "Za novye pobedy mirnogo kommunisticheskogo dvizheniia," *Kommunist* 1 (Jan. 1961): 3–37, esp. p. 22.

73. The best account of the 1961 Berlin crisis is Robert M. Slusser, *The Berlin Crisis of 1961: Soviet-American Relations and the Struggle for Power in the Kremlin* (Baltimore, Md., 1973). Wolfe, *Soviet Power and Europe*, p. 95, describes the construction of the Berlin Wall in the context of the crisis as "a defensive device . . . which subsequently came to be regarded by many on both sides as a stabilizing factor."

the Kennedy administration, on the assumption that greater access to data makes the momentum of choice easier to establish. More is known about Soviet policy during the crisis than ever before, however, and much of the information reflects badly upon Khrushchev, whose high-risk venture in Cuba proved to be badly misconceived.

The gradual warming of Soviet-Cuban relations that followed Castro's accession to power was anchored upon the Soviet willingness to provide the Cuban revolution security assistance. Soviet arms transfers to Cuba began during 1960, and in July Khrushchev made the ambiguous assertion that, "speaking figuratively," Soviet rockets might be used in Cuba's defense.[74] The CIA-sponsored invasion of Cuba at the Bay of Pigs on April 1961 was defeated by Cuban forces acting on their own, but the episode could only have reinforced Castro's awareness of his island's strategic exposure.

The decision to place intermediate-range ballistic missiles in Cuba would subsequently be justified as an attempt to guarantee Cuban security.[75] At the time of the missile crisis there were approximately 40,000 Soviet military personnel in Cuba in addition to the Cuban army's 240,000 effectives. These forces were sufficient to make a U.S. intervention difficult and bloody, but far from adequate to defeat Washington were it intent upon prevailing. There was therefore a sound military logic for the deployment of nuclear weapons as a deterrent force. Given the risks involved, however, it is likely that the defense of Cuba was not the sole Soviet motive. Taking into account the United States' large strategic advantage, the failure of arms control initiatives, and the new emphasis being placed upon the nuclear rocket weapon in Soviet military doctrine, it may be assumed that an additional goal was to take advantage of American embarrassment at the Bay of Pigs in order to legitimize the deployments and thus to set right the strategic balance

74. "Rech' tovarishcha N. S. Khrushcheva na Vserossiiskom s"ezde uchitelei," *Pravda*, 10 July 1960, p. 2. Wayne S. Smith, *The Closest of Enemies: A Personal and Diplomatic Account of U.S.–Cuban Relations since 1957* (New York, 1987), pp. 49–54, and Levesque, *The USSR and the Cuban Revolution*, p. 10, argue that Castro's shift toward a pro-Soviet position was originally intended as a calculated bid for support on the eve of the Bay of Pigs invasion. It was not until December 1961 that Castro declared himself to be a Marxist-Leninist.

75. Khrushchev offered this explanation to the Supreme Soviet in a speech of 19 Dec. 1962 and indicated that the initial request for the missiles came from Cuba. N. S. Khrushchev, *Predotvratit' voinu, otstoit' mir!* (Moscow, 1963), pp. 374–90. Castro denied the latter assertion in an interview with Claude Julien conducted several weeks later. See "Sept heures avec M. Fidel Castro," *Le Monde*, 22 March 1963, pp. 1 and 6. Khrushchev returned to the theme of defending Cuba in his memoirs, arguing in *Khrushchev Remembers*, p. 495: "The main thing was that the installation of our missiles in Cuba could, I thought, restrain the United States from precipitous military action against Castro's government."

"overnight."[76] The forty launcher units that Khrushchev sought to install would have moved the Soviet Union considerably closer to the kind of nuclear capacity that its military leaders deemed to be essential.

In purely formal terms the basis for the Soviet action was unassailable. The United States had acted unilaterally in ringing the USSR with military installations, including medium-range missile sites adjacent to Soviet territory in Turkey. Indeed, part of Khrushchev's motivation in Cuba may have been the desire to "balance" these forces, considered an insult to Soviet national pride as well as a security threat, with comparable deployments in the western hemisphere. But Khrushchev was well aware that such arguments would carry no weight in Washington, and he did his best to disguise the work of installation for as long as possible. Predictably, when the missile sites were discovered by U-2 reconnaissance on 16 October, the Kennedy administration responded firmly, declaring a naval blockade of the island and threatening air strikes unless the sites were dismantled. After a harrowing week of esoteric diplomatic communication, the two sides arrived at an agreement: the missile sites would be eliminated, the Soviets would pledge never again to station offensive weapons in Cuba, and the United States would promise in return to sponsor no further invasions of the island. In addition, Washington signaled its intention to withdraw U.S. Jupiter missiles from Turkey and Italy.

Khrushchev called the Cuban crisis a "great victory" because it resulted in a U.S. no-invasion commitment.[77] In retrospect, however, it is difficult to interpret the outcome as anything less than a humiliating defeat. To begin, Havana was far from pleased with the Soviet decision to pull back, made unilaterally and without consultations. "What we contend," editorialized Che Guevera with the crisis still unresolved, "is that we must walk by the path of liberation even when it may cost millions of atomic victims."[78] In the light of such hair-raising extremism Khrushchev appeared as a champion of peace, but it was his decision to risk the

76. This is the way that Castro explained the decision in his interview with Julien: "It was explained to us [by the Soviets] that in accepting them [the missiles] we would be reinforcing the socialist camp on the global level." Le Monde, 22 March 1963, p. 1. See also Horelick and Rush, Strategic Power and Soviet Foreign Policy, p. 154.

77. Khrushchev Remembers, p. 500.

78. Cited in Carla Anne Robbins, The Cuban Threat, (Philadelphia, 1983), p. 47. Guevara's editorial was withheld from publication by the Cuban government during the crisis and did not appear in print until 1967. Convinced that a U.S. attack was imminent, the Cuban government was ready to support a preemptive strike—a counsel that Khrushchev rejected with horror. See Khrushchev Remembers: The Glasnost Tapes, pp. 170–83; Castro's correspondence with Khrushchev during the crisis published in "Castro, Khrouchtchev et l'apocalypse," Le Monde, 24 Nov. 1990, pp. 1 and 3.

deployments that had caused the problem. For the first secretary's political opponents the incident provided a whole cache of ammunition. Khrushchev had placed the USSR in an untenable position, had been found out, and had been intimidated into a shameless retreat. The Soviet Union's military inferiority vis-à-vis its main global rival, its inability to face down the Americans when vital interests were at stake, were laid bare for all the world to see. Beijing mocked the Soviets for moving from "adventurism to capitulationism" and inflicting "unprecedented shame and humiliation on the international proletariat." Perhaps the most telling comment of all was that reportedly made shortly after the crisis by the Soviet diplomat Vasilii Kuznetsov to John McCloy: "You will never do that to us again."[79]

The U-2 incident and the collapse of the Paris summit, the Berlin crises of 1958 and 1961, and the Cuban missile crisis of 1962 undermined the Soviet coexistence offensive. Although for the time being Khrushchev remained in the saddle, his audacity had not served him well. The defeats suffered as a result of the competitive edge of his policies raised serious questions about his judgment, weakened the momentum of his reform project, and ultimately prepared the ground for his ouster and political defeat.

Khrushchev's Last Stand

The Cuban missile crisis demonstrated that even when the best of intentions prevailed, nuclear war remained within the range of possibility. In the wake of the stand-off, steps were taken to restore something of the "Spirit of Geneva." The result was a process of accommodation that might well have gone further had not both Kennedy and Khrushchev, the main protagonists on each side, been torn from the scene in 1963–1964.

79. Kuznetsov's remark is cited in Charles Bohlen, *Witness to History* (New York, 1973), p. 495, and the Chinese remark in Gittings, *Survey of the Sino-Soviet Dispute*, pp. 181–83. For evaluations incorporating the results of recent Soviet-American consultations on the event see James G. Blight and David A. Welch, *On the Brink: Americans and Soviets Reexamine the Cuban Missile Crisis* (New York, 1989); the insightful account by Raymond L. Garthoff, *Reflections on the Cuban Missile Crisis* (Washington, D.C., 1989). The first important Soviet academic evaluation of the crisis by Anatolii A. Gromyko, "Karibskii krizis," *Voprosy istorii* 7 and 8 (1971): 132–44 and 121–29, emphasized the serious threat of escalation. Accounts produced in the era of *glasnost'* became considerably more self-critical. See particularly S. Chugrov, "Politicheskie rify Karibskogo krizisa," *Mirovaia ekonomika i mezhdunarodnye otnosheniia* 5 (1989): 19–32.

The Soviet Union signaled its desire for a renewed dialogue in December 1962 by liberalizing its position on inspection arrangements for a comprehensive nuclear test ban. During 1963 talks aimed at a comprehensive ban within the U.N.'s eighteen-nation disarmament conference in Geneva broke down, but on 2 July, Khrushchev reshuffled the deck by announcing the Soviet Union's willingness to conclude a partial test ban according to the terms favored by the West.[80] In June the "hot line" agreement providing for direct telephone communication between the White House and the Kremlin in the event of an international crisis was announced, and Soviet jamming of Voice of America radio broadcasts was reduced.

Kennedy came toward these gestures with a major speech at American University in Washington on 10 June that in some ways echoed the Soviet line of peaceful coexistence. According to the U.S. president, in the age of nuclear weapons "total war makes no sense." Armed conflict between the United States and the USSR was not inevitable, and areas of tensions could be reduced by conscious political action. Kennedy urged the American people to strive for a deeper understanding of the Soviet Union and in conclusion announced a U.S. moratorium on atmospheric testing. The speech was received with real enthusiasm in Moscow and privately described by Khrushchev as "courageous."[81] With Soviet-American relations on the upswing, negotiations for a limited test-ban treaty were brought to a successful conclusion, and a treaty was signed by the foreign ministers of the United Kingdom, United States, and USSR on 5 August 1963.

The Limited Test Ban Treaty was followed by other steps in the direction of arms limitations. On 17 October 1963 a U.N. resolution approved jointly by the United States and the USSR outlawed the placement of nuclear weapons in outer space. During 1963 and 1964 Moscow addressed numerous proposals to the U.N. disarmament forum focused on the problem of European security, including the familiar call for a NATO–Warsaw Pact nonaggression pact, the reciprocal stationing of observers at control points and other measures to reduce the risk of surprise attack, and force reductions in the two Germanies. In January 1964 Khrushchev sent an open letter to all world heads of state

80. Already prior to the Cuban crisis in August and September 1962 the Soviet Union softened its position in the U.N.'s eighteen-nation disarmament conference. In a letter to Kennedy of 19 Dec. 1962 Khrushchev agreed to accept "two or three" onsite inspections per year or the emplacement of automatic seismic stations on Soviet territory as part of a comprehensive test-ban treaty. Bloomfield et al., *Khrushchev and the Arms Race*, pp. 185–89.

81. The text of the speech appears in "Text of Kennedy's Address offering 'Strategy of Peace' for Easing the Cold War," *New York Times*, 11 June 1963, p. 16; Khrushchev's formal response, in "Ukrepliat' delo mira," *Pravda*, 15 June 1963, pp. 1–2.

proposing the renunciation of the use of force in resolving territorial disputes. These initiatives were not all equally convincing, but cumulatively they expressed a desire to reassert the premises of peaceful coexistence in the wake of the Cuban debacle.

These modest advances were not adequate to overcome growing resentment within the ranks of the Soviet hierarchy against the willful and unpredictable dimensions of Khrushchev's leadership. Discontent was focused upon the problematic consequences of institutional and economic reforms. The rapid succession of administrative restructurings had created a considerable amount of bureaucratic confusion. By 1963 the virgin lands campaign, launched with such fanfare during the 1950s, had turned sour. Overeagerness to produce bumper crops, lack of infrastructure, and poor agronomic methods aggravated by a spell of poor weather turned the 1963 harvest into one of the worst in memory. The result was large-scale grain purchases on international markets, a step unprecedented in Russia's modern history. De-Stalinization also had the effect of alienating many senior cadre who felt themselves to be compromised personally. By 1963 Khrushchev appears to have become nearly isolated politically.[82]

Foreign and security policy also contributed to Khrushchev's discomfiture. The blow administered to his prestige by the Cuban missile crisis was one from which he never fully recovered. Relations with China were disintegrating steadily. De-Stalinization had the effect of undermining the unity of the international communist movement and reducing Moscow's ability to control it. Dissent was particularly visible in Europe, where the desire of the most important Communist parties to distance themselves from the Soviet example, well illustrated by the testament of Palmiro Togliatti written just prior to his death in the summer of 1964 and published in *Pravda* on 10 September, provided the foundation for what would become a major challenge to Moscow's leadership. The exercise in personal diplomacy undertaken by Khrushchev's son-in-law Aleksei Adzhubei during a visit to the FRG in July 1964, possibly intended to prepare the way for a raprochement, seems to have been resented by the more conservative members of the hierarchy, no doubt at the end of their tether with Khrushchev's unpredictable personalist direction.[83]

In the end Khrushchev became the victim of a conspiracy hatched within the Presidium and set into motion during one of his frequent

82. The growth of opposition to Khrushchev is described in Carl A. Linden, *Khrushchev and the Soviet Leadership, 1957–1964* (Baltimore, Md., 1966), pp. 146–221.

83. Tatu, *Power in the Kremlin*, pp. 361–423. According to Adzhubei, in an interview published as "La chute de Khrouchtchev racontée par son gendre," *Le Monde*, 19–20 Feb. 1989, pp. 1 and 5, the desire to block the possible consequences of his scheduled trip to Germany was a significant factor in the intrigue leading to Khrushchev's ouster.

absences from Moscow in October 1964. In 1957 Khrushchev had faced a similar challenge and won out. Seven years later his political base was too weak, and perhaps at age seventy and with a host of battles behind him his personal energy too low, to repeat the performance. When the assembled Soviet power elite demanded the first secretary's retirement, he chose not to resist. The explanation he later gave to his son has the ring of truth:

> I'm already old and tired . . . I've accomplished the most important things. The relations between us, the style of leadership has changed fundamentally. Could anyone have ever dreamed of telling Stalin that he no longer pleased us and should retire? He would have made mince-meat of us. Now everything is different. Fear has disappeared, and a dialogue is carried on among equals. That is my service. I won't fight any longer.[84]

The style of leadership had indeed changed. Unfortunately, the goals to which the new collective leadership sought to apply the exercise of power would prove to be very different from those favored by Khrushchev. His key successors, including First Secretary Leonid Brezhnev, Chair of the Council of Ministers Aleksei Kosygin, and President Nikolai Podgornyi, promised continuity in the broad lines of policy together with the elimination of Khrushchev's notorious excesses. In reality the fall of the dynamic reformer meant the beginning of a conservative reaction that would soon lead to the defeat of many of the causes for which he had fought so hard and so long.

Soviet accounts of the Khrushchev period published under the aegis of the reformist leadership of Mikhail Gorbachev emphasized the well-intentioned but essentially inadequate character of his attempt to move Soviet society away from the legacy of Stalinism. Khrushchev's fall is said to have been occasioned by his failure to push the momentum of reform toward its logical culmination: "Not one single step was taken with the required resolution, not one undertaking was carried through to

84. Cited by Sergei Khrushchev, "Pensioner soiuznogo znacheniia," *Ogonek* 40 (Oct. 1988): 27. According to Sergei Khrushchev's account, during the Politburo session that decided his father's dismissal the most severe criticisms were directed against failures in foreign policy. The recollections of one of the key anti-Khrushchev conspirators confirms that foreign policy issues were part of the indictment but places more emphasis upon Khrushchev's "unreflective and impulsive" leadership style. A. N. Shelepin, "Istoriia—uchitel' surovyi," *Trud*, 14 March 1991, p. 4. For a good summary see Werner Hahn, "Who Ousted Nikita Khrushchev?" *Problems of Communism* 3 (May–June 1991): 109–15.

the end.''[85] Such judgments contain a kernel of truth, but on balance they are probably too harsh. Khrushchev dared to raise the Stalin question even if he could not resolve it. He emptied Stalin's Gulag, acknowledged the Soviet Union's most evident failings, and ventured reform upon reform in an effort to rectify them. But Khrushchevite reformism never reached beyond piecemeal change toward a thoroughgoing alternative to the political regime and ideology, as opposed to the criminal excesses and distasteful methods, of Stalinism.[86] Because his authority lacked a democratic foundation, Khrushchev was always vulnerable to the kind of bureaucratic coup that eventually defeated him.

Similarly ambiguous conclusions may be drawn concerning Khrushchev's impact upon Soviet security policy. His years in power correspond to a period of transition during which the Soviet Union was required to come to terms with the realities of the nuclear age and break the spiral of confrontation inherited from the Cold War. These proved to be difficult goals to pursue simultaneously. Under Khrushchev, Soviet strategic doctrine was adjusted to take account of the impact of nuclear weaponry, and the foundations for a modern strategic arsenal were put in place. Peaceful coexistence was expanded into the centerpiece of an approach to security that sought rapprochement with the West, but that remained committed to a competitive international posture and to a doctrine of peace through strength. Khrushchev may nonetheless be described as a sincere advocate of peace. His brief remarks to the World Youth Forum in September 1964 just prior to his ouster have the ring of a *cri du coeur*: "The chief thing in deciding 'who will win' is economic competition, economic competition. I repeat it a third time—economic competition."[87]

At the moment of Khrushchev's ouster the Soviet-American relationship was no less adversarial than it had been under Stalin. The East-West divide in Europe remained frozen, and the Soviet security posture continued to rest upon coercive control over the "bloc," now institutionalized as the Warsaw Pact. In Asia the Sino-Soviet rift represented a major degradation in the USSR's overall international situation. Although some of the intensity had been bled away from Cold War rivalries, the

85. Iurii Levida and Viktor Sheimis, "1953–1964: Pochemu togda ne poluchalas'," *Moskovskie novosti*, 1 May 1988, pp. 8–9.

86. As put by Alexander S. Tsipko, *Is Stalinism Really Dead?* (San Francisco, 1990), p. vi: "Why did the perestroika that Khrushchev launched in 1956 fail to produce a new vision of socialism and its destinies? For the simple reason that his criticism of Stalin's crimes did not evolve into criticism of the philosophical and economic foundations of the political regime that Stalin had built."

87. "Vystuplenie N. S. Khrushcheva na prieme v chest' uchastnikov Vsemirnogo foruma molodezhi," *Pravda*, 22 Sept. 1964, p. 1.

Cold War system, characterized by ideological polarization, high levels of militarization, and confrontational bilateral diplomacy, had if anything been reinforced. Although it would be unfair to place exclusive blame upon Khrushchev, it is possible to argue that an approach to security built upon the assumptions of competitive coexistence was creating as many problems as it was able to solve. Even in the economic sphere, where Khrushchev's hopes for the future were always placed, his last years in office saw the beginning of a slide backward. Much had been ventured, but the promise of peaceful coexistence and hopes for a fundamental reform within Soviet society itself remained unfulfilled.

CHAPTER SEVEN

The Rise and Fall
of Détente, 1964–1982

The problems of the conscience—
Before them, how not to sin?
Here and there tin soldiers—
How to decide who should win?
——Vladimir Vysotskii, 1968

Leonid Brezhnev's eighteen-year tenure as general secretary of the CPSU seems to resist balanced judgments. Increasingly the object of an artificially manufactured personality cult inside the USSR during his waning years, Brezhnev was simultaneously being portrayed in the West as the grim embodiment of an expanding empire bent upon world domination. Since his death in 1982 the picture has been reversed, but the judgments have not been tempered. The Brezhnev period is reviled by Russian reformers as an era of "stagnation" marked by political immobility and rampant corruption, whereas western commentators who once spoke fearfully of Soviet ambitions now revel in the collapse of communism.

Brezhnev's record is above all contradictory. In the wake of Khrushchev's "hare-brained scheming" and administrative upheavals, the new leadership promised stability, and it kept its word. Brezhnev's authority rested upon the support of a bureaucratic elite of leading party functionaries traumatized by reform and determined to reassert a conservative consensus. His backers moved quickly to undo much of Khrushchev's work, and the February 1966 trial of the writers Iulii Daniel and Andrei Siniavskii, accused of publishing anti-Soviet literature abroad under pseudonyms and punished with lengthy prison terms, signaled a revival of tight political standards in society as a whole. To describe the Brezhnev period as "neo-Stalinist" is nonetheless unfair. The extreme abuses that Khrushchev eliminated from Soviet political life were not revived, and serious, though substantially frustrated, efforts were made to reform the economic mechanism, improve living standards, and create a more equitable social environment.

In the realm of foreign relations a similar ambiguity was apparent. Brezhnev rose to power as a Khrushchevite, and his key lieutenants had all worked comfortably with the peaceful coexistence line associated with the fallen chieftain. *Competitive coexistence* therefore remained the dominant paradigm informing Soviet security policy. Brezhnev inherited Khrushchev's cautious optimism concerning the potential of Soviet power and the belief that it was possible to combine stable relations with the United States with an ambitious striving for enhanced influence.

The problem was that while according to its own standards the Soviet Union continued to make halting progress, the terms of the international competition to which it was subject were changing dramatically. The Soviet Union over which Brezhnev presided, predominantly urban, uniformly educated, and increasingly aware of the world around it, was completely different from the society of villages that had won the Great Patriotic War. At home, urbanization and the transformation of social norms that it brought in its train demanded new approaches to public policy. Internationally, a proliferation of weapons of mass destruction was qualitatively altering the very essence of security. Confronted with sweeping changes that often transcended their grasp. Brezhnev and his associates strove ever more doggedly and ever more futilely to consolidate their regime around tried and true principles.

In some ways Brezhnev successfully fulfilled his mandate. His government achieved and maintained approximate strategic parity with the United States, managed to give positive content to peaceful coexistence under the rubric of détente, and made the Soviet Union a formidable world power. Domestically his policies offered real though faltering economic growth and a slow but perceptible improvement in living standards. Unfortunately many of these accomplishments were unsustainable, and the price paid for them was unacceptably high. Economic gains were achieved at the expense of a rapid depletion of raw materials and rampant ecological damage. Heavy-handed coercion and ideological rigidity provided for a modicum of order but also provoked a virtual collapse of public morale. And the fundaments of security policy were built upon levels of military preparedness that exceeded the state's long-term ability to pay.

In the end the repressive character of Brezhnev's domestic policies and the increasingly costly attempt to pursue a competitive relationship with the United States globally became recipes for frustration. Although the Soviet state border remained inviolable, the failure to carry on the positive reform initiatives of Khrushchev, to achieve the much-discussed transition from quantitative to qualitative economic growth, and to break free from the paralyzing spirit of the Cold War led to a dangerous erosion of the foundations upon which the Soviet Union's long-term interests rested. Robin Edmond's assertion that "at the moment of his [Brezhnev's] death the Soviet Union was no more secure, in reality, than it was eighteen years earlier" is an understatement.[1] The Brezhnev period led to a disintegration in the USSR's security situation that his successors would be hard-pressed to make good.

The Torrents of Spring

In March 1966 the 23rd party congress of the CPSU confirmed Brezhnez as first among equals with the restored title of general secretary (the congress also rechristened the Khrushchev-era Presidium as the Politburo). Brezhnev's personal authority was still constrained, however; part of the logic of Khrushchev's ouster was the desire to eliminate unpredictable personalist direction. More than ever before, the new Soviet power elite deserved to be called a collective leadership.

The first initiatives of the post-Khrushchev leadership in foreign affairs reflected the desire to maintain a degree of continuity. In his Revolution Day address of November 1964 Brezhnev signaled that the premises of competitive coexistence were still in place. "The Soviet Union has conducted and will conduct a Leninist policy of peaceful coexistence of states with different social systems," he intoned. "A situation of peaceful coexistence will facilitate the success of the liberation struggle and the achievement of the revolutionary task of the people."[2] Brezhnev's first major foreign policy speech, delivered on 29 September 1965, offered no significant concessions, but it was moderate in tone.[3] On 20 January the Political Consultative Committee of the Warsaw Pact revived the idea of a European security conference in a statement on behalf of European détente, reiterated by the "Declaration on Strengthening Peace and Security in Europe" issued in Bucharest on 7 July 1966 and by the conference of European Communist parties at Karlovy Vary on 26 April 1967.[4] A mission to Beijing led by Kosygin in February 1965 ended without results, but the Soviet Union strengthened its hand in Asia at the expense

1. Robin Edmonds, *Soviet Foreign Policy: The Brezhnev Years* (Oxford, 1983), p. 5.
2. L. I. Brezhnev, *Leninskim kursom: Rechi i stat'i*, 8 vols. (Moscow, 1970–81), 1: 27.
3. Ibid., pp. 206–32.
4. "Kommunike soveshchaniia Politicheskogo Konsul'tativnogo Komiteta gosudarstv—uchastnikov Varshavskogo Dogovora," *Pravda*, 22 Jan. 1965, p. 1; "Deklaratsiia ob ukreplenii mira i bezopasnosti v Evrope," *Pravda*, 9 July 1966, p. 1; "Konkretnaia programma bor'by za bezopasnost'narodov," *Pravda*, 26 April 1967, pp. 1 and 4.

of China by successfully mediating between India and Pakistan at a conference in Tashkent in January 1966. Perhaps most tellingly, in an era of expanding social activism worldwide the USSR and the pro-Soviet wing of the international communist movement remained remarkably passive. The Kremlin was clearly not interested in storming barricades.

The road to Brezhnev's emergence as dominant leader was paved by a contest over economic reform. Under Khrushchev it was widely acknowledged that the centralized command model of economic planning developed under Stalin had become too constraining. A public debate over alternatives was opened on 9 September 1962 with the publication in *Pravda* of a manifesto by the economist Evsei Liberman that proposed an ambitious reform based upon a reduction in the number of centrally determined plan indicators and the replacement of quantitative indices by other standards, including deliveries and profits. The exchange of views that followed culminated with the announcement by Kosygin at a September 1965 Central Committee plenum of a comprehensive reform in the spirit of Liberman's proposal, including the restitution of the ministerial system that had been jettisoned under Khrushchev, price reform, and a redrawing of incentive mechanisms designed to encourage innovation and attention to quality standards.

Despite the fanfare with which they were announced, the "Kosygin reforms" failed to accomplish their most important goals. The point of administrative restructuring was to restore past procedures rather than to encourage innovation. Price and incentive reforms were not begun until 1967 and then progressed at a snail's pace. Foot dragging, artificially inspired delays, and outright deceit were used to good effect to frustrate the reform effort, which in the end proved to be a major disappointment.[5] The failure was a victory for conservative forces within Soviet society at large, and a political defeat for Kosygin. In June 1967 it was the Soviet premier who was chosen to represent his country at the summit with U.S. president Lyndon Johnson in Glassboro, New Jersey. By the 1970s, though he retained some symbolic stature, Kosygin had been effaced by Brezhnev.

Who was Leonid Brezhnev? A party loyalist and man of the apparatus whose strengths, in his own estimation, were "organizational and psychological" rather than theoretical, the new general secretary had not made his career as an independent leader or original thinker.[6] He would

5. The experience is summarized in Ed A. Hewett, *Reforming the Soviet Economy: Equality versus Efficiency* (Washington, D.C., 1988), pp. 227–45.
6. Brezhnev's self-evaluation is cited by Fedor Burlatskii, "Brezhnev i krushenie ottepeli: Razmyshleniia o prirode politicheskogo liderstva," *Literaturnaia gazeta*, 17 Sept. 1988, p. 13.

cast his lot unambiguously with the forces of bureaucratic conservatism only when forced to choose by the Czechoslovak crisis of 1968, a major event in Soviet domestic as well as international policy and one whose outcome would fix the course of the Soviet ship of state for a generation to come.

The Czechoslovak crisis was triggered when student demonstrations in Prague on All Saint's Eve in October 1967 grew spontaneously into a rowdy manifestation of discontent. Red lights now switched on in the Kremlin, where Soviet leaders remained hypersensitive to the threat of destabilization on their western marches. Following a two-day visit to Prague by Brezhnev, the conservative party leader Antonín Novotný was forced to step down. He was replaced on 5 January 1968 by Alexander Dubček, a provincial leader from Slovakia with liberal credentials but educated in the Soviet Union and presumed to be loyal to Moscow. The Soviets appeared to be following a tried and true strategy by opting for controlled reform from above in order to head off destabilization.

Moscow's well-laid plans were to go seriously astray. The Dubček appointment, rather than calming the waters, had the effect of galvanizing a movement for renewal. With Dubček's enthusiastic support, an April plenum of the Czechoslovakian Communist party's (CPCz) Central Committee approved wholesale personnel changes that placed the party firmly in the hands of its reformist wing. An "Action Program" was promulgated as an agenda for change featuring calls for democratization, an end to censorship, and open borders—"socialism with a human face" in the expressive phrase that would soon come to characterize the movement's aspirations worldwide.[7] An extraordinary party congress was also scheduled for September to formalize a liberal agenda that seemed to have triumphed across the board.

The "Prague Spring" was composed of a series of overlapping projects for change. In addition to the political reforms outlined in the Action Program, the full implementation of a contested economic reform package drawn up by the liberal Ota Šik was targeted. Dubček was committed to a movement for constitutional reform on behalf of expanded Slovak autonomy and an authentically federal state. Less often referred to but critically important, a reform current surfaced within the Czechoslovak military, whose leaders publicly raised the issues of national control over defense policy, the professional status of Czechoslovak officers within the Warsaw Pact, and the implications of pact

7. The text of the Action Program is given is Robin Allison Remington, *Winter in Prague: Documents on Czechoslovak Communism in Crisis* (Cambridge, Mass., 1969), pp. 88–137.

nuclear policy.[8] When combined with the impressive popular mobilizations that followed the April plenum, the Prague Spring took on the contours of a challenge to the entire Soviet image of socialism. Against its will the Brezhnev leadership was forced to choose. Was change on such a scale compatible with the exigencies of the Soviet security system in central Europe?

Only a small minority within the group of leaders surrounding Brezhnev was capable of considering the Prague Spring in the way that Dubček perceived it, as a hopeful experiment in the liberalization of communist systems within the confines of loyalty to the USSR and the party-state model. Although a considerable amount of dissent within the Soviet leadership has been documented, it concerned how best to reverse the movement, not whether or not to identify with it.[9] Even prior to the promulgation of the Action Program, on 25 March 1968, a Dresden meeting of delegations from the USSR, the GDR, Poland, Hungary, Bulgaria, and Czechoslovakia (with the notable absence of an increasingly uncooperative Romania) signaled the bloc's preference for a hard-line response. On 4 May the Czechoslovak leadership was summoned to Moscow for consultations, where according to Vasil Bilák they were instructed unceremoniously that the proposed reforms meant "the betrayal of socialism and the annulling of the results of the Second World War."[10] In the months to come the Soviets resorted to every imaginable sort of pressure to convince Dubček of the need to "bring events under control," including minatory public statements, unscheduled troop movements, a major Warsaw Pact exercise conducted on Czechoslovak territory, and a sequence of bloc summits and bilateral consultations.

Dubček struggled to control the reform movement without capitulating to external pressure. Following a tête-à-tête with Brezhnev at Čierna-nad-Tisou on the Czechoslovak-Soviet border on 29–30 July and the issuance of a conciliatory declaration by the Warsaw Pact member states (again minus Romania) on 3 August at Bratislava, he appeared to

8. Condoleezza Rice, *The Soviet Union and the Czechoslovak Army, 1948–1983* (Princeton, N.J., 1983), pp. 94–110; Josef Hodic, "Military-Political Views Prevalent in the Czechoslovak Army: 1948–1968," in Zdeněk Mlynář, ed., *The Experience of the Prague Spring* (Vienna, 1979), pp. 14–16.

9. For accounts of the dissent see Grey Hodnett and Peter J. Potichnyi, *The Ukraine and the Czechoslovak Crisis* (Canberra, 1970), pp. 77–89; Jiri Valenta, *Soviet Intervention in Czechoslovakia 1968: Anatomy of a Decision* (Baltimore, Md., 1978). Karen Dawisha, *The Kremlin and the Prague Spring* (Berkeley, Calif., 1985), pp. 341–66, places greater emphasis upon the elements of accord among key Soviet leaders.

10. Cited in Dawisha, *The Kremlin and the Prague Spring*, p. 76. The Dresden communiqué is given in Remington, *Winter in Prague*, pp. 55–57.

have pulled off the feat.[11] But the show of reconciliation was the sheerest of deceptions. On 20–21 August, one week prior to the date set for the CPCz's party congress, no less than twenty-four divisions representing the Soviet Union, Hungary, Poland, and Bulgaria rolled across the border at eighteen points and, after making short work of Czechoslovak passive resistance, brought the reform project to a screeching halt.

Why had Moscow opted to use force? Dubček never considered himself less than a loyal communist perfectly willing to defer to Soviet interests, authority remained firmly in the hands of the CPCz, and there was no trace of public disorder. It is true that certain special constituencies, including the Soviet provincial administration in the Ukraine and the East German and Polish governments of Walter Ulbricht and Wladyslaw Gomulka, felt threatened by a spillover effect and urged preemptive action. But there were also calmer heads present anxious to avoid destabilizing military measures and willing to ride the tide of controlled change. The decision to use armed force was not only a response to events in Prague; it meant a settling of accounts with would-be reformers inside the Kremlin.

The official justification issued by TASS on 22 August claimed that Moscow was responding to a call for help to block "counterrevolutionary forces that have entered into collusion with external forces hostile to socialism."[12] In subsequent weeks an attempt was made to build the explanation into a general premise of Soviet foreign policy. In the event that socialist regimes in power found themselves threatened by externally sponsored counterrevolution, it was proposed, the Soviet Union had both the right and the duty to intervene in defense of socialism, if need be in defiance of the narrowly construed principle of national sovereignty.[13] Labeled the "Brezhnev Doctrine" by the western press, the dubious rationalization would be accorded a considerable amount of attention in the years to come. The Soviets themselves never acknowledged the existence of a "doctrine" of limited sovereignty, but the argument revealed a good deal about their specific motives during the Czechoslovak crisis. At stake, in addition to the integrity of the

11. The texts of the Bratislava and Čierna-nad-Tisou statements are provided in Remington, *Winter in Prague*, pp. 255–61.

12. Ibid., pp. 299–23. The text was published as an editorial statement, "Vernost' bratskomu dolgu," *Pravda*, 22 Aug. 1968, p. 1.

13. The key statement is the editorial signed by S. Kovalev, "Suverenitet i internatsional'nye obiazannosti sotsialisticheskikh stran," *Pravda*, 26 Sept. 1968, p. 4. The critical sentence reads: "The sovereignty of each socialist country cannot be opposed to the interests of the entire socialist community or of the world revolutionary movement." For the text in English see Remington, *Winter in Prague*, pp. 412–16.

eastern European security zone, was the kind of socialism that Soviet leaders considered to be compatible with their own claim to a right to rule. The decision to invade was a victory for conservative forces who thereby signaled their complete lack of interest in meaningful reform, whether among the Soviet satellite states or within the USSR itself. The Soviet incursion, according to Jerry Hough, "ended not only the Dubček experiment, but also any hope of major economic reform in Russia in the Brezhnev era."[14]

To the extent that there was a single, critical explanation for the decision to invade, it probably concerned the implications of Czechoslovak reformism for Soviet security. One direction in which Brezhnev did not follow Khrushchev's lead was that of military policy. Brezhnev's relationship with the high command was not entirely free of friction, but he was more receptive to military council than his predecessor and from 1965 onward defense spending increased steadily.[15] By the late 1960s the changing balance of forces in the European theater also contributed to heightened professional military concern over Soviet preparedness for the contingency of war. Faced with the disintegration of its margin of strategic superiority and declining European confidence in the reliability of the American nuclear umbrella (dramatized by France's withdrawal from NATO's military arm in 1966), NATO moved in 1967 to implement a new strategic doctrine of "flexible response." Rather than hinging the defense of western Europe upon the intimidating effect of the American nuclear arsenal, flexible response emphasized forward defense and conventional warfighting capacity, with nuclear weapons reserved as a last resort should conventional defense fail. Viewed from Moscow, flexible response meant a new palette of military options for NATO, including a greatly enhanced conventional and tactical-nuclear threat.

Michael MccGwire has argued that the years 1967–1968 represented "a watershed in Soviet defense policy" during which, in part as a reaction to flexible response, the conclusions that had emerged from the strategic debate of the 1950s were thoroughly revised.[16] The foundation

14. Jerry Hough, *Russia and the West: Gorbachev and the Politics of Reform* (New York, 1988), p. 139.

15. For analyses of party-military relations in the Brezhnev period see Colton, *Commissars, Commanders, and Civilian Authority;* Michael J. Deane, *Political Control of the Soviet Armed Forces* (New York, 1977), pp. 169–91.

16. Michael MccGwire, *Military Objectives in Soviet Foreign Policy* (Washington, D.C., 1987), pp. 3 and 13–66. MccGwire attempts to date the revision precisely to a Central Committee plenum decision of 12–13 Dec. 1966 (pp. 381–405). Harry Gelman, *The Brezhnev Politburo and the Decline of Detente* (Ithaca, N.Y., 1984), p. 80, argues that the shift occurred during 1965. See the discussion in Herspring, *The Soviet High Command,* pp. 56–59.

for the revisions was the realization that in a situation of rough strategic parity, all antagonists would make the avoidance of nuclear strikes a first priority. The escalation of a war between the superpowers to the nuclear strategic level need not, therefore, be considered inevitable. Nuclear parity created the possibility of a protracted global conflict fought out exclusively with conventional means. The key to winning such a war from Soviet perspective would be the ability to defeat NATO forces in place, to occupy continental Europe, and to defend it against an American counteroffensive in order to deny the adversary a platform for operations against the USSR. In such a scenario the importance of the Warsaw Pact and of the conventional combined arms theater offensive was obviously enhanced. From the mid-1960s onward Soviet military-technical planning emphasized the possibility of winning a war for Europe at the conventional level with an overwhelming *Blitzkrieg* across the central front. Among the consequences were the reversal of Khrushchev's force cutbacks, a qualitative upgrading of tactical air capacity, new training procedures stressing preparation for conventional combat, and a reassertion of the coalition warfighting doctrine animating the Warsaw Pact.[17]

The program articulated by Czechoslovak military reformers prior to and during the Prague Spring worked at cross-purposes to the new Soviet priorities. The Czechoslovaks resisted a more integrated Warsaw Pact joint command, refused to accept Soviet forces on their national territory, and questioned the implications of pact doctrine for the smaller nations situated in the line of fire. The fact that only the Romanians, who were themselves in the process of asserting greater military autonomy, refused actively to oppose Dubček within the pact was a bad omen.[18] Events in Prague, according to Karen Dawisha, "presented the worrying prospect of another Romania-style defection, this time from the very

17. See Garthoff, *Deterrence and the Revolution in Soviet Military Doctrine*, pp. 52–64. These priorities are spelled out in the entry for military doctrine of the *Sovetskaia voennaia entsiklopediia*, 8 vols. (Moscow, 1976–80), 3: 225–29, and reflected in the series of lectures from the Soviet General Staff Academy dating to 1973–75 published in the West as Ghulam Dastagir Wardak, comp., *The Voroshilov Lectures: Materials from the Soviet General Staff Academy*, vol. 1: *Issues of Soviet Military Strategy* (Washington, D.C., 1989). The new emphasis upon conventional operations did not bring an end to planning for the contingency of nuclear war on either the operational-tactical or global levels. See the remarks in M. M. Kir'ian, ed., *Voenno-tekhnicheskii progress i vooruzhennye sily SSSR: (Analiz razvitiia vooruzheniia, organizatsii i sposobov deistvii)* (Moscow, 1982), pp. 311–15.

18. On Romania's challenge see Aurel Braun, *Rumanian Foreign Policy since 1965: The Political and Military Limits of Autonomy* (New York, 1978), pp. 1–44; Jones, *Soviet Influence in Eastern Europe*, pp. 156–58.

heart of the Pact's central front and thus a conspicuous threat to the unity of the socialist camp and to the security of the Soviet Union itself."[19]

Whatever the motives that led to the decision of August 1968, its consequences were considerable. First, the conservative orientation of the Brezhnev leadership was reinforced. Coupled with the collapse of the Kosygin reforms, the Kremlin had opted to oppose meaningful change both at home and abroad. The use of force likewise contributed to a widening rift within the international communist movement. The Communist parties of France and Italy, to name only the most significant, openly condemned the action, stepping closer to what would become the Eurocommunist challenge of the 1970s.[20] Finally, the European security system was frozen around a confrontational status quo. Five Soviet divisions remained in Czechoslovakia following the repression, all Soviet forces stationed in Europe saw a significant upgrading in the weaponry at their disposal, and the non–Soviet Pact members were pressured to accept increases in military spending.

Six months after the incursion the Warsaw Pact's Political Consultative Committee met in Budapest and announced sweeping organizational changes. The spirit of the reforms was conciliatory, but their most important effect was to give the pact a more complex structure commensurate with its expanding importance.[21] The disproportionate size of the Soviet military establishment, the Soviet monopoly of nuclear weapons, the fact that eastern European national armies were highly dependent upon Soviet sources for munitions, fuel, and lubricants, and not least the admonition provided by the Brezhnev Doctrine all ensured that the Warsaw Pact would remain primarily an instrument of Soviet defense policy. The Czechoslovak crisis only reiterated how vital the eastern European glacis was to the Kremlin's security outlook. According to Zdeněk Mlynář, a member of the Dubček government who was present during the confrontation in the Kremlin between Soviet and Czechoslovak leaders that followed the invasion, Brezhnev's justifications were based upon precisely this point. "Brezhnev spoke at length," Mlynář recalled, "about the sacrifices of the Soviet Union in the Second World War: the

19. Dawisha, *The Kremlin and the Prague Spring*, p. 87. The implications of Czechoslovak reformism for Soviet military strategy in Europe were perceived at the time by insightful observers. See Lawrence L. Whetten, "Military Aspects of the Soviet Occupation of Czechoslovakia," *World Today* 25 (Feb. 1969): 60–68.

20. Lilly Marcou, *Les pieds d'argile: Le communisme mondial au présent 1970–1986* (Paris, 1986), pp. 196–303.

21. Tiedtke, *Die Warschauer Vertragsorganization*, pp. 93–99. The issue of organizational reform was precipitated by the repression of the Prague Spring, but the need for such a reform had already been hinted at by Brezhnev in his foreign policy speech to the 23rd party congress during 1966. Brezhnev, *Leninskim kursom*, 1: 226–27 and 271–73.

soldiers fallen in battle, the civilians slaughtered, the enormous material losses, the hardships suffered by the Soviet people. At such a cost, the Soviet Union had gained security, and the guarantee of that security was the postwar division of Europe, and, specifically, the fact that Czechoslovakia was linked with the Soviet Union 'forever.' "[22] Although "forever" is an inappropriate term in political analysis, Brezhnev's remarks provide a revealing commentary upon the deepest sources of his approach to the Soviet security dilemma.

Coexistence and Détente

Brezhnev's international policies were justified on the basis of a highly codified theory of international relations. The central concept remained peaceful coexistence, with the advocacy of peace professed to be the first goal of policy, but with a simultaneous commitment to a competitive worldview grounded in the inflexible tenets of Soviet Marxism-Leninism.[23] Because peaceful coexistence applied only to relations between states with opposing social systems, space remained for the notion of "limited sovereignty" as a rationale for enforced conformity within the socialist camp. Meanwhile, class struggle on an international scale was said to proceed as an "objective process" that the Soviet Union was pledged to support. And the long-term goal of prevailing over the West was reiterated on a theoretical plane even if it was acknowledged that self-interest dictated a policy of cooperation in the short term.

Coexistence did not carry the static connotation of a balance of power. The most resonant concept in international theory under Brezhnev became the "shifting correlation of forces," a concept familiar since Lenin's day but now given new emphasis as a measure of the long-term trends presumed to be working to the advantage of the socialist camp in its historical rivalry with imperialism.[24] Evaluating the correlation of forces at any given moment required subtle calculations; economic capacity, popular morale, social cohesion, and the quantitative military factor all had

22. Zdeněk Mlynář, *Night Frost in Prague: The End of Human Socialism* (London, 1980), pp. 239–40.

23. Margot Light, *The Soviet Theory of International Relations* (Brighton, 1988), pp. 53–68. For a formal Soviet definition of the concept of peaceful coexistence reflecting the priorities of the Brezhnev era see A. M. Rumiantseva, ed., *Nauchnyi kommunizm: Slovar'*, 3d ed. (Moscow, 1980), pp. 154–56.

24. See G. Shakhnazarov, "K probleme sootnosheniia sil v mire," *Kommunist* 3 (1974): 86. Also of interest are the discussions in Lynch, *Soviet Study of International Relations*, pp. 89–103; Seweryn Bialer, *Stalin's Successors: Leadership, Stability and Change in the Soviet Union* (New York, 1980), pp. 241–53.

to be factored together to arrive at a rough indication of overall strength. The difficulty of actually measuring a "correlation" in such terms was self-evident, but Soviet theorists did not shy away from using the concept to arrive at an unambiguous conclusion. If it could be maintained, it was argued, the shift in the correlation of forces would eventually culminate in a "fundamental restructuring of international relations" characterized by the triumph of socialist institutions and ideals.[25]

Brezhnev's international theory bore the marks of the cloistered intellectual environment within which it was formulated; dogmatic inflexibility, vulgar anti-Americanism, and shallow apologies for the exercise of Soviet power abounded. The concepts of peaceful coexistence and the shifting correlation of forces remained fixed to the premises of competitive coexistence; Soviet international theory after Khrushchev refused to abandon a confrontational, two-camps frame of reference. But the changing realities that the Soviet Union encountered on the international stage also left their traces; the nuclear dilemma could not be ignored, peace was an objective necessity, and there was no reasonable alternative to a pragmatic East-West dialogue. This was the partially contradictory conceptual foundation upon which the most significant international initiative of the Brezhnev era, the policy of détente, was to unfold.

The term "détente" became a point of reference in Soviet foreign policy analysis from the late 1960s onward. Originally it did not refer to a policy in its own right, but rather described the consequence of the successful pursuit of peaceful coexistence. "Détente became possible," Brezhnev remarked in 1975, "because a new correlation of forces in the world arena has been established . . . and we can say that the decisive impetus to détente was the combined effort of the Soviet Union and the other countries of the socialist commonwealth, their consistent struggle against the forces of aggression and war."[26] As the Brezhnev leadership's détente orientation evolved into the 1970s, however, it became a more ambitious framework for the simultaneous pursuit of a number of specific and interrelated foreign policy goals. At the risk of some oversimplification, the most important of these goals may briefly be summarized.

(1) *To stabilize the arms race once approximate strategic parity with the United States was achieved.* Throughout the 1960s the Soviet Union worked purposefully to reduce the strategic advantage built up by the United States under Kennedy. The third generation of Soviet ICBMs, notably the SS-9 with its large throw weight and monstrous 25-megaton

---

25. R. Judson Mitchell, "A New Brezhnev Doctrine: The Restructuring of International Relations," *World Politics* 3 (1978): 388–89.

26. Brezhnev, *Leninskim kursom*, 5: 317.

warhead deployed beginning in 1965, represented a turning point of sorts in the arms race.[27] Henceforward the Soviet capacity to inflict unacceptable damage in a retaliatory strike was more or less unquestionable. Given the superior technological capacity of its American rival, Moscow had every incentive to use arms control as a means of achieving constraint once parity was in place.

(2) *To win international acceptance of the postwar security order in Europe.* Despite its brutality, the intervention in Czechoslovakia was a defensive gesture to the extent that the goal was to preserve the European status quo. The transfer of power in the FRG during the autumn of 1969 to a center-left coalition headed by the social democrat Willy Brandt opened up prospects for winning the West's approval for postwar European borders. Brandt's pursuit of *Ostpolitik* (political opening to eastern Europe) led in short order to an exchange of visits with East German president Willi Stoph (19 March and 27 May 1970), a USSR-FRG treaty acknowledging postwar territorial arrangements (12 August 1970), an FRG-Poland treaty putting to rest the issue of the former German eastern territories (7 December 1970), a quadripartité agreement liberalizing the status of Berlin (3 September 1971), and a basic principles agreement between the FRG and GDR (21 December 1972). In the summer of 1970 the Warsaw Pact encouraged the trend by issuing yet another call for a European security conference.[28] Moscow's hope was to use détente as a complement to *Ostpolitik* in order to reinforce its hegemonic status east of the Elbe.

(3) *To create a more propitious climate for East-West trade and technology transfer.* After the failure of the Kosygin reforms new approaches to the problem of stimulating the Soviet economy were mandatory. By the early 1970s hopes had begun to be placed upon the potential for expanded trade to inject from without the dynamism that could not be generated from within, by "substituting western commerce for the pursuit of major internal reform."[29] The 1970 treaty with the FRG opened a door to the West, and the Soviets made clear their desire to extend such arrangements to other leading economic powers, including the United States.

27. Robert P. Berman and John C. Baker, *Soviet Strategic Forces: Requirements and Responses* (Washington, D.C., 1982), pp. 53–55; Robbin F. Laird and Dale R. Herspring, *The Soviet Union and Strategic Arms* (Boulder, Colo., 1984), pp. 19–20. The SS-9 was maintained horizontally, in a hardened silo, with a mounted warhead—all advances over its predecessors. Alan B. Sherr, *The Other Side of Arms Control: Soviet Objectives in the Gorbachev Era* (Boston, 1988), p. 85.
28. Gromyko and Ponomarev, *Istoriia vneshnei politiki SSSR,* 2: 352.
29. Bruce Parrott, "Soviet Foreign Policy, Internal Politics, and Trade with the West," in Bruce Parrott, ed., *Trade, Technology and Soviet-American Relations* (Bloomington, Ind., 1985), p. 40.

(4) *To neutralize the threat of U.S.-Chinese collusion by giving the West a greater stake in positive relations with the USSR.* Brezhnev inherited the problem of disintegrating Sino-Soviet relations. During his first years in power, with China in the throes of its Great Proletarian Cultural Revolution, the situation reached its nadir. In March 1969 the two countries' armed forces clashed in a bloody encounter along their disputed border on the Ussuri River in the Far East. Thereafter, China moved toward a new foreign policy by seeking closer ties to the West. In February 1972 U.S. president Richard Nixon visited China, in September of the same year Beijing reestablished diplomatic relations with Japan, and from 1972 onward the Chinese deployed a small nuclear strike force targeted against the USSR. The prospect of an anti-Soviet alliance combining the United States, the PRC, and Japan represented a worst-case scenario for Soviet security planners, reviving fears of isolation and exposure on two fronts. An important goal of Soviet détente policy therefore became to improve Soviet-American relations in order to pre-empt the emergence of a Sino-American security tie.[30]

The critical factor that made a détente orientation not only desirable but also possible was greater American openness to cooperation. Upon assuming office in January 1969, contemplating what one historian calls "the most disastrous international situation any President had confronted since Pearl Harbor," President Nixon and his national security advisor Henry Kissinger discretely sought Soviet help in disengaging from the Indochinese quagmire.[31] With the United States facing a difficult post-Vietnam transition and accumulating economic woes, and with a growing awareness of the potential virtues of an arms control dialogue, a home-grown version of détente was expanded into the flagship of the entire U.S. foreign policy.

The shift in U.S. policy was accompanied by polemics over the propriety of closer relations with the USSR. At their worst the arguments degenerated into vulgar anti-Sovietism, with all sorts of malicious intentions willfully attributed to the leaders of the Kremlin.[32] More

30. Mike Bowker and Phil Williams, *Superpower Detente: A Reappraisal* (London, 1989), p. 24, argue that the rift "may have been the most important single consideration impelling the Soviet Union towards an East-West détente."

31. William G. Hyland, *Mortal Rivals: Superpower Relations from Nixon to Reagan* (New York, 1987), p. 3. The point is documented in Raymond L. Garthoff, *Détente and Confrontation: American-Soviet Relations from Nixon to Reagan* (Washington, D.C., 1985), pp. 248–61.

32. R. Judson Mitchell, *Ideology of a Superpower: Contemporary Soviet Doctrine on International Relations* (Stanford, Calif., 1982), pp. 58 and 69, finds significance in the fact that the Russian term for détente derives from a term also describing "the relaxation of tension in the trigger mechanism accompanying the firing of a gun."

sophisticated critics emphasized the competitive foundations upon which Soviet policy rested and warned against appeasement. According to Harry Gelman, Moscow's détente orientation was best described as "an island in the stream of continuous Soviet efforts . . . to displace the United States in the world."[33] Détente's partisans countered by emphasizing the importance of encouraging a dialogue that at least held out the hope of movement away from Cold War confrontation.[34] In retrospect, however, all parties to the debate seem to have been guilty of attaching to détente a greater significance than was ever really appropriate. Brezhnev's policies were not radical new departures, and in Soviet usage the term "détente" was never allowed to take on a life of its own.[35] In the United States, in contrast, détente was ballyhooed as a revolutionary transformation of the U.S.-Soviet relationship, "not the consequence of U.S. foreign policy . . . but the foreign policy itself."[36] The resulting imbalance in expectations may well have contributed to détente's eventual collapse.

Brezhnev preferred to define détente in terms of specific international agreements. In 1969 the United States and USSR began a series of Strategic Arms Limitations Talks (SALT), and by May 1972 a SALT treaty was ready to be signed, the first significant arms-limitation agreement of the nuclear era. The signing was accomplished in the course of a visit by Nixon to Moscow during which no less than ten additional documents were approved. The most important was a so-called basic principles agreement in which both sides pledged allegiance to a twelve-point program of civilized conduct, phrased in diplomatic language and including an incongruous commitment to abjure the quest for "unilateral advantage."[37] On 18 October 1972 a U.S.-Soviet trade agreement was concluded including an implied promise of most-favored-nation status for the USSR. During Brezhnev's visit to the United States in June 1973 an "Agreement on the Prevention of Nuclear War" was reached which emphasized crisis management procedures, and in July 1974 Brezhnev publicly moved away from what had once been a central tenet of Soviet

33. Gelman, The Brezhnev Politburo, p. 116.

34. The monument to such interpretations is Garthoff, Détente and Confrontation. See also Bowker and Williams, Superpower Detente, pp. 30–59.

35. The much-touted "Peace Program" promulgated by the 24th party congress in November 1971 was intended to give détente a boost, but its premises never went beyond those of competitive coexistence. The program is discussed in Peter M. E. Volten, Brezhnev's Peace Program: A Study of Soviet Domestic Process and Power (Boulder, Colo., 1982), pp. 49–75.

36. Edmonds, Soviet Foreign Policy, p. 137.

37. "Text of Basic Principles, May 29," Department of State Bulletin 66 (June 5, 1972): 943–44. See also the discussion in Garthoff, Détente and Confrontation, pp. 290–93.

strategic doctrine by hinting that only universal ruin could result from nuclear war.[38] The Moscow summit also resulted in an agreement to proceed with plans for the oft-invoked Conference on Security and Co-operation in Europe (CSCE), which was finally held at Helsinki, Finland, from July 1973 to July 1975. Despite considerable controversy, the conference concluded by approving a final act encompassing three "baskets" touching respectively upon the problems of security, economic cooperation, and human rights. The Helsinki treaty crowned decades of Soviet effort by formally sanctioning postwar European boundaries. SALT, the U.S.-Soviet basic principles agreement, and the Helsinki accords became the major pillars of Soviet détente policy, and each was in its own way a respectable accomplishment.

Détente demanded concessions and risks on the part of the USSR, and Brezhnev was forced to fight battles to overcome resistance to his policies at home.[39] In the end he prevailed, and with the cooptation of the leading figures of the national security establishment (Foreign Minister Gromyko, Defense Minister Andrei Grechko, and KGB Secretary Iurii Andropov) into the Politburo in April 1973, the possibility of significant institutional resistance to his policies was eliminated. The fact that hawks such as Grechko could be "brought into line" was in its way revealing. Brezhnev's détente orientation did not imply a reformulation of basic foreign policy goals. Competitive coexistence, with its harsh insistence upon rivalry between antagonistic systems as the axis of world politics, continued to inform the Soviet approach to security affairs.

A Touch of SALT

The arms-control dialogue was conceived of as the most important pillar of détente, but it proved to be a weak reed. The climate of mistrust that continued to condition superpower relations assured that agreements would not come easy, but perhaps the most important

38. Brezhnev, *Leninskim kursom*, 5: 120. Brezhnev repudiates the formula "If you want peace, prepare for war," regrets the phenomenon of nuclear overkill, and pledges the USSR to a policy of peace. Subsequently the Brezhnev leadership would officially endorse the position that a nuclear war could only lead to universal disaster. The key text is Brezhnev's address delivered in Tula during January 1977 in ibid., 6: 284–99.

39. Perhaps the best known reference to these battles is that made during 1977 by Gromyko's deputy Georgii Kornienko to U.S. negotiator Paul Warnke that "Brezhnev had to spill political blood to get the Vladivostok [arms control] accords." Cited in Strobe Talbott, *Endgame: The Inside Story of SALT II* (New York, 1979), p. 73. According to the sometimes unreliable testimony of Arkady Shevchenko, *Breaking with Moscow* (New York, 1985), p. 202, Defense Minister Grechko and the high command were vocal opponents outside the public domain.

inhibition was the inherent dilemma of arms control itself. Achieving arms limitations in the nuclear age was an unprecedented challenge for which all parties were in some measure unprepared.

The Soviet attitude toward arms control through the 1960s is not difficult to interpret. The Kennedy administration's strategic buildup gave the United States an overwhelming advantage which the Soviet Union was pledged to overcome. Awareness that its lead could not be maintained indefinitely moved Washington to propose a "verified freeze" on strategic systems to the eighteen-nation European disarmament conference in January 1964, an offer that the Soviets curtly refused. Only when progress toward a parity relationship was considerably more advanced did the tone change, and in June 1968 Moscow finally agreed to an "exchange of opinion." In November 1969, after a brief delay caused by the intervention in Czechoslovakia, what would become known as the SALT I talks began. Seven sessions and two and one-half years later the talks concluded with the signing of the SALT I treaty.

Soviet negotiating goals in SALT I were also relatively transparent. Although some of the aggressive rhetoric of Sokolovskii's *Military Strategy* lingered on into the early 1970s, by the time that the SALT process was launched, responsible figures in the Soviet national security establishment had grasped the fact that loose talk about "fighting and winning" a nuclear war was counterproductive. The only rational function for nuclear weapons was to deter their use by adversaries; controlled and monitored strategic competition was therefore preferable to an anarchic arms race.[40] SALT, it was hoped, would institutionalize a parity relationship at levels that would keep the deterrent function of mutual assured destruction secure.

An immediate concern was posed by the impending deployment of an American anti-ballistic missile (ABM) system. Although the Soviets had begun deployment of their own "Galosh" ABM system around Moscow in 1966, there was good reason to be cautious about the potential of American ABM capacity to destabilize the strategic balance. The ability to limit damage by warding off a percentage of the enemy's retaliatory blow after a successful first strike could open the door to scenarios for a surprise nuclear blitz, or at least so it was feared. Washington shared such concerns, and controlling ABM systems became a first priority for SALT.

40. There is a considerable western literature discussing the Soviet conception of deterrence. John Erickson, "The Soviet View of Deterrence: A General Survey," *Survival* 6 (Nov.–Dec. 1982): 242–51, convincingly argues that Soviet views have always been broadly comparable with those held in the West. See also Garthoff, *Deterrence and the Revolution in Soviet Military Doctrine*, pp. 34–48; for an attempt to synthesize divergent interpretations, John van Oudenaren, *Deterrence, Warfighting and Soviet Military Doctrine*, Adelphi Papers no. 210 (London, Summer, 1986).

The SALT I agreement encompassed three parts. The first was an ABM treaty restricting each side to two deployment sites (later reduced to one) with one hundred launchers each. Monitoring was to be accomplished by unhindered national technical means of verification (essentially satellite reconnaissance). Second, the "Interim Agreement" established guidelines for a new round of SALT II negotiations aimed at limiting offensive systems. Finally, the Standing Consultative Committee was created to resolve complaints concerning noncompliance. Altogether these were impressive accomplishments. The destabilizing potential of ABM was voided, a blueprint for continuing negotiations set in place, and a cooperative mechanism for resolving disputes established that would go on to function successfully.[41]

Unfortunately, SALT I also brought new problems to the surface and provoked criticisms that would make comparable successes more difficult to achieve. An implicit acknowledgment of parity was resented by many in Washington, who argued that it represented a one-sided concession by the West. The ABM tradeoff was condemned as unilateral to the extent that a promising U.S. system was sacrificed for an inadequate Soviet "equivalent." And the inadequacy of verification procedures was cited, a charge that would be a major barrier to progress in future negotiations.

The Interim Agreement also posed problems. The approach to arms control that it embodied took full account of both sides' strong reluctance to sacrifice existing or planned systems capable of reinforcing their overall capacity. In order to facilitate accord, the Interim Agreement adopted the negative strategy of establishing ceilings for key categories of strategic arms beyond which the negotiating partners agreed not to build. In effect, the agreement rested upon an implicit bargain according to which a Soviet quantitative advantage in numbers of launchers would be balanced by an American technological advantage and by the elimination from consideration of American Forward Based Systems (tactical aircraft and attack bombers based in Europe and capable of launching nuclear strikes against Soviet territory). The approach enabled both sides to engage in the arms-control process without committing themselves to important reductions, and it added a note of subjectivity to calculations that would prove to be endlessly troublesome.

41. For the texts of the agreements see Roger P. Labrie, ed., *SALT Hand Book: Key Documents and Issues, 1972–1979* (Washington, D.C., 1979), pp. 15–23. Descriptions of the SALT I talks are provided by John Newhouse, *Cold Dawn: The Story of SALT* (New York, 1973); Gerard C. Smith, *Doubletalk: The Story of the First Strategic Arms Limitations Talks* (Garden City, N.Y., 1980).

SALT II would in fact become the Calvary of arms control. After tortuous negotiations a treaty was drawn up and signed by U.S. president Jimmy Carter and Brezhnev on 18 June 1979. In the seven years since the talks commenced, however, the political foundation upon which the arms-control dialogue originally rested had collapsed. Although its provisions would continue to be respected informally by both sides, the SALT II treaty was never ratified by the U.S. Congress.[42]

Many of the problems that swamped SALT II were unavoidable given the competitive context within which the negotiations unfolded. The American decision early in the SALT process to exclude multiple independently targetable reentry vehicles (MIRV) from consideration created a short-term U.S. advantage, but it opened a Pandora's box of troubles as the Soviet Union began to master the same technique. By the mid-1970s a fourth generation of Soviet missiles was being tested. Of particular note were the SS-18 and SS-19 "heavy" missiles capable of carrying ten and six independently targetable warheads, respectively.[43] With improved accuracy, a large throw-weight advantage, and MIRV capacity, it was feared that the Soviet Union might eventually find itself in a position to threaten or venture a disarming first strike against the U.S. Minuteman force. The deployment of the intermediate-range Backfire bomber led to complications when U.S. negotiators sought to have it classified as a strategic system and counted against the Soviets' allotted launcher total. Moscow responded by threatening to reopen the issue of American Forward Based Systems, to establish range limits for the U.S. "cruise" missile (a pilotless drone), and to demand that air-launched cruise missiles be counted as strategic systems. Complaints concerning Soviet civil defense procedures, methods of silo construction, and alleged impediments to verification were also dragged into the talks as time went on.

The foundations for a treaty were laid as early as November 1974 in an agreement negotiated by Kissinger and signed by Brezhnev and U.S. president Gerald Ford in Vladivostok. The Vladivostok accord moved a step beyond the SALT I Interim Agreement by establishing the principle of "equal aggregates" according to which each side would be permitted an equal number of launchers (now extended to include

42. The story of the negotiations is recounted with flair by Talbott, *Endgame.* Soviet goals are explored in Thomas Wolfe, *The SALT Experience: Its Impact on U.S. and Soviet Strategic Policy and Decision Making* (Santa Monica, Calif., 1974). Samuel B. Payne, *The Soviet Union and SALT* (Cambridge, Mass., 1980), attempts to detect rivalry behind the scenes over arms-control strategy between Soviet "hawks" and "doves."

43. Berman and Baker, *Soviet Strategic Forces*, p. 65. The Soviet "fourth generation" included the SS-17, SS-18, and SS-19 ICBMs, the SS-20 IRBM, the Yankee and Delta class strategic submarines, and the SS-N-8 and SS-N-18 SLBMs.

long-range bombers), which could be "mixed" variously among designated subcategories. The Soviets dropped the issue of Forward Based
Systems and accepted numerous limitations upon their MIRVed ICBM
force without achieving equivalent constraints on U.S. cruise missiles,
but the failure to move quickly to a final treaty proved to be fatal. When
the Carter administration took office in January 1977, it opted for a new
approach, demanding deep Soviet cuts in key strategic categories. Gromyko was quick to label the proposals an attempt to "obtain unilateral
strategic advantage," and the conclusion of a SALT II treaty was set back
once again.[44]

The SALT II treaty became the target of insistent attacks in the United
States, but in retrospect one might well ask what all the fuss was about.
So that both sides would be happy, ceilings were raised to the point
where neither was required to give up anything that it considered useful.
The momentum of research, development, testing, and deployment
was virtually unaffected. In the five years between the Vladivostok accord and the conclusion of a treaty, even though the number of nuclear
weapons in the arsenals of the superpowers nearly doubled, no violation
of the terms of the treaty itself occurred. SALT II was truly the lowest
common denominator of arms limitation. In practice that meant no limitations at all.

Despite its inadequacies, the SALT II process at least kept a strategic
arms negotiating forum in place. That, too, would be lost as the controversy surrounding SALT contributed to the general decline of détente.
In the last years of the Carter administration, with an anti-détente offensive by the right wing of the political establishment in full swing,
U.S. military spending leaped upward. In Presidential Directive 59,
signed by Carter on 25 July 1980, the United States unveiled a "coun-
tervailing" strategy that emphasized counterforce capacity and nuclear
war fighting scenarios. With the election of the conservative Ronald
Reagan to the presidency in November 1980, after a campaign in which
he berated SALT, blithely lamented U.S. military inferiority, and asserted
the goal of recapturing strategic superiority, an era of arms control had
come to an end.

The strategic arms dialogue finally shattered on the issue of
intermediate-range nuclear force modernization in Europe. In 1976 the
Soviets began deployment of a solid-fueled and partially mobile SS-20
IRBM in the European theater to replace the aging SS-4s and SS-5s put
into place nearly twenty years before. The SS-20 was denounced as a major escalation of the arms race, even though many observers perceived it

44. For Gromyko's remark see "Press-konferentsiia A. A. Gromyko," *Pravda*, 1 April
1977, p. 2.

as an overdue modernization with a "compelling military-technical rationale."[45] West German chancellor Helmut Schmidt added fuel to the fire with a lecture delivered during October 1977 in which, without mentioning the SS-20 by name, he regretted the potential for Soviet-American agreements on strategic arms to leave an imbalance of forces in Europe unaffected.[46] Schmidt's remarks became the pretext for a campaign within NATO in favor of new Intermediate Nuclear Force (INF) deployments to balance the SS-20 and reinforce "linkage" between the United States and its European allies. In December 1979 a "Dual Track Decision" committed NATO to deploy 108 Pershing II IRBMs in the FRG and 464 ground-launched cruise missiles in Great Britain, the Netherlands, Belgium, and Italy beginning in 1983 if progress toward negotiating the removal of the SS-20 had not been achieved. It was now Moscow's turn to cry escalation. Although the range of the Pershing II was disputed, Soviet sources cited its ability to strike Moscow and noted correctly that its deployment would mean drastically reduced warning time in the event of an actual nuclear rocket attack.

The INF negotiations opened on 30 November 1981 in Geneva. Beginning on 29 June 1982 Switzerland's center for international diplomacy also became the venue for a new round of Strategic Arms Reduction Talks (START) designed to take the place of what had originally been planned as SALT III. In the prevailing political climate these negotiations were bound to fail.[47] Although the negotiators managed to generate a number of interesting options, all of them were rejected by their respective capitals. NATO's INF deployments began in November 1983, and soon thereafter the Soviets suspended their participation in both the INF and START forums.

Fourteen years after it had opened with SALT I, the arms-control dialogue between the superpowers was once again at point zero. In March 1983, to the surprise of his closest associates as well as the general public, President Reagan announced a plan for using futuristic technology to

45. Garthoff, *Détente and Confrontation*, p. 878. See also Stephan M. Meyer, *Soviet Theater Nuclear Forces*, Adelphi Papers nos. 187–188 (London, 1984); Jonathan Haslam, *The Soviet Union and the Politics of Nuclear Weapons in Europe, 1969–87* (Ithaca, N.Y., 1990), pp. 42–88; G. M. Kornienko, "Pravda i domysly o raketakh SS-20," *SShA: Politika, ekonomika, ideologiia* 4 (1989): 42–52. Kornienko's account is critical of the Soviet deployment decision, but it asserts that the original deployments were never intended to be perceived as a provocation.

46. Helmut Schmidt, "The 1977 Alastair Buchan Memorial Lecture, October 28, 1977," *Survival* 1 (Jan./Feb. 1978): 3–4.

47. Sherr, *The Other Side of Arms Control*, pp. 151–53; for a more general account, Strobe Talbott, *Deadly Gambits: The Reagan Administration and the Stalemate in Nuclear Arms Control* (New York, 1985).

build a space-based defensive system that would purportedly make nuclear weapons obsolete. Dubbed the Strategic Defensive Initiative (SDI) by its friends and "Star Wars" in the public imagination, Reagan's program threatened to undermine the one real accomplishment that arms control had to its credit—the ABM treaty negotiated as a part of SALT I. With the entire arms-control component of détente in ruins, the Soviet Union confronted the unsettling prospect of an unconstrained arms race that it was less and less capable of pursuing. The failure could not be attributed entirely to Brezhnev, but the results of his policies spoke for themselves.

The China Card

As the arms-control process stuttered toward an impasse, new problems loomed on the horizon. One of the most troubling as viewed from Moscow was the increasingly confrontational nature of its relationship with China. Moscow's rift with the PRC in the early 1960s occasioned a buildup of the forces stationed in Soviet far-eastern military districts, and the bizarre radicalism of the Cultural Revolution, begun in earnest in August 1966 and characterized by extreme anti-Soviet rhetoric, only heightened concern. The Soviet reaction was to intensify military pressures even more. In January 1966 Moscow signed a new defensive treaty with Ulan-Bator and began to rebuild its military garrisons on Mongolian territory. By 1968 approximately twenty-four divisions stood guard in the Sino-Soviet border area, double the force in place during 1961.

Tensions along the Sino-Soviet frontier led to an explosion on 2 March 1969 when Chinese troops ambushed without provocation a Soviet patrol on Damanskii Island (Zhenbao Island to the Chinese) in the Ussuri River some 300 kilometers south of Khabarovsk. The barren island was of no intrinsic importance, but it was located in a strategically vital region and symbolized disputed territories throughout the border zone. On 15 March, with a force approximately one battalion strong including tanks and artillery, the Soviets counterattacked. When the smoke cleared, they had retaken the island and administered a punishing blow to their antagonists.[48] Soviet forces had won a battle and reasserted the territorial status quo, but the political ramifications of the incident would prove to be immense.

---

48. For background and the details of the encounter see Thomas W. Robinson, "The Sino-Soviet Border Conflict," in Kaplan et al., *Diplomacy of Power*, pp. 273–83; Richard Wich, *Sino-Soviet Crisis Politics: A Study of Political Change and Communication* (Cambridge, Mass., 1980), pp. 97–112 and 163–92.

The motives that prompted the Chinese action are not entirely clear to this day. They appear to have involved the declining fortunes of Defense Minister Lin Biao, whose grip on power was slipping as the Cultural Revolution wound down, and may have included the desire to "send a message" to the Kremlin following the repression in Czechoslovakia.[49] To the Soviets the provocation underlined the dangerous volatility of China's policies and the relative exposure of neuralgic points along the frontier, and the immediate response was blustering. During the spring and summer of 1969 a series of provocative Soviet maneuvers unfolded along the Amur River and in Xinjiang as part of a campaign of intimidation that included scarcely veiled threats of a preemptory nuclear strike.[50] Under pressure, China agreed to resume talks on the border dispute in October 1969. Thereafter the incidence of military confrontation declined, and no further incidents on the scale of the Ussuri clash were to occur. The year 1969 nonetheless became a watershed in the evolution of Sino-Soviet rivalry.

In the wake of the Ussuri incident the Soviets recast their China policy around the premises of containment and intimidation. The most visible manifestation of the new approach was a rapid military buildup. In August 1970 a new Central Asian military district was created to unify the command function in the regions abutting upon China. By 1973 the division count in the theater leapt to forty-five, with a sixfold increase in the number of tactical aircraft, significant upgrading of equipment, and a modernization of nuclear forces. Moscow was transforming its Far Eastern theater into a self-sustaining arena for combat operations that would eventually absorb no less than one-third of total Soviet military assets.[51]

In addition, long-term strategies for managing the China problem were considered. Pessimistic voices insisted that China now represented a permanent threat that must somehow be nipped in the bud. Although the option of a preemptory strike was probably never considered seriously, it was argued with some force that a minimum defensive posture demanded a clear margin of military superiority in the Far East and active preparation for the worst-case scenario of a two-front war in the European and Asian theaters. More positive assessments emphasized the need to mollify China and suggested that a combination of military

49. Garthoff, *Détente and Confrontation*, p. 203.

50. See the unsigned editorial statement "Avantiuristicheskii kurs Pekina," *Pravda*, 28 Aug. 1969, p. 2, and the article by Victor Louis in the *London Evening Times*, 16 Sept. 1969. Louis is generally believed to have functioned as a voice for the Soviet government.

51. Garthoff, *Détente and Confrontation*, p. 208; Robinson, "The Sino-Soviet Border Conflict," pp. 286–95.

pressure with openness to dialogue could eventually draw the PRC back toward the Soviet camp.[52] Although they were partially contradictory, both of these scenarios reinforced the logic of a policy of intimidation based upon armed force.

China's reaction to Soviet military pressure took the form of an effort to build bridges to the West. The changing balance of power in Chinese politics by the early 1970s probably made some kind of foreign policy reorientation inevitable, but the Soviet diplomacy of intimidation lent force to the arguments of those pressing for a more vigorous courting of Washington. The Nixon administration's openness to new options in Asia after its decision to throw in the towel in Vietnam was also important. Following an initial opening in the cultural and sporting domains quaintly characterized as "ping-pong diplomacy" and the preparatory work accomplished by Kissinger during two secret visits to Beijing, Nixon was officially received in the Chinese capital en route to the Moscow summit in February 1972. The results encouraged the Soviets' worst fears. On the very eve of the greatest achievements of the détente era Washington betrayed its spirit by offering China concessions in exchange for access to facilities for monitoring Soviet nuclear launching sites.[53] Warding off attempts to use China as an instrument of intimidation against the USSR—"playing the China card" in American political parlance—now became an essential goal of Soviet policy.

The turn to the West was a diplomatic revolution that would eventually move China well beyond a rebalanced relationship with the superpowers to a clear tilt in the direction of the United States. The deaths of Mao Zedong and Zhou Enlai in 1976 and the emergence of a reform-oriented leadership under Deng Xiaoping virtually negated the original ideological foundations of Sino-Soviet rivalry, but it did not dampen the anti-Soviet tenor of Chinese policy. In August 1978 China signed a friendship treaty with Japan, and on 1 January 1979 U.S.-Chinese relations were normalized. Moscow responded with a wave of hostile rhetoric and yet more military deployments, including the emplacement beginning in 1978 of SS-20 IRBMs in the Lake Baikal region.[54] This was

52. Discussed in Seweryn Bialer, "The Soviet Perspective," in Herbert J. Ellison, ed., *The Sino-Soviet Conflict: A Global Perspective* (Seattle, Wash., 1982), pp. 29–49; Jonathan D. Pollack, "Sino-Soviet Relations in Strategic Perspective," in Douglas T. Stuart and William T. Tow, eds., *China, the Soviet Union, and the West: Strategic and Political Dimensions in the 1980s* (Boulder, Colo., 1982), pp. 282–85.

53. André Fontaine, *Un seul lit pour deux rêves: Histoire de la "détente" 1962–81* (Paris, 1981), pp. 180–81.

54. These moves are discussed in Garthoff, *Détente and Confrontation*, pp. 710–13.

the same policy of intimidation that had helped to conjure up the China problem. As events were to show, it was quite incapable of resolving it.

At the world conference of Communist parties in June 1968 Brezhnev made a brief reference to the need for an Asian collective security pact, but his project generated very little support.[55] Instead of collective security, a broadening net of U.S. military deployments throughout Asia and increasing U.S.-Chinese collusion culminating in U.S. Secretary of Defense Harold Brown's visit to China in the summer of 1979 threatened to leave the Soviets completely isolated and badly exposed. After toying briefly with the idea of disengagement from South Korea, the Carter administration surrendered to the geostrategic logic of national security advisor Zbigniew Brzezinski, who perceived Asia as a weak link in the Soviet security system that the United States could profitably exploit. In 1978 Washington refused Vietnam's plea for assistance to contain the aggression being launched by neighboring Kampuchea at the behest of Pol Pot and the murderous Khmers Rouges. Faced with intolerable provocations, Hanoi was forced to conclude a treaty of friendship with Moscow in November 1978 as a prelude to its invasion of Kampuchea one month later.[56] In February–March 1979, immediately following Deng Xiaoping's return from a visit to Washington and with obvious American encouragement, Chinese forces attacked Vietnam in order to "punish" its offending neighbor. Although the action was repulsed with heavy losses, the entire episode exposed the potential consequences of intensifying superpower confrontation.

The implications of Sino-Soviet rivalry also spilled over into the northwest Pacific, an immense region including Japan, northwest China, the eastern USSR, and the Koreas as well as the seas of Japan and Okhotsk. By the 1970s the northwest Pacific was the only region outside of Europe where the armed forces of the superpowers confronted one another directly. It was also an area of potential Soviet exposure. The Soviet Pacific fleet, the largest of the four Soviet fleets, in full expansion during the 1970s and charged with increasingly wide-ranging responsibilities, was based in the Soviet Maritime Province near Vladivostok. Its access to the high seas depended upon control of the Tsushima and La Perouse straits leading past the Japanese islands. Farther to the north significant forces based on the Kamchatka Peninsula at Petropavlovsk and in the Sea of Okhotsk, chosen as a sanctuary for over 30 percent of the Soviet

---

55. Brezhnev, *Leninskim kursom*, 2: 366–415.
56. Nayan Chanda, *Brother Enemy: The War after the War* (San Diego, Calif., 1986), pp. 263–96.

sea-based nuclear deterrent force, confronted the need to survive in inaccessible regions far removed from major communications lines and population centers. In the islands and waters surrounding these facilities the United States was concentrating an imposing strike force including jet fighter squadrons based in Japan and South Korea capable of covering the La Perouse and Tsushima straits.[57] With the turn toward a more assertive military posture under Reagan, voices were raised on behalf of a "maritime strategy" of "horizontal escalation" that targeted the northwest Pacific as a region of special opportunity. The United States should respond to a major Soviet provocation or in the event of war, it was argued, by striking where the enemy could be most severely wounded. Moscow's vital but nearly indefensible Pacific installations seemed to fill the bill.

The real possibility of a preemptive strike against Soviet facilities in the northwest Pacific was always slim. The case for horizontal escalation was nonetheless forcefully argued, and it corresponded to an emerging pattern of U.S. deployments.[58] Washington also placed pressure upon Japan to expand military spending and force procurement, provide more aid to other U.S. Asian allies such as the Philippines and South Korea, and assume more of the financial burden for maintaining U.S. troops in Japan. Soviet-Japanese relations were frozen over the question of the Kuril Islands, territories annexed by the Soviet Union after World War II and since revindicated by Tokyo as Japan's "northern territories." Japan made the return of the islands a prerequisite for improved relations, but given the problem of strategic exposure (the Kuril Islands cover access to the Sea of Okhotsk), Moscow insisted, and with some reason, that their status was not negotiable. Japan's military potential was immense and the poor state of Soviet-Japanese relations, combined with Tokyo's strategic ties to the United States, represented yet another dilemma for Soviet security planners.

The high level of military competition in the northwest Pacific region, accompanied by constant aerial surveillance, eventually became the background for a tragedy. On 1 September 1983 Soviet air defense forces shot down Korean Airlines flight 007, a civilian airliner that for reasons never adequately explained had strayed far off course and passed directly over a number of significant Soviet military installations. The Soviet reaction, and its horrifying consequences, revealed major deficiencies in air

57. Michael Klare, "Asia's Theater of Nuclear War," *South* 37 (Nov. 1983): 9–14; Frank C. Langdon and Douglas A. Ross, "Superpower Conflict," in Frank C. Langdon and Douglas C. Ross, eds., *Superpower Maritime Strategy in the Pacific* (London, 1990), pp. 12–23.
58. MccGwire, *Military Objectives in Soviet Foreign Policy*, pp. 176–78.

defense procedures, reinforced arguments stressing Soviet callousness, and underlined the kind of unplanned contingencies that unconstrained strategic rivalry could create.[59]

As the 1980s dawned, it was clear that a strategy of intimidation had not cowed the Chinese, but rather pushed them toward a degree of strategic cooperation with the West that was harmful to Soviet interests. Although Brezhnev's Asian policy had secured certain minimal objectives, the Soviets' overall strategic posture in the region was weakening. Brezhnev had no answer to the ominous turn of events. The 1980s saw a gradual moderating of Chinese hostility, symbolized by the decision of the CCP's 12th party congress in 1982 to "rebalance" China's international alignments yet again, but it would remain for his successors to come toward emerging opportunities with more positive and creative responses.

Global Commitment, Regional Conflict

A forward policy in the Third World was another inheritance from Khrushchev that took on a life of its own during the Brezhnev years. By the 1970s the ideological framework provided by the noncapitalist path of development scenario was giving way to a more precise variant whose central concept was "socialist orientation."[60] The noncapitalist path as an option for Third World development was retained, but the prerequisites were made more demanding. According to the foreign policy analyst Evgenii Primakov, four criteria for the successful pursuit of socialist orientation could be specified: (1) *Economic criteria*, including the need to expand the state sector of the national economy via land reform, nationalization, and industrialization; (2) *social criteria* emphasizing the need for a "cultural revolution" including literacy campaigns and the politicization of the masses; (3) *political criteria* calling for the creation of a vanguard party at home and "alliance with the countries of victorious socialist revolution" abroad as "the fundament without which a noncapitalist transition of underdeveloped nations

59. For accounts of the KAL incident see Alexander Dallin, *Black Box: The KAL Incident and the Superpowers* (Berkeley, Calif., 1985); Seymour M. Hersh, *"The Target Is Destroyed": What Really Happened to Flight 007 and What America Knew about It* (New York, 1986); R. W. Johnson, *Shootdown: Flight 007 and the American Connection* (New York, 1986). An update on the continuing controversy is provided by Patrice de Beer, "Six ans àprès, le mystère du vol KE-007," *Le Monde*, 1 March 1990, p. 7.

60. Light, *The Soviet Theory of International Relations*, pp. 111–41; Sylvia Edgington, "The State of Socialist Orientation: A Soviet Model for Political Development," *Soviet Union/Union Soviétique* 2 (1981): 223–51; Iu. I. Iudin, *Gosudarstvo sotsialisticheskoi orientatsii* (Moscow, 1975).

to socialism is impossible"; and (4) *ideological criteria* requiring a gradual shift from the petty bourgeois ideology characteristic of the national democratic stage to a more orthodox variant of scientific socialism.[61] Thus defined, socialist orientation represented a relatively precise blueprint for development which made alliance with the USSR a sine qua non for progress. Soviet social theory rejected north-south or Third Worldist perspectives that refused to grant the Soviet Union a special exemption from responsibility for the Third World's plight, expressed skepticism toward calls for a New International Economic Order on the grounds that capitalist imperialism was in essence unreformable, and in general maintained a rigorous two-camps approach to the "struggle for the Third World."[62]

The theoretical lens through which the Soviets chose to view the Third World was revealing of long-range aspirations, but not always helpful as a guide to policy formation. When necessary, the injunctions of socialist orientation were allowed to conflict with an opportunistic diplomacy geared to expanding Soviet state interests and open to a variety of compromises with principle in pursuit of allies. The Soviet diplomatic approach to the Third World was pragmatic and low-key; for all of the pontificating about the vital role of national liberation movements, Foreign Minister Gromyko paid not a single visit to Africa or Latin America (with the exception of Cuba) during his entire tenure in office. The dozen treaties of friendship and cooperation concluded with Third World allies under Brezhnev did not make ideological affinity a decisive criterion. Though a star pupil in the school of socialist orientation such as Cuba was apparently never offered a treaty, the honor could be accorded to such politically ambiguous but tactically useful allies as India, the Congo-Brazzaville, and Iraq. Opportunistic motives dominated on both sides, and in the cases of Egypt and Somalia (in 1971 and 1974, respectively) treaties were abrogated as relations soured.

Efforts to increase economic interaction between the USSR and the less-developed countries were disappointing. According to Soviet calculations, economic exchange with less-developed countries more than tripled during the 1970s, but the USSR still accounted for less than 5 percent of total world trade with the Third World. Nor was Moscow a particularly generous aid donor. Under Brezhnev the Soviet Union

61. E. Primakov, "Strany sotsialisticheskoi orientatsii: Trudnyi no real'nyi perekhod k sotsializmu," *Mirovaia ekonomika i mezhdunarodnye otnosheniia* 7 (1981): 13–14.

62. L. Goncharov, "Afrika v bor'be za novyi mezhdunarodnyi ekonomicheskii poriadok," *Mirovaia ekonomika i mezhdunarodnye otnosheniia* 6 (1981): 49–62. A somewhat contrasting view, with more emphasis upon the relevance of the concept of nonalignment, is presented by Roy Allison, *The Soviet Union and the Strategy of Non-alignment in the Third World* (Cambridge, Mass., 1988), pp. 41–59.

proffered only 3 percent of all foreign aid received by Third World countries.[63] The one important exception was the arms trade. Arms sales represent between two-thirds and three-quarters of all Soviet economic exchange with the Third World since 1955, and the USSR has been impressively successful in penetrating the lucrative world arms market.[64] Arms sales became a significant means for balancing deficits with Third World trading partners and a major source of hard currency earnings. Whether they have also been a useful means of achieving political influence is perhaps necessarily left as an open question.

There is no question, however, that military power was an important foundation for the dynamic Soviet Third World policy of the 1970s. In addition to arms sales, the Soviet capacity to use armed force as a policy tool expanded; humiliations such as that suffered in Zaire during 1960 were no longer unavoidable. Airlift and naval transport capacity were improved, a mobile infantry force was groomed as the possible spearhead for small-scale interventions, and the ability to project air power was increased. These trends were noted in the West, and the purported priority being attached to power projection in Soviet global strategy became a major item in the bill of indictment drawn up by the anti-détente wing of the U.S. policy establishment.[65]

Moscow's Third World ambitions were real, and consistent with the logic of competitive coexistence, but they were not unlimited. First, although Soviet power projection capacity did expand, it never came close to matching the corresponding U.S. capacity. Second, the common assertion that increased power projection meant an attempt to revive the idea of the "revolution from without" in the volatile circumstances of the Third World was repeatedly refuted, both by Soviet conduct and declaratory policy. For a brief period during the early 1970s some voices were raised within the military establishment on behalf of a more assertive use of armed force as a means of influence in the Third World, a perspective

63. *Postroeno pri ekonomicheskom i tekhnicheskom sodeistvii Sovetskogo Soiuza* (Moscow, 1982), p. 16; Rajan Menon, *Soviet Power and the Third World* (New Haven, Conn., 1986), p. 58. Aid was not predominantly granted on the basis of ideological considerations. From 1954 to 1981 only 20% of Soviet foreign aid was received by states designated as states of socialist orientation. According to Susan Strange, *States and Markets: An Introduction to International Political Economy* (London, 1988), p. 216, CMEA aid to the less developed countries during the 1980s constituted less than 0.2% of total GNP.

64. Orah Cooper and Carol Fogarty, "Soviet Military and Economic Aid to the Less Developed Countries, 1954–1978," in Morris Bernstein, ed., *The Soviet Economy: Continuity and Change* (Boulder, Colo., 1981), p. 254; for a statistical portrait of the phenomenon, Michael Brzoska and Thomas Ohlson, *Arms Transfers to the Third World, 1971–1985* (Oxford, 1987).

65. See, for example, Harriet Fast Scott and William F. Scott, eds., *The Soviet Art of War: Doctrine, Strategy and Tactics* (Boulder, Colo., 1982), pp. 241–86.

that was summarized in the 1972 collection *Military Force and International Relations* edited by V. M. Kulish.[66] The Kulish text became a favorite source for hawkish western commentators, but its conclusions were criticized inside the USSR, where Kulish himself was eventually dismissed from his position as a researcher with the Institute for World Economy and International Relations.[67] Third, too much has been made of the case presented by Admiral Sergei Gorshkov on behalf of a Soviet blue water fleet with global reach. In his published work Gorshkov is careful to define the mission of the Soviet navy in such a way as to exclude the imposition of Soviet power by force of arms. The tasks of the Soviet navy, he specifies, are nuclear deterrence, strategic strikes in the event of nuclear war, countering enemy aircraft carriers, and the promotion of state interests in peacetime through port calls and the maintenance of a permanent presence in various areas."[68] This is a fair list of Soviet naval priorities throughout the Brezhnev era, a recipe for enhanced strategic deterrence and an active naval diplomacy rather than adventuristic expansionism. In fact, Soviet naval forces were never configured to carry out large-scale interventions in the Third World. According to the 1987 edition of the Pentagon's *Soviet Military Power*, hardly a source prone to underestimate the Soviet threat: "Sustained combat operations in Third World areas . . . would require underway replenishment ship support of a kind that the Soviets currently lack."[69] The task that Soviet planners assigned to military force in crafting their Third World policy was essentially demonstrative, "as a means of communicating Soviet interests, building prestige, and reassuring friends."[70]

The various Third World engagements into which the Soviet Union was drawn under Brezhnev revealed an ambition to assert global power status, but also the limited means and inherent constraints that made that ambition so difficult to realize. The most important of these engagements was in the Middle East, where geographical proximity, shared ethnic and religious identities, and pragmatic political and economic

66. V. M. Kulish, ed., *Voennaia sila i mezhdunarodnye otnosheniia: Voennye aspekty vneshnepoliticheskikh kontseptsii SShA* (Moscow, 1972), pp. 136–39.

67. See the references to Kulish in Harriet Fast Scott and William F. Scott, *The Armed Forces of the USSR*, 2d ed. (Boulder, Colo., 1981), pp. 56–59; for a subtle Soviet critique, V. V. Zhurkin and E. M. Primakov, *Mezhdunarodnye konflikty* (Moscow, 1972), pp. 55–69. See also Mark N. Katz, *The Third World in Soviet Military Thought* (Baltimore, Md., 1982), pp. 66–69.

68. Sergei Gorshkov, *The Sea Power of the State* (Annapolis, Md., 1976), p. 111. See also MccGwire, *Military Objectives in Soviet Foreign Policy*, pp. 448–76.

69. *Soviet Military Power 1987* (Washington, D.C., March 1987), p. 87.

70. Menon, *Soviet Power and the Third World*, p. 83, and the entire discussion in pp. 90–129.

interests combined to make the Soviet desire to achieve a voice in regional affairs particularly strong.[71] Khrushchev's link to Nasir made the USSR a credible regional actor, but influence was purchased at the price of considerable exposure. In the Arab-Israel war of 1967 the Soviets were humiliated by the swift Israeli victory; during the "Canal war" of 1970–1971 Moscow offered its Egyptian ally a large number of combat aircraft as well as pilots, airfields, and surface-to-air missiles; and when the Kremlin threatened intervention on behalf of Egypt's beleaguered third army during the Arab-Israel war of 1973, it was met with a worldwide U.S. nuclear alert. The subsequent shift toward the West by Nasir's successor Anwar Sadat voided twenty years of effort and left Moscow with no option other than to rebuild a regional presence around whatever allies of convenience it could find, including such mercurial actors as Baathist Syria and Iraq, Yasir Arafat's Palestine Liberation Organization, and Mu'ammar al-Qaddhafi's Libya. Soviet proposals for a comprehensive regional peace settlement to be negotiated by an international conference in Geneva were scuttled by U.S. and Israeli resistance.[72] In place of the Geneva conference format Washington opted for a policy of exclusion, the centerpiece of which became the separate peace between Egypt and Israel negotiated under the auspices of President Carter during 1978 at Camp David, Maryland. Although U.S. policy would soon be plagued by contradictions of its own, the fact remained that Brezhnev's Middle East policy left the Soviet Union marginalized in the one Third World region where it had significant national security interests at stake.

Comparable frustrations became evident elsewhere. Vietnam's occupation of Kampuchea in 1979 proved to be the beginning of yet another protracted armed conflict in long-suffering Indochina. A Kampuchean national resistance based upon the remnants of Pol Pot's forces succeeded in establishing base areas inside Thailand, where with discrete Chinese assistance it began a campaign of harassment against the pro-Vietnamese successor regime in Phnom Pehn. Soviet assistance to Vietnam was granted in exchange for a number of concessions that contributed to extending Moscow's global reach, including access to the former U.S. naval base at Camh Ran Bay, but it was not sufficient to break the Kampuchean resistance or to efface completely Vietnam's spirit of independence. The result was a stand-off that locked the Soviets

71. R. Craig Nation, "The Sources of Soviet Involvement in the Middle East: Threat or Opportunity?" in Mark V. Kauppi and R. Craig Nation, eds., *The Soviet Union and the Middle East in the 1980s: Opportunities, Constraints, and Dilemmas* (Lexington, Mass., 1983), pp. 41–70.

72. At least according to Soviet interpretations. See E. M. Primakov, *Anatomiia blizhnevostochnogo konflikta* (Moscow, 1978), pp. 161–90.

into support for a difficult regional ally in a conflict for which no solution was in sight.

The most successful Soviet moves in the Third World during the 1970s came in Africa. In 1975–1976 the USSR logistically supported the intervention of more than 15,000 Cuban soldiers on behalf of the Marxist Popular Movement for the Liberation of Angola (MPLA) faction in the civil war that accompanied Portugal's withdrawal from its former colony, an intervention that proved to be the key to the MPLA's eventual triumph. A second, equally decisive intervention by Cuban forces in support of revolutionary Ethiopia during an interstate conflict with its neighbor Somalia followed in 1977–1978. These actions may not have represented what one commentator has called a "major departure in Soviet foreign policy," but they were at the least provocative.[73] In retrospect it is quite clear that they did not lead to the creation of secure bastions of Soviet influence in the Horn or sub-Saharan Africa. Despite its protestations of allegiance to orthodox Marxist-Leninism, the Ethiopia of Mengistu Haile Marian was not able to overcome the ravages of drought and famine, or the challenge of separatist movements in Tigray and Eritrea provinces. The victory of liberation movements in Mozambique and Angola became the prelude to a broadened regional conflict propelled by South Africa's attempts to destabilize its uncongenial neighbors. Pretoria's reaction to the Cuban presence in Africa made progress toward bringing an end to the apartheid tragedy nearly impossible, and at the time of Brezhnev's death the entire southern Africa region was locked into a cycle of violence.

In general, "national liberation" as viewed from Moscow increasingly appeared as a two-edged sword. The Sandinista revolution in Nicaragua during 1979, supported in the years to come by both Cuba and the USSR, was a blow to U.S. pride, but it brought the Soviets little concrete gain. The Sandinistas' hopes to pursue progressive social goals were frustrated by the campaign of subversion waged by the U.S.-backed "contras" operating from base areas in Honduras, and their hold on power was precarious. Beginning in December 1979 a full-fledged Soviet military occupation of neighboring Afghanistan gave rise to yet another open-ended confrontation, between the pro-Soviet regime in power in Kabul and a U.S.-supported resistance with sanctuaries in Pakistan's northwest frontier province. By the 1980s the phrase "regional conflict" had taken on the precise connotation of a U.S.-Soviet clash, in the first person or by proxy, in Third World crisis zones. A series of such conflicts, waged with

73. Jiri Valenta, "Soviet Decision Making on the Intervention in Angola," in David E. Albright, ed., *Communism in Africa* (Bloomington, Ind., 1980), p. 97.

terrible ferocity, created a steady drain on Soviet resources, undermined the spirit of détente, and posed a permanent threat to global stability.

According to the terms of Soviet international theory, détente should have provided a positive context for the progress of revolutionary change in the Third World. By the end of the Brezhnev period, however, evidence of real movement in the direction of socialist orientation was hard to find. Nor was a forward policy contributing to the larger purposes of Soviet diplomacy. In the Middle East the Soviets remained excluded from the core of a region where they possessed truly vital interests. In Southeast and Central Asia, southern Africa, and Central America socialist-oriented regimes linked to the USSR were being forced to fight cruelly destructive wars of survival, the costs of which made a mockery of their aspirations to accomplish progressive change. By the early 1980s the United States was promulgating the Reagan Doctrine, which unabashedly justified the use of military force to roll back socialist orientation and Soviet influence in the less-developed world.[74] It did not really matter that in many cases the USSR did indeed stand on the side of progress against an array of U.S. allies—the Islamic resistance in Afghanistan, the Khmers Rouges in Kampuchea, the South African apartheid state, or the Central American contras—whose credentials were extremely compromised. Brezhnev's ambitious global commitments had led to a series of draining stalemates whose perpetuation was in no one's best interests.

The New Cold War

The Soviet occupation of Afghanistan in December 1979 is sometimes described as the final straw that collapsed the rickety edifice of détente.[75] Coming as it did at the culmination of a phase of growing U.S.-Soviet tensions, the event was clearly important, but the fact remains that well before Afghanistan, both as a policy and as a way of characterizing the U.S.-Soviet relationship, détente had ceased to exist. In the latter years of the Carter administration the very term "détente" was purged from American public discourse. Carter's presidency was won over by a conservative reaction that highlighted the Soviet threat, and it had already moved to sponsor substantial increases in military spending.

74. See Fred Halliday, *Beyond Irangate: The Reagan Doctrine and the Third World* (Amsterdam, 1987), pp. 18–31.

75. Bowker and Williams, *Superpower Detente*, pp. 230–31. Garthoff, *Détente and Confrontation*, p. 887, argues that although détente was "admittedly faltering badly" by the time of the Afghanistan decision, the event nonetheless represented a "watershed in American-Soviet relations."

Most of the areas of cooperation laboriously assembled earlier in the decade were rapidly breaking down.

From the Soviet perspective it had long been clear that the détente orientation was not accomplishing the specific ends for which it had been conceived. Prospects for congressional ratification of the SALT II treaty were dim. Hopes for expanded economic interaction were frustrated by the so-called Jackson-Vanik and Stephenson amendments linking the granting of most-favored-nation trade status to a liberalization of Soviet emigration policy and placing low ceilings on Export-Import Bank credits to the USSR. The United States had played the China card. The Soviets faced a wall of exclusion in the Middle East and dogged resistance to their attempt to extend influence elsewhere in the Third World. Under the circumstances little incentive remained for Moscow to be solicitous of American sensitivities. The occupation of Afghanistan did not occasion détente's failure. It was, rather, a product of that failure, the first important example of what the absence of the mutual constraint provided by some degree of cooperation and dialogue could lead to.

The move into Afghanistan marked the first appearance of major Soviet combat forces outside the eastern European security zone since World War II. Proponents of a global expansionism thesis concerning Soviet foreign policy motivation immediately leapt forward to argue that, encouraged by American weakness in the post-Vietnam period and after having tested the water with a series of low-level provocations, Moscow was crossing a threshold. The warm waters of the Arabian Sea, the oil riches of the Gulf, a chronically unstable Pakistan, and an Iran in the throes of revolution had been moved within reach of the outstretched arm of Soviet military power.[76] In retrospect, such extravagant explanations seem overwrought, but there is no question that the Soviet action was highly destabilizing. In opting for a military solution to the Afghanistan problem, Brezhnev and the clique of leaders surrounding him revealed that they perceived the stakes to be high.

Since Chicherin's dealings with Khan Amin Amanullah in 1920 the Soviet Union had been content to tolerate an independent and nonaligned Afghanistan as a buffer on its southern flank. When in April 1978 the government of president Mohammed Daoud was overthrown in a violent coup led by the pro-Soviet People's Democratic party of Afghanistan (PDPA) under the leadership of Noor Mohammed Taraki, however, Moscow elected to commit itself to its support. Although there is no evidence of Soviet involvement in the coup, which was apparently

76. For arguments to this effect see Alfred L. Monks, *The Soviet Intervention in Afghanistan* (Washington, D.C., 1981), pp. 18–39; Edward Giradet, *Afghanistan: The Soviet War* (New York, 1985), pp. 12–29.

launched as an attempt to preempt a crackdown against the left by Daoud, the event was immediately hailed as Afghanistan's "April Revolution." The de facto alliance between Moscow and the revolutionary government in Kabul was sealed by a treaty of friendship and cooperation on 5 December 1978.

The Taraki government upon which Moscow placed its bets proved to be a poor risk. When a series of ill-conceived and clumsily implemented reforms created swelling popular resistance, the Soviets found themselves ever more engaged in the effort to keep the head of their newly embraced ally above water. As the internal situation disintegrated, two high-level Soviet military delegations conducted fact-finding missions in order to identify options.[77] A last attempt to avoid military action by forcing a more moderate course upon Kabul backfired when a plot to eliminate Taraki's ultra-radical lieutenant Hafizullah Amin ended in September 1979 with a preemptive coup sponsored by Amin himself, during which Taraki and his closest associates were seized and killed. These bloody events triggered the denouement that was to follow. During the last week in December, Soviet troops airlifted into Kabul completed the sequence of coups by murdering Amin in turn and installing a new government under Babrak Karmal, the leader of a rival wing of the Afghan communist movement, exiled by Taraki but now returned in the train of a Soviet military contingent that would soon count more than 100,000 troops. The April Revolution had survived even if its leaders had not. Soviet forces now confronted the daunting task of stabilizing the situation and beating down a growing popular insurrection.

In Afghanistan, Moscow acted to avoid a foreign policy humiliation by propping up a beleaguered regime to which, wisely or not, it had made a strong commitment. The decision-making process seems to have typified the modus operandi of the Brezhnev years, concentrated within a handful of top leaders, conducted without extensive consultations, and prone to military solutions.[78] The variables that determined Brezhnev and his lieutenants in their course must remain objects of speculation.

77. Harry S. Bradsher, *Afghanistan and the Soviet Union* (Durham, N.C., 1983), pp. 148–88. Voices within the Soviet military establishment have subsequently suggested that at the time responsible military professionals opposed an armed incursion. The decision for a military option is said to have been made behind their backs, "in Brezhnev's office." See A. Oliinik and A. Efimov, "Vvod voisk v Afganistane: Kak prinimalos' reshenie," *Krasnaia zvezda,* 18 Nov. 1989, p. 4; the interview with Iu. V. Ganovskii, "Urok, kotoryi stoit usvoit': Voina v Afganistane glazami istorika," *Izvestiia,* 4 May 1989, p. 5.

78. See the letter by Academician Oleg Bogomolov, "Kto zhe oshibalsia?" *Literaturnaia gazeta,* 16 March 1988, p. 10, where it is claimed that the advice of Soviet area specialists was neither solicited nor respected. Of special interest is Andrei Gromyko's version of the decision as recounted by his son, in "Tak my voshli v Afganistan," *Literaturnaia gazeta,* 20 Sept. 1989, p. 14.

The Iranian revolution of 1979 weakened America's strategic posture in the area and made the use of force easier to contemplate. It also raised the specter of Islamic fundamentalism in a region where, with its own large Islamic population, the Soviet Union could not help but feel exposed. With détente on the rocks, Brezhnev may have sought to demonstrate that he would not suffer passively a continuing disintegration of the USSR's international standing. The most important contributing factor, however, was probably concern for the consequences of the PDPA's defeat. Brezhnev phrased the problem lucidly in the immediate aftermath of the incursion. Soviet forces had entered Afghanistan, he claimed, because "a real threat of Afghanistan's losing its independence has appeared, of its transformation into a military platform for imperialism on the southern border of our country. . . . To have acted otherwise would have meant to look on passively while the source of a serious threat to the security of the Soviet government took shape on our southern border."[79] The presumptions upon which this judgment rests are dubious, but its relevance as an explanation for Soviet actions is not. The occupation of Afghanistan is best understood as an effort to prevent the loss of control in a sensitive border zone. Against the background of the collapse of détente, Moscow was not about to surrender strategic terrain to its rivals.

Whatever its motives, the consequences of the Afghanistan incursion were dramatic. The Soviet expeditionary force was sufficient to prop up the Karmal regime, but not to defeat a burgeoning resistance possessed of considerable international sympathy and support. The action left the USSR at odds with much of the Islamic world and isolated it within multilateral forums. The hue and cry raised in the United States helped to propel the conservative wave that would bring Ronald Reagan to office later in the year. A virtual orgy of anti-Sovietism erupted in the western media, summed up by Reagan's March 1983 reference to the USSR as an "evil empire."[80] And Reagan's words were accompanied by deeds: an unprecedented increase in U.S. defense spending, the promulgation of the Reagan Doctrine, the Strategic Defense Initiative, and a host of other measures both threatening and insulting to the aging leadership in the Kremlin.

Fast on the heels of the Afghanistan imbroglio came a new challenge in Soviet-dominated eastern Europe. On 31 August 1980, after a wave of strikes and factory occupations, the Polish government of Edward Gierek signed the Gdansk Accords legalizing the independent trade union

79. Brezhnev, *Leninskim kursom*, 8: 246–47.
80. President Reagan, "Remarks at the Annual Convention (of the Evangelicals) in Orlando, Fla., March 8, 1983," *Weekly Compilation of Presidential Documents* 19 (March 14, 1983): 369.

Solidarity.[81] Official sanction for an opposition forum on such a scale was unique for the eastern bloc, but the gesture did not suffice to channel popular discontent. In the months that followed much of Polish society used the banner of Solidarity to mobilize against the status quo. With international reaction to the occupation of Afghanistan still at a fever pitch, Moscow found itself confronted by yet another difficult crisis.

At the heart of the problem in Poland was the chronic dilemma of Soviet power in all of eastern Europe: the inability of the postwar communist regimes to achieve any real legitimacy. Poland was the largest, most populous, and most vigorously anti-Soviet of all the bloc states. In both 1956 and 1970 it produced impressive popular mobilizations forcing changes of government, it possessed a powerful Catholic tradition capable of providing a moral foundation for dissent, and throughout the 1970s it was a society in ferment. The failure of Gierek's economic program, and the burden of foreign debt which was its most significant legacy, made some kind of explosion virtually inevitable. That the Brezhnev leadership stood by passively while the storm gathered in the heart of its eastern European security zone was a measure of the growing inflexibility that characterized its decline.

The Soviet response to Solidarity was predictably blinkered and negative. In a manner that recalled reactions to the Czechoslovak crisis a dozen years before, a combination of admonitions and intimidating gestures was resorted to as a means of encouraging retrenchment. On 24 October the new Polish party leader Stanislaw Kania and Prime Minister Józef Pinkowski were summoned to Moscow and privately instructed to "reverse the course of events."[82] During December all the elements of a Warsaw Pact invasion were drawn into place. It is impossible to determine whether the mobilization was intended from the first as an elaborate bluff or postponed at the last minute as a result of Polish pleading. Whatever the case, the widely publicized preparations established the awareness that military occupation was an outcome to be reckoned with.

On 10 February Defense Minister Wojciech Jaruzelski received a joint appointment as Poland's prime minister. He was simultaneously presenting Moscow with plans for the outlawing of Solidarity and the imposition of martial law. The summer of 1981 was filled with turmoil as contestation spread in all directions. Solidarity's moderate leaders struggled to prevent provocations, but the die had already been cast.

---

81. The text is in William F. Robinson, ed., *August 1980: The Strikes in Poland* (Munich, 1980), pp. 423–35.

82. For Brezhnev's references to the need to "reverse" events see Nicholas G. Andrews, *Poland 1980–81: Solidarity versus the Party* (Washington, D.C., 1985), p. 149. The best account of Soviet reactions to the Polish crisis is Sydney Ploss, *Moscow and the Polish Crisis: An Interpretation of Soviet Policies and Intentions* (Boulder, Colo., 1986).

Jaruzelski replaced Kania as first secretary of the Polish United Worker's party on 18 October, thus uniting in his person all significant leadership posts. After careful preparations a "state of siege" was declared on 13 December 1981. The arrest at a stroke of more than five thousand opposition leaders, the massive presence of armed forces in the streets, the implicit threat of Soviet intervention should martial law fail to hold, and the conciliatory posture adopted by the Polish primate Cardinal Józef Glemp, who reiterated appeals for nonviolence, all contributed to a successful outcome. Whether Jaruzelski had betrayed the nation or taken upon his shoulders the responsibility for the only action that could save it from Soviet occupation is a question that no doubt will never be resolved. In the end Moscow got its way, and an uneasy peace was imposed upon Poland by sheer coercion.

Once again the Brezhnev leadership had warded off the worst while utterly failing to address the sources of the problem. Solidarity, though temporarily squelched, maintained a precarious underground existence. The rage of a nation of 30 million citizens could not permanently be suppressed by armed force alone. And yet stability in Poland was critical to the viability of the Soviet security posture in Europe. Brezhnev died on 10 November 1982, less than a year after the crackdown and with martial law still in effect. He had concluded his exercise of power in the same way in which it had been consolidated, with a crude military gesture sufficient to hold the lid on a boiling pot but completely inadequate as a response to the long-term dilemmas of Soviet power.

Brezhnev's final years were painful, punctuated by the gradual disappearance of an entire generation of leaders who had clung to power too long and weighed down by the general secretary's increasingly visible senility. At the moment of his death Soviet foreign and security policies had arrived at a dead end. Détente had collapsed, the CSCE follow-up conference in Madrid was paralyzed by disputes over human-rights violations, and what remained of the arms-control dialogue was about to disappear altogether. The world communist movement, once a meaningful arm of Soviet policy, was riven by multiple wounds, with China outspokenly hostile, a state of permanent crisis in Soviet eastern Europe, and the Eurocommunists rejecting the relevance of the entire Soviet experience. Military intimidation had only reinforced rivalry with Beijing, hopes to extend Soviet influence in the Third World had run into the sands of open-ended regional conflicts, and the Soviet expeditionary force was mired in a debilitating war in Afghanistan. The Polish crisis exposed a terrifying instability at the core of the European security zone to which the leadership appeared incapable of responding in a positive and foresightful manner.

Perhaps most significantly, the promise of a better future for Soviet citizens was beginning to appear compromised. The failure to impose economic reforms had by the 1980s begun to make itself felt with a vengeance. Rather than overtaking and surpassing the West, the Soviet economy was plagued by a widening technology gap, declining rates of growth, persistent shortages, poor work morale, and chronic inefficiency. Juxtaposed with greater public awareness, the inability to progress economically contained potentially explosive social consequences.

By the 1980s interpretations of Soviet international policy in the West had begun to emphasize the threat of a *fuite en avant*. The USSR was described as a dysfunctional society, bound to a socioeconomic model that had exhausted its potential, drawn toward military adventurism as the only means to ward off decline.[83] The more apocalyptic scenarios of this type could become highly unrealistic. Indeed, from the mid-1970s onward, in part as a response to economic pressures, Soviet military spending was in relative decline.[84] But the argument contained more than a grain of truth. Military power was the key to the USSR's international stature, and maintaining its arsenal imposed a burden that the Soviet economy was less and less capable of bearing. One of the more insightful western commentators speaks of a "paradoxical militarism," the quest for superpower status without an adequate socioeconomic base and exaggerated reliance upon armed force in order to compensate.[85] Brezhnev had no desire to conquer the world, but he accepted a competitive image of world politics that sapped efforts to build détente and dictated levels of military preparedness that were destructive of long-term economic well-being. This was the Achilles' heel of Soviet security policy during the entire Brezhnev era, a paradox that grew from the conservative reaction against Khrushchev and that the leadership generation attached to Brezhnev, secure in their positions and insulated from popular concerns, could neither recognize nor begin to resolve.

Western observers sympathetic to the promise of détente have tended to blame both the United States and the USSR for betraying its spirit, and to look for ways in which the original concept might somehow be revived.[86] The case for a "controlled rivalry" as an alternative to un-

---

83. A sophisticated variant of this interpretation is presented by Seweryn Bialer, *The Soviet Paradox: External Expansion, Internal Decline* (New York, 1986).

84. Richard F. Kaufman, "Causes of the Slowdown in Soviet Defense," *Soviet Economy* 1 (Jan.–March 1985): 9–41; *Allocation of Resources in the Soviet Union and China— 1984 Hearings before the Subcommittee on International Trade, Finance, and Security Economics*, 99th Cong., 2d sess., part 10, 21 Nov. and 15 Jan. 1985, pp. 53–54.

85. Jacques Sapir, *Le système militaire soviétique* (Paris, 1988), p. 303.

86. See, for example, Garthoff, *Détente and Confrontation*, pp. 1068–89.

bridled superpower competition certainly made good sense, but the inherent limitations of the canon of détente as it was developed during the 1970s should not be ignored. Détente did not expire because its premises were inadequately defined or insufficiently respected. It failed because the premises themselves were fundamentally flawed.

The source of the Soviet Union's frustration with détente may be traced to the assumptions of competitive coexistence. No matter how often they might be repeated by Soviet ideologues, by the 1980s these assumptions were not being borne out by the facts. The global correlation of forces was not shifting to the advantage of the Soviet Union. Coexistence could not permanently be combined with a confrontational diplomacy and a two-camps mentality that had never entirely shed the notion of *la lutte finale*. Emphasis upon the competitive edge of East-West relations played into the hands of western hawks and lost the Soviet Union a good deal of international good-will. Real arms control was incompatible with the hostility that reigned between the superpowers and with an unrepentant commitment to achieving security through strength. The foreign policy dogmas of the Brezhnev leadership did not correspond to realities. What is more, the growing distance between Soviet aspirations and real capacity had become fraught with peril.

More subjectively, it is possible to suggest that the Soviet Union had ceased to believe in itself. Even during the worst of the Stalin years, in part because of a residual respect for the ideals of the revolution and in part because of the barbarity of its enemies, the Soviet state could inspire its partisans with an idealistic sense of purpose. Under Brezhnev the pervasiveness of official hypocrisy, the crude and extraneous methods used to muzzle dissent, the filth within the Augean stables of corruption accumulated at every level of society gave rise to a deep moral crisis. Vladimir Vysotskii became the poet of this crisis, and his themes fairly expressed its essence: a combination of frustrated patriotism, embryonic pacifism, scornful rejection of official cant, and militant attachment to personal integrity as the key to a revival.

The pervasive atmosphere of alienation that Vysotskii describes pertains to the realm of security policy as well. What was the point of endless sacrifices on behalf of a cause whose justice could no longer be assumed, or even fairly credited, the logic of a system whose only claim to legitimacy rested upon a cultivated hypocrisy, the sense of a strategic rivalry that seemed to lead inexorably toward the unfathomable darkness of nuclear war? By 10 November 1982 answering these questions had become the essential first step toward reformulating a viable Soviet security policy. To their credit, Brezhnev's eventual successors would not shy from the task.

CHAPTER EIGHT

New Thinking, New Dilemmas, 1982–1991

The course of intensification is dictated by objective conditions, by the entire course of the country's development. There are no alternatives. Only an intensive economy, developing on the most up-to-date scientific-technical basis, can serve as a reliable material base for an improvement in the well-being of the workers, a successful resolution of the problems confronting society. Only an intensive, highly developed economy can guarantee a strengthening of the position of the country in the international arena, enabling it to enter the new millennium with dignity as a great and prosperous world power.

—Mikhail Gorbachev, 10 December 1984

The leadership transition that followed Brezhnev's death occurred in stages. Already in the course of 1982, with the exposure of a bizarre scandal implicating Brezhnev's daughter, Galina Churbanova, in a smuggling racket, the general secretary's reputation—and legacy—was coming under siege. The revelations were organized by the KGB, and it was its long-time director, Iurii Andropov, who now stepped forward as potential successor. In January 1982 the death of Mikhail Suslov removed one of the most important props of the leadership. On 24 May, Andropov assumed Suslov's post as Central Committee secretary in charge of ideology and established himself as the heir apparent. Within two days of Brezhnev's demise on 10 November, Andropov was appointed the new general secretary.

In subtle ways Andropov pledged his government to a policy of reform. But the collapse of his health, leading to a virtual withdrawal from public life in August 1983 and his death on 9 February 1984, prevented the emergence of a coordinated reform agenda. Andropov's successor became Konstantin Chernenko, at age seventy-two the very embodiment of Brezhnevite "stagnation." The choice of Chernenko represented a concession to the party's old guard, but it came with a price attached. Chernenko was in poor health, and his appointment was tolerated by the party's liberal wing upon the understanding that the broad lines of Andropov's policies would be maintained and that Mikhail Gorbachev, a Politburo member since 1980, at age fifty-three still its Benjamin and the rising star of Soviet reformism, would be recognized as next in line.[1] Historically the Chernenko interlude was of little importance. His death on 10 March 1985 marked the end of an interregnum. One day later, with the appointment of Gorbachev as general secretary, a new era had begun.

The new leadership styled its program *perestroika* ("restructuring") and promised to pursue reform. The source of perestroika was not a magician named Gorbachev, however, but rather the maturation of Soviet society itself.[2] By the mid-1980s the Soviet state mechanism had become a creaking anachronism, desperately in need of revitalization if it hoped to respond to the aspirations of an increasingly self-aware population. The implications of perestroika for Soviet security policy grew directly from the urgent need for internal renewal, and they were profound. Gorbachev summed up the connection on the eve of his accession to office, remarking that only major reform would allow the Soviet Union to enter the new century "with dignity" as a great world power.[3] By the mid-1980s, in the minds of Gorbachev and his supporters, successful reform had become an essential prerequisite for continued international competitiveness, for a viable Soviet security posture apt to the demands of the twenty-first century.

In line with these priorities, under the rubric of "new thinking" about international relations, Gorbachev sought to recast the most basic postulates of Soviet security policy as it had unfolded since the October revolution. Taken as a whole, Soviet new thinking represented nothing less than a carefully articulated alternative security paradigm that was characterized by Gorbachev himself as *mutual security*.[4] In our time, it was argued, security must be conceived in terms of humanity's common interest in survival, placed at risk by new kinds of threats for which

1. Dev Murarka, *Gorbachov: The Limits of Power* (London, 1988), pp. 102–3; Christian Schmidt-Häuer, *Gorbachev: The Path to Power* (London, 1986), pp. 96–98; Michel Tatu, *Gorbatchev: l'URSS va-t-elle changer?* (Paris, 1987), pp. 104–5.

2. See esp. Moshe Lewin, *The Gorbachev Phenomenon: A Historical Interpretation* (Berkeley, Calif., 1988); David Lane, *Soviet Society under Perestroika* (Boston, 1990), pp. 1–19.

3. M. S. Gorbachev, *Izbrannye rechi i stat'i*, 7 vols. (Moscow, 1987–90), 2:86.

4. For an attempt to apply the concept to a series of practical problems see Richard Smoke and Andrei Kortunov, eds., *Mutual Security: A New Approach to Soviet-American Relations* (New York, 1991).

national egoism, the sterile dogmas of "official" Marxism, and raw military power offer no remedies. The contours of new thinking remained to some extent ill defined, but the inherent attractiveness of its central concepts was beyond dispute. Gorbachev was the first Soviet leader since Lenin convincingly to articulate a visionary image of the future of international society. His sheer intellectual daring, coupled with the capacity to link words to deeds earned him tremendous accolades. It also imparted to Soviet international policy a dynamism scarcely imaginable only several years before.

Soviet security policy under Gorbachev is nonetheless not correctly perceived as quixotic, as a blind leap forward into yet another brave new world. This is so for at least two reasons. First, for all its idealistic trappings, Gorbachev's foreign policy retained a hard core and was firmly attached to a realistic appraisal of national interests. It was a policy that had been conditioned by Brezhnev's failures and that retained the goal of reasserting Soviet power and prestige. Second, in rejecting the legacy of Stalin and Stalinism, the group of reformers attached to Gorbachev did not turn exclusively to western models as an alternative. Their image of international security, and of the Soviet Union's vocation in a community of states, was anchored within the Soviet experience itself. Gorbachev's security policy was not strictly speaking a new start. It was tied to the Soviet past by a thousand threads, visible and invisible. The weight of that past, with its tortuous complexities, continues to bear heavily upon the struggle for the future to which perestroika has given rise.

To Be or Not to Be

The six years of Gorbachev's reforms, culminating with the failure of the coup d'état of August 1991, can be divided into two phases, with the Central Committee plenums of January and June 1987 as approximate turning points. During the first phase, change was pursued in the Andropov manner. The most visible innovations, in addition to the dynamic new spirit imparted by the general secretary himself, were the gradual phasing out of the leading figures of the old Brezhnev hierarchy, a controversial campaign to fight alcohol abuse by restricting supply and access, and an exhortatory approach to economic reform conveyed by the term "acceleration." The second phase of "revolutionary" perestroika characterized by far-reaching institutional reforms did indeed conclude in a decisive break with the past, though not necessarily of the kind that Soviet reformers originally desired.

It is not clear to what extent perestroika was launched on the basis of a carefully considered scenario. Though radical transformations were on the agenda from the start, change was also accelerated by its own self-generated momentum. Whatever the case may be, the Gorbachev reformers required a period of time in order to consolidate their position, and the first phase of perestroika was used to good effect to prepare the ground for the more difficult confrontations that would follow. This was particularly the case in the domain of ideology. The political order that Gorbachev inherited was an ideological system, where official canons rigidly delineated the limits of the acceptable in terms of innovative social thought and public policy. Ideological renewal was an essential prerequisite for reform, and a process of renewal began with Gorbachev's first day in office.[5]

The phrase "new thinking" was coined by the foreign policy specialists Anatolii Gromyko and Vladimir Lomeiko during 1984 at a low point of the "new Cold War." Against a background of disintegrating East-West relations, Gromyko and Lomeiko argued that a redrawing of international priorities had become a necessity of the nuclear age.[6] Originally voiced as a *cri du coeur* in light of the spiraling nuclear arms race, the phrase was eventually picked up by Gorbachev as the basis for a no-holds-barred assault upon established orthodoxies.

Speaking before the French parliament on 3 October 1985 during his first visit abroad as general secretary, Gorbachev sought to make the premises of the new Soviet approach to international affairs clear. The first Soviet priority, he explained, was henceforward to be economic revitalization. This required, "not only a reliable peace, but also calm, normal international circumstances. These are the priorities that inform our foreign policy," which "like the foreign policy of any government is determined first of all by internal demands."[7] Gorbachev's appeal for international reconciliation as a basis for domestic reform was pragmatic, but it was also attached to a number of more ambitious generalizations. In the modern age, he proposed, the very essence of international relations was changing. Increased international interdependence, threats to the well-being of all peoples posed by health and environmental problems,

5. "Perestroika needs an ideological renewal," wrote the philosopher R. G. Ianovskii, "an ideology based upon dialectical method, foreign to dogmatism and scholasticism, negating fanaticism and the cult of authority." R. G. Ianovskii, "Filosofskie problemy perestroiki," *Filosofskie nauki* 9 (1988): 4.

6. Anatolii Gromyko and Vladimir Lomeiko, *Novoe myshlenie v iadernyi vek* (Moscow, 1984), p. 6. The phrase itself derives from a 1954 manifesto sponsored by Bertrand Russell and Albert Einstein to inaugurate the Pugwash peace movement.

7. Gorbachev, *Izbrannye rechi*, 2:459–60.

and the overarching nuclear menace placed humanity as a whole before the fateful question that Hamlet applied to his personal destiny: To be or not to be? "There can be only one answer," Gorbachev insisted, "humanity, civilization must survive whatever it takes. But this can only be achieved by learning to live together, to cohabit side by side on this small planet, mastering the difficult art of taking into account each other's mutual interests. This we call the policy of peaceful coexistence."[8]

Although the punchline was familiar, this was a new language for a Soviet leader. Gorbachev's variant of peaceful coexistence, hinged upon the concept of interdependence, was very different from the competitive brand marketed by both Khrushchev and Brezhnev. The confrontational image of world politics passed down in the Soviet tradition from the civil war to the present, Gorbachev implied, conflicted with the pressing need of Soviet society for reform, and was moreover out of step with the entire evolution of international society. Within months of taking office the general secretary had laid the foundation for a radically new approach to the Soviet security dilemma.

New thinking was not offered as a new orthodoxy. One of the most striking aspects of Gorbachev's Soviet Union was the degree to which it became possible to articulate alternative viewpoints and to debate openly vital issues of public policy. New thinking is perhaps best characterized as a set of propositions concerning international society specifically associated with Gorbachev and his entourage, propositions that have continued to be developed and refined.[9] As the basis for the new Soviet approach to security affairs, new thinking nonetheless made a certain number of primary assumptions, which at the risk of some oversimplification may briefly be summarized.

8. Ibid., p. 461. Gorbachev also uses the phrase "to be or not to be" in his political report to the 27th party congress. See ibid., 3:198.

9. For concise summaries of Soviet new thinking see Bruce Parrott, "Soviet National Security under Gorbachev," *Problems of Communism* 6 (Nov.–Dec. 1988): 1–36; Richard Sakwa, *Gorbachev and His Reforms* (New York, 1990), pp. 315–56. The most complete high-level expositions of the new line were offered in Gorbachev's best-selling book, M. S. Gorbachev, *Perestroika i novoe myshlenie dlia nashei strany i dlia vsego mira* (Moscow, 1987), pp. 135–267, and in his speech to the United Nations of 7 Dec. 1988, Gorbachev, *Izbrannye rechi*, 7:184–202. See also Foreign Minister Edvard Shevardnadze's address to a special conference of the Soviet foreign ministry, "XIX vsesoiuznaia konferentsiia KPSS: Vneshniaia politika i diplomatiia," *Mezhdunarodnaia zhizn'* 10 (1988): 3–35. More skeptical appraisals, which emphasize the roots of new thinking in the late Brezhnev period and interpret the exercise as a "tactic" in an ongoing competition with the West, are presented by V. Kubálková and A. A. Cruickshank, *Thinking New about Soviet "New Thinking"* (Berkeley, Calif., 1989); Stephen Shenfield, *The Nuclear Predicament: Explorations in Soviet Ideology* (London, 1987).

(1) *The dynamics of world politics are no longer primarily a function of narrow national or class interests. The essential attribute of the contemporary international system is interdependence.*

Our world, Gorbachev explained before the United Nations on 7 December 1988, is radically different from that which emerged from World War II. The source of change has been the scientific-technical revolution in communications, transportation, and modes of production. The achievements of modern science have created the prerequisites for a truly global community, the interdependent international society of the twenty-first century. The reality of interdependence, the increasingly complex interlinkages that bind states and peoples together and force them to contemplate their mutual interests, is the source from which almost all of the conclusions of Soviet new thinking flow.

Interdependence means that the vital problems confronting the international community have become global in scope. They include, most notably but not exclusively, the threat of a nuclear holocaust, ecological disintegration, and the widening gap between haves and have-nots in the global political economy. The contemporary international system is characterized by its fragility, by a vulnerability to new kinds of threats that set at risk not only the narrowly defined self-interest of individuals and nations but the interests of humanity as a whole.[10] The problem of security becomes coterminous with the problem of survival; at stake is the fate of the earth and all those who inhabit it.

The call is therefore raised to restructure the international political agenda on a foundation of universal human values and moral norms. In the Soviet context, where international theory since Lenin was premised upon the primacy of class interests, and where "normative" analysis was dismissed as foreign to the scientific foundations of Marxism-Leninism, the conclusion was radical. Though conflicting class and national interests remain influential, they must be transcended precisely because humanity as a whole confronts the urgent need to cooperate or perish. The most terrifying manifestation of the problem is the nuclear dilemma. For Bovin, humanity's new-found capacity to "commit suicide" in a nuclear holocaust necessitates "qualitatively new approaches to the entire problematic of war and peace . . . the nuclear age dictates new political thinking."[11]

10. For the concept of "fragility" see Iu. A. Zamoshkin, "Ideal iadernogo razoruzheniia i problema ego realizatsii (filosofskie i psikhologicheskie aspekty)," *Voprosy filosofii* 1 (1988): 92–93.

11. A. Bovin, "Novoe myshlenie—trebovanie iadernogo veka," *Kommunist* 10 (July 1986): 114, 117.

The alternative is described as a "universal" system of international security that acknowledges the immediacy of global threats, the need for mechanisms capable of assuring mutual security in the face of such threats, and the importance of broadening the security agenda beyond its traditional military preoccupations to include social, economic, and ecological dimensions as well.[12] Security is described, in a conscious invocation of Litvinov's collective security policy of the 1930s, as "indivisible."[13] Only a comprehensive approach to world order, it is concluded, is capable of guaranteeing "the future of the planet and the preservation and development of civilization on earth."[14]

(2) *War can no longer be considered an "extension of politics." Force is becoming less relevant as a mechanism for resolving interstate conflicts and should be deemphasized in favor of political means.*

Disarmament was one of the most insistently proclaimed goals of perestroika, and the "powerlessness of force" in grappling with the dilemmas of contemporary world politics was a leitmotif of Soviet new thinking. Once again the foundation of the problem was perceived to be the new state of affairs created by nuclear arms. The nuclear age was said to require a "new philosophy" of war and peace in which Lenin's dictum, paraphrased from Clausewitz, that "war is a continuation of politics by other means" would have no place.

The most challenging dimension of the Soviet argument was its rejection of deterrence as a means for managing the nuclear dilemma and a call for complete nuclear disarmament as an alternative. First outlined by Gorbachev in a policy statement of 15 January 1986, a program for achieving nuclear disarmament "by the year 2000" soon became the basis of the Soviet arms-control agenda.[15] A strategic philosophy grounded upon the principles of assured second-strike capacity and mutual assured destruction, it was argued, rests upon numerous fallacies. First, the need to maintain a margin of safety in a competitive strategic environment has not led to stability but rather to an open-ended arms race that "sooner or

12. In his address to the 27th party congress Gorbachev outlined the basic premises of the "universal" security system in four categories: military, political, economic, and humanitarian. Gorbachev, *Izbrannye rechi*, 3:256–57. See also V. Petrovskii, "Dialog o vseob"emliushchei bezopasnosti," *Mezhdunarodnaia zhizn'* 10 (Oct. 1989): 3–13.

13. The phrase "indivisible security" is used by I. Usachev, "Obshchechelovecheskoe i klassovoe v mirovoi politike," *Kommunist* 11 (July 1988): 118, and Iu. Kirshin, "Politika i voennaia strategiia v iadernyi vek," *Mirovaia ekonomika i mezhdunarodnye otnosheniia* 11 (1988): 40.

14. A. M. Serdiuk, *Neprostye zaboty chelovechestva: Nauchno-tekhnicheskii progress, zdorov'e cheloveka, ekologiia* (Moscow, 1988), p. 5.

15. Gorbachev, *Izbrannye rechi*, 3:133–44.

later is capable of spinning out of control."[16] It has made politics captive to technology by generating a technological arms race that proceeds according to a logic of its own. It fails to account for human fallibility and for the proneness of complex systems eventually to fail, with the possible consequence of nuclear war by accident.[17] Finally, deterrence is rejected because the need to ensure "credibility" dictates a policy of threat, bluff, and intimidation. Such a policy undermines confidence, breeds fear and hostility, and ultimately makes the political accommodation that is the only lasting foundation for real security more difficult to achieve.[18]

The revision of attitudes toward conventional military competition was equally radical. In populous industrial regions such as Europe a resort to conventional war was described as being no less irrational than a resort to nuclear war. The Soviet Union always emphasized its peaceful intentions, but on a military-technical level its planning through the early 1980s emphasized the need for Warsaw Pact forces to take the offensive in the event of a European war. On 29 May 1987 a policy statement issued by the pact's Political Consultative Commission redefined the traditional orientation substantially, asserting that "the military doctrine of the Warsaw Pact, and each of its members, is subordinated to the problem of preventing war, both nuclear and conventional."[19] In place of the overwhelming combined arms offensive that had been the foundation for warfighting contingencies in the past, Soviet planners began to speak of preparing for a twenty- to thirty-day defensive phase in the

16. Ibid., p. 245.

17. See V. M. Gavrilov and S. V. Patrushev, "Gonka vooruzhenii v ierarkhii global'nykh problem," *Voprosy filosofii* 5 (1984): 99–107; A. A. Kokoshin and V. V. Larionov, *Predotvrashchenie voiny: Doktriny, kontseptsii, perspektivy* (Moscow, 1990), pp. 153–63.

18. The argument is summarized in Gorbachev's address to the international forum "For a World without Arms, For the Survival of Humanity," Gorbachev, *Izbrannye rechi*, 4:383–85, and by I. S. Shatilo, "Razoruzhenie: Real'naia vozmozhnost' ili nes"ytochnaia mechta," *Filosofskie nauki* 8 (1987): 3–11. In Soviet policy literature the case for total nuclear disarmament was subsequently tempered though not abandoned. E. Agaev, "K novoi modeli strategicheskoi stabil'nosti," *Mezhdunarodnaia zhizn'* 2 (1989): 103–11, developed the concept of "defensive deterrence" as an interim position that was realistically achievable. A. A. Kokoshin, "Sokrashchenie iadernykh vooruzhenii i strategicheskaia stabil'nost'," *SShA: Ekonomika, politika, ideologiia* 2 (1988): 3–12, used simulation modeling to calculate reductions of between "50% and 95%" consistent with stability. Gorbachev adopted these views, and in his address before the Council of Europe in Strasbourg on 6 July 1989 he embraced the goal of "minimal deterrence" as an interim goal. "Obshcheevropeiskii protsess idet vpered," *Pravda*, 7 July 1989, p. 2.

19. "O voennoi doktrine gosudarstv-uchastnikov Varshavskogo Dogovora," *Pravda*, 20 May 1987, p. 1. See also the statement by chief of the Soviet General Staff S. Achromejew, "Doktrin zur Verhütung eines Krieges, zum Schutze des Friedens und des Sozialismus," *Probleme des Friedens und des Sozialismus* 12 (Dec. 1987): 1614–22; the statement "Doktrina predotvrashcheniia voiny," *Krasnaia zvezda*, 23 June 1987, p. 3.

event of war accompanied by negotiations to terminate conflict. "Averting world war now took precedence over not losing it," writes Mcc-Gwire, "thereby legitimizing a defensive posture."[20]

The new Soviet emphasis upon defensive doctrine was summarized by the phrase "reasonable defensive sufficiency." There was never total accord within military circles concerning the practical implications of the concept, but in the most general terms its tenets may be said to include: (1) a definitive renunciation of any intent to initiate armed confrontation; (2) mutual arms reductions to a level at which neither side has the capacity successfully to launch an invasion; (3) the repositioning and reequipping of troops to ensure that they are capable of fulfilling uniquely defensive functions; and (4) military *glasnost'* ("openness") in the form of greater access to information about opposing armed forces, more effective verification procedures, and various kinds of confidence-building and stabilization measures.[21] A vigorous debate was launched concerning the relative importance of the counteroffensive in defensive strategy, the kinds of force configurations most appropriate to defensive planning, and the degree to which the Soviet Union could hope to pursue a defensive orientation unilaterally, but the general orientation of the new Soviet military thinking away from the "primacy of the offensive" was quite clear.[22]

The challenge to the long-standing traditions of Soviet military doctrine implicit in the concept of reasonable defensive sufficiency was striking. The ideology of the offensive had dominated Soviet military thought since the civil war. Now it was stated unambiguously that real

20. Michael MccGwire, *Perestroika and Soviet National Security* (Washington, D.C., 1989), p. 42. MccGwire's work provides the best elucidation of this transformation in Soviet military doctrine. He traces the shift to the Central Committee plenum of January 1987 and calls it "the final step in a process of doctrinal evolution that had been underway for some thirty years" (p. 307).

21. Iu. Lebedev and A. Podberezkin, "Voennye doktriny i mezhdunarodnaia bezopasnost'," *Kommunist* 13 (Sept. 1988): 117–18. For controversial attempts to use the concept as the justification for radical force reductions see Al. Arbatov, "O paritete i razumnoi dostatochnosti," *Mezhdunarodnaia zhizn'* 9 (Sept. 1988): 80–92, and "Skol'ko oborony dostatochno?" *Mezhdunarodnaia zhizn'* 3 (1989). In an influential article by A. Kokoshin and V. Larionov, "Kurskaia bitva v svete sovremennoi oboronitel'noi doktriny," *Mirovaia ekonomika i mezhdunarodnye otnosheniia* 8 (1987): 32–40, the battle of Kursk is used as a model for the successful application of a defensive strategic orientation.

22. The evolution of the debate is demonstrated by a later article by A. Kokoshin and V. Larionov, "Protivostanie sil obshchego naznacheniia v kontekste obespecheniia strategicheskoi stabil'nosti," *Mirovaia ekonomika i mezhdunarodnye otnosheniia* 6 (1988): 23–31. The authors present four models for conventional force configurations, the most ambitious of which moves far beyond their earlier "Kursk" scenario by calling upon both sides to negotiate force levels making any and all offensive operations impossible.

security could not be built upon an accumulation of military capacity that contributed to a feeling of insecurity among one's neighbors.[23] The emphasis in military doctrine had shifted from the contingency of war to the necessity of peace, and assuring an adequate and nonprovocative defense had become the armed force's primary military-technical task.

(3) *The character of international relations has changed fundamentally. East-West competition is no longer the main axis of world politics. The Cold War is over.*

New thinking included a sweeping revision of traditional interpretations of Soviet history, the essence of which was an uninhibited confrontation with the "Stalin question." How did the positive ideals of the October revolution give rise to the personal dictatorship of Stalin and the terror of Stalinism? Gorbachev and his supporters sought to keep the image of Lenin above the fray by describing Stalin's emergence as a despot as a sharp break with the positive core of the Bolshevik tradition.[24] In discussing the evolution of the Soviet approach to security, however, one cannot possibly ignore the decisive break with the past that was wrought by Lenin's revolution.

The great distinctiveness of the October revolution was its commitment to the priority of internationalism. Bovin notes correctly that "*all* of the remarks of V. I. Lenin on the eve of the October transformation that are known to us, *all* of the actions of the leader of the revolution bear witness that he regarded the Russian revolution only as the prologue to the world revolution." The post-October situation, that of declining revolutionary prospects and capitalist stabilization, "transcended the framework of the theoretical presumptions" offered by classical Marxism.[25] The need for an isolated revolutionary polity to achieve security within a community of states once the "age of world revolution" had come to an end was a problem for which Lenin and his comrades were unprepared both emotionally and intellectually.

23. See the strong statement by G. Trofimenko, "Kakaia voennaia doktrina nam nuzhna?" *Mezhdunarodnaia zhizn'* 12 (1990): 39–51. For an evaluation that emphasizes the degree to which the Soviet Union's attempt to maintain military capacity for which it lacked an adequate material base actually damaged long-term security interests see S. Blagovolia, "Voennaia moshch'—skol'ko, kakaia, zachem?" *Mirovaia ekonomika i mezhdunarodnye otnosheniia* 8 (1989): 5–19.

24. Comparable interpretations are posed from Soviet and western perspectives by A. Simoniia, "Stalinizm protiv sotsializma," and S. Koen, "Bol'shevizm i stalinizm," *Voprosy filosofii* 7 (1989): 28–72. The former article is a translation of the essay "Bolshevism and Stalinism" in Stephen F. Cohen, *Rethinking the Soviet Experience: Politics and History since 1917* (Oxford, 1985), pp. 38–70. See also G. Smirnov, "K voprosu o leninskoi kontseptsii sotsializma," *Politicheskoe obrazovanie* 1 (1989): 12–21; for a summary of the more cautious official position, V. Medvedev, "K poznaniiu sotsializma: Otvet na voprosy zhurnala 'Kommunist,'" *Kommunist* 17 (Nov. 1988): 3–18.

25. A. Bovin, "Novoe myshlenie—novaia politika," *Kommunist* 9 (June 1988): 116.

The shift toward a policy of accommodation after 1921 did not eliminate the Soviet security dilemma. The legitimacy of Soviet power continued to rest upon the claim to represent a revolutionary alternative to the corrupt world order of capitalist imperialism. As a result the October revolution gave rise to what the theorists of perestroika called an "ideologization" of international relations, with the rivalry between the world views of capitalism and socialism expressed as an interstate conflict between the Soviet Union and its many enemies.[26] The dilemma of maintaining Soviet power in a hostile world was an essential theme of the Soviet experience, and it gave rise to broadly contrasting approaches that continually reemerged as the foundation for alternative policy options at critical junctures in Soviet history. The first was a discourse of accommodation, introduced by Lenin in his final writings, carried on by Chicherin, Bukharin, and Litvinov during the 1920s and 1930s, and expressed in new forms by Khrushchev's special variant of peaceful coexistence and by the Soviet commitment to peace and disarmament. The second, and historically dominant, alternative was a discourse of confrontation, embodied in Stalin's encirclement thesis, in Zhdanov's two-camps rhetoric, in the Brezhnev era codification of international theory, and in the entire spirit of the Cold War.

Though it may to some extent have been justified at a time when the Soviet state was faced with imminent external threats, the confrontational strain in Soviet security policy was now condemned as a destructive anachronism. Once again the new realities of the nuclear age were perceived to dictate change. The "logical" outcome of the ideologically driven East-West conflict, according to Georgii Shakhnazarov, was a "universal St. Bartholomew's Night."[27] A vital goal of perestroika must therefore be to deideologize the Soviet approach to international relations by rejecting once and for all the claim to embody the "future that works." According to Evgenii Primakov: "Inter-state relations in their totality cannot be the domain within which the fate of the global conflict between world socialism and world capitalism will be decided."[28] Contemporary capitalism, it was argued, had proven its ability to adapt and successfully *completed* the transition to an intensive model of development, a transition that the planned economies had in most cases yet to begin.[29] Nor could contemporary capitalism be described as an

26. Usachev, "Obshchechelovecheskoe i klassovoe v mirovoi politike," p. 111.

27. G. Shakhnazarov, "Vostok-Zapad: K voprosu o deideologizatsii mezhgosudarstvennykh otnoshenii," *Kommunist* 3 (Feb. 1989): 67.

28. Evgenii M. Primakov, "Novaia filosofiia vneshnei politiki," *Pravda*, 10 July 1987, p. 4.

29. Evgenii Primakov, "Kapitalizm v vzaimosviazannom mire," *Kommunist* 13 (Sept. 1987): 101–10.

inevitable source of war; Vadim Medvedev writes of a new era of "ul-traimperialism" in which the cooperative management of the world economy by the leading capitalist powers will provide the basis for an enduring peace.[30] The very idea of a military threat from the West, the bedrock of Soviet security policy since the revolution, was dismissed by some analysts as a chimera, negated by inexorable changes in the nature of strategy itself.[31] The capitalist mode of production was still consid-ered to be flawed, but much greater importance was placed upon the ut-ter failure of the Soviet model to generate a positive alternative. Under the circumstances to speak of East-West conflict as the "main axis" of world politics had become incongruous. The Cold War, it was con-cluded, was over.

The effort to transcend the legacy of the Cold War required a decisive rejection of Stalinism (whether regarded as a "distorted" model of so-cialism or as a negation of the very idea of socialism), an abandonment of claims to a monopoly of historical understanding based upon a pseudo-science of "Marxism-Leninism," and a commitment to the pre-mises of empowerment and democracy. It required a special effort to build bridges between the United States and the USSR, the two major protagonists of the Cold War and the only world powers that main-tained the capacity to unleash a nuclear holocaust. And it required a commitment to construct cooperative mechanisms capable of making mutual security a reality. As the first trained lawyer to occupy the post of general secretary since Lenin, Gorbachev made his personal priorities clear. "Our goal," he explained before the United Nations, "is a world community of states of law which submit their external political activi-ties to the rule of law."[32] Soviet new thinking emphasized the role of in-ternational organizations, and especially the United Nations, as forums for conflict management, and praised the regulatory and disciplinary function of international legal bodies. Again according to Gorbachev, "the concept of universal international security is founded on the prin-ciples of the U.N. charter and derives from the fact that international law is obligatory for all states."[33]

---

30. See V. Medvedev, "Velikii Oktiabr' i sovremennyi mir," *Kommunist* 2 (Jan. 1988): 5–6; for the summation of a lengthy academic debate on the point, A. Shapiro, "Eshche raz k voprosom o teorii vsemirnogo khoziaistva," *Mirovaia ekonomika i mezhdunarodnye ot-nosheniia* 3 (1985): 91–102.

31. V. Zhurkin, S. Karaganov, and A. Kortunov, "Vyzovy bezopasnosti—starye i novye," *Kommunist* 1 (Jan. 1988): 42–50.

32. Gorbachev, *Izbrannye rechi*, 7:195.

33. Ibid. See also V. S. Vereshchatin and R. A. Miullerson, "Novoe myshlenie i mezh-dunarodnoe pravo," *Sovetskoe gosudarstvo i pravo* 3 (1988): 3–9.

Taken as a whole, new thinking represented a serious effort to recast the most basic assumptions of Soviet international policy. It should nonetheless be noted that in many ways the new Soviet approach to international affairs remained disconcertingly vague. In the context of the Soviet domestic debate Gorbachev's ideas offered a compromise position, located somewhere between traditional dogmas and the anticommunist certitudes of radical revisionists. Gorbachev's identity as a "centrist" may have been a source of strength politically, but it was not conducive to theoretical clarity. What are "universal human values" and how are they to be determined? How can such values be reconciled with the harsh realities of a world order where the imperatives of power and survival remain primordial? One commentator cites Raymond Aron's criteria for *raison d'état* as a guide. Sergei Rogov of the Institute for the USA and Canada refers to Marx's appeal to the "simple laws of morality and justice." Deputy Foreign Minister Anatolii Adamishin suggests that "in the final analysis it is simply justifiable to be guided by the ten commandments."[34] Such assertions reveal a certain intellectual disorientation. Soviet new thinking was obviously much more than the foundation for a self-serving "charm offensive," but it was much less than a compelling theory of international relations.[35]

What emerges unambiguously from a survey of Soviet new thinking are the practical goals that inspired it. The attempt to move beyond the disastrous legacy of Stalinism was obviously sincere, but it was undertaken in such a way as to preserve certain core values that gave the Soviet experience a claim to legitimacy in spite of all. The plea for international reconciliation was justified in terms of the changing nature of world politics, but it was also described as a necessary prerequisite for Soviet domestic reform. Arms reductions were championed on behalf of universal values, but justified on the basis of a rigorous evaluation of the military-technical prerequisites for an adequate defense. And the "ideological" component of traditional Soviet security policy was rejected in conjunction with a pragmatic campaign to reintegrate the USSR into the dominant international political and economic order. Gorbachev's program promoted ambitions as well as ideals, and the fact that it could be

34. The citations are drawn from E. Agab-Ogly, "Real'nosti novogo myshleniia: Ot konfrontatsii k sotrudnichestvu," *Kommunist* 2 (Jan. 1988): 55; S. M. Rogov, "O vzaimodeistvii interesov SSSR i SShA," *SShA: Ekonomika, politika, ideologiia* 8 (1988): 10; A. Adamishin, "U chelovechestva edinaia sud'ba," *Mezhdunarodnaia zhizn'* (Jan. 1989): 6.

35. Gerard Holden, *Soviet Military Reform* (London, 1991), pp. 8–17, gives a good summary of new thinking's contradictions and inadequacies. An appeal for more systematic theoretical approaches to the problems of international relations is made by G. N. Novikov, "Novoe myshlenie i sovremennaia teoriia mezhdunarodnykh otnoshenii," *Novaia i noveishaia istoriia* 1 (1991): 199–203.

defended as a means for achieving long-standing national goals helped to account for its initial success.

The Common European Home

Nowhere were the changes set to work by perestroika greater than in Europe. Already during his visit to London in December 1984 Gorbachev had begun to speak of Europe as a "common home," and to intimate that the Cold War system that divided the continent and left it the most militarized region in world politics was an "abnormal state of affairs."[36] Soon an appeal for the construction of the common European home became a leading theme of Gorbachev's new approach to foreign policy.[37]

The theme of the common home was greeted in the West with considerable skepticism. Gorbachev's superficially appealing slogan, it was noted, proposed a European rather than an Atlantic orientation for the key European pillars of the Atlantic alliance and thereby threatened to undermine the foundations of western security. Moderate scholars such as Pierre Hassner argued that, given its sheer size, the Soviet Union must be regarded as a potential threat regardless of its declared intentions in regard to a Europe that was not closely bound to the United States. More severe critics found in Gorbachev's phrase the implication "that the United States, as a trans-atlantic power, really had no business" in the common home. Even potentially sympathetic observers such as France's François Mitterrand dismissed the concept as "a very beautiful expression, but a very long term perspective."[38]

It remained for Gorbachev to demonstrate good-will. His chosen vehicle, and the real flagship of Soviet foreign policy during the first years of perestroika, became arms control. Although the negotiating forums

36. Gorbachev, *Izbrannye rechi*, 2:114–15. Hannes Adomeit, "Gorbatschows Westpolitik: 'Gemeinsames europäisches Haus' oder atlantische Orientierung," *Osteuropa* 6 (June 1988): 419–34, traces Soviet use of the concept "common home" to the 1960s.
37. The theorists of perestroika preferred the Gaullist concept of a Europe "from the Atlantic to the Urals." Europe was described as a "historical-cultural entity" resting upon a "serious material base" of economic and scientific-technical cooperation, with the "historical, cultural, political, and economic prerequisites" for the creation of a common European home "already in place." Cited from G. Vorontsov, "Ot Khelsinki k 'obshcheevropeiskomu domu,'" *Mirovaia ekonomika i mezhdunarodnye otnosheniia* 9 (1988): 43–44.
38. Pierre Hassner, "Europe between the United States and the Soviet Union," *Government and Opposition* 1 (1986): 17–35; *The Gorbachev Challenge: A Report from the European Strategy Group* (Baden-Baden, 1988), p. 105; "M. Mitterrand et les 'progrès' de l'URSS," *Le Monde*, 27–28 Nov. 1988, p. 5.

abandoned by Andropov following NATO's INF deployments had been restored on 7 January 1985 just prior to Gorbachev's accession to office, the arms-control agenda remained completely blocked. The task of reversing the arms spiral appeared to be monumental, but it would be tackled with exemplary energy and intelligence.

Gorbachev took the initiative on 7 April 1985 by announcing the suspension of Soviet countermeasures applied in response to the NATO INF deployments, and a moratorium on further deployments of SS-20s. On 20 August 1985 he proclaimed a unilateral moratorium on nuclear testing, which was to be extended "indefinitely" should the United States agree to join. Eventually maintained through March 1987 without any reciprocal action by the United States, the moratorium was an important symbolic gesture that set the stage for much that was to come. On 19–20 November 1985 Gorbachev met with President Reagan in Geneva. No concrete results were obtained, but Gorbachev's comments reinforced his credibility as a man of peace. The American attachment to the SDI program, the Soviet leader hinted, had become the last major barrier to dramatic arms reductions. For its own part, the Soviet Union was determined to avoid an "extension of the arms race into outer space" and frustrated by a U.S. administration that was "unprepared for major decisions."[39]

On 15 January 1986 Gorbachev unveiled his program for complete nuclear disarmament, to be achieved in three stages by the year 2000.[40] Though dialogue with the United States continued to stick on the issue of SDI, Gorbachev had seized the high ground in the contest for international opinion. Another step forward was taken on 22 September 1986 when the CSCE Conference on Confidence and Security-Building Measures in Stockholm approved a series of impressive confidence-building measures. The agreements required forty-two-day notification for military exercises involving more than 13,000 men and 300 tanks (the Helsinki treaty called for twenty-one-day notification for exercises involving more than 25,000 men), sanctioned the presence of international observers during major exercises, and required the submission of annual calendars of important military activities. The signatories also agreed to broaden the verification function by confirming their right "to carry out inspections on the territory of any other participant" conforming to certain established procedures.[41] The acceptance of the much-disputed right

39. Gorbachev, *Izbrannye rechi*, 3:64–82.
40. Ibid., pp. 133–44.
41. The Stockholm talks opened under CSCE sponsorship in January 1984. For an account of the negotiations see Sherr, *The Other Side of Arms Control*, pp. 268–69.

of onsite inspection and willingness to allow considerably greater access to military data represented a dramatic break with the traditional Soviet preoccupations with secrecy and control.

In the aftermath of the Stockholm agreements the second Reagan-Gorbachev summit, held on 10–13 October 1986 in Reykjavik, Iceland, began under the best auspices. Given the high initial expectations, the outcome was chastening. Gorbachev arrived with a long list of proposals, including an offer entirely to eliminate the SS-20 missile in Europe and to limit the number deployed in Asia to 100, and a program for 50 percent reductions in the strategic nuclear arsenal. Hopes for an agreement broke down, however, upon Reagan's commitment to SDI, which the Soviets continued to regard as incompatible with progress in other domains. In some ways Reykjavik was another public relations triumph for Gorbachev. Following the sessions the impression remained that a tremendous opportunity had been lost because of Reagan's irrational fixation upon the chimera of "Star Wars." The U.S. delegation was visibly unprepared to deal with the Soviet proposals, and Reagan's counter offer of the total elimination of nuclear arms seemed improvised and insincere.[42]

On 16 February 1987 the Soviet-sponsored international forum "For a World Without Arms, For the Survival of Humanity" gave another boost to what had become a Soviet disarmament campaign.[43] The exercise in media politics was followed on 28 February by an essential concession. After long insisting that without an SDI accord no progress in other arms-control dossiers was possible, Moscow now granted that separate U.S.-Soviet negotiations on the euromissile question could go forward, and that the total elimination of intermediate-range nuclear forces, that is, a variant of Reagan's 1981 proposal known as the "zero option," was a feasible goal. The gesture, though spectacular, was also a logical next step in view of past Soviet inflections on the matter. The 1985 moratorium on SS-20 deployments was followed in December 1985 by a statement that the euromissile case could be treated as a separate category for the purpose of negotiations. Gorbachev's January 1986 disarmament plan agreed to leave the British and French nuclear arsenals out of the INF equation. At Reykjavik the idea of a zero option was broached, but only in conjunction with progress on other disarmament fronts. Now the concept of "linkage" had been abandoned as well.

42. The eyewitness account by Donald T. Reagan, *For the Record: From Wall Street to Washington* (San Diego, Calif., 1988), pp. 345–55, though sympathetic to President Reagan, confirms the impression of improvisation.

43. For the text of Gorbachev's keynote address see Gorbachev, *Izbrannye rechi*, 4: 376–92.

Moscow was embracing a radical solution to the euromissile contro-versy, a solution that was originally proposed by the American side with the specific intention of placing the bar so high as to preclude an accord.

During a conversation with U.S. Secretary of State George Shultz on 14 April 1987 Gorbachev upped the ante once again by offering the reciprocal elimination of both intermediate-range nuclear forces (all So-viet SS-20s including those based in Asia and the U.S. Pershing II and Europe-based ground-launched cruise missiles, systems with a range of 1,000–5,000 kilometers) and an additional category of short-range in-termediate forces (or, in Soviet parlance, "tactical-operational" forces, with a range of 500–1,000 kilometers, including the Soviet SS-22 and SS-23). The proposal was dubbed the "double-zero option," and it was on this basis that an agreement in principle was announced on 19 Sep-tember 1987. During Gorbachev's visit to Washington for his third en-counter with Reagan on 8 December the INF treaty was signed, marking the conclusion of the first major arms-reduction accord of the entire nu-clear era.[44]

By agreeing to accept the double-zero option, the western alliance sac-rificed deployments that had been won at great political cost. According to some the Reagan administration had been caught in a trap of its own making and was pressured to accept reductions that were potentially damaging to western interests.[45] In the wake of the INF treaty an at-tempt was made to regain the initiative by "calling Gorbachev's bluff" and demanding more vital concessions. The Soviet reform program, it was argued, was "arbitrarily reversible."[46] What is more, the Soviet arms-control agenda was perceived to contain three major flaws. First, it left intact a threatening imbalance in conventional and short-range nu-clear forces in Europe. In response the West was urged to modernize its own short-range nuclear forces while testing Moscow's intentions with the demand for unilateral Soviet reductions.[47] Second, the content of the Soviet commitment to a defensive strategic orientation was questioned; military restructuring, it was argued, could also result in "leaner and meaner" forces that would be *more* capable of conducting a successful

44. The text and protocols are in Honoré M. Catudal, *Soviet Nuclear Strategy from Sta-lin to Gorbachev: A Revolution in Soviet Military and Political Thinking* (Berlin, 1988), pp. 313–68.

45. See, for example, Pierre Lellouche, "'Double zéro,' double péril," *Le Monde,* 1 Oct. 1987, pp. 1 and 6.

46. In the words of U.S. Under Secretary of State John Whitehead at an East-West se-curity conference in St. Paul, Minn., in October 1987, cited from "Comment l'Occident doit-il réagir au gorbatchévisme?," *Le Monde,* 14 Oct. 1987, p. 4.

47. See, for example, Graham T. Allison, Jr., "Testing Gorbachev," *Foreign Affairs* 1 (Fall 1988): 18–32

offensive.[48] Finally, the ingenuousness of the concept of the common home in a continent whose division still rested squarely upon Soviet coercion was underlined.

Arguments stressing the instability of Gorbachev's position would have to cope with his evident political skills. Even the Soviet high command, long regarded as a critical source of opposition to reform of any kind, was not immune to the pressures of perestroika. On 28 May 1987 a West German amateur pilot managed to fly a small private plane all the way to Red Square, where he landed in the shadow of the Kremlin and disembarked with a grin before the gaze of astonished onlookers. The freakish incident, humiliating for an air defense command whose reputation had already been tarnished by the KAL tragedy and for a military hierarchy that had to some degree discredited itself in Afghanistan, provided the pretext for a shake-up. Within days seventy-six-year-old Defense Minister Sergei Sokolov (who had succeeded Dmitrii Ustinov following the latter's death in 1984) was replaced by Dmitrii Iazov, at that moment a Gorbachev supporter who leapfrogged upward in the hierarchy over numerous ranking opponents. Other replacements would follow, culminating in December 1988 with a thorough restaffing of high command positions. Gorbachev apparently had secured a military leadership broadly supportive of his policies.[49] In October 1988 a comparable shake-up struck the KGB. Its director Viktor Chebrikov was replaced at Gorbachev's behest by Vladimir Kriuchkov, and in subsequent months the organization attempted to improve its image with a mini-perestroika of its own.[50] Both Iazov and Kriuchkov would eventually become leaders of the foiled August 1991 coup attempt, but for the time being the key organs of Soviet power seemed to be harnessed to the wagon of reform.

Meanwhile, Gorbachev pushed his arms-control offensive into the domain of conventional arms. Speaking before the Polish parliament on 11

48. Holden, *Soviet Military Reform*, pp. 46–47.

49. The attitude of the Soviet high command toward perestroika was not consistent and remains difficult to interpret. Arguments that emphasize the willingness of Gorbachev's reformed military hierarchy to accept the price of reform, considered to be an essential prerequisite for the economic modernization needed to maintain an adequate defense, are presented by Russell Bova, "The Soviet Military and Economic Reform," *Soviet Studies* 3(July 1988): 385–405; Raymond L. Garthoff, "New Thinking in Soviet Military Doctrine," *Washington Quarterly* 3 (Summer 1988): 131–58; Stephen Larrabee, "Gorbachev and the Soviet Military," *Foreign Affairs* 5 (Summer 1988): 1002–26. For an opposing point of view that stresses continuity in the Soviet military tradition see Stephen P. Adragno, "A New Soviet Military? Doctrine and Strategy," *Orbis* 2 (Spring 1989): 165–79.

50. A program for reform is outlined by O. Kalugin, "Razvedka i vneshniaia politika," *Mezhdunarodnaia zhizn'* 5 (1989): 61–71. The author's criticisms subsequently led to his dismissal from the intelligence services.

July 1988, he proposed a "pan-European Reykjavik" with the goal of "breaking the viscous circle" of the conventional arms stand-off. The idea was refused point-blank by NATO Secretary General Manfred Woerner, according to whom Soviet proposals ignored "the fundamental cause of military instability in Europe," namely, "the massive deployment of Soviet ground forces in numbers largely superior to legitimate defensive needs."[51] Gorbachev turned to the objection in a dramatic manner during his 7 December U.N. address by announcing a major unilateral reduction of Soviet conventional forces. Cutbacks to be completed by 1991 were to amount to 12 percent of the Soviet manpower total, including 20 percent of forces stationed west of the Urals and six divisions counting over 50,000 men and 5,000 tanks to be withdrawn from the groups of Soviet forces stationed in the GDR, Czechoslovakia, and Hungary. Though reductions of such magnitude struck hard at the traditional priorities of the armed forces, they corresponded to the exigencies of the emerging doctrine of reasonable defensive sufficiency and could be defended in terms of both economic rationalization and military modernization.[52]

December 1988 also saw the winding down of the protracted MBFR (Mutual and Balanced Force Reduction) negotiations in Vienna. The epitome of the futility of arms control as practiced by both East and West during the Brezhnev era, MBFR had been paralyzed since its inception by the "counting problem," the inability of the two sides to arrive at mutually acceptable estimates of NATO and Warsaw Pact forces in place. Moscow took a step toward greater openness on 30 January 1989 by publishing a detailed accounting of the military balance in Europe that was widely acknowledged to be a more accurate estimate than anything made available in the past.[53] On 6 March 1989 the MBFR mandate was transferred to a new CFE (Conventional Forces in Europe) forum in Vienna under the aegis of NATO and the Warsaw Pact. Simultaneously a follow-up CSCE conference on confidence-building measures was

51. Gorbachev's address to the Polish Sejm appears in Gorbachev, *Izbrannye rechi*, 6:426–40. For Woerner's remark see Thierry Maliniak, "Le secrétaire général de l'OTAN appelle les Soviétiques à négocier 'sérieusement' à Vienne," *Le Monde*, 16 July 1988, p. 20.

52. The most visible proponent of a "high tech" army was the former chief of the general staff Marshal Nikolai Ogarkov. See his seminal article "Na strazhe mirnogo truda," *Kommunist* 10 (July 1981): 80–91; the accounts in Herspring, *The Soviet High Command*, pp. 145–54; Mary F. Fitzgerald, *Marshal Ogarkov on Modern War, 1977–1985*, Professional Paper 443.10, Center for Naval Analysis (Alexandria, Va., 1986). A cogent Soviet analysis of the exigencies of modern warfare emphasizing the centrality of technology is offered by F. F. Gaivoronskii, ed., *Evoliutsiia voennogo iskusstva: Etapy, tendentsii, printsipy* (Moscow, 1987), pp. 187–245.

53. "Zaiavlenie Komiteta oborony gosudarstv—uchastnikov Varshavskogo Dogovora," *Pravda*, 30 Jan. 1989, p. 5.

convened, also in the Austrian capital. In large measure because of the impetus provided by perestroika, a new round of conventional arms-reduction talks had been launched with considerable prospects for success.

During his first years in office Gorbachev used the cause of disarmament to good effect in order to bolster his international reputation and to reverse the momentum of the "new Cold War." The INF treaty was a limited but real achievement, and it provided a basis for further progress. Coupled with the unilateral conventional force reductions announced in December 1988, it made hopes for a process of reconciliation along the front line of the Cold War seem much more realistic. But as 1989 dawned the front line was still very much in place, a line composed of cement walls, barbed wire, and imposing military fortifications. By the end of the year this, too, would have changed. The Cold War system in Europe was about to end, with both a bang and a whimper.

The "Revolutions" of 1989

Since the creation of the Soviet bloc the states of eastern and central Europe had been simultaneously a vital pillar of Soviet security policy and a security problem in their own right. The Warsaw Pact, and particularly the twenty-division-strong Group of Soviet Forces in Germany, was the key to Soviet warfighting strategy in Europe. But the foundation of coercion upon which the pro-Soviet regimes in power rested and the demoralization created by an increasingly evident gap in well-being between East and West made the pact a source of chronic instability and crisis.

The decisive impetus for change came from within the region itself. After suffering the military crackdown of December 1981, the Polish opposition gradually reemerged, buoyed by nearly uniform popular support, tacit encouragement from the Catholic church, and the eventual decision of the Jaruzelski government to reopen the political spectrum with a policy of national reconciliation. The defeat of a government-sponsored referendum on economic reform on 29 November 1987 and a wave of bitterly contested strikes in the summer of 1988 made it clear that only a government with a broader popular base could hope successfully to impose necessary but painful economic austerity measures.

A breakthrough arrived in the spring of 1989 with the convening of a "roundtable" bringing together representatives of the government with opposition leaders to discuss the country's future. On 4 and 18 June 1989 legislative elections conducted according to a "semi-democratic" formula that guaranteed the Polish United Workers party a majority a priori nonetheless resulted in a debacle for the ruling party and called its ability to build a viable parliamentary majority into question. The impasse was broken in August by the appointment of a noncommunist government with the Catholic intellectual Tadeusz Mazowiecki as prime minister. The Mazowiecki government was a hybrid; the lower house of the national parliament, the presidency, and the interior and defense ministries remained under communist control. It was nonetheless the first noncommunist government in eastern Europe in over forty years.

A comparable process of halting reform went forward simultaneously in Hungary. In May 1988 a congress of the ruling Hungarian Socialist Worker's party (HSWP) cleared the way for change by ousting János Kádár, and in January 1989 the Hungarian parliament legalized the creation of opposition groups. In June a roundtable began to discuss the means for coordinating general elections. The HSWP's party congress on 6–9 October 1989 ended in a schism, with the reform communists led by Imre Pozsgay founding a new Hungarian Socialist party pledged to the values of "democracy, legality, and socialism."[54] At this point more than fifteen opposition groups had been registered and the stage was set for parliamentary elections.

By the autumn of 1989 the former east bloc was split into two camps. Gorbachev's Soviet Union, Poland, and Hungary were oriented toward reform, while Bulgaria, Czechoslovakia, the GDR, and Romania clung to established orthodoxies. With Moscow urging change, however, there could be little doubt about where the balance of power lay. The real configuration of forces became brutally clear when between October and December the remaining bastions of "really existing socialism" collapsed like a row of dominoes.

Communist reformers in Hungary set events to work during the summer with the decision to open their border, thereby permitting East German visitors to defect to the West without risk. By October a flood of refugees was the result, accompanied by mass demonstrations in Berlin, Leipzig, and other urban centers. The decision by the Socialist Unity party (SED) Politburo on 18 October to replace seventy-seven-year-old party boss Erich Honecker with his lieutenant Egon Krenz was a futile gesture. On 9 November the Krenz Politburo threw in the towel, agreeing to restructure the government and announcing that henceforward GDR citizens would have the unrestricted right to travel abroad. During the night of 9–10 November the Berlin Wall, quintessential symbol of

54. Cited from "Le congrès du PC mettra aux prises réformateurs radicaux et centristes," *Le Monde,* 7 Oct. 1989, p. 4.

the Cold War division of Europe, opened its gates to the euphoric residents of what had become a single city in celebration.

Almost unnoticed amidst the high drama set off by the collapse of the wall, on 10 November 1989 the Politburo of the Bulgarian Communist party divested Todor Zhivkov, after thirty-five years in power, of all his official functions. A new leadership headed by the former foreign minister Petŭr Mladenov promised thorough reform and convened yet another roundtable to prepare for free elections. Next in line was Czechoslovakia, where the dramatic events elsewhere in the region caused long-simmering resentments to overflow. Late October and November saw a crescendo of popular demonstrations in Prague. On 21 November the reformist Prime Minister Ladislaw Adamec agreed to meet formally with opposition leaders, and four days later party boss Miloš Jakeš and his entire Politburo resigned. Within days Alexander Dubček, still honored as the protagonist of reform in 1968, and the dramatist Václav Havel, symbol of resistance and imprisoned as a "dissident" only several months before, were carried in honor to the seat of government at Prague Castle.

Of the former people's democracies only Romania remained in place, but the days of its *conducator* ("supreme leader") Nicolae Ceauşescu were numbered. On 16 December, Romanian security forces intervened to repress demonstrations in the provincial capital of Timişoara, with some loss of life. The events that followed—Ceauşescu's televised loss of control over the crowd gathered to celebrate his "victory" over subversion, the appearance of a Front of National Salvation as an interim government following the dictator's arrest, the summary execution of Ceauşescu and his wife Elena after a mock trial on Christmas Day, and the establishment of the Front, led by former Interior Minister Ion Iliescu, in power after several days of sporadic fighting—have yet to be satisfactorily elucidated.[55] Their consequences, however, were immediately clear. Ceauşescu was gone, and Romania, too, committed to what promised to be a difficult transition to a new political order.

In the four months following the appointment of the noncommunist Mazowiecki government in Poland every pro-Soviet communist regime in eastern and central Europe had collapsed! The motive forces of what have been dubbed the "revolutions of 1989" will remain a subject of investigation for some time.[56] It is already possible to suggest, however,

55. Some of the misperceptions concerning events in Romania encouraged by irresponsible reporting are exposed in Michel Castex, *Un mensonge gros comme le siècle: Roumanie, histoire d'une manipulation* (Paris, 1990).
56. A summary and interpretation is provided by J. F. Brown, *Surge to Freedom: The End of Communist Rule in Eastern Europe* (Durham, N.C., 1991).

that far from having been caught by surprise and overtaken by events, Moscow actively encouraged and at critical junctures perhaps even provoked them.

A compelling case can be made that from Moscow's perspective the game of maintaining the eastern European security glacis inherited from the Cold War had ceased to be worth the candle. In this regard the Solidarity crisis and the INF controversy of the early 1980s may well have been cathartic. Though it did not in the end result in a Soviet intervention, the Polish crisis contained the possibility of such an outcome, with the most unforeseeable consequences. Nor had the dilemma of chronic instability inside the region been solved. The very existence of the bloc, and the military threat that it was presumed to embody, remained a pretext for the massive U.S. military presence in Europe.[57] In an age when control of a territorial buffer no longer brought invulnerability, when the primary military threat was represented by NATO's theater nuclear forces and state-of-the-art "emerging technologies" capable of carrying the battle to the east, and when war prevention rather than warfighting had become the foundation for Soviet military doctrine, it could convincingly be argued that the Warsaw Pact had become more of a liability than an asset.

The continued existence of the bloc could also be portrayed as a barrier to the progress of reform within the USSR. Gorbachev's domestic program, which by 1989 had begun to grapple with the problems of democratization and economic transition, was becoming incompatible with the continued existence of dependent satellite regimes embodying the very system that the Soviet Union was seeking to discard.[58] Eastern European communist leaders, blinded by arrogance and privilege, who forgot the degree to which their exercise of power rested upon Soviet support, did so at their own peril. The cynical remark concerning the implications of perestroika for the GDR made in 1987 by SED ideologue

57. The conclusion is drawn by Viacheslav Dashichev, "Vostok-Zapad: Poisk novykh otnoshenii. O prioritetakh vneshnei politiki sovetskogo gosudarstva," *Literaturnaia gazeta*, 18 May 1989, p. 14. Dashichev interprets the U.S. presence in western Europe as a dimension of an "anti-coalition" drawn together to resist the Soviet imperial presence in the east. "The military and political presence of the United States on the European continent," he notes, "has become a powerful, and long-lasting until our day, instrument of anti-Soviet policies."

58. The point is made by V. L. Musatov, "Vostochnaia Evropa: Vzgliad na peremeny," *Voprosy istorii KPSS* 11 (1990): 105–17, who describes the collapse of communism in eastern Europe as "the historically necessary consequence of the postwar development of this region, exposing the bankruptcy of the administrative-command model of socialism imposed upon it" (p. 108). V. K. Volkov, "Revoliutsionnye preobrazovaniia v stranakh Tsentral'noi i Iugo-vostochnoi Evropy," *Voprosy istorii* 6 (1990): 21–35, arrives at similar conclusions.

Kurt Hager that "just because the neighbor wallpapers his apartment, there is no reason for us to do so too" was a self-imposed death warrant.[59] The "neighbor" was in fact the proprietor, and more was in the works than a change of decor.

Not least, the bloc system could be represented as a barrier to Soviet access to the new Europe being constructed on the basis of the European Community (EC) Single European Act. Maintaining its Warsaw Pact allies had long since become an economic burden for the USSR, and the CMEA was moribund.[60] The logic of division embodied in the bloc system worked at cross-purposes to Gorbachev's project for drawing the USSR closer to the European and world economy; it saddled Moscow with costly and recalcitrant "fraternal allies"; and it threatened to cause the Soviets to miss the boat at a vital juncture of European history. In sum, though the Cold War system in Europe may have suited the bipolar vision of competitive coexistence, in the age of mutual security it had become an anachronism.[61]

Far from being shocked by the fall of the "iron curtain," Soviet leaders repeatedly invoked the event. In January 1989, greeting the opening of the new CFE talks in Vienna, Foreign Minister Shevardnadze remarked that progress toward disarmament "has shaken the iron curtain, weakened its rusting foundation, pierced new openings, accelerated its corrosion."[62] Speaking in Strasbourg on 6 July 1989, Gorbachev remarked that the common European home "excludes all possibility of armed confrontation, all possibility of resorting to the threat or use of force, and notably military force employed by one alliance against another, within an alliance, or whatever it might be."[63] A more straightforward repudiation of the Brezhnev Doctrine could scarcely be imagined, and the message, conveyed to eastern European reformers through both formal and informal channels, would not be missed.

At every critical juncture during the breakdowns culminating in changes of regime the Soviet Union acted (or refrained from acting) in

59. Cited from an interview in *Stern* magazine in Bundespressamt, *DDR-Spiegel* 69 (9 April 1987): 20–23.

60. Valerie Bunce, "The Empire Strikes Back: The Evolution of the Eastern Bloc from a Soviet Asset to a Soviet Liability," *International Organization* 1 (Winter 1985): 1–46; for a good evaluation of the CMEA's dilemmas, Laszlo Csaba, "CMEA and the Challenge of the 1980s," *Soviet Studies* 2 (April 1989): 266–89.

61. An interesting perspective to this effect, written in April 1989 by Viacheslav Dashichev with reference to the case of East Germany, appears as "Enormer Schaden für Moskau," *Der Spiegel* 6 (5 Feb. 1990): 142–58.

62. "K novym masshtabam i kachestvu obshcheevropeiskogo dialoga," *Pravda*, 20 Jan. 1989, p. 5.

63. Cited from "Obshcheevropeiskii protsess idet vpered," *Pravda*, 7 July 1989, p. 2.

order to accelerate change. The choice for free elections in Poland and Hungary was made with muted Soviet encouragement. During the days preceding Honecker's fall in the GDR Soviet forces are reported to have refused to engage themselves against demonstrators, and Egon Krenz flew to Moscow for consultation one week prior to the decision to open the wall. Gorbachev is likewise rumored to have met with Bulgaria's Mladenov in a Soviet airport in late October during an unprogrammed transit stopover, and the role of the Soviet embassy in the coup that overturned Zhivkov remains to be clarified. Ceauşescu's fall was preceded on 17 November by a mocking editorial in *Izvestiia,* and the involvement of Soviet security forces in the plot to topple the dictator is a distinct possibility.[64]

The collapse of the communist regimes of eastern and central Europe was not "made in Moscow," but it was at least encouraged by Moscow. Once Soviet support was unmistakably withdrawn, the regimes in power, overnight, became too weak to sustain themselves. The old order collapsed like a house of cards, voluntarily bowing to the inevitable in Poland and Hungary, surrendering in the face of determined popular resistance in the GDR and Czechoslovakia, and disappearing as the result of a palace coup, peacefully in Bulgaria and with marginal violence in Romania. The role of communist reformers close to Gorbachev in preparing the ground for the transition, such as Poland's Mieczyslaw Rakowski, Hungary's Imre Pozsgay, the GDR's Hans Modrow, Czechoslovakia's Ladislaw Adamec, Bulgaria's Mladenov, and Romania's Ion Iliescu, was critical in every case. The "revolutions" imploded the region's discredited Communist parties, but they did not really resolve the question of long-term socioeconomic orientation. Establishing stable democratic institutions, finding new social equilibriums, and managing a myriad of accumulated problems promised to leave plenty of space for political confrontations, and for the foreseeable future.

In opting to abandon its former allies, Moscow must have concluded that the transition could be managed without provoking uncontrollable instability. This was a calculated risk. The depth of anti-Soviet feeling within the region provided fertile ground for extremism, and forty years of *pax Sovietica* had done little to heal its many indigenous rivalries. Not least, the demonstration effect of people in the streets sweeping away hated dictatorships overnight promised to complicate the gradual and controlled reform program that Gorbachev was crafting for the USSR. After vain attempts to slow down the course of events, the Soviet leadership bowed to the inevitable and agreed to accept the unification of

64. V. Volodin, "Svetlye perspektivy, bol'shie zadachi," *Izvestiia,* 17 Nov. 1989, p. 5.

Germany within NATO. The disbanding of the Warsaw Pact in May 1991 was a logical, though probably regretted, consequence. These events were disturbing to traditionally minded forces in the national security establishment, but they did not conflict with the reformist thrust of Moscow's new European policy. The key task was no longer preparation for an impossible war, but rather the attempt to integrate the Soviet Union more closely with Europe's "common home."

The disappearance of the people's democracies made the need to consider alternative images of European security more urgent than ever before. The Cold War system and the entire postwar order were gone, even if their institutional relics for the time being remained in place. The Gorbachev leadership was not reticent about articulating its own project: a renewed commitment to disarmament and denuclearization, expanded economic cooperation on a European scale, and an enlarged and institutionalized security function for the CSCE. Should even an approximation of such an outcome have been achieved, the Soviet Union would have drawn closer to several "classic" national security goals: an inevitably reduced role for the United States in Europe, a reduction of the military threat posed by NATO, and an opening to the West's economic dynamism and prosperity. In a game played for high stakes the "sacrifice" of eastern and central Europe might well have appeared to have been a fair wager.

Asia and the Third World

For all of its traumas, Europe has become a zone of relative stability where the eruption of interstate war on the scale of the past is virtually unthinkable. Asia and the Third World, by way of contrast, remain torn by murderous rivalries that show no sign of abating. With a territory that abuts upon the Middle East, Central Asia, and the Far East, and with security interests that overlap with the politics of each of these regions, the USSR was not in a position to ignore these conflicts.

Gorbachev outlined his agenda for Asia in a major speech delivered in Vladivostok on 28 July 1986. Noting that the majority of Soviet territory lies in Asia and that Moscow intended to be fully engaged in the "renaissance of world history" occurring along the Pacific rim, Gorbachev asserted an ambitious program for Siberian development and for Soviet involvement in the Asian-Pacific region.[65] Compared with the caution that had characterized the Soviet approach to Asia in the past, the Vladivostok address was a significant departure.

65. Gorbachev, *Izbrannye rechi*, 4:9–34.

The most serious of the Soviet Union's Asian dilemmas was its rivalry with the PRC, which had driven Beijing toward a form of security cooperation with the West during the 1970s and created a military stand-off along the Sino-Soviet frontier. American engagement in the Asian-Pacific region, including close security cooperation with Japan and wide-ranging military deployments, represented another complex of problems. The Afghanistan imbroglio, where Soviet soldiers were dying to no clear purpose in a costly and unpopular war, was a foreign policy disaster of the first order. Despite the steady expansion of the Pacific fleet during the 1970s, Soviet allies in the region were relatively few, and those states that might be considered friendly (India, Vietnam, Kampuchea, Laos, North Korea, Mongolia, and Afghanistan) were often unstable or unreliable. The Kampuchean conflict pitted the Soviets' regional allies against western- and Chinese-backed rivals in what had long since become an exercise in futility, and the division of Korea mirrored the division of Germany with even less historical or cultural logic. The Cold War system in Asia appeared to be alive and well.

The Soviets' first priority was normalizing relations with the PRC. The honeymoon of the late 1970s between China and the West had begun to sour after the CCP's 12th party congress in 1982, as the Chinese struggled with the social consequences of their reforms. A gradual improvement in Sino-Soviet relations was already under way when Gorbachev came to office, but it was impeded by what Beijing called the "three obstacles": the large Soviet troop presence on the Chinese border and in Mongolia, the Vietnamese occupation of Kampuchea, and the Soviet expeditionary force in Afghanistan.[66]

Gorbachev's Vladivostok speech contained a number of gestures toward China. Asserting the "shared values" that bound together the world's two largest socialist states, the general secretary praised the Chinese modernization program and proffered Soviet support. More concretely, he pledged an eventual withdrawal of the majority of Soviet forces from Mongolia, announced the immediate pullout of six Soviet combat regiments from Afghanistan, and suggested that the Amur-Ussuri River thalweg (rather than the Chinese shore, as Moscow had heretofore demanded) could be acknowledged as the border demarcation line, thus eliminating at a stroke a long-standing point of contention. The INF treaty in December 1987 included an important concession to Asia with the pledge to liquidate all SS-20s stationed east of the Urals, and the conventional force reductions announced in December 1988 called for the

---

66. George Segal, *Sino-Soviet Relations after Mao*, Adelphi Paper no. 202 (London, Autumn 1985), provides a portrait of Sino-Soviet relations at the time of Gorbachev's arrival in office.

elimination of more than 200,000 soldiers from Asian military districts. Moscow also pressured its Vietnamese ally to adopt a more flexible attitude toward the Kampuchean problem, and on 26 September 1989 Hanoi completed the withdrawal of its combat forces from Kampuchea.

Most dramatically, Gorbachev cut the Gordian knot in Afghanistan by committing the USSR to negotiate the elimination of its military contingent. Talks opened under U.N. auspices in Geneva on 25 February 1987, and by April 1988 they had produced an agreement that required a complete Soviet pullout over the next nine months.[67] The commitment was carried out to the letter, with the last Soviet troops marching across the frontier on 15 February 1989. Contrary to widespread expectation, the withdrawal did not provoke the collapse of the pro-Soviet government of President Najibullah in Kabul, and Afghanistan's civil war went on. The achievement was substantial all the same. Gorbachev's ability to put the Afghan episode behind him and to close what had become a bleeding wound for Soviet foreign policy without submitting to a humiliating defeat spoke highly of his diplomatic skill.

Sino-Soviet relations also improved. By 1988 both sides were committed to their own specific variants of reform: commercial relations, including experiments with open-trading regimes along the common border, were developing positively; both had signed a nuclear no-first-use pledge and supported the 1985 Rarotonga treaty calling for the denuclearization of the South Pacific; and both shared a common position on the Taiwan question. On 13 October 1988 Deng Xiaoping, much of whose political career had been built around resistance to Soviet "hegemonism," announced that a Sino-Soviet summit was scheduled for the coming spring. Gorbachev arrived in Beijing for four days of encounters on 15 May 1989. After thirty years of nearly unbroken hostility the Sino-Soviet schism seemed on the way to being healed.

Gorbachev's sojourn in Beijing was lent an air of unreality by the huge prodemocracy demonstrations unfolding simultaneously on Tienanmen Square. The turmoil disrupted the diplomatic agenda, but it did not prevent the larger purposes of the visit from being accomplished. The Soviet delegation sought to ignore the Chinese drama to the degree possible. After a cordial personal encounter Deng and Gorbachev announced the normalization of Sino-Soviet relations, and in a joint declaration the two sides renounced aspirations to hegemony in Asia and expressed the desire to continue border negotiations.[68] Although no substantial agreements

67. Rosanne Klass, "Afghanistan: The Accords," *Foreign Affairs* 5 (Summer 1988): 922–45, gives the texts of the accords as well as a skeptical appraisal.

68. Stephen M. Goldstein, "Diplomacy Amid Protest: The Sino-Soviet Summit," *Problems of Communism* 5 (Sept.–Oct. 1989): 49–71.

were concluded, the symbolic importance of the meetings was great. Of course, not all problems had been resolved. China's effort to regularize relations with the USSR did not mean an abandonment of ties to the West.[69] Beijing's support for the Khmers Rouges faction in Kampuchea was by 1989 the single greatest obstacle to the negotiated settlement that Moscow very much desired. Most of all, China's unrealized potential and independent geostrategic orientation remained long-term security dilemmas for the USSR. After May 1989, however, they were much less pressing dilemmas than during the previous decades of unbridled rivalry.

The Soviet Union's second major security problem in the Far East was Japan, whose expanding economic and military potential remained attached to a rigorously anti-Soviet international orientation. In December 1986 Japan's military budget temporarily crept above the constitutionally defined limit of 1 percent of GNP, prompting Gorbachev to comment upon "the stubborn buildup of [Japanese] military potential within the framework of 'burden sharing' with the United States."[70] Japan's security link to the United States was an important foundation for a polity of global containment directed against the USSR, and a legitimate subject of Soviet concern.[71]

In search of accommodation with the its wealthy and powerful Asian neighbor, the Gorbachev team offered a series of positive gestures.[72] Soviet military forces stationed in the region were reduced, and in May 1986 Moscow appointed a new ambassador to Tokyo who was described by one Japanese newspaper as "the most pro-Japanese in the entire Soviet foreign ministry."[73] Diplomatic exchanges brought Foreign Minister Shevardnadze to Tokyo in January 1986 and December 1988, and Gorbachev's advisor Aleksandr Iakovlev in November 1989. The culmination of these feelers was the state visit by Gorbachev himself on 16–19 April 1991, the first appearance ever by a Soviet head of state in

69. See Michel Chossudovsky, "L'alliance militaire Washington–Pékin ne faiblit pas," *Le monde diplomatique* 443 (April 1990): 7.

70. Cited from Gorbachev's address at Krasnoiarsk on 17 Sept. 1988 in Gorbachev, *Izbrannye rechi*, 6:559.

71. See Gregory P. Corning, "U.S.-Japan Security Cooperation in the 1990s," *Asian Survey* 3 (1989): 268–86; Kenneth Hunt, "Japan's Security Policy," *Survival* 3 (May–June 1989): 201–7; Paul D. Scott, "The New Power of Japan," *Pacific Review* 3 (1989): 181–88.

72. Mikhail G. Nossov, "The USSR and the Security of the Asia-Pacific Region: From Vladivostok to Krasnoyarsk," *Asian Survey* 3 (March 1989): 262–67; Masahiko Asada, "Revived Soviet Interest in Asia: A New Approach," in Langdon and Ross, *Superpower Maritime Strategy in the Pacific*, pp. 41–43; Hiroshi Kimura, "Gorbachev's 'New Thinking' and the Asian-Pacific Region," in Peter Juvilier and Hiroshi Kimura, eds., *Gorbachev's Reforms: U.S. and Japanese Assessments* (New York, 1988), pp. 149–70.

73. Cited by Rajan Menon, "New Thinking and Northeast Asian Security," *Problems of Communism* 2–3 (March–June 1989): 8. The individual in question is ambassador Nikolai Solov'ev.

Japan. Talks with Japanese Prime Minister Toshiki Kaifu proved to be difficult. Although it is in some ways a contrived issue that is amenable to a variety of negotiated arrangements, the Kuril problem continued to defy diplomatic resolution.[74] Tokyo made clear its skepticism toward Soviet projects for a new Asian security order and refused to commit itself to a substantial economic aid program. Twelve modest accords regulating commercial exchange were signed nonetheless, a joint communiqué noted a commitment to work on resolving outstanding differences, and the spirit of the exchanges was positive. By expanding areas of dialogue, the visit kept alive Soviet hopes that a consistent policy of gradual rapprochement might eventually bear fruit.

Gorbachev's image of a "new Asian-Pacific security order" was often accompanied by references to the Helsinki process in Europe. Movement toward a collective security order in Asia is considerably less advanced than in Europe, but Moscow offered a number of practical proposals to further the process. These included calls for the phasing out of all foreign military bases, proposals for conventional arms reductions, suggested limitations upon the deployment of sea-launched cruise missiles, and support for the creation of nuclear free zones in the South Pacific, Southeast Asia, the Korean peninsula, and elsewhere.[75] Various confidence-building measures were likewise proposed, including limits on the size of military exercises, increased access for foreign observers, and more effective verification procedures.[76] Such suggestions will eventually stand or fall on their individual merits, but cumulatively they made clear that the search for expanded cooperation had become a foundation for Soviet Asian policy. Controlled demilitarization, a rapprochement with key regional actors on both sides of the ideological divide (including Australia, South Korea, and the ASEAN [Association of South-East Asian Nations] group as well as the PRC and Japan), and advances toward significant multilateral regional forums such as the Asian Development Bank and the Pacific Cooperation Conference pointed toward significantly changed priorities.[77]

74. For Soviet perspectives on the Kuril problem see B. N. Slavinskii, "Na puti k sovetsko-iaponskomu mirnomu dogovoru," *Problemy Dal'nego Vostoka* 3 (1989): 132–45; E. Prokhorov and L. Shevchuk, "O territorial'nykh pretenziiakh Iaponii k SSSR," *Mezhdunarodnaia zhizn'* 1 (Jan. 1989): 47–52.

75. Gorbachev's Krasnoiarsk address outlined a seven-point program embodying these proposals. Gorbachev, *Izbrannye rechi*, 6:540–64. See also Henry Trofimenko, "Long-term Trends in the Asia-Pacific Region: A Soviet Evaluation," *Asian Survey* 3 (March 1989): 237–51.

76. Trevor Findlay, "North Pacific Confidence-Building: The Helsinki-Stockholm Model," in Langdon and Ross, *Superpower Maritime Strategy in the Pacific*, pp. 72–88.

77. For a good summary of the new Soviet orientation see M. S. Kapitsa, "Novoe myshlenie i mezhdunarodnye otnosheniia v ATR," *Narody Azii i Afriki* 3 (1990): 3–9.

The need to pursue diplomatic solutions to Third World conflicts became another leading theme of Soviet new thinking.[78] In the Middle East, Afghanistan, Indochina, southern Africa, and Central America, U.N. or regionally sponsored peace plans received active Soviet support. Although the embittered confrontations born during the era of the "Reagan doctrine" continued to claim victims, varying degrees of progress toward negotiated settlements were achieved. Perestroika dictated a significant Soviet disengagement from the Third World, an area once regarded by many on both sides as the critical front where the outcome of the Cold War would eventually be decided. Already under Brezhnev, Soviet academic analysis had begun to express pessimism concerning the prospects for autonomous revolutionary development under Third World conditions and to question the USSR's capacity meaningfully to assist such development.[79] In the Gorbachev period Moscow sought to reduce its financial commitments, distanced itself from the call for revolutionary change, became more selective in the support accorded to Third World causes in the United Nations, and pressured its Third World allies toward various kinds of concessions and reforms.

Had Gorbachev "abandoned" the Third World by giving priority to the quest for a cooperative relationship with the West?[80] However one chooses to assign responsibility, there is little doubt that the Third World did become a primary victim of Soviet reform, deprived of the ability to play off the superpowers against each other and consigned to what one commentator described with brutal frankness as "the dark seas of competition and struggle on an international scale, amidst the crises associated with the first phase of becoming subjects of the capitalist world, struggling for the right to exist."[81] The assumption that exacerbated

78. For examples of an extensive literature see A. Kislov, "Novoe politicheskoe myshlenie i regional'nye konflikty," *Mirovaia ekonomika i mezhdunarodnye otnosheniia* 8 (1988): 39–47; V. P. Sudarev, "Regional'nye konflikty: Problemy razblokirovaniia," *Latinskaia Amerika* 1 (1989): 6–18; E. Primakov, "Sovetskaia politika v regional'nykh konfliktakh," *Mezhdunarodnaia zhizn'* 5 (May 1989): 3–9.

79. See Galia Golan, *The Soviet Union and National Liberation Movements in the Third World* (Boston, 1988), pp. 96–154; Jerry F. Hough, *The Struggle for the Third World: Soviet Debates and American Options* (Washington, D.C., 1986); Elizabeth Valkenier, *The Soviet Union and the Third World: An Economic Bind* (New York, 1983). A key Soviet work is N. A. Simoniia, *Strany Vostoka: Puti razvitiia* (Moscow, 1975).

80. The problem is posed by Fred Halliday, *Cold War, Third World: An Essay on US-Soviet Relations* (London, 1989), pp. 112–18.

81. V. Sakharov, "'Sotsialisticheskaia orientatsiia' na slovakh i na dele," *Aziia i Afrika segodnia* 1 (1990): 17. The concept of "socialist orientation" was also critically reevaluated. See A. Kiva, "Razvivaiushchiesia strany, sotsializm, kapitalizm," *Mezhdunarodnaia zhizn'* 2 (Feb. 1989): 57–67; V. Maksimenko, "Sotsialisticheskaia orientatsiia: Perestroika predstavlenii," *Mirovaia ekonomika i mezhdunarodnye otnosheniia* 2 (1989): 93–103.

East-West conflict was somehow a positive spur to Third World development is at any rate quite specious. Nor had Moscow entirely lost sight of its own priorities. In the spirit of mutual security a new emphasis was placed upon political rather than military instruments as tools of influence. Dependency relationships with radical "garrision" states were downplayed in favor of more conventional relations with significant regional actors regardless of their real or professed ideological coloration. Pragmatic economic policies were recommended in place of flawed models of "noncapitalist" development. And a particular importance was attached to the cultivation of a positive relationship with the United States as a foundation for conflict management.[82] On balance, however, it is clear that, compared with the policies of Khrushchev and Brezhnev, Gorbachev's approach to the Third World was singularly unambitious. In a period of transition attended by considerable domestic unrest, an assertive Third World policy had become entirely too risky to justify.

Beyond the Cold War

The foundation of Gorbachev's foreign policy was an effort to transform the nature of Soviet-American relations. Perestroika posed a special challenge for American leaders, whose worldviews were often structured around the presumed centrality of a Soviet threat, and elite opinion in the United States concerning Gorbachev proved to be extremely volatile. Prior to 1985 the majority of specialists argued that a substantial reform in Soviet-type systems was impossible. For a time Gorbachev was dismissed as the purveyor of a "charm offensive" designed to delude the West and garner unilateral concessions. When the evidence of far-reaching reform became undeniable, the emphasis was shifted to Gorbachev's vulnerability and the likelihood that perestroika would eventually wreck upon the contradictions to which it was giving rise. It soon became incontrovertibly clear, however, that regardless of how one interpreted Gorbachev's intentions, perestroika was imposing a change of agenda that Washington was obliged to take seriously.

Reagan's visit to Moscow in May 1988 and Gorbachev's brief sojourn in New York during December of that year culminated a remarkable series of five summits in the space of three years. As a consequence of these sessions the momentum of the "new Cold War" was almost entirely reversed. The new U.S. administration of President George Bush came to

82. See R. Craig Nation, *Conflict Reduction in Regional Conflicts: Restructuring Soviet-American Relations in the Third World* (Bologna, 1990).

office with the conviction that in his haste to make history Reagan had allowed the Soviets to dominate the diplomatic agenda to their advantage, and it sought to slow down the pace of change by conducting an extended policy review. In view of the insistent pressures emerging from Moscow, however, a policy of inaction was impossible to maintain. In December 1989, with the world still vibrating from the opening of the Berlin Wall, Bush and Gorbachev met on the island of Malta in a "presummit" and in a joint declaration solemnly announced, "The Cold War is over."[83]

Some analysts perceived the new emphasis in Soviet policy upon Europe and Japan as the sign of a "multilateral" approach that sought to downplay the importance of the U.S.-Soviet axis, but the centrality of the superpower relationship was never lost upon Moscow.[84] A central goal of perestroika became to replace the confrontational relationship born of competitive coexistence with a more balanced one taking into account common interests as well as differences, and to "win over" Washington to the cause of Soviet reform. The Soviet-American relationship, it was asserted, should not be perceived as "zero sum." Both parties had divergent and conflicting interests but also parallel interests that offered a basis for cooperation. These interests included the goals of maintaining peace, managing potentially explosive regional conflicts, reducing the burden of military spending, and developing mutually beneficial economic ties. In order to forward their mutual concerns, the superpowers were urged to restructure their relationship in the spirit of security cooperation, built upon the identification of a balance of interests and coordinated efforts to master common problems.[85]

The most substantial progress came in the domain of arms control. Though it was an impressive achievement, the INF accord concerned peripheral weapons systems that both sides could eliminate without affecting their overall force structures. After the Malta summit the ground was cleared for more ambitious negotiations concerning chemical, conventional, and nuclear arms. Agreements or mutual understandings were achieved in all these fields, though their implications remain unclear

83. "Zaiavlenie M. S. Gorbacheva i Dzh. Busha," *Pravda*, 4 Dec. 1989, p. 1. The same conclusion was written into the "Declaration of Paris" promulgated by the second CSCE summit in Paris on 21 Nov. 1990. See "La Charte de Paris pour une nouvelle Europe," *Le Monde*, 23 Nov. 1990, p. 4.

84. The notion of a multipolar policy is developed in Hough, *Russia and the West*, pp. 216–38.

85. S. M. Rogov, *Sovetskii Soiuz i SShA: Poisk balansa interesov* (Moscow, 1989), pp. 259–324; V. Udalov, "Balans sil i balans interesov," *Mezhdunarodnaia zhizn'* 5 (1990): 16–25.

because of political turmoil within the former USSR. It is obvious all the same that the arms control process as conducted by Gorbachev succeeded in moving the former Cold War rivals toward a qualitatively different kind of military relationship.

The least complex of the arms-control forums was that concerned with chemical arms; from the perspective of both superpowers the production and stockpiling of large numbers of such weapons had become anachronistic.[86] The START treaty, signed in the Kremlin by Bush and Gorbachev on 31 July 1991 and aimed at achieving deep cuts in strategic nuclear arsenals, and the CFE-I treaty, negotiated during 1990 and 1991 in Vienna, aspired to more complex goals. One of the most striking aspects of the entire arms control agenda became the virtual disappearance of the SDI issue. Although it remained an unsolved problem, SDI was no longer considered to be a significant barrier to progress in other domains.

After only twenty months of deliberations the CFE-I negotiators produced a formal treaty, which was signed in Paris by twenty-two countries including the United States and the USSR on 19 November 1991.[87] The keys to the achievement included Moscow's willingness to include Soviet territory west of the Urals in the scope of the treaty and to accept highly asymmetrical reductions calculated at about 68 percent for the Soviet Union compared with 12 percent for NATO. The accord limits both personnel and military equipment, includes a "sufficiency rule" that places further constraints upon the USSR by forbidding any individual country from maintaining disproportionately large forces, and makes provisions for a Joint Consultative Group to monitor compliance.

There is also much that the CFE-I treaty does not do. Even with its provisions in effect, Europe will remain the most militarized region in world politics. No important restrictions on the modernization of conventional arms are included, and the size of military exercises is not constrained. What is more, the entire CFE agenda has to some extent been overtaken by the regime changes in eastern Europe during 1989 and by the breakdown of the Soviet Union. With or without CFE, Moscow is committed to withdrawing its armed forces from central Europe. Present plans call for the pursuit of negotiations in the context of CFE-IA and CFE-II follow-ups, eventually to expand to a pan-European format

86. For a succinct outline of the Soviet position see Shevardnadze's address to the January 1989 Paris conference on the problem of chemical arms, "Navsegda pokonchit' s khimicheskim oruzhiem," *Pravda*, 9 Jan. 1989, pp. 1 and 5.

87. For the text of the treaty and an analysis of its terms see the special supplement "Treaty on Conventional Armed Forces in Europe: Analysis, Summary, Text," in *Arms Control Today* 1 (Jan./Feb. 1991).

under the auspices of the CSCE. An ongoing arms reduction process on the basis of the CFE treaty is considered to be a necessary foundation for a new European security order, but the shape that this process will take will importantly depend upon the decisions concerning military priorities made by the leaders who will eventually inherit authority over the territory of the former USSR.

START's announced goal was a 50 percent reduction in strategic arms, with each side to build down to a force of no more than 1,600 launchers and 6,000 "accountable" warheads, including a sublimit of 4,900 on the aggregate number of ICBM and SLBM warheads (intended to restrain the Soviet "heavy" missile category). The real extent of the reductions defined by the accord is considerably more modest in view of the complicated counting rules applied at American insistence that "discount" bombers transporting gravity bombs and short-range attack missiles. It is estimated that reductions of 50 percent on paper will amount to cutbacks of about 30 percent or less on the gound.[88]

Perhaps more important than quantitative reductions is the restructuring of arsenals that the START accord should enforce. The seven-year period allotted for the START build down coincided with the scheduled deployment of a fifth generation of Soviet strategic forces including the rail-mobile, MIRVed SS-24 (although Moscow announced that it did not intend to add to the thirty-six SS-24s already deployed) and the road-mobile, single-warhead SS-25. According to the Soviet deployment schedule, more than one-third of the arsenal could be mobile in 1995, as opposed to 10 percent at present. The new emphasis upon mobile forces was in part a response to U.S. "counterforce" programs such as the MX and D-5 missiles, and an attempt to overcome the "use them or lose them" syndrome that had led Soviet strategic planning toward the dangerous options of preemption and launch under attack in the past, but it also corresponded to the new spirit of the strategic regime defined by START. For both sides the START treaty demands smaller, more stable, and more survivable strategic triads. Even assuming that the United States will continue to place relatively more emphasis upon sea- and air-launched systems, and Moscow more emphasis upon the ICBM, according to the terms of the treaty the gap between the configurations of the rival arsenals will grow smaller. START's fundamental goal is to raise the costs of preemptive counterforce strategies and to encourage an emphasis upon survivability and retaliation. Despite the rhetoric of Soviet new thinking, therefore, the logic of deterrence is reinforced. Indeed, given the extent of Gorbachev's verbal challenge to conventional

88. Jack Mendelsohn, "Why START?" *Arms Control Today* 3 (April 1991): 3–9.

strategic thought, the START treaty, which culminated his arms-control agenda, was cautious to an extreme.

Even if imperfect, the CFE and START treaties represented real achievements and paved the way for further advances. Perhaps most significantly, their verification was programmed to require the coordinated efforts of thousands of inspectors, an exchange of data that will provide each side with an unprecedentedly complete portrait of the rival's military means, and extensive confidence-building and stabilization measures. The verification regime that is an integral part of the accords will be a functioning model for security cooperation of a very practical kind. Whatever the outcome of the political battles under way in Moscow, the START treaty provides an element of stability in a time of chaotic change that all parties have a vested interest in preserving.

The challenge to the traditional prerogatives of the Soviet military-industrial complex implicit in Gorbachev's ambitious program for security cooperation with the United States may have been the single most important factor that pushed his conservative opponents toward the desperate attempt to seize power in August 1991. The U.S. invasion of Panama during December 1989 demonstrated that the strictures of Soviet new thinking carried little weight when Washington perceived its own interests to be at stake, and it gave rise to a certain amount of opposition to a policy of security cooperation within the Kremlin.[89] The Gulf War during January–March 1991 was a more severe test. Gorbachev unambiguously supported the U.N. coalition's policy of using armed force to expel the Iraqis from Kuwait, but he also persisted, to Washington's annoyance, in urging a negotiated solution right up to the eve of the final assault. These futile gestures only served to reveal how limited Moscow's influence over events had become. Soviet policy during the conflict gave rise to a pointed debate, during which conservative opposition to an overly subservient posture toward the United States was strongly articulated.[90] In the end, the U.S-Soviet relationship weathered the storm and even emerged strengthened from a Third World crisis in which,

89. See the comment by Iu. Subbotin, "Po dvoinomu standarta," *Sovetskaia Rossiia*, 3 Jan. 1990, p. 5.

90. Stanislav Kondrashov, "Boinia v pustyne," *Izvestiia*, 14 Feb. 1991, p. 5, charged that the war "is not a 'desert storm' but a desert massacre . . . and we are on the side of the assassins," while V. Beliakov, "Muchitel'nye voprosy," *Pravda*, 25 Feb. 1991, p. 6, described the operation as "morally identical" to America's "dirty war" in Vietnam. E. Gudkov, "Te li garantii?" *Krasnaia zvezda*, 20 Feb. 1991, p. 5, argued that the conflict made clear the United States' readiness "to employ any means, including military means, in the pursuit and consolidation of its interests." Criticisms such as these were probably influential in motivating the surprise resignation of Soviet Foreign Minister Shevardnadze in the midst of the Gulf crisis during December 1990.

almost uniquely in the postwar period, both superpowers were aligned on the same side. But the feeling of betrayal that emerged on the right-wing of the Soviet political spectrum during the crisis was an ill omen.

Gorbachev made rapprochement with the United States the keystone of an ambitious program for international pacification. Political recon-ciliation, intensified dialogue, and positive cooperation in helping to re-solve "hot spots" of international confrontation were the elements of what was posed as a new global collective security system inspired by the visionary tenets of new thinking, with the United Nations as its central forum and the U.S.-Soviet axis as its underlying support. The need for such a rapprochement, it could be argued, was determined by long-term historical trends. The Cold War was originally a function of a particular configuration of power, a bipolar world order characterized by intense ideological rivalry and highly militarized geostrategic competition. Its foundations had been sapped not only by the crisis of Soviet power to which perestroika was a response, but by changes in the nature of inter-national society. The reality of increased interdependence, the relative decline of the United States as an economic force, the emergence of real multipolarity among the world's leading nations, and the crisis of de-velopment transforming much of the Third World into a tinderbox of latent conflicts made the Cold War system, and the military confronta-tion that was its essence, increasingly irrelevant.

What Soviet reformers seem to have underestimated was the depth of the crisis that had matured within the Soviet Union itself. Gorbachev's program was conceived as a means for reinvigorating the Soviet super-power by recasting its policies on a new, more positive foundation. The implosion of the Soviet Union under the strain of reform has brought an end to such hopes, and makes images of East-West cooperation as a foundation for a more viable international security regime seem unreal-istic. Whether the consequences of the crisis into which the Soviet fed-eration has now entered will eventually culminate in more viable international security arrangements is likely to remain an open question for some time to come.

The Crisis of Perestroika

Perestroika emerged from the perception that the greatest threat to the Soviet Union's security was of its own making. Although the fear of an imminent external threat that haunted Soviet power since its in-ception had lost much of its force, the "pre-crisis" situation inherited from Brezhnev was understood to contain the seeds of disaster. After a generation of stagnation the Soviet leadership contemplated a secular decline in economic performance, a widening technology gap, increasing demoralization among the population at large, and a foreign policy primed for confrontation. Without a thorough domestic renewal, it was concluded, the Soviet Union's stature in the community of nations would inexorably decline. For a regime whose entire international existence had been shaped by the primacy of external threats, perestroika demanded a kind of Copernican revolution in understanding.

The leading themes of Gorbachev's project may be characterized as democratization, economic restructuring, demilitarization, and socialist renewal. The basis for democratization was *glasnost'*, a progressive broadening of freedom of expression that eliminated the sterile and fear-ridden public discourse of the Brezhnev period in favor of a vibrant and conflictual political debate. Institutional reform proceeded chaotically, but the various innovations that were attempted, including the creation of a new Congress of People's Deputies and autonomous parliamentary forums on the republic level that quickly became important centers of contestation, the progress toward the negotiation of a union treaty intended to place relations between republics on a new foundation, and the measures to reduce the political and social role of the Communist party all aimed at a greater degree of authentic pluralism. By 1990 the goal of radical economic reform had moved onto the policy agenda despite strong disagreements over the shape that such reforms should take. Demilitarization was an essential theme of new thinking, and attempts to move forward with arms cutbacks and defense industry conversion were accompanied by a significant reduction in Soviet military spending.[91] The renewal of socialism was perhaps the least viable of Gorbachev's aspirations, but it remained a goal to which his leadership was committed for a variety of reasons. First, because the political generation that Gorbachev represented, successful products of the Soviet system but horrified by the abuses of Stalinism and the implications of Brezhnev-era stagnation, no doubt retained some personal allegiance to socialist ideals. Second, because the Soviet Union's identity as a socialist state, however broadly defined, was still considered to be too important a source of legitimacy and cohesion to sacrifice. And third, because the conservative wing of the political establishment, still a force to be reckoned with,

---

91. On 30 May 1989 Gorbachev announced a figure for Soviet defense spending that was considerably higher than anything admitted by the Soviets in the past. See "Ob osnovnykh napravleniiakh vnutrennei i vneshnei politiki SSSR," *Krasnaia zvezda*, 31 May 1989, p. 2. Cuts of 14% in the defense budget and of 19.5% in the production of armaments were targeted for 1990–91.

continued to make allegiance to "socialism" a last line of defense for tra-ditional Soviet values.[92]

The attempt to revitalize the Soviet economy was always perestroika's first priority.[93] An efficient, technologically sophisticated economy was considered to be an essential prerequisite for security in an inter-dependent world order in which the logic of confrontation between antagonistic systems no longer dominated. Economic reform also became Gorbachev's greatest challenge. Perestroika was probably launched upon the assumption that after a brief period of adjustment the energies unleashed by reform would lead to a rapid economic ame-lioration. Instead, an accumulation of errors and false starts, accentuated by disagreements over policy options, the inherent difficulty of disman-tling the administrative-command system, active and passive resistance to change, and the loss of control promoted by national separatism, led to a major economic crisis.[94] Popular frustrations fueled by poor eco-nomic performance undermined Gorbachev's personal popularity and fed the flames of separatism and political confrontation.

In almost every way perestroika proved to be strong medicine. By seek-ing to preempt a gathering crisis of Soviet power it precipitated one of its own, a crisis of order for which there could be no easy solution. *Glasnost'* and institutional reforms began to create an authentic Soviet political culture reflected in a diversity of movements and viewpoints, but they did not succeed in imposing new equilibriums. Indecision and misjudgment pushed the economy into free fall, separatist movements became increasingly vocal and uncompromising, an important part of the Soviet intelligentsia broke with Gorbachev in the name of radical an-ticommunism, and in a society without deeply rooted democratic tradi-tions the space for irresponsible demagoguery proved to be large. After six years of sound and fury, and despite prodigious achievements,

92. A summary of Gorbachev's position is offered in M. Gorbachev, "Sotsialisticheskaia ideia i revoliutsionnaia perestroika," *Pravda,* 26 Nov. 1989, pp. 1–3. Bovin writes of the need to "save" socialism by "replacing its historically exhausted form with an alternative." Aleksandr E. Bovin, "Perestroika i sud'by sotsializma," *Izvestiia,* 11 July 1987, p. 4.

93. A concern for the possibility of inexorable economic decline haunts the entire liter-ature of perestroika. N. Spasskii, "Natsional'naia bezopasnost'?—deistvitel'naia i mni-maia," *Mezhdunarodnaia zhizn'* 6 (1989): 3–14, states revealingly: "In the final analysis a nation's wealth, as banal as it may sound, is determined by its economic well-being," and refers to the best-seller by Paul Kennedy, *The Rise and Fall of Great Powers: Economic Change and Military Conflict from 1500 to 2000* (London, 1988), as an illustration of historical decline produced by overextension and economic weakness. In the same vein see N. Dolgopolova and A. Kokoshin, "Chemu uchat sud'by velikikh derzhav," *Kommunist* 17 (Nov. 1988): 115–21.

94. See the analysis in Anders Aslund, *Gorbachev's Struggle for Economic Reform* (Ith-aca, N.Y., 1991).

perestroika arrived at a point of crisis. For all of its national existence the Soviet Union had purchased stability at the price of centralized authoritarian controls. Such controls had become a barrier to progress, but the attempt to dismantle them by means of what one commentator called a "policy of directed chaos" contained acute dangers.[95]

Gorbachev responded to increasing social tensions by attempting to reinforce his authority as Soviet president. Between September 1990 and April 1991 he also drew closer to the conservative wing of the policy establishment, probably in an attempt to buy time without altogether sacrificing the momentum of reform. By the spring of 1991 Gorbachev had realigned once again with the most visible symbol of radical change, the newly elected Russian president, Boris Eltsin, and seemed to be poised to launch a new wave of innovations. A blueprint for comprehensive economic reform was finally in place, a union treaty transferring considerable powers from the central government to the individual Soviet republics was ready for signing, and traditionalist elements within the Communist party were under siege.

The commitment to press ahead with reform in defiance of conservative opposition and in an atmosphere of pervasive social crisis was the immediate prelude to the attempted coup d'état launched by the eight-member State Committee for the State of Emergency in the USSR on 17 August 1991. Perhaps the most striking thing about the committee was the degree to which it was dominated by representatives of the traditional national-security establishment. Its members included Minister of Defense Dmitrii Iazov, KGB chair Vladimir Kriuchkov, head of the Ministry of Internal Affairs Boriss Pugo, a deputy chair of the Soviet Defense Council with a professional background in defense industry, Oleg Baklanov, and a leading party bureaucrat with experience as an industrial manager in defense industry, Aleksandr Tiziakov. The plotters isolated Gorbachev by placing him under house arrest at his vacation resort in the Crimea and attempted to impose martial law, but confronted by dramatic resistance spearheaded by Eltsin in Moscow and by defiance within the upper levels of the military command structure, the ill-conceived project quickly collapsed. The authoritarian adventure ended ignominiously, but its immediate consequences were immense all the same.

On one level the failure of the coup simply accelerated trends that had long been apparent. The authority of the central organs of Soviet power was further weakened, and the autonomy of the individual republics, and particularly the Russian federation headed by Eltsin, was enhanced. The Baltic states moved quickly to consolidate full independence, and

95. Jerry F. Hough, "The Politics of Successful Economic Reform," *Soviet Economy* 1 (Jan.–March 1989): 42.

the pressures exerted by separatist movements throughout the Union were strengthened. More substantially, the coup marked the end of perestroika itself as an experiment in peaceful and managed reform from above. All the key actors were for the moment still in place, but the rules of the game had changed. The incarnation of an authoritarian threat, even if temporarily foiled, gravely destabilized the entire reform agenda and created a vacuum of authority that leaders espousing radical anticommunism and uncompromising nationalism stepped forward to fill. In the wake of the coup the political center of gravity in Russia shifted toward self-styled democratic reformers, who moved to suspend the activities of the Communist party, confiscate its considerable properties, and launch an attack against the entire legacy of Soviet power. It will be some time before the consequences of these monumental initiatives, and the resolution of the struggle for power that accompanies them, become clear. For our purpose the failed coup provides a convenient point at which to conclude. Perestroika had led to a decisive break with the past, though it remained unclear whether it should be considered a partial success, a magnificent failure, or an unmediated disaster. It had also led to the end of the Soviet Union in its traditional configuration, and perhaps to the end of the Soviet experiment, understood as a direct continuation of the Bolsheviks's Red October. In a certain sense the contradictions of the Soviet past, and of its dark Stalinist core, had overwhelmed prospects for managed reform that sought to pursue change in continuity.

Gorbachev's security policy highlighted the need to reduce international exposure in order to concentrate all available energies upon domestic reform. It was presumed that for the time being the Soviet Union could neither afford nor hope to pursue an assertive international orientation. Some analysts portrayed the foreign policy of perestroika as a "diplomacy of decline" motivated primarily by a sharpened awareness of radically reduced capacity, but from the start Gorbachev's project also promised a new idealism whose watchwords were peace, ecology, and development.[96] Gorbachev himself was a consummate realist, but he struggled to preserve an identity as the heir of Lenin and the positive aspirations of the October revolution.[97] His supporters were certainly not partisans of the mystified Lenin cult that has been one of the most

96. See Stephen Sestanovich, "Gorbachev's Foreign Policy: A Diplomacy of Decline," *Problems of Communism* 1 (Jan.–Feb. 1988): 1–15.

97. The playwright Mikhail Shatrov made the point in describing the political confrontation accompanying Gorbachev's appointment, speaking of "a struggle for a return to the ideals of October." Mikhail Shatrov, "Neobratimost' peremen," *Ogonek* 4 (24–31 Jan. 1987): 5.

bizarre and tasteless emblems of Soviet power. They did not seek to revive a revolutionary program that was completely irrelevant to contemporary circumstances. But they did acknowledge the legitimacy of the revolutionary origins of the Soviet state, its positive historical achievements, and the ethical values inherent in its founding ideology. Perestroika was conceived by reform communists who refused entirely to burn their bridges to the past and whose policies were designed, at least in part, to redeem what remained in the Soviet experience that could be considered worth saving.

One should hasten to add that Soviet reformers kept their feet firmly planted on the ground. One of the words that recurred in discussions of perestroika was "normal." The Soviet Union sought to become a "normal" state, with a rational market-based economy, a pluralistic political order reflective of its own diversity, and a respected role within the community of states. New thinking offered a vision, but it did not exhort to a crusade. Ultimately, perestroika sought to eliminate the terms of the Soviet security dilemma altogether by bringing the country in from the cold, voiding its claim to embody the future, and facing up to the realities of international society as it is. The terrible burden of representing a cause imbued with revolutionary messianism, either sincerely or as a callous justification for the exercise of power, had defined much of the Soviet experience and cost the Soviet peoples dearly. By the 1980s the pretense to stand for such a cause had become a pathetic farce that strained the state's resources beyond measure and undermined popular morale by encouraging a pervasive cynicism. The two-camps mentality that such pretense perpetuated frustrated the search for real security without bringing the ideals in question, more often than not long since forgotten, one iota closer to realization. Perestroika sought to close the gap between the Soviet Union and the rest of the world opened up by the October revolution by affecting a lasting accommodation with the dominant international order.

Many of Gorbachev's policies were designed to reinforce the international status quo. The literature of perestroika nonetheless offered a positive image of security that may be described at Kantian. It posited the existence of a community of states evolving gradually toward more benign patterns of interaction and greater sensitivity to problems of universal human concern, toward a federation of peoples in which the concepts of world citizen and world government might eventually take on substance. It envisioned the emergence of a thoroughly reformed variant of the old USSR, perhaps reduced by secessions, but with a revitalized economy, new sources of social consensus, viable confederative structures, and a stable democratic polity, capable of playing a vital and progressive role in world affairs. The goals were tremendously ambitious, and the attempt to shepherd reform from above without provoking a breakdown or abandoning the foundations of Soviet power, to be simultaneously "both Luther and the Pope," was arguably misconceived. One of the great strengths of perestroika was nonetheless the extent to which it was inspired by an integrated image of international security that was alert to the changing nature ot the security problem itself. Part of what was perceived to be at stake was the struggle for a new world order actually worthy of the name, a world of mutual security in which "people may live, not like wild beasts fighting over a piece of bread, but as brothers in harmony." Gorbachev and his backers pledged their country to wage this struggle, not from the vanguard but in the ranks.

The eventual outcome of Gorbachev's project and its consequences for the international security regime are unclear; the failure of the coup d'état of August 1991 did not solve any of the underlying dilemmas that created the crisis of perestroika. The red flag that once defined the substance of the Soviet experience is no longer flying, but the black earth of the Slavic east remains, and the security problems generated by a collapse or restructuring of the Soviet federation will be no less preoccupying than the security dilemmas of the past. Time will tell whither the Russian troika is now dashing, how the disintegrative forces unleashed by reform will eventually be contained, whether new thinking ever expressed anything more than a misguided utopia. It may at any rate be concluded that the effort to prepare the Soviet peoples for new kinds of challenges in a changing world and to contribute to the emergence of a more peaceful international order in which the forces of socialism and progress can evolve in their own way without the bad example of the USSR to constrain them was a part, and not the least part, of what the promise of perestroika was all about. If the promise is not realized, it will not have been for lack of trying.

Index of Published Sources

As an aid to the reader in following up citations, an index of most of the published primary and secondary sources used in this book has been compiled. Most of the references are listed alphabetically by author. The page reference indicates the first citation of a work, and a short title is provided when more than one work by an author is cited.

General Index

Acheson, Dean, 192
Adamec, Ladislav, 306, 309
Adamishin, Anatolii, 297
Adenauer, Konrad, 207
Adzhubei, Aleksei, 241
Afghanistan, occupation of, 276–80
Akhmatova, Anna, 174
Alekseev, Mikhail, 21
Amin, Hafizullah, 279
Andropov, Iurii, 260, 285–87, 299
Anti-Ballistic Missile (ABM) treaty, 261–62, 266
Anti-Comintern Pact, 80
Antonov, Aleksandr, 31
Antonov-Ovseenko, Vladimir, 21
Aron, Raymond, 297
Atlantic Charter, 139
Austrian State Treaty, 206–7, 219

Baghdad Pact, 226–27
Baklanov, Oleg, 324
Balance of power, 72, 111, 255
Bandung conference, 229
Barthou, Louis, 43n.17, 84
Baruch, Bernard, 169
Basic principles agreement, 259
Battle of the Bulge, 148, 151
Bay of Pigs invasion, 237
Belorussia, battle of, 144
Beneš, Edvard, 97, 146, 178
Beria, Lavrentii, 119, 124, 185, 204
Berlin: crisis of 1948–1949, 179–82; crisis of 1958–1961, 235–36; fall of Berlin Wall, 305–6, 317
Bliukher, Vasilii, 21, 31, 71, 91–92
Blum, Leon, 94
Bonch-Bruevich, M. A., 18

Bordiga, Amadeo, 61–62, 69
Brandt, Willy, 257
Brest-Litovsk, peace of, 9–15, 17, 22, 35, 42–43
Brezhnev, Leonid: Afghanistan decision, 278–80; détente policy, 255–60, 263, 266, 271; legacy, 321; political program, 245–49, 282–84, 287, 289, 315; successor to Khrushchev, 242; Third World policy, 272, 274
Brezhnev Doctrine, 222, 251–52, 254, 308
Brockdorff-Rantzau, Ulrich, 44, 46
Brown, Harold, 209
Brusilov, Aleksei, 28
Brussels Pact, 180, 182
Brzezinski, Zbigniew, 269
Budennyi, Semen, 25–26, 50, 127, 136
Bukharin, Nikolai, 10–11, 13, 17, 19–20, 44, 56–59, 63–64, 90, 295
Bulganin, Nikolai, 124, 204, 206–7, 225
Bullitt, William, 26
Bush, George, 324
Byrnes, James, 164, 168, 198

Carter, Jimmy, 263–64, 269, 275, 277
Castro, Fidel, 228, 237
Ceauşescu, Nicolae, 306, 309
Chamberlain, Neville, 97–98
Chebrikov, Viktor, 302
Chernenko, Konstantin, 285–86
Chicherin, Grigorii, 38, 40–42, 46, 52, 75–76, 78, 111, 278, 295
Chinese Eastern Railway, 71, 80
Chuikov, Vasilii, 133
Churchill, Winston, 24, 124, 151–52, 156, 162, 165